MW01009874

THE
EIGHT
KING
HENRYS
OF
ENGLAND

TO JOYCE

Come be with me in a land of golden dreams
Where the western winds brings messages of love and happiness
Singing, Forever true, there is only you, Forever you
In you alone I know time's Forever love.

THE
EIGHT
KING
HENRYS
OF
ENGLAND

PHILIP J. POTTER

PEN & SWORD
HISTORY

AN IMPRINT OF PEN & SWORD BOOKS LTD.
YORKSHIRE – PHILADELPHIA

First published in Great Britain in 2024 by
PEN AND SWORD HISTORY
An imprint of
Pen & Sword Books Ltd
Yorkshire – Philadelphia

ISBN 978 1 39900 935 5

Typeset in Times New Roman 10/12 by
SJmagic DESIGN SERVICES, India.
Printed and bound in the UK by CPI Group (UK) Ltd.

Pen & Sword Books Limited incorporates the imprints of Atlas, Archaeology,
Aviation, Discovery, Family History, Fiction, History, Maritime, Military,
Military Classics, Politics, Select, Transport, True Crime, Air World, Frontline
Publishing, Leo Cooper, Remember When, Seaforth Publishing, The Praetorian
Press, Wharncliffe Local History, Wharncliffe Transport, Wharncliffe True Crime
and White Owl.

For a complete list of Pen & Sword titles please contact
PEN & SWORD BOOKS LIMITED
George House, Units 12 & 13, Beevor Street, Off Pontefract Road,
Barnsley, South Yorkshire, S71 1HN, England
E-mail: enquiries@pen-and-sword.co.uk
Website: www.pen-and-sword.co.uk

or

PEN AND SWORD BOOKS
1950 Lawrence Rd, Havertown, PA 19083, USA
E-mail: uspen-and-sword@casematepublishers.com
Website: www.penandswordbooks.com

Contents

Legend: b. — born   r. — reigned

Image Sources

1. Henry I: British Library, Henry I – Cotton Claudius D, i i f 45v (This work is in the public domain in its country of origin and other countries and areas where the copyright term is the author's life plus 100 years or fewer)

2. Henry II: Wikipedia Henry II (This work is in the public domain in its country of origin and other countries and areas where the copyright term is the author's life plus seventy years or less, Wikimedia)

3. Henry III: Coronation of King Henry III (This work is in the public domain in its country of origin and other countries and areas where the copyright term is the author's life plus 100 years, Wikimedia)

4. Henry IV: Illumination of Henry IV (The National Archives UK – Illumination of Henry IV from the Records of the Duchy of Lancaster – catalogue reference DL 42/1 Wikimedia)

5. Henry V: Henry V of England – public domain (This work is in the public domain of its country of origin and in other countries and areas where the copyright term is the author's life plus 100 years – Dulwich Pictures Gallery – Wikimedia Commons)

6. Henry VI: King Henry VI crowned as King of France (Bibliotheque National de France, MS Francais 83 – Wikimedia Commons)

7. Henry VII: Young Henry VII (Public domain – PD-Old-PD-Art – Wkimedia Commons)

8. Henry VIII: Henry VIII of England by Joos Van Cleve (Public domain – Wikimedia Commons – Royal Collection)

9. Westminster Abbey: Photo by author

10. Coffin of Henry II: Fontevraud Abbey France (photo by author)

11. Battle of Agincourt: (This work is in the public domain in its country of origin and other countries and areas where the copyright term is the author's life plus seventy years or fewer – Wikimedia)

12. Field of the Cloth of Gold: (This work is in the public domain in its country of origin and other countries and areas where the copyright term is the author's life plus seventy years or fewer – Wikimedia)

Genealogical Charts

CHART 1

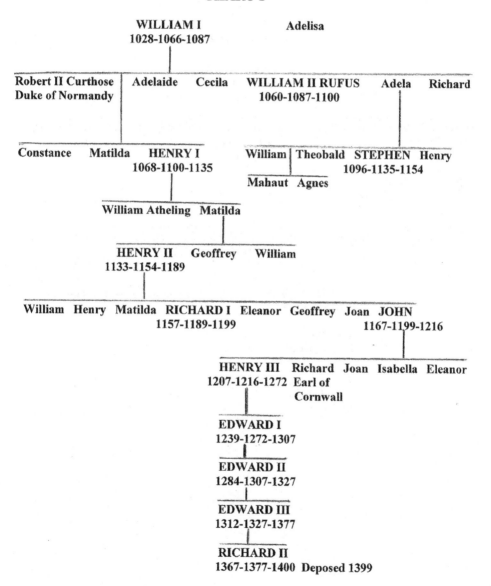

WILLIAM I
1028-1066-1087
      Adelisa

Robert II Curthose Duke of Normandy   Adelaide   Cecila   **WILLIAM II RUFUS** 1060-1087-1100   Adela   Richard

Constance   Matilda   **HENRY I** 1068-1100-1135   William   Theobald   **STEPHEN** Henry 1096-1135-1154

Mahaut   Agnes

William Atheling   Matilda

HENRY II 1133-1154-1189   Geoffrey   William

William   Henry   Matilda   **RICHARD I** 1157-1189-1199   Eleanor   Geoffrey   Joan   **JOHN** 1167-1199-1216

HENRY III 1207-1216-1272   Richard Earl of Cornwall   Joan   Isabella   Eleanor

EDWARD I
1239-1272-1307

EDWARD II
1284-1307-1327

EDWARD III
1312-1327-1377

RICHARD II
1367-1377-1400 Deposed 1399

vii

CHART 2

HOUSE OF LANCASTER

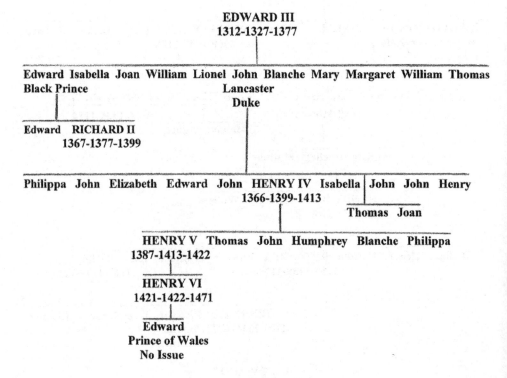

EDWARD III
1312-1327-1377

Edward Isabella Joan William Lionel John Blanche Mary Margaret William Thomas
Black Prince   Lancaster
                                                 Duke

Edward   RICHARD II
          1367-1377-1399

Philippa John Elizabeth Edward John HENRY IV Isabella John John Henry
                                          1366-1399-1413
                                                             Thomas Joan

          HENRY V Thomas John Humphrey Blanche Philippa
          1387-1413-1422

          HENRY VI
          1421-1422-1471

          Edward
          Prince of Wales
          No Issue

CHART 3

HOUSE OF YORK

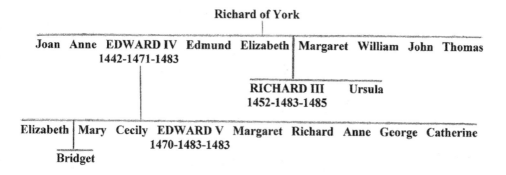

Richard of York

| Joan | Anne | EDWARD IV 1442-1471-1483 | Edmund | Elizabeth | Margaret | William | John | Thomas |

RICHARD III 1452-1483-1485   Ursula

| Elizabeth | Mary | Cecily | EDWARD V 1470-1483-1483 | Margaret | Richard | Anne | George | Catherine |

Bridget

CHART 4

HOUSE OF TUDOR

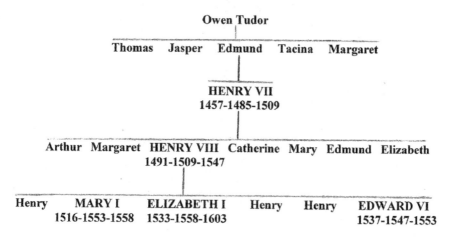

Owen Tudor

| Thomas | Jasper | Edmund | Tacina | Margaret |

HENRY VII 1457-1485-1509

| Arthur | Margaret | HENRY VIII 1491-1509-1547 | Catherine | Mary | Edmund | Elizabeth |

| Henry | MARY I 1516-1553-1558 | ELIZABETH I 1533-1558-1603 | Henry | Henry | EDWARD VI 1537-1547-1553 |

Maps

PLANTAGENET EMPIRE, 1200

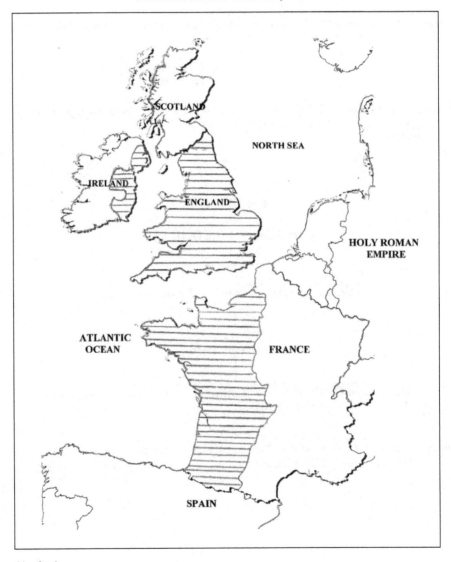

(Author)

BATTLE OF LEWES, 14 May 1264

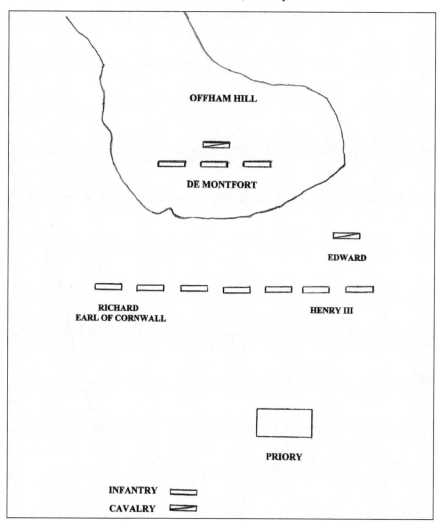

(Author)

BATTLE OF EVESHAM, 4 AUGUST 1265

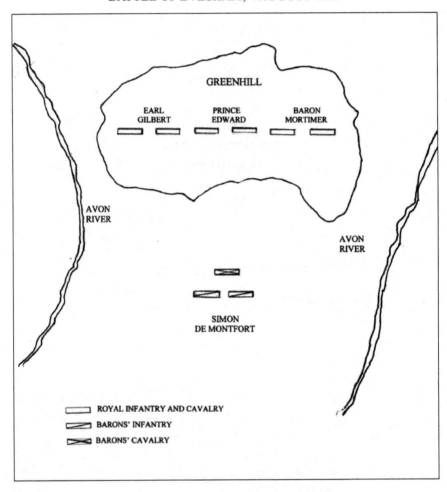

(Author)

BATTLE OF SHREWSBURY, 21 JULY 1403

(Author)

BATTLE OF AGINCOURT, 25 OCTOBER 1415

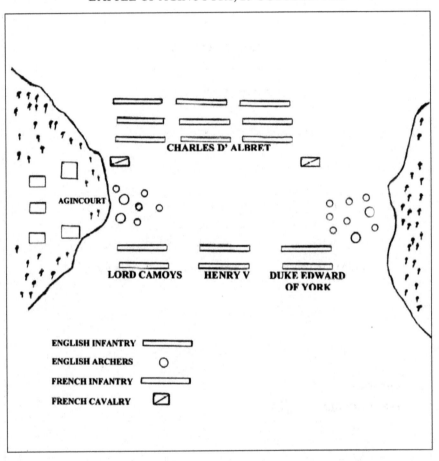

(Author)

BATTLE OF TOWTON 29 MARCH 1461

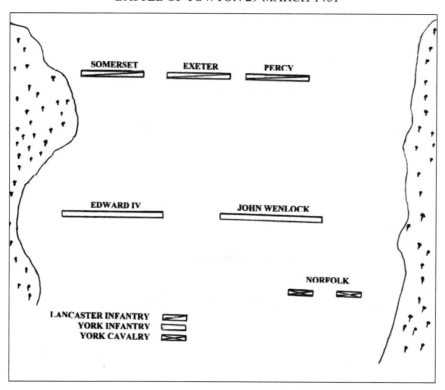

(Author)

BATTLE OF STOKE FIELD, 16 JUNE 1487

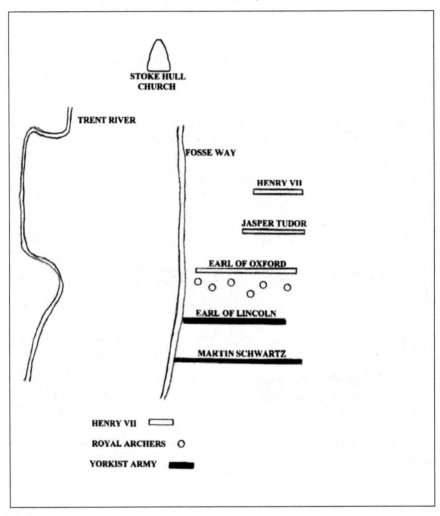

(Author)

Overview

In the nearly 450 years between 1100 and 1547, England was ruled by eight kings who were enthroned with the name of Henry. Under their reigns, the Kingdom of England emerged from the Dark Ages into the light of the Renaissance. The Henrys guided the English nobles, Church and populace through times of demographic, economic and governmental deterioration into the formation of a unified state governed by an all-powerful king. The Henrys held the reins of power through the Norman, Plantagenet and Tudor houses. In 1066, the Normans defeated the reigning Anglo-Saxons at the Battle of Hastings, creating a new dynasty that ruled over England. The first Henry claimed the English crown in 1100 after his childless brother, King William II, was accidently killed while hunting. He governed over the kingdom for thirty-five years, enforcing his English sovereignty, while fighting his older brother, Robert Curthose, for control of the Duchy of Normandy. Following the death of Henry I in 1135, the previously peaceful Kingdom of England erupted into anarchy during the weak regime of Stephen until order was finally restored by Henry II's acquisition of power. Henry II of the Plantagenet family became the English king in 1154, and by the end of his reign in 1189 had brought peace to the kingdom, while creating the Angevin Empire through inheritances, political intrigues and military might and thus holding supremacy over England, Normandy, Aquitaine and Anjou. The greatest threat to Henry II's throne came from his four sons, who repeatedly challenged their father for control over his vast empire.

Following the death of two of Henry II's sons, Henry III succeeded to the English monarchy in 1216 aged just 9, governing the English for the next 56 years. During his long kingship, his regime was forced to fight two bloody civil wars against his recalcitrant warlords, who were seeking greater independence and a voice in the administration of the government. The fourth Henry was not in the direct line of succession to the English monarchy, seizing the throne through force of arms. After his earlier exile from England for alleged acts of treason, he returned at the head of an army of volunteers to overthrow the reigning King Richard II. In October 1399, Henry IV was anointed monarch at Westminster Abbey, vowing to defend the laws and rightful customs of the kingdom with all his might. He presided over the English nation for the next thirteen years.

Henry V succeeded his father to the English throne in 1413 at the age of 25, and for the next ten years governed England with justice and virtue. He inherited a peaceful realm from Henry IV, and leaving a brother to govern England as regent was drawn into the reconquest of the lost lands of the Angevin Empire in France. In August 1415, Henry V crossed the English Channel with an army of

10,000 men-at-arms and foot soldiers, defeating the French at Agincourt in one of Medieval Europe's greatest battles. The triumph at Agincourt created the legend of an unconquered warrior-king. Henry V died in Vincennes, France, at the age of 32 and was followed on the English throne by his infant son, Henry VI, during whose long kingship the power and grandeur of the English realm fell to its lowest level. Henry VI's regime was dominated by long bouts of mental illness which left him incapable of ruling his kingdom. As king, he was indecisive and easily influenced as his nobles battled each other for control of the crown. Beginning in 1452, he exhibited signs of increasing mental illness, leaving him in a nonresponsive catatonic state. He was murdered, while at his prayers in the Tower of London, on the order of King Edward IV.

Henry VII, the first Tudor monarch, assumed the English crown by defeating the ruling King Richard III at the Battle of Bosworth Field in 1485. Following years of unrest and civil turmoil, he eventually brought peace to England and restored the fabric of the battered monarchical power. He was the last English monarch to win his crown on the battlefield. As king, his monetary and financial policies brought a revival of England's economy and trade with Europe. Henry VII's reign marked the beginning of what is known as England's Glorious Age and the passage into a modern state. The final Henry came to the throne in 1509 and ruled for the next 38 years. The monarchy of Henry VIII was dominated by his pursuit of an heir and the reacquisition of lost English domains in France. During his quest for a male successor, he broke with the Holy See of Rome by creating the Church of England under the authority of his monarchy, while taking six wives in an attempt to secure the continued supremacy of his family over England with the birth of a son. Under the reign of Henry VIII, England became a dominant force in European politics and was sought as an ally by the major powers on the continent.

Henry I

In late September 1066, following the death of King Edward the Confessor, Duke William of Normandy crossed the English Channel with his army to enforce his birthright to the Kingdom of England. After landing unopposed at Pevensey, he advanced his forces to meet the English troops of King Harold II at Hastings. On 14 October, William led his men to victory, being crowned king on Christmas Day at Westminster Abbey in London. By 1071, he had subdued the rebellious feudal barons and towns to solidify his rule, creating the Norman dynasty that reigned in England for the next seventy-four years through four monarchs. Upon his death in September 1087, William the Conqueror's possessions were divided among his three surviving sons. He bequeathed to his first-born, Robert Curthose, the Norman Duchy, and granted his second son, William Rufus, the English realm. Henry, the third son, received a large payment in silver. William II ruled over England for nearly thirteen years, in spite of sporadic uprisings of dissident warlords. At the height of his power in 1100, William II was killed by an errant arrow while hunting in the New Forest, making possible Henry of Normandy's usurpation of the English throne.

Unlike his two surviving brothers, Henry was born in England, at Selby in Yorkshire during the summer of 1068, and was the eighth child of the four sons and five daughters born to William I and Queen Matilda of Flanders. He spent his early years in England, while frequently travelling to his father's lands in Normandy. Henry was sent to Salisbury Cathedral by the king to be educated by Bishop Osmund, a renowned scholar. Under the tutelage of the bishop, the young Norman prince studied reading, writing, Latin and religion, becoming fluent in the French language. Near the age of 7, he began training for knighthood under the instruction of Sir Robert Achard. He spent long hours practicing with the sword and shield of an infantryman, mastering archery and charging against an enemy on horseback with the lance of a cavalryman. Henry took part in martial sports and games, learning the skills of a knight. In May 1086, the Norman prince knelt before the king at Westminster and was tapped on the shoulders, rising to his feet as a knight.

Following his knighthood ceremony, Prince Henry remained with the royal court, and in July 1087 he accompanied William I to Rouen, the capital of Normandy, to prepare for a retaliatory attack against the nobles of the French County of Vexin. At the encouragement of King Philip I of France, the Vexin warlords had repeatedly crossed the frontier, sacking Norman villages and plundering the land. In July, the English king led his troops to the south-east to attack the Vexin capital of Mantes.

Prince Henry rode with his father, participating in the assault against the city. During the sortie, William I was severely wounded and taken back to Rouen. As his condition grew worse, he granted his dominions to his first two sons, while Henry was bequeathed 5,000 pounds of silver.

Henry had been the favorite child of Queen Matilda, and before she died she bequeathed to him her English properties in Gloucestershire and Buckinghamshire. At the time of her death in 1083, Henry was still a minor and the inheritance stayed under the protection of William I. When his father died in 1087, Henry still had not yet reached the age of majority and the queen's lands remained under the control of the new monarchy. In 1088 at the age of 20, Henry crossed the Channel from Normandy to England, petitioning King William II Rufus for possession of his inheritance from Queen Matilda. Despite the pleas of his younger brother, the monarch refused to grant the request and the Norman prince remained landless. As part of the royal court and brother of the ruling king, Henry possessed a status superior to other English nobles, but his lack of properties lessened his standing among them. Considering the absence of a lordship as unfitting for a member of the royal household, the acquisition of suitable lands now became his primary goal.

Following the death of William the Conqueror, the 19-year-old Henry remained in Normandy, joining Robert Curthose's court and serving as his chief counsellor. At the time of William I's death, Curthose, as the eldest son, had expected to receive both Normandy and the English kingdom. Disappointed with only the Norman duchy, he began plotting with friends and allies in England to seize the monarchy. In March 1088, a rebellion erupted in support of Robert's quest for the English throne, led by his powerful and influential uncle, Bishop Odo of Bayeux. While the rebels attacked the English king's castles and towns, they expected the duke to assemble his Norman army and join the uprising, but his money was exhausted before the invasion could be launched. Desperate for funds, Robert asked Henry to lend him part of his inheritance. When the youngest brother promptly refused the request, Duke Robert offered to sell him part of his Norman lands. The young prince accepted the proposal, and for 3,000 pounds of silver – over half of his legacy – acquired Cotentin County in western Normandy with the title of count.

After receiving the deposit of silver from Henry, Duke Robert began preparations to invade England and dethrone his brother. While he assembled a formidable army and navy, an advance force of knights and infantrymen set out to England to reinforce the ongoing rebellion against William II. During the Channel crossing, however, the Norman fleet was intercepted by English ships and decimated. Following the loss of his men and vessels, Curthose abandoned his campaign to claim England and stayed in Normandy. Henry had remained at the ducal court, aiding his brother with the arrangements for the conquest of England, becoming exposed to the preparations for war and acquiring political and administrative skills. While Robert had lost his opportunity to once again reunite his father's great realm, the aborted English invasion gave Henry the opportunity to acquire nearly a third of Normandy and to become a count.

In the wake of the failed English campaign, Henry set out to impose his rights over his newly acquired countship. The Cotentin barons and churchmen willingly accepted the rule of the young count, with the exception of Robert of Mowbray, who remained loyal to Duke Robert and intrigued to overthrow Henry. Count Henry's properties were located in current-day north-western France, 200 miles west of Paris and bordering the English Channel. Henry's authority reached beyond the borders of Cotentin and included the properties of his vassals outside the countship. The great Abbey of Mont-Saint-Michel was part of his demesne, giving him possessions throughout the Norman duchy. During Robert Curthose's reign, the Cotentin region was poorly governed by the duke, with widespread dissidence among the nobles, bishops and towns. Under Henry's new administration, the government was reorganized and qualified agents appointed to enforce the count's laws. To gain the loyalty of the powerful Cotentin warlords, the count made grants of strategic lands and paid large bribes in silver. While the Norman duchy under the rule of Robert Curthose continued to suffer from widespread turmoil and insecurity, Henry's reign provided security and stability to the countship's magnates, towns and Church.

By mid-summer 1088, William II had suppressed the rebellion of Duke Robert's English allies, allowing Henry to safely cross the Channel to England and petition his brother for the release of his mother's properties. Before leaving Cotentin, the count secured his remaining silver treasure, placing it under the custody of trusted nobles and churchmen, and in early July set sail for England. Upon appearing at the royal court, he received a cordial welcome from the king and spent the remainder of the summer with him. During his stay in England, Henry asked his brother for possession of his inheritance from his mother, but the lands had been earlier granted to Robert FitzHamon to secure his continued support during the recent revolt. In the autumn, Henry returned to Normandy without Matilda's estates, rejoining the court of Duke Robert and serving as his principal advisor.

While Henry was in England, his uncle, Bishop Odo of Bayeux, had returned to Normandy after the failed rebellion against William II, joining Duke Robert's court. The bishop's properties in England had been confiscated by the English regime for his involvement in the revolt, and he feared a retaliatory attack on Normandy by William II. While Odo had lost his English lands, he still retained large lordships in Normandy, but Henry – as Count of Cotentin – was overlord for most of them and a threat to seize them. It was now in the best interest of the bishop for Henry to be overthrown as count. Odo had little difficulty convincing Curthose that Henry had formed an alliance against him with Rufus while at the English court. When the count's ship landed in the duchy, Henry was imprisoned along with Robert of Belleme, who held large holdings in southern Normandy and was implicated by Odo in the conspiracy against Curthose. Henry was placed in the custody of Odo and held prisoner at Bayeux. While he remained imprisoned, his countship of Cotentin was seized by the duke, along with his other lands in western Normandy.

Henry remained the captive of Duke Robert for over six months before he was finally freed, but still landless. In the aftermath of his release, he stayed in Normandy and began to conspire with his allies and friends in the western fiefdoms to regain his lost lordships. When Curthose was distracted with his military campaigns in the south to reclaim the lost County of Maine and his ducal lands became beset with turmoil and private wars due to his poor government, the younger brother reasserted his right as count for the Cotentin region and fortified his castles against an attack by his eldest brother.

Meanwhile, in England, William II Rufus had not forgiven Robert Curthose's attempt to seize his crown and began negotiating with dissident Norman barons for their support in the overthrow of his older brother. The king remained in his kingdom but garrisoned the strongholds of his Norman friends with his knights, who repeatedly ravaged the enemy's lands and villages. By 1090, Rufus' control over the north-eastern region of Normandy was intensifying. William II continued to intrigue against his older brother, employing promises and large bribes to negotiate an alliance with the inhabitants of the ducal capital at Rouen. Led by Conan Pilatus, the rebels sent messengers to the king's allies calling on them to join their planned uprising. When Robert's spies informed him of the danger at Rouen, he mustered his loyal magnates, while summoning Henry and Robert of Belleme for armed assistance. Seeking to regain his favorable relationship with his eldest brother, the young Norman prince agreed to join him in the defense of the ducal capital. In early November, he arrived at the castle at Rouen with his armed retainers, uniting his forces with the ducal army. On 3 November, hostilities erupted when the troops of Conan Pilatus clashed with a force of the duke's soldiers at the city's Cauchoise Gate. As the fighting at the gate spread into the narrow streets of Rouen, Henry and the duke led their knights and foot-soldiers into the castle, smashing into Conan's men with their swords and spears in savage hand-to-hand fighting. During the bloody melee, Robert Curthose panicked and fled the city, taking refuge in a monastery. The count remained in Rouen, leading the duke's men-at-arms and infantrymen in the fierce and brutal fray. When ducal reinforcements arrived, Henry renewed his assault, a tidal wave of troops surging forward to overwhelm Conan's men and compel the royalists to retreat, leaving their wounded and dead in the bloody-soaked streets of Rouen. As his men fell back in disarray, Conan was captured and placed in the custody of Henry.

Following the withdrawal of the insurgents, Henry seized Conan and, accompanied by several knights, forced his prisoner up the spiral stairway to the top of the castle's tower. Angered by Conan's treason, the young Norman prince yelled at him: 'By my mother's soul, there shall be no ransom for a traitor only swifter infliction of the death he deserves.' He then grabbed Conan and pushed him over the side of the tower to his death. As a warning to other would-be defectors, Conan's body was tied behind a horse and dragged through the streets of the city. While Henry was inflicting his punishment on the traitor, Robert of Belleme and other barons captured wealthy Rouen citizens for ransom, holding them in dungeons until payment was made.

Henry had fought with bravery and determination in defense of his brother's principal city, while Robert had fled in fear. For his spirited resistance at Rouen, Henry was hailed as the hero of the battle, while Duke Robert's knightly reputation was severely damaged. Instead of showing gratitude to his brother for his actions and victory, however, Curthose ordered him to leave the city.

On 2 February 1091, William Rufus assembled a large army in England to cross the Channel and overthrow Robert after his ducal allies had failed to seize the duchy. He established his headquarter at the city of Eu on the coastline north of Rouen. In Eu, the king joined his English forces with his Norman allies and mercenary soldiers and prepared to attack the duke. Confronted by the formidable royal army, Robert sent envoys to Eu to negotiate a peace. Under the terms of the ensuing treaty, Robert agreed to transfer to the English king the lordship of much of Upper Normandy, including the County of Eu, the town of Cherbourg, the great abbey at Mont-Saint-Michel and the castles and lands of all warlords who had supported him in the revolt. In return, William promised to assign English territories to his older brother and aid him in the reconquest of Maine and all other Norman properties lost since the death of their father. Finally, the agreement stipulated that if either died without a legitimate son, he would be succeeded by the other brother, effectively eliminating Henry from any Norman lands.

From western Normandy, Henry soon learned the terms of his brothers' treaty and expressed his strong opposition, while preparing his castles for war and hiring Norman and Breton mercenary troops. Many of Henry's once-loyal allies now abandoned him, giving their allegiance to the powerful king. As William II and Robert proceeded with their large army into western Normandy, Henry's forces were greatly depleted by desertions to his approaching brothers. Garrisoning his strongholds with his remaining loyal soldiers, Henry pulled back with his household guards and mercenaries to the monastery of Mont-Saint-Michel. When Rufus and Curthose learned their brother had withdrawn to the abbey, in early March 1091 they hastened after him and besieged the great fortress.

The abbey of Mont-Saint-Michel was located on a large rock rising from the coastline of the bay. At high tide, the abbey became an island surrounded by the waters of the English Channel. The island fortification was virtually impregnable, compelling the two older brothers to lay siege to it. As Henry repelled their attacks, he sent his men to harass his brothers with constant sorties, ravaging the surrounding countryside, taking captives and raiding his enemies' encampments. Henry relentlessly pursued his pillaging forays against his brothers but was unable to drive them off. Realizing that continued resistance was useless, and with water and food supplies running low, he was compelled to negotiate a peace agreement. Under the terms of their treaty, Henry agreed to surrender Mont-Saint-Michel and abandon his castles and properties in western Normandy. Following the settlement, he departed from the abbey with his troops, first travelling to Brittany, where his mercenaries were paid-off. In the summer of 1091, he proceeded across the border into the Vexin County of France, once again landless.

Accompanied by several companions and servants, Henry remained in Vexin for almost a year, journeying from castle to castle, while his two brothers stayed together in Normandy. Rufus had pledged to support Robert's recovery of the lost County of Maine but made no attempt to honour the terms of the treaty. While William II took no measures to comply with their agreement, Curthose granted large regions of Normandy to him. In early August 1091, Robert sailed to England with Rufus to claim his promised properties as stipulated in the Rouen treaty.

He stayed in the kingdom for the next five months, travelling with his younger brother to Wales and north through the realm to Scotland. They met the Scottish king, Malcolm III, and Curthose helped negotiate a truce between the two kingdoms. The Norman duke had met the major conditions of the Rouen treaty, but William II had failed to aid in the conquest of Maine and now refused to transfer the promised English lands to his brother. Curthose grew increasingly enraged at his brother's lack of compliance, and just before Christmas abruptly returned to Normandy, severing his friendship with Rufus.

Henry had meanwhile remained in France, an impoverished landless nobleman travelling from town to town with his few friends and servants. After wandering for nearly a year, his future suddenly changed when the residents of the fortified hilltop town of Domfront revolted against their overlord, offering to recognize Henry as their liege. Domfront, located in south-western Normandy, was protected by a strong castle built on a promontory. When the prince met with the city officials, he pledged to retain possession of the lordship and honour their laws and customs. After establishing his rule, Henry recruited wayward knights and hired mercenaries, unleashing fierce pillaging raids against Duke Robert of Normandy to recover his lost lordships. From his secure fortress, Henry led his men into Normandy to plunder towns and burn farms and crops. As he continued to expand his land holdings, his previous allies and friends in Cotentin rejoined his army, allowing him to extend his control once again through his former territories. With his power in the duchy spreading, Henry became a growing threat to Duke Robert, and after William II's break with Curthose in late December 1091, the king realigned himself with his youngest brother and supported Henry's campaigns against Robert with generous financial backing.

As Henry expanded his overlordship in Normandy, Robert remained hostile toward the English king for violating their 1091 treaty, threatening to repudiate it. In December 1093, Robert sent messengers across the Channel to the English court at Gloucester, demanding King William II immediately transfer the promised lordships to him or he would cancel the treaty. He challenged his brother to either honour the agreement or submit to the judgment of the twenty-four jurors who had earlier confirmed the Rouen treaty. The English king answered the duke's defiance by preparing for war against Normandy.

In mid-March 1094, William Rufus crossed over to Normandy to meet with Robert. He held talks with his brother but negotiations ended without any resolution, and the king departed to his properties in Eu to muster his military forces. With lavish payments of gold and promises of plunder, knights and foot-soldiers from far and wide rushed to join his growing army. As William II's military might grew, Robert negotiated the support of King Philip I of France to bolster his defences. When hostilities broke out, Rufus unleashed pillaging attacks into the duke's lands, Curthose responding by capturing several of the king's Norman castles, but their skirmishing remained inconclusive. While the two brothers fought each other for possession of Normandy, Henry stayed at Domfront, involved with the administration of his growing fiefdom.

In the early autumn of 1094, as William's war against Duke Robert dragged on without resolution, messengers from the king were dispatched to Henry at

Domfront, seeking his armed intervention against their older brother. The king had made little progress against Robert and had returned to England to raise more money and recruit additional soldiers. In late December, Henry crossed the Channel to meet Rufus in London. The Norman prince lingered at the royal court until spring before returning to Normandy with a large treasury to renew the conflict against Curthose. Henry led his brother's campaign, sending his knights and infantrymen to repeatedly hammer the duke's towns and lands, inflicting great damage. Over the next few years, Henry continued to expand and strengthen his powerbase in western Normandy, while crossing the Channel occasionally to England to attend the royal court.

Henry relentlessly pressed his campaign against Curthose's ducal lands, expanding the king's authority over a large section of Normandy, while the duke struggled to hold his surviving demesne. As Henry harassed his eldest brother's domains, in the autumn of 1095 Pope Urban II summoned the knights of Europe to free the Holy City of Jerusalem from Saracen control in what became the First Crusade. Bishop Odo of Bayeux, along with several Norman prelates, attended the Church assembly at Clermont in central France, where the pontiff issued his call for a crusade against the Muslims. Beset with the loss of territories in the eastern and central regions of his ducal lands, and with private wars and turmoil raging in the area still under his possession, Duke Robert was convinced by his bishops to turn over the duchy to the English king and 'take the cross'. In need of money to finance his participation in the crusade, he arranged to borrow the funds from William II, giving Normandy as his guarantee for future repayment. In September 1096, Curthose set off on his journey to Constantinople and then on to the Levant. The English king now ruled all the lands formerly controlled by William the Conqueror. For his loyalty and success in defeating Robert, William II granted Henry his former countship of Cotentin and authority over western Normandy as vassal to his eldest brother.

In the wake of Curthose's departure on the journey to the Holy Land, Henry joined William II in Normandy, remaining with the king during the following months. In 1097 and 1098, the restored Count of Cotentin participated in his brother's campaigns in the Vexin against King Louis VI of France, enlarging the territory under the control of the English monarch. When the count was not serving in the royal army, he was in western Normandy ruling his demesne. In late May 1099, he followed Rufus to London to attend the royal court.

By 1100, William Rufus was at the summit of his power, ruling both England and Normandy, and had just gained possession of Aquitaine in western France after taking it as collateral for a loan to Duke William IX for his participation in the crusade. To inhibit Curthose from reclaiming his duchy, the king amassed a large treasury of silver for the defence of Normandy. In early August 1100, William II's grand plans to reign over north-western Europe suddenly ended in the New Forest of southern England.

On the afternoon of 2 August, the English king, accompanied by several noblemen, set out to hunt deer in the New Forest. Count Henry was again visiting the English court and was in the royal entourage. During the hunt, a wayward arrow struck William II in the chest, killing him instantly. When informed of the monarch's death, Henry rode quickly to Winchester to take possession of the royal treasury and gain the English barons' approval for his succession to the throne. By right of birth, Robert Curthose was the next in line to the crown, but when challenged by a supporter of the duke, Henry drew his sword and declared he would allow no one to prevent his seizure of the throne. The gathered warlords now declared their allegiance to Henry of Normandy as King of England. To ensure his kingship, Henry travelled to London, being crowned by Bishop Maurice on Sunday, 5 August, in Westminster Abbey. During the ceremony, he pledged before the altar to keep the peace and maintain all just laws, while promising to put right all the injustices of his brother. When the assembled magnates, prelates and high officials were asked by the bishop whether they accepted Henry as the new monarch, they loudly acclaimed their approval. After prayers, the bishop anointed Henry I with holy oil and placed the English crown on his head. As the ordained king sat on his throne, the coronation ceremony was concluded with a Mass.

After claiming the crown of England, Henry I initiated a series of measures to secure his hold on the realm. With Robert Curthose reportedly on his way back from Jerusalem, his younger brother needed the full support of the nobles and churchmen to prevent the usurpation of his regime. He granted wide-ranging concessions and conferred numerous favours to secure their endorsement. Under the reign of Rufus, the popular Archbishop of Canterbury, Anselm, had been compelled to abandon the kingdom; to gain the favour of the Church, Henry invited him to return. Anselm, an Italian monk, abbot and philosopher, had been enthroned as Archbishop of Canterbury by Pope Urban II in 1093. He was later canonized as a saint in 1163 by Pope Alexander III.

To further solidify his hold on the throne, King Henry intervened to end the private wars fought among his vassals, thereby bringing peace to England. In November 1100, he negotiated his marriage to Matilda, sister of King Edgar of Scotland, to insure his northern borders against an attack by the Scots. The king's marriage to Matilda, who was directly related to several Anglo-Saxon kings, bound his Norman monarchy to the old English ruling dynasty. To prevent Robert from gaining allies in France and Flanders, Henry formed a coalition with them, limiting the potential military power of his brother. The king wrote to Pope Paschal II, telling him: 'I wish to preserve unimpaired in my kingdom those privileges, usages and customs which my father had.' Papal compliance was guaranteed by a large sum of money sent by the English throne to the court of the pope. To further gain the support of the magnates and churchmen, the highly unpopular Bishop of Durham, Ranulf Flambard, was charged with corruption and exploitation of ecclesiastic offices, and held captive in the Tower of London on orders from the English crown.

On 11 November 1100, Henry I was married in Westminster Abbey to Matilda of Scotland. Matilda, born in 1080 into the ruling royal Scottish dynasty, was the daughter of King Malcolm III and Queen Margaret. Through her mother's bloodlines, she was a descendant of the Saxon kings Edward the Confessor and Edmund Ironside. She received a well-rounded education, attending school at the nunnery of Romsey and later at the Wilton Convent. Henry I likely first met

Matilda when she visited the court of William II. He was attracted to her and she reciprocated his feelings. As the plans for their matrimonial union developed, many members of the clergy considered her a nun and thus canonically ineligible for marriage. She had indeed spent many years in convents and was suspected of taking holy orders. To overcome the obstacle to her marriage to the king, Anselm intervened by convening an ecclesiastic council to determine if she had taken vows. When the council members declared she was not a holy sister, Anselm accepted the decision. Shortly after, he performed the wedding ceremony and crowned her Queen of England. Matilda was described by her contemporaries as intelligent and well-educated, while possessing a common beauty. As queen, she resided at Westminster Palace and travelled with the king on his many journeys throughout England. At the royal court, she was an ardent patron of literature and music, being surrounded by noted poets, musicians and scholars. The queen became renowned for her devotion to religion and the poor. She often conferred with the monarch on government decisions, and during his prolonged absences presided over council meetings, serving as regent. Matilda bore Henry I two children: Matilda, born in 1102, and the heir to the English crown, William Atheling, born the following year at Winchester. In 1115, after Henry I reimposed his rule over Normandy, William Atheling received pledges of fealty from the rebel barons as the successor designate. Queen Matilda died in 1118 at the age of 38, leaving a large void in the life of the king and the administration of his regime.

In September 1100, Robert Curthose returned to Normandy from the First Crusade with an Italian wife, Sybilla of Conversano, and a large dowry. After landing in his duchy, he quickly reasserted his overlordship over his barons and churchmen without a fight, and with the money from the dowry began preparations for the conquest of Henry's kingdom to enforce his rightful claim to the realm as William II's eldest surviving son. Most of the Norman warlords preferred the disorderly rule of Robert and willingly rallied to his call to arms. While Curthose was organizing his army, in England Bishop Ranulf Flambard escaped from the Tower of London and fled to Normandy. Residing at the Norman ducal court, the bishop pressed the lethargic duke to challenge his brother's claim to the English throne. Robert had made little progress in preparing for the invasion of England, but after Flambard was named counsellor to the duke the situation rapidly changed. Flambard, a skilled and experienced organizer, quickly assembled ships, troops, weapons and supplies for the attack against Henry.

In England, Henry I was initiating measures to defend his crown and strengthen his support among the English magnates, Church and populace. He negotiated an agreement with Robert II, Count of Flanders, for the use of 1,000 knights against his enemies in return for an annual retainer of 500 pounds. The king held court in April and June, where his nobles renewed their assurances of fealty, but their allegiance remained tepid and unenthusiastic. During the summer, the king sent letters to every shire confirming his subjects' laws and rights, while requiring them to swear oaths to defend his realm.

When the king received reports that his older brother was mobilizing an invasion army, he summoned his soldiers to arms. Despite their repeated pledges of fealty, many of Henry's warlords failed to appear with their troops, but the ecclesiastic forces of the bishops assembled at the king's call. With numerous barons ignoring Henry's order, Archbishop Anselm met with many of them individually and in large groups, convincing them to participate in the campaign. Summons were also sent to the towns for the farmers and merchants to muster in defence of England.

In late June, the assembled English army, led by Henry I, marched to Robert's anticipated landing site at Pevensey Bay in south-eastern England to await the arrival of his brother. While the royal troops waited for the invasion, Henry moved through their camps, encouraging them to fight for their lands and king. As Duke Robert made his final preparations for the invasion, Flambard convinced him to disembark his fleet at Portsmouth. The Norman ships crossed the Channel in fair weather, and on 20 July 1101 the small ducal army of knights, infantrymen and archers landed unopposed. As news of the invasion quickly spread, many English nobles disregarded their pledges of loyalty, deserting their sovereign-lord to join Curthose's forces. Robert now led his reinforced host north toward Winchester to seize the royal treasury. Instead of immediately advancing on the city, however, he ordered his men to encamp, giving Henry the opportunity to hasten west and intercept his brother. As the ducal army remained in its encampment, Henry approached with his soldiers.

The two armies met at Alton in Hampshire, where the brothers delayed unleashing their attacks. As the stalemate continued, Norman and English knights began to meet to discuss a settlement. King Henry and Duke Robert joined the negotiations, working out a peace treaty. Under the terms of the resulting agreement, Henry renounced his rights to western Normandy, with the exception of Domfront, and pledged to pay his brother 3,000 marks a year, while Robert released him from his prior oaths of fealty and acknowledged him as King of England. It was further agreed that all lands seized during the conflict would be restored to their previous owners. Curthose remained in England for several months, attending court and royal council meetings with his brother before sailing back to his duchy with many gifts.

While King Henry was struggling to impose his rule over his recalcitrant English warlords and repel the invasion of Robert Curthose, he was embroiled in an investiture controversy with the Church. In 1099, Pope Urban II had issued a papal decree banning lay investiture of the clergy and the offering of homage to the ruler. Traditionally, English kings had ordained the realm's abbots and bishops with the ring and staff of office and received their pledge of fealty, but now only the papacy was authorized to perform the ceremony. The ruling was ignored by Henry I, but when Archbishop Anselm returned from exile in 1100, he notified the sovereign that he would comply with the papacy's wishes. Despite Henry's attempts to win over the archbishop, Anselm refused to abandon the pope's orders. As the disagreement escalated, Anselm travelled to Rome in 1103 to present his position to the pope. After Pope Paschal II supported the archbishop, the king refused to permit Anselm to return to England and seized his sizable ecclesiastic properties. The conflict escalated further when the pope threatened to excommunicate Henry. The religious crisis was finally resolved in July 1105 when the king and archbishop negotiated a compromise. Under their agreement, Henry renounced lay ordination, while retaining the custom of receiving the homage of the abbots and bishops for their fiefdoms. The final treaty was signed at Laigle, south-east of Paris.

Meanwhile, the king was moving against the powerful English barons who had rallied to support Robert Curthose during his invasion of England. In 1102, he advanced against Robert of Belleme and his two brothers. Robert of Belleme, a wealthy landowner in both England and Normandy, had repeatedly sided with the enemies of the crown. When the English regime proclaimed Robert of Belleme a traitor, the rebellious warlord gathered his retainers and troops, and along with Welsh mercenaries plundered royal lands in Staffordshire. In April, the king responded to Robert's attacks by assembling an army of knights and foot-soldiers, first advancing against Belleme's castle at Arundel. The stronghold was besieged and assailed with siege towers and battering rams. While the siege at Arundel continued, Henry sent part of his army under the command of the Bishop of Lincoln against Lord Robert's fortress at Tickhill, which submitted without opposition. Following three months of attacks and with provisions running low, Arundel's defenders surrendered. The king resumed his campaign in the summer, taking the castle at Bridgnorth after a three-week siege. Through his offensive of aggressive attacks against Robert's fortifications and the generous use of bribes to his allies, Henry I greatly weakened the resolve of Belleme's followers. When the royalists next marched into Shrewsbury, Robert of Belleme realized the hopelessness of his situation, the rebel lord surrendering all of his English lands to the crown and going into exile in Normandy. Belleme's brothers, Roger the Poitevin and Arnuly of Montgomery, who had joined the revolt against the English monarch, suffered a similar fate, losing all their properties in England. The remaining Norman landowners in England, not willing to risk the seizure of their lordships, duly proclaimed their loyalty to Henry I.

With his hold over England now secure, Henry moved against Duke Robert in Normandy. He cultivated the support of the Anglo-Norman warlords by granting them lordships and arranging their marriages to wealthy English ladies. In August 1104, the king crossed the Channel with a great fleet and entourage, visiting his enclave at Domfront in a show of force and grandeur. During his journey through Normandy, he was joined by numerous Norman noblemen, who deserted Curthose to seek his friendship. When Henry returned to England in the autumn, he had secured the fealty of numerous Norman barons, leaving his brother with the allegiance of only two families with large powerful lordships, the magnates of Belleme and Mortain.

Upon his return to his kingdom, Henry I began to prepare for a definitive conquest of Normandy. To finance the expeditionary force, taxes were raised and the kingdom's fiscal systems reorganized. Large bribes were paid to retain his Norman supporters and gain new lords to his banner. In Normandy, the rule of Duke Robert was beset by private wars among the nobility, with crops laid to waste, widespread lawlessness and attacks against the Church and towns. Henry sent his agents into the duchy to spread the word that his reign would bring peace and prosperity to the region. To reinforce his army, Henry negotiated alliances with the neighbouring rulers of Normandy, gaining troops from Maine, Anjou and Brittany, while securing an agreement with the French king, Philip I, for his neutrality.

In the spring of 1105, the English king marshalled his army and crossed the Channel, landing unopposed at Barfleur on the Cotentin Peninsula. Most of the warlords in western Normandy were supporters of the English crown and offered no resistance to the invasion. Henry marched his men to the town of Carentan, and on Easter Sunday attended religious services led by the Bishop of Sees. The bishop exhorted him to end the turmoil of Duke Robert's reign and bring peace to the duchy. Following the Easter service, the monarch led his army east to attack the city of Bayeux. When the inhabitants refused Henry's demands to surrender, the king besieged the city. The English, with their allies from Anjou and Maine, then unleashed a savage assault to break into Bayeux and set many buildings on fire. The flames spread rapidly through the city from rooftop to rooftop, compelling the defenders to submit. The magnificent Cathedral of Notre Dame, built by Bishop Odo, was destroyed by the raging fire but later rebuilt by Henry I. The garrison captain and many of his men were taken prisoner, with the soldiers from Maine and Anjou allowed to plunder the remains of Bayeux.

In the aftermath of the destruction of Bayeux, the royal army renewed its offensive, hastening toward Caen. When the invading forces had first landed in the Cotentin, Robert Curthose travelled north to Caen and was still in the city as the English advanced from Bayeux. Learning that the populace intended to submit, he fled in haste to avoid capture. News of the devastation at Bayeux had reached the Caen townspeople, and to avoid the same fate, the ruling council sent envoys to Henry surrendering the city. With his victories at Bayeux and Caen, Henry had regained control of most of western Normandy and was determined to continue his campaign to recreate the empire of his father.

From Caen, the royalists proceeded south to seize the town of Falaise. Unlike Caen, the Falaise garrison refused to surrender, forcing the English and their Norman allies to besiege the town. While the investment continued, the king made plans to take Falaise by storm, but when his Maine and Anjou allies suddenly withdrew from the expeditionary force, he was forced to abandon the attack. After failing to take the town, he suspended his campaign and arranged to meet his brother at Cintheaux to negotiate a peace. Their meeting lasted for two days but ended without any agreement, after which Henry returned to England.

In the spring of 1106, Henry resumed his campaign against Robert Curthose, assembling his army and recrossing the English Channel. After landing in Normandy, he moved his army against the fortified Abbey of Saint-Pierre sur Dives. Advancing at night, the English and their allies unleashed a surprise morning assault against the abbey, overrunning the defenders and setting the buildings on fire. The garrison was forced to surrender, the royalists next marching against the town of Tinchebray and its hilltop citadel.

Tinchebray castle was the property of Lord William of Mortain, who had maintained his loyalty to Duke Robert. Henry proceeded against the town with a large force of English and Norman soldiers, laying siege to the citadel. As the siege wore on, Lord William sent messengers to his uncle, Robert of Belleme, and

Duke Robert Curthose to petition their intervention. The two Roberts answered the call by assembling their knights and foot-soldiers and advancing to relieve the investment. On 28 September 1106, the two armies clashed at Tinchebray. Before the battle, Henry I sent emissaries to the duke, offering to pay him the yearly revenues of Normandy for the surrender of his duchy. Robert quickly rejected the terms and the armies prepared to fight.

Henry ordered the majority of his troops to fight on foot, while a force of mercenary cavalry led by Count Helias of Maine was hidden out of sight behind some hills. The royal army was aligned into three divisions of knights and infantrymen. Henry took command of a contingent of Englishmen and Normans, advancing against the enemy on foot. The battle began with a cavalry charge by Duke Robert's mounted soldiers, led by William of Mortain, who crashed into the royalists' line, whereupon his infantry joined the fierce and bloody melee. As fighting continued across the battlefield, Count Helias unleashed a savage charge into the foe's flank from his concealed position, his horsemen thundering into the duke's foot-soldiers. The ducal troops were unable to withstand the combined onslaught of the royal cavalry and infantry. As their line began to break, Curthose's men fled, leaving hundreds of their dead and wounded on the bloody field. Lord Robert of Belleme, in command of the rearguard, panicked and abandoned the battlefield as the Norman soldiers fled. After less than an hour of fighting, Henry I had won a complete victory over his brother. Robert Curthose was captured during the battle and spent the remainder of his life as the king's prisoner, dying in 1134, while Lord William of Mortain was also seized and imprisoned. The total defeat of Curthose's army secured Henry's control over Normandy and reunited his father's Anglo-Norman domain. Following the Battle of Tinchebray, the English king sent a message to Archbishop Anselm announcing his victory and claiming he had captured 400 knights and 10,000 infantrymen, while a countless number had died by the sword.

Many of the leading Norman followers of Duke Robert were present at the Battle of Tinchebray, and their death or capture ensured the remainder of the magnates quickly acknowledged the overlordship of Henry I. While Curthose and William of Mortain remained in confinement, most of the captured warlords were soon released after pledging allegiance to the English king. Before the clash at Tinchebray, the duke's soldiers at Falaise had sworn to surrender only to the duke or his personal representative. To gain the peaceful submission of the garrison, Henry – accompanied by his brother – rode to Falaise, where Robert arranged to meet with the garrison captain and townspeople to negotiate their pledges of submission and loyalty to his brother. While at Falaise, the king was introduced to William Clito, the young son of Duke Robert. Henry believed the boy was no threat to his reign and released him, placing his nephew in the custody of Helias of Saint-Saens, who had been a devoted friend and follower of Curthose. Henry's decision at Falaise would later lead to conflict with the rulers of France, Flanders and Anjou, who supported William Clito as the rightful successor to the ducal throne of Normandy.

After peacefully gaining control of Falaise, King Henry, accompanied by the duke, travelled to the ducal capital at Rouen, where the city surrendered to the royalists without resistance. With control of the city, Henry I revalidated William the Conqueror's laws and privileges to the Norman citizens. With the assistance of his brother, the king secured the submission of the remaining ducal castles and the homage of the townspeople. While remaining in Normandy strengthening his overlordship, he summoned the ducal warlords to meet in October at Lisieux, in north-western France, to restore the administration of Normandy to its state during the rule of his father. He decreed that peace should be enforced throughout the duchy, that plundered Church properties should be returned and that robbery and pillage should cease. He met with bishops and abbots, settling outstanding disputes between them and the warlords. During his stay in the duchy, Henry restored an orderly government that would enforce law and order and end the turmoil of his brother's reign.

In the spring of 1107, Henry returned to England after an absence of nearly a year. He had previously finalized his ecclesiastic agreement with Archbishop Anselm at Laigle, thereby ending the investiture controversy, and after arriving in England moved to formally present its terms to the English nobles, abbots and bishops. A grand council was summoned to Westminster Palace on 1 August 1107 to gain the approval of the English prelates and magnates. Henry defended his decision to renounce investiture and announced before the assembled body that no English prelate would now receive ordination to his office from the king, while Archbishop Anselm accepted their pledging of homage to the crown. During the investiture crisis, numerous vacancies in the English Church had remained unfilled. With the Laigle Treaty now formally accepted, the king, with the advice of the archbishop, began naming churchmen to fill the positions. When Anselm later wrote to Pope Paschal II reporting that the king was now making his choices for ecclesiastic offices with the advice of religious men, the pontiff became satisfied with the terms of the Laigle settlement.

Following his conquest of Normandy and the end to the investiture dilemma, Henry I became embroiled in reforming the government of England. He issued decrees increasing the penalties for numerous crimes and made robbery a capital offence. To improve the economy of the kingdom, the coinage system was redesigned and standardized. The ell was the standard unit of length in the realm, but there was no official dimension for the measurement. On orders from the sovereign, the length of his arm was set as the benchmark for an ell and all tradesmen were now required to use it. To curtail ongoing abuses in the shire courts, the royal regime issued strict regulations forbidding courtiers from stealing or plundering, setting the penalties for such acts at blinding and castration. The royal courts now served as the principal administer of justice. The position of exchequer was created by the king to record, safeguard and disburse royal taxes, while the local sheriffs were made responsible for the collection of funds. The reform measures served to reduce corruption and greatly increase the amount of money flowing into the crown's coffers.

In 1108, King Philip I of France died and was succeeded by his son, Louis VI. Under the reign of Philip I, his Capetian regime had remained neutral during Henry I's seizure of Normandy, but the new king adopted a more aggressive policy toward western France. The Capetian king now demanded Henry's pledge of fealty for Normandy and the abandonment of his two castles bordering French lands. Henry refused to relinquish control of the strategic strongholds, and in the summer of 1108 sailed across the Channel to Normandy to defend his demesne. As the Normans prepared their defences, in early 1109 the Capetian crown plundered and burned the French possessions of Henry I's vassal, Count Robert of Meulan. As Louis VI stayed along the border threatening to attack Normandy, the English king mobilized his army and hastened to the eastern frontier to protect his lands and support his allies.

While the English-Norman army approached Meulan, Henry I encountered the French monarch near the River Epte in northern France. Envoys were exchanged between the two realms and peace talks begun. Louis VI again demanded Henry I pay homage for Normandy and surrender his two border castles, but the English king defiantly refused. Nevertheless, the meeting did end with a truce, and soon after the English and their allies returned to Normandy.

Undeterred by his first confrontation with Henry I, the French king remained determined to enforce his overlordship in the fiefdoms bordering his realm. He sent his Capetian troops across the border to attack Norman strongholds and towns. Many Norman warlords still preferred the weak rule of Robert Curthose and now began to promote William Clito as the rightful successor to the ducal crown. To secure the allegiance of the rebel lords, Louis VI declared his support for the young prince. As news of the French throne's declaration spread in western France, the Count of Anjou, Fulk V, joined the French king along with Robert of Flanders. In Normandy, numerous barons now broke their pledges of fealty, abandoning Henry and fortifying their fortresses in defiance of his ducal government.

As the rebellion spread across Normandy, the English king's nephew, Count Theobald IV of Blois, ordered his soldiers to attack Louis VI's castles to distract the French away from Normandy. Theobald was the second son of Henry I's favourite sister, Adela, and had succeeded his father as count in 1102. By 1112, many French warlords had broken with Louis VI to unite with Theobald IV in his revolt against the Capetian regime. The Count of Blois' uprising grew larger when Norman knights joined with him and the allies struck out against the French. Meanwhile, in Normandy, with his martial resources spread between the recalcitrant Norman barons and raids along his border with France, the English king was forced to avoid a pitched battle and concentrate his efforts on defeating the individual rogue lords. After more than a year of fighting, Henry I's strategy had defeated many of the rebel warlords and his hold on Normandy seemed secure again.

During the struggle with the French and the recalcitrant Normans, Count Robert of Belleme again broke his oath of homage and joined the uprising. In November 1112, he attended the Anglo-Norman court at Bonneville claiming to be an emissary from Louis VI. Henry refused to recognize him as a foreign ambassador, condemning him as a rebel who had joined his regime's enemies. The count was also charged with failing to attend court following a summons and refusing to remit collected tax revenues. Belleme was sentenced to imprisonment and spent the remainder of his life in captivity in England. The count's border fortress at Alencon was besieged by the king's men and following a short investment was captured, ending the prolonged defiance of the Belleme family against the English throne.

While the English and their Norman allies were aggressively overpowering the dissident lords, the king ordered the arrest of William Clito. Viscount Robert of Beauchamp was sent to capture the young lord at the castle of Saint-Saens. As the viscount approached the fortress, Clito was carried away by friends across the Normandy border. Under the continued guardianship of Count Helias of Maine, William was taken from castle to castle before finding refuge at the Flemish court of Count Baldwin VII. Remaining with the Flemish regime, Helias aggressively sought support for Clito from Louis VI and other great French princes.

After securing his rule in Normandy, Henry I aggressively pursued the allegiance of the fiefdoms surrounding his lands. Utilizing a policy of granting bribes of land and arranging marriages to royal illegitimate daughters, the English king won over many magnates from Maine. The English crown acquired the strategic fortress at Sourches north-west of Le Mans by the transfer of properties in England to Lord Patrick. King Henry gained the support of the powerful lord of Beaumont-le-Viscomte, Roscelin, by his marriage to a royal daughter. The marital union with Roscelin brought his strategic castle in Maine under Henry I's control and away from possible alliance with the French. In early 1113, Henry arranged the marriage of his 9-year-old son, William Atheling, to the daughter of Count Fulk V of Anjou, as well as the matrimonial union between the English princess, Maud, to Conan II of Brittany, drawing two powerful countships away from the French.

Following the English peace agreements with Anjou and Brittany, Louis VI became increasingly isolated, forcing him to pursue terms with Henry I's regime. Henry met the French king in late March near Gisors to discuss a resolution to their conflict. Under their negotiated treaty, both realms agreed to keep the peace and form an alliance of friendship. The French conceded the overlordships of Maine, Brittany and Belleme to King Henry.

Despite his recent alliances with neighbouring fiefdoms and the submission of the Norman rebels, Henry I still had one significant pocket of resistance to his rule. The southern Norman county of Robert Belleme's son, Count William II Talvas, remained hostile. The English king thus summoned his army and allies, advancing against Talvas' stronghold. The captain of the garrison refused to submit, withdrawing his soldiers into the formidable hilltop citadel. Count Fulk V and Theobald IV had answered the royal call, joining their troops with Henry at the castle. The Anglo-Normans then stormed the town, breaking through the gate and attacking the garrison in the citadel. As William's garrison continued to resist, the soldiers of Henry I and his allies set the fortification ablaze, forcing the defenders to surrender. This victory gave Henry unchallenged control over Normandy and solidified his hold on the nearby strategic County of Maine.

King Henry returned to England in July 1113, assuming control of the kingdom from Matilda, who had acted as regent during his absence. While he governed over England and Normandy, in December the royal court celebrated the Christmas season at the newly constructed castle at Windsor. The king continued to fill the vacant ecclesiastic offices, meanwhile attending to the routine governing of the realm. In 1114, he sent his army into Wales to quell the fighting between several local princedoms and to enforce his suzerainty. The king divided his forces into three columns and personally led the most easterly advance into Wales. The Welsh princes of Powys and Gwynedd quickly ended their belligerence and submitted without resistance. In the aftermath of their surrender, the remaining princedoms agreed to terms with the English crown. Henry's triumphant Welsh campaign brought years of peace along the frontier.

Henry returned to Normandy in the autumn of 1114 to safeguard the continued loyalty of the barons, prelates and towns. He summoned the Norman magnates to Rouen in the spring of 1115, where they pledged their fealty to the king's son and heir, William Atheling. From his Norman capital, he sent emissaries to the court of Louis VI offering a large sum of silver for the French throne's acceptance of his son's succession to the Norman duchy. On the advice of his counsellors, the Capetian monarch quickly rejected the offer and announced his support for William Clito as the rightful duke. With its denial of William Atheling's legitimacy as ruler, the French regime had set the stage for the renewal of hostilities between the two monarchies.

Henry I crossed the Channel to England again in July 1115, assuming the reins of government from his regent. Several months later, he summoned a great council, with the magnates and prelates meeting at Westminster to resolve outstanding ecclesiastic and government issues. During his stay in England, Henry provided military support for his nephew, Theobald IV of Blois, who continued his pillaging attacks against Capetian lands, drawing French troops away from Normandy. As Louis VI expanded his raids into the duchy, Baldwin VII of Flanders sent knights and soldiers into Normandy to ravage isolated villages and castles in support of the French. King Henry stayed in England for less than nine months before returning to Normandy to defend his lands as hostilities with the French and their allies increasingly spread along his Norman frontier, threatening to unravel his overlordship. Henry would spend the following four years defending his rights to the Duchy of Normandy against the repeated attacks of the French throne and his rebellious Norman warlords.

After arriving in Normandy, the English king marched his army east to assail the Capetian town and citadel at Saint-Clair-Epte on the French side of the River Epte. The Anglo-Normans launched a surprise assault that quickly overwhelmed the enemy forces and captured the fortress. Louis VI retaliated by seizing the village of Gasny in Norman territory. When the English monarch built two new castles to reinforce his borderland security, the French attacked the stronghold at Malassis, while ravaging the countryside for miles as they established a foothold in Normandy. As the French moved deeper into the duchy, Louis VI summoned Count Fulk V, who had broken his pledge of fealty to the English, and Baldwin VII of Flanders to join his army with their troops. The French and their allies continued their plundering and burning attacks in the summer of 1117, while Henry I remained in the fortress at Rouen with his army.

The following year, the Capetian king and his vassals intensified their border attacks across southern and eastern Normandy as a growing number of recalcitrant

Norman warlords joined their campaign of pillage and destruction. In the west, Count Baldwin VII persuaded the Norman lords of Eu and Aumale to rebel against the rule of Henry I and participate in the assaults against his lands, while to the south, Count Fulk V rallied dissidents to the French cause. In the summer of 1118, Robert Giroie merged his troops with the rebellion and fortified his castle at Saint-Ceneri against an attack by Henry I. With Giroie's stronghold threatened by the barons loyal to the Anglo-Norman throne, Fulk V rode with 500 knights and infantry to reinforce his ally. After reaching Saint-Ceneri, to distract the enemy the Count of Anjou took his troops to besiege the English-held fortress at La Motte Gautier, which was garrisoned with soldiers from Henry's personal household guard. When Henry learned of the siege, he assembled his men and advanced south-west, meanwhile ordering reinforcements from his vassals. Overwhelmed by repeated attacks, the garrison troops at La Motte Gautier surrendered before Henry arrived with his relief forces, compelling him to remain at Alencon.

With his southern demesne under escalating attacks by Louis VI and his allies, Henry I transferred to Theobald IV's overlordship his strategic castles at Alencon, Sees and La Roche Mabile, plus several other fortified towns, from the deposed Robert of Belleme to shore up his defences. The properties were soon ceded by the count to his younger brother, Stephen, who would later succeed his uncle as King of England. The continued loyalty of the Norman barons remained questionable and the king was under persistent attacks on several fronts.

In 1118, Lord Richer of Laigle rebelled against his Norman overlord after King Henry ceded English lands to his younger brother instead of him. When Henry learned of Richer's agreement with the French crown in August, he rescinded the grant to the younger brother to win back the barons' fealty. Now with possession of the English properties, Richer attempted to withdraw from his treaty with the Capetian throne, but Louis VI refused, attacking and destroying his town of Laigle while occupying the citadel with his men to expand the lands under his overlordship.

While the French were plundering the southern Normandy lordships, King Henry led his army north-east from Rouen in a bid to force his recalcitrant barons to abandon the French crown and pledge their fealty to him. He first attacked the stronghold of Robert of Neubourg, who had recently joined the uprising against his rule. The king sent his troops over the castle's walls, subduing the garrison and burning the town to the ground. As Henry renewed his barbaric pillaging campaign against the dissidents in the north-east, in September 1118 Baldwin VII of Flanders was mortally wounded while attacking loyal Norman lords and was compelled to retire. The count died in mid-1119 and was succeeded by Charles the Good, who abandoned the Norman war and kept the peace along the north-eastern border with Normandy.

In the aftermath of the withdrawal of the Flemish forces, the hostile pressure against English rule was decreased along the north-eastern frontier, allowing Henry I to lead his army of knights, infantrymen and archers against the French at Laigle. He besieged the citadel but the garrison repeatedly repelled his assaults. During the fighting, the king was almost killed when he was struck in the head by a stone thrown from the walls, while his ally, Theobald IV of Blois, suffered injuries after he was thrown from his horse when charging the enemy. Unable to force the surrender of the garrison, Henry abandoned the siege and moved south against the strategic stronghold of Alencon.

Theobald IV's younger brother, Stephen, had been granted Alencon by the count, but his repressive policies led to the revolt of the townspeople, who now offered Fulk V of Anjou the lordship of the town. The Count of Anjou accepted the tender and hastened to the stronghold with his army to defend his new possession. In late December, he took control of the town and laid siege to the citadel garrison, which remained loyal to the ducal regime. When King Henry learned of the attack, he summoned his English forces and loyal Norman lords and advanced to relieve the siege. Theobald IV led the advance force of soldiers, but moved too far ahead of the main body and was attacked by Fulk V, being beaten back with heavy losses. The reunited royal army proceeded forward, soon clashing with the Count of Anjou's men. During fierce fighting, Count Theobald IV was wounded and the royal Norman forces were pushed back. Overwhelmed by the relentless and determined assaults of the Anjou knights and foot-soldiers, Henry I was compelled to retreat, leaving his wounded and dead on the battlefield of Alencon. In the wake of this victory, Fulk V continued to besiege the castle, eventually forcing the garrison to surrender. Alencon was now occupied by troops faithful to Count Fulk and Henry had suffered another humiliating loss of authority.

The English king's defeat at Alencon prompted additional Norman barons to abandon him and join the rebellion. In February 1119, Eustace of Breteuil, who was married to the king's illegitimate daughter, Juliana, threatened to defect to the French if he was not granted the stronghold of Ivry. Henry gave Eustace a vague assurance of the property's transfer, and to ensure his continued loyalty forced his son-in-law to exchange hostages. The king received his two granddaughters, while Eustace was given the son of Ralph Harnec, the Constable of Ivry. After gaining possession of the constable's son, Eustace ordered him blinded and sent back to his father to enhance his new alliance with the French. Ralph Harnec, enraged by the mutilation, appealing to his overlord for vengeance. Harnec avenged his son by blinding the two young granddaughters of Eustace and cutting off portions of their noses. When Eustace heard of the girls' fate, he prepared his fortresses for an attack by the English and their allies. He sent Juliana with a contingent of knights and infantry to defend the Breteuil stronghold. Despite the occupation of the citadel by Juliana, the town's burghers remained loyal to the ducal crown and offered Breteuil to the king. Royal forces duly entered the town and attacked Juliana and her soldiers, who fled to the citadel. The fortress was besieged, and as sorties against the defenders continued, Juliana asked to meet with her father. When he approached his daughter, she drew a crossbow and quickly fired a bolt at him, but missed. Juliana was seized by the king's men and confined to the castle, but she soon leapt from the tower into the frozen waters of the moat to escape back to Eustace's encampment.

After receiving pledges of loyalty from the populace of Breteuil, Henry was forced to resume the war to retain his lands in western and eastern Normandy.

He waged a brutal campaign, ravaging his foes' properties, burning their villages and crops, and killing their followers. To finance his war against the rebels, Henry imposed a heavy taxation on his English subjects, who in spite of the financial burden remained loyal. Despite the defection of many Norman warlords, the English monarch still had a loyal force of powerful barons, plus household troops and soldiers from the episcopal cities. As the fighting continued, Henry I tirelessly pursued peace with his enemies, offering them grants of lordships and money which won back many of the defectors, while seeking terms with the neighbouring independent countships.

In May 1119, the English throne sent envoys to Fulk V to negotiate his defection from the French. An agreement was worked out that removed the count from the French alliance in return for a large sum of money and the marriage of his daughter, Matilda, to the king's heir, William Atheling, with the lordship of Maine as her dowry. The withdrawal of the Count of Anjou from the French coalition resulted in the cessation of the revolt along the southern frontier of Normandy.

With the rebellion in the south suppressed, in the summer of 1119 Henry I led his army in a campaign of destruction, burning villages and farmlands along the eastern border of his Norman realm. In July he advanced against the town of Evreux, defended by Lord Amaury III of Montfort, who had repeatedly rejected the ducal regime's offers of peace. With the support of Stephen of Blois and the Bishop of Evreux, Audoin, the Anglo-Norman army attacked the castle of Amaury III but failed to penetrate the defensive works, despite repeated assaults. The king ordered his men to burn the town to the ground, including Bishop Audoin's cathedral. The royalists again assailed the citadel, but the garrison repeatedly repelled their advances. Lord Amaury III was away from the town at the fortress of Eustace and Juliana, and after learning of the siege at Evreux sent messengers to Louis VI asking for his intervention. The French king marched a large army to support Amaury III's defence of his lands, and as his soldiers approached the fortification at Noyon-sur-Andelle in the Norman Vexin, they clashed at Bremule with the Anglo-Normans, who had recently abandoned the siege at Evreux. Warned of the fast-approaching French by his scouts, Henry I divided his forces into infantry and cavalry formations and awaited the enemy. The Capetian army was personally led by Louis VI and included William Clito and William Crispin, who was a well-known adversary of Henry I. The mounted French troops initiated the battle, charging into the Anglo-Norman cavalry and smashing through their front line. However, when they struck the next line of dismounted knights and foot-soldiers, the Capetian forces were thrown back in disarray. The English and their Norman allies now surrounded the enemy, killing many men and taking a large number prisoner. During the savage fighting at Bremule, William Crispin identified Henry I on the battlefield and galloped toward him, striking the dismounted king on the helmet with his sword. Henry survived the blow when the blade of the sword was deflected by his armour. Roger FitzRichard came to his overlord's rescue, knocking Crispin off his warhorse and taking him captive. With the battle lost, the surviving Frenchmen, including Louis VI and Clito, escaped into the dense woodlands.

In the aftermath of his defeat at Bremule, Louis VI returned to France and recruited a large but poorly armed and trained army to renew the campaign against the Anglo-Normans. In mid-September, he crossed the border and hastened toward Breteuil to recover the town for Eustace and Juliana. The French attacked the defenders of Breteuil, who were led by Lord Ralph of Gael. The Capetian knights and foot-soldiers charged the defensive works but were repeatedly repulsed. As Ralph of Gael continued to throw back the assaults, Louis VI was compelled to withdraw. The battle at Breteuil was the final attempt by the Capetian monarch to take Normandy, and Louis thereafter remained at his court in France. Without the strong military support of the Capetians, the Norman revolt faltered.

On 18 October 1119, Pope Calixtus II convened a great papal council at Reims. The gathering of high churchmen gave Louis VI the opportunity to address the prelates to secure their support against Henry I's English regime. He condemned the English king for his illegal seizure of Normandy and relentless attacks against his Norman lords, while supporting the inheritance rights of William Clito. Calixtus II responded by urging peace between the two realms and ordered the Anglo-Normans and their French adversaries to observe the Truce of God, a temporary cessation of hostilities promoted by the Church from the eleventh century in an attempt to end the epidemic of private wars occurring in Western Europe. Shortly after the synod ended, many Norman rebels deserted the Capetian crown and began negotiating a reconciliation with Henry I to resolve their differences. As the Norman warlords' uprising unravelled, Henry met with William Clito and offered his nephew three English counties and a place at the royal court for his renunciation of Normandy, but the proposal was rejected.

Henry I had continued to fend off attempts by the French and their Norman allies to overthrow him, but the pope's call for the observance of the Truce of God now prompted many of the rebels to submit to him as their overlord. Following the loss of most of his allies, Louis VI agreed in June 1120 to negotiate peace with his great rival. Under the terms of the resulting treaty, the French crown ceded Normandy to the son of Henry I, who in turn offered fealty to Louis VI as his overlord. William Atheling was now acknowledged as king and duke designate. Henry I and his 18-year-old heir remained in Normandy for several more months, ruling the duchy without opposition. On 25 November 1120, the king sailed from the port of Barfleur back to England after an absence of four years, during which he had been occupied with the suppression of the Norman barons' rebellions and fending off encroachments by the French. Before embarking on his vessel, he was asked by a sea captain to sail with him in his newly constructed vessel, the *White Ship*. Henry I's preparations were already made and the offer was declined, but he agreed to send his son, William Atheling, on the *White Ship*. The new vessel put to sea on a moonless night, and as the helmsman steered away from the shoreline, the *White Ship* crashed into a large hidden rock that tore open the hull and caused the ship to capsize. The heir to the English and ducal thrones was drowned, meaning Henry's skilfully crafted peace with France and Anjou was in shambles. In addition to William Atheling, Richard, Earl of Chester – the king's illegitimate son – was drowned, along with many young lords and ladies from the royal court. William Clito was now the recognized rightful successor to both England and Normandy.

Shortly after Henry I resumed personal rule in England, he was compelled to muster his barons and militiamen to advance against the Prince of Powys in northern Wales, who was ravaging the lands across the Welsh border. When the Welsh prince, Bleddy ap Bleddyn, learned of the death of the Earl of Chester on the *White Ship*, he began pillaging and destroying the castles and towns in his Chester earldom. To bring peace to his realm, the king led a large army into northern Wales to subdue the rebels. As the English pursued the Welsh, they were ambushed by a contingent of archers. During the fighting several royalists were killed, while Henry was hit in the chest by an arrow, which was deflected by his armour. The royal troops remained in Wales, attacking the rebellious Welsh and forcing Bleddyn to agree to end his plundering and accept peace terms.

Henry I's wife, Matilda, had died in 1118, and with the death of William Atheling on the *White Ship*, it was now vital to the succession of his family that he marry again to secure a legal heir. Negotiations were thus opened with Godfrey VI, Duke of Lower Lorraine and Count of Louvain, for a marital union with his daughter, Adeliza. On 6 January 1121, after a meeting in London with his barons and prelates to secure their approval, the king announced his marriage to Adeliza. The wedding ceremony took place at Windsor Castle on 20 January, followed by Adeliza's anointment as queen by the Archbishop of Canterbury. The new queen was described by contemporaries as young, beautiful and a direct descendent of Charlemagne, which generated added status for the English court and brought the monarchy closer to its strategic Duchy of Normandy.

After arranging the marriage of his daughter, Matilda, to William Atheling, Fulk V of Anjou had gone on a pilgrimage to Jerusalem seeking salvation for his many sins. In late 1121, he returned to Anjou and requested the return of his widowed daughter from the English court. The king sent Matilda back to Anjou, but kept control of her Maine dowry. The following year, the count sent emissaries to the English demanding the release of Maine, but Henry again declined to abandon the strategic countship. The rebuff by Henry resulted in the dissolution of the alliance between the two realms.

While Fulk V was negotiating the return of Maine, Lord Amaury III of Montfort rebelled again against the increasingly intrusive rule of the Anglo-Normans. Amaury III arranged an alliance with Fulk V, who had already severed his friendly relationship with the English regime. The Montfort lord persuaded the count to negotiate the marriage of his second daughter, Sibyl, to William Clito, with a dowry of Maine. The matrimonial union was consecrated in 1123, and with the full support of the Count of Anjou, Amaury III organized a revolt of numerous Norman barons against the rule of the English crown.

In late 1123, William Clito – with the support of Angevin troops – began attacking Henry I's forces in southern Normandy, while the Anglo-Normans strengthened their fortresses in preparation of the renewal of the barons' uprising. In October, Henry I led a large army out of Rouen in defence of his lands. He marched against Hugh of Montfort, attacking his castle at Montfort-sur-Risle.

They burned the town to the ground and laid siege to the citadel. After battering the walls for a month, the garrison captain was compelled to submit. The king resumed his campaign to quell the rebellion by attacking the great hilltop fortress at Beaumont in late October. With military assistance from Charles the Good of Flanders, he besieged the castle and destroyed the town, sending his cavalry to ravage the surrounding countryside. As the investment wore on, Henry I ordered a large siege tower to be built. The tower was rolled to the walls, allowing archers to fire down deadly flights of arrows on the defenders. Under the relentless assaults of the Anglo-Normans, the garrison finally surrendered. The revolt continued into the winter, the royalists capturing additional rebel strongholds and imposing their overlordship.

Despite the defeat of numerous rogue barons, the anti-Anglo-Norman coalition continued its quest for independence from the rule of Henry I. In late March 1124, the rebels assembled a large army under the command of Amaury III of Montfort and hastened to relieve the royalist siege of the castle of Vatteville in north-eastern Normandy. Amaury III's forces attacked the royal encampment in the early morning, forcing the king's troops to abandon the siege.

Meanwhile, at Evreux, loyal baron Ranulf of Chester was informed of the rebels' attack at Vatteville. He quickly sent messengers to nearby fortress captains, arranging an ambush against the rebels as they withdrew from Vatteville. On 26 March, the royalists were deployed along an open field at Bourgtheroulde, waiting for the enemy forces to emerge from dense woodlands. The king's men were divided into three divisions, with the dismounted knights holding the front line, followed by the cavalry, and the archers on the flanks. When Amaury III's troops came out of the forest, they saw Ranulf's men aligned in front of them. As the Norman dissidents charged forward, they were struck by wave after wave of arrows. Many knights were unhorsed before delivering a blow and were captured or killed, while the survivors fled to safety. The decisive victory marked the end of the uprising, any warlords who were considering joining the rebellion now remaining loyal to Henry. When Amaury later lost his lands, he took the cross of a crusader, dying in the Holy Land in 1137.

In the months prior to the Battle of Bourgtheroulde, the English monarch had mounted a diplomatic initiative to reduce the support of France and Anjou in the renewal of his campaign against the rebels. Henry sent representatives to Rome to arrange the annulment of William Clito's marriage to Sibyl. After the payment of large bribes, Pope Calixtus II issued a bull annulling the marriage on 26 August 1124. When Fulk V learned of the papal bull, he was enraged, briefly imprisoning the pope's envoy; for his actions, he was excommunicated by the Holy See. Shortly after the pope's decree, Fulk V submitted and William Clito was forced to leave the Angevin court.

While the English regime's negotiations with the Holy See were in progress, Henry I sent envoys to the imperial court of his son-in-law, Henry V – King of Germany and Holy Roman Emperor – to encourage him to attack the French from the east. In the summer of 1124, a German army crossed the border, marching toward Reims. This compelled Louis VI to remain in his kingdom, limiting his support for the rebel Norman warlords against the Anglo-Norman campaign of submission.

During the Norman rebellion of 1123–24, Henry I's second wife, Adeliza, travelled with him in the hope of conceiving a child. By 1125, after four years of marriage, it was likely the marriage was going to be childless and Henry I would die without a legitimate son to succeed him. Stephen of Blois had become the favourite nephew of the king, being ceded grants of large lordships in Normandy and England. He was now the likely choice as the heir to Henry I's realms. Speculation around Stephen's succession grew when he was married to Matilda, daughter of the Count of Boulogne, which brought him great wealth and power.

Henry I's only surviving legitimate child, also named Matilda, had married Henry V of Germany, but in 1125 he died and she returned to her father's court. In the following year, Henry I sailed to England with his daughter and soon met with his counsellors, convincing them to support the appointment of Matilda as heiress to the crown. On Christmas Day 1125, the English and Norman barons swore homage to Matilda, with Stephen of Blois pledging his fealty to her.

When Louis VI received reports of Matilda's recognition as successor-designate, he renewed his support for William Clito's claim to the Anglo-Norman lands. After Charles the Good was assassinated, the French king granted Clito the Countship of Flanders to enhance his power and prestige. As this new threat to his Norman lands escalated, Henry crossed the English Channel to Normandy and assembled his army. To discourage the French from their continued patronage of Clito, he marched his knights and soldiers to the frontier to reinforce the Flemish who had revolted against the succession of William Clito.

While the English and their Norman allies were demonstrating against France, Henry I renewed his alliance with Count Fulk V. As part of their agreement, the king's heiress, Matilda, was betrothed in late August 1127 at Rouen to Geoffrey, the son and heir of Count Fulk. Matilda opposed the union as it diminished her imperial status as empress, also objecting to marrying someone only 14 years old. She was finally persuaded by the Archbishop of Tours, Hildebert, to accept the marriage. On 10 June 1128, in Rouen, Henry I knighted Geoffrey, who received a sword, a pair of golden spurs and shield decorated with lions from the English king. The wedding ceremony took place in Le Mans Cathedral one week later, in the presence of Henry and Count Fulk V. Soon after the ceremony, Geoffrey was associated with the government of Anjou, and the following year, when his father travelled to the Holy Land, Geoffrey assumed control of the countship as ruler designate.

Meanwhile, in Flanders, William Clito was pursuing his quest for recognition as count. With financial and military aid from the English regime, Thierry of Alsace led the armed resistance against William. Thierry was the youngest son of Theoderic II of Lorraine and Gertrude, daughter of Count Robert I of Flanders. Following the murder of his cousin, Charles the Good, Thierry claimed the Flemish countship as the grandson of Robert I, contesting the rights of William Clito. During his conflict with the Flemish rebels, Clito fought with great skill against Thierry and was slowly gaining control of the countship. In late July 1128, Clito led an assault against Thierry's castle at Aalst, but during the fighting there was mortally wounded. Before his death, Clito wrote a letter to Henry I asking for his forgiveness and a pardon for all who had supported him. Many of William Clito's allies were now welcomed to the royal court by King Henry. The death of Clito eliminated the last serious threat from the Norman warlords to Henry's rule. In the following months, the Anglo-Norman throne negotiated peace with the French king, ending many years of hostility, and peace thereafter reigned in England and Normandy for the remainder of Henry I's life.

Shortly after Matilda's marriage to Geoffrey, she quarrelled with him and left his court, establishing her residence in Normandy. Geoffrey soon renounced Matilda, ruling his demesne without her. With his heiress and husband separated, Henry's plans for his succession again lay in ruins. During the following two years, the king's daughter remained in Normandy, but the political status quo changed in 1131 when Fulk V died. Geoffrey was now acknowledged as Count of Anjou and sent envoys to the English court asking Henry for the return of his wife. The king summoned Matilda from Normandy and she reached England in August. To secure his daughter's inheritance to his realm, Henry assembled his great royal council at Northampton, where the lords and prelates swore their fealty to Matilda. With his heiress' rights protected, Henry sent his daughter back to Anjou. Matilda was now the recognized inheritor of England and Normandy, while Geoffrey was to rule as Count of Anjou. Two years later, Matilda gave birth to a long-awaited son, Henry Plantagenet, who would take the throne as Henry II in 1154. The following year, a second son, Geoffrey, was born in Rouen. Soon after the birth of her second child, Matilda became seriously ill and her imminent death was feared, but during the following days she found the strength to recover. The birth of the two royal sons assured the continuation of Henry I's Norman line.

During the next few years, England and Normandy remained at peace and Henry I was occupied with the affairs of state. He travelled extensively through his lordships in England and Normandy imposing his justice and overlordship, while settling local disputes. While in Normandy in 1135, the king became estranged from his daughter and Geoffrey over their request for the transfer of previously promised frontier castles. As part of his daughter's dowry, Henry had pledged to assign several strongholds on his southern border to the Anjou court, but had repeatedly refused to deliver them, enraging Geoffrey.

Matilda's support among the Norman warlords was tenuous, so the transfer of the strategic fortresses while her father was alive would strengthen her hold on Normandy. While Geoffrey pressed his demands for the strongholds, Norman barons on the southern border with Anjou began preparations to revolt against the king in support of Geoffrey. The Count of Ponthieu, William Talvas, broke his oaths of allegiance, joining the Count of Anjou late in 1135. As additional barons abandoned the Anglo-Normans, Henry I mustered his forces and marched to the southern frontier to defend his castles. He stayed in the south for nearly four months, capturing the rebel strongholds at Alencon and Almenesches, while reinforcing the defensive works of his own southern castles. With winter approaching, he retired to his stronghold at Lyons-la-Foret to hunt and rest. In late

November, the monarch arrived at his fortress, planning to hunt in the morning, but during the night he became severely ill. Over the following days, Henry's health grew increasingly worse and he summoned his chaplain to confess his sins. Before he died, he assigned all of his properties in England and Normandy to Matilda as his lawful successor. On 1 December 1135, King Henry I died at the age of 68 after a reign in England of 35 years. The monarch's body was escorted to Rouen, where the corpse was prepared for burial. It was next taken to Caen for transfer to England, but stormy weather in the Channel delayed the voyage until late December. Henry I was eventually buried in the monastery at Reading, which had been largely funded by him.

Before returning to Normandy in 1135, Henry I had secured oaths of homage for his daughter's succession from the land's high magnates and churchmen. Yet despite their pledges of allegiance, Matilda's support among the barons was questionable and weak, allowing Stephen of Blois to outmanoeuvre her followers and take the crowns of England and Normandy. On 22 December 1135, Stephen was anointed King of England by the Archbishop of Canterbury at Westminster Abbey. Following the consecration of Stephen as sovereign, Henry I's demesne was plunged into seventeen years of bloody civil war as the followers of Matilda challenged the new regime for control of England and Normandy. The succession crisis was finally resolved in November 1153 when Henry Plantagenet and Stephen signed the Treaty of Winchester, recognizing Henry I's grandson as inheritor of the crown.

Selected Sources

Ackroyd, Peter, *Foundation – The History of England from its Earliest Beginnings to the Tudors* (Thomas Dunne Books, 2011).

Ashley, Mike, *British Kings and Queens* (Carroll and Graf, 2004).

Brooke, Christopher, *The Saxon and Norman Kings* (Fontana and Collins, 1967).

Cannon, John and Hargreaves, Anne, *The Kings and Queens of Britain* (Oxford University Press, 2001).

Chambers, James, *The Norman Kings* (Weidenfeld & Nicholson, 1981).

Gillingham, John, 'Henry I', in Fraser, Antonia, *The Lives of the Kings and Queens of England* (Alfred A. Knopf, 1975).

Hollister, C. Warren, *Henry I* (Yale University Press, 2001).

King, Edmund, *Henry I* (Allen Lane, 2018).

Roberts, Clayton and Roberts, David, *A History of England – Volume 1* (Prentice Hall, 1991).

Henry II

By 1152, the 19-year-old Duke Henry Plantagenet had enforced his rule over the western French fiefdoms of Normandy, Anjou, Maine and Aquitaine and was now challenging his uncle, Stephen of Blois, for possession of the Kingdom of England. In early 1153, he mobilized his Norman forces, crossing the Channel and landing on the southern coast of England to launch his invasion. As he marched inland to assail the king's strategic stronghold at Malmesburg, many English lords abandoned their overlord to join the forces of Henry. Following the defection of his barons, Stephen arranged a temporary truce with his nephew, giving up control of Malmesburg. When the truce expired, Duke Henry resumed his offensive, while the English king proceeded to the rebel castle at Wallingford with his army and began siege operations. As his campaign steadily gained momentum, Henry hastened north to relieve the siege of Wallingford. Weakened by the desertion of his warlords and facing the reinforced army of the duke, Stephen decided to negotiate a reconciliation. He rode out to meet Henry and reached a settlement agreeing to a permanent peace. Under the terms of the treaty, Stephen was to reign as English sovereign for the remainder of his life, while Henry Plantagenet was acknowledged as heir to the throne. In late October 1154, Stephen died; Henry II was crowned king on 19 December that year at Westminster Abbey.

In November 1120, William Atheling, heir to England and Normandy, had died in a shipwreck crossing the English Channel, creating an inheritance crisis for King Henry I. The king's only surviving legitimate child was a daughter, Matilda, and her acceptance as sovereign by his barons and churchmen was questionable. To secure the succession of his dynasty, Henry I arranged the marriage of the widowed Matilda to the son of the Count of Anjou, Geoffrey, in the hope their union would result in the birth of a male successor. The wedding took place on 17 June 1128, and five years later a son, named Henry, was born at Le Mans in the County of Maine. When Matilda was in Argentan in southern Normandy with her son, King Henry I saw his long-awaited heir for the first time. Prince Henry spent his first nine years in the household of the Count of Anjou at Angers with his two younger brothers, Geoffrey and William. The young lord routinely attended Mass every day, a practice continued throughout his life. When the prince was 10 years old, Aquitainian scholar Peter of Saintes was brought to court to assist in his education. Under the tutelage of Peter, Henry was taught to read and write and studied the basics of Latin, law and religion. During his adolescent years, he received military training from renowned knights and was taught the skills of jousting, horsemanship, fencing and hunting. Henry spent long hours drilling with the weapons of a warrior, learning to fight with the sword and lance, while also mastering archery. As part of his military education, he was exposed to castle warfare, learning the strategies of laying siege to and storming a fortress.

King Henry I died on 1 December 1135 while hunting at Lyon-da-Foret, but the planned succession of his daughter quickly fell apart. Stephen of Blois was in his ancestral county when he learned of his uncle's death; he broke his oath of fealty to Matilda, quickly sailing to England to usurp her kingdom. Landing on the south coast of England, he made his way to London, where the people acknowledged him as their new king. After acquiring the allegiance of the London populace, Stephen hastened to Winchester to seize the royal treasury, and with the help of his brother, Bishop Henry of Winchester, convinced the Archbishop of Canterbury to anoint him monarch. On 22 December 1135, Stephen was crowned king and later recognized as Duke of Normandy, despite the pledges of loyalty to Matilda from the bishops and magnates. In the wake of his coronation, the English barons and churchmen offered little opposition, and by April 1136 Stephen had gained widespread support across England, greatly reducing Matilda's chances of assuming the monarchy.

At the time of Henry I's demise, Geoffrey of Anjou and Matilda, who earlier had been married to Emperor Henry VI and preferred to be called empress, were at their capital in Angers occupied with the governing of the countship. When the news of the king's death reached them, they assembled their Angevin army, crossing into southern Normandy to seize the duchy. After taking control of several castles near the town of Argentan, they prepared to advance against Rouen to claim Matilda's inheritance. Before they departed for Rouen, the Norman barons and bishops made clear their intention to accept Stephen as duke, ending the short-lived civil war and forcing Matilda and her husband to return to Angers, leaving the new English king firmly in control of the duchy.

While Matilda's attempts to seize the Norman duchy had failed, she still had many supporters in England, who urged her to fight for her inheritance. In 1138, Matilda's half-brother, Earl Robert of Gloucester, repudiated his oath of fealty to Stephen and formed an alliance of barons in opposition to the king. In September 1139, Matilda sailed across the Channel, landing at Arundel to enforce her claim to the monarchy. While she organized the resistance to Stephen's reign, Henry Plantagenet remained in Angers with his father. The young Angevin lord followed the reports of his mother's English campaign, which was enthusiastically discussed at court. Henry frequently travelled with Count Geoffrey in Anjou, visiting towns across the county and learning the skills of statesmanship by observing his father enforcing his laws and justice, while meeting with advisors and foreign envoys.

Meanwhile, in England, Empress Matilda hastened into the West Country from Arundel, where she had considerable support among the warlords and churchmen. She joined her half-brother, Robert, at Gloucester, and with his support pressed her inheritance rights to the English crown. Over the next two years, she gained control over large parts of southern England, receiving pledges of allegiance from the barons, clergy and townspeople.

During her campaign for the English throne, Matilda had gained the fealty of the Earl of Chester, Ranulf, compelling Stephen to recapture the earl's fortress at Lincoln to strengthen his weakened defences in the Midlands. The royal army advanced to lay siege to the castle. As the investment continued, Matilda's forces rushed to Lincoln to relieve the siege, unleashing a surprise attack. Stephen ignored the advice of his counsellors to retreat, and instead prepared to attack. On 2 February 1141 the two armies clashed at Lincoln, where the empress's allies ploughed into the royal troops and quickly overwhelmed them in the town's narrow streets. During the battle, King Stephen was taken captive.

While Henry Plantagenet continued his martial training and academic education in Angers, Matilda's campaign of conquest in England gained momentum. Following the capture of the king at Lincoln, his wife, Queen Matilda, seized the reins of power and demanded the barons and churchmen honour their oaths of allegiance to Stephen. The queen utilized the political powers of her office and the resources of the loyal parts of the kingdom to defend her husband's realm. With money from the royal treasury, she hired Flemish mercenary soldiers and bribed many warlords to remain loyal to the crown, while Stephen remained in captivity.

Meanwhile, Matilda of Anjou manipulated the ambitions of prominent warlords by offering them properties and titles for their support. Despite the queen's attempts to protect the kingship of Stephen, in the summer of 1141 Empress Matilda gained the support of the populace of London and was granted entry to the city for her coronation as monarch. Arriving at the capital, she was acclaimed successor to the throne by the great barons and ecclesiastic lords. Matilda ruled from London for several months as the unanointed queen. As ruler, Matilda's behaviour quickly became arrogant and overbearing, and when she demanded a large sum of money from the Londoners to fund the war against Stephen's supporters, her quest for the kingdom suffered a grievous blow, the citizens abandoning her and making an agreement with Queen Matilda to restore Stephen to the throne. When the empress attended a banquet at Westminster Palace, the Londoners attempted to arrest her, but with the intervention of several supporters she escaped to the safety of Oxford.

While Matilda was in Oxford, the Bishop of Blois, Henry, cancelled his previously issued excommunication of the followers of Stephen in response to her recent overthrow in London, and transferred his allegiance to the king. The bishop was in Winchester, and the empress travelled to the city to compel him to reinstate his excommunication decree. Under threats from her, Bishop Henry appealed to Queen Matilda for help. The English queen responded quickly, sending Viscount William of Ypres with a contingent of knights and infantry to protect the bishop. William of Ypres was a second cousin of King Stephen and had followed him to England from Boulogne in support of his usurpation of the crown. William had earlier taken part in the battle against the empress at Lincoln, leading a force of troops and repelling an attack against the royalists' flank by the Welsh allies. Upon reaching Winchester, William launched a surprise assault against the supporters of Empress Matilda who were led by Earl Robert of Gloucester. Ypres' men quickly overran the troops of the empress, but Robert managed to hold off the royalists long enough for her to escape the onslaught. After the battle, the Earl of Gloucester attempted to flee, but was pursued and captured by William and his Flemish soldiers at Stockbridge. Robert was later exchanged for the captive King Stephen.

By the end of 1141, Empress Matilda's campaign to enforce her rights to England lay in tatters. While she remained in England pursuing her quest for the monarchy, she sent Robert of Gloucester to Anjou for reinforcements from Geoffrey. The earl carried a letter for the count from his wife asking him to send Prince Henry to England to boost the morale of her supporters and encourage new magnates to join her forces. Later in the year, Robert recrossed the Channel, bringing with him the 9-year-old Henry along with 300 mounted warriors. Prince Henry spent the next two years in Bristol at the court of his uncle. In the household of the earl, Henry's education was continued and he was exposed to the powerful martial warlords, who came to discuss the campaign to overthrow Stephen with Earl Robert. From his close association with the lords, the young Henry learned the skills of diplomacy, campaign preparations, logistics, war finances and battle strategy. At the earl's court, he also met many of the English ecclesiastic lords, who uncompromisingly opposed the rule of King Stephen. Henry came to know many of the high Church prelates and discussed with them the kingdom's political disorder. The Archbishop of Canterbury, Theobald, was a frequent visitor, working tirelessly to bring an end to the civil war between the two factions. Talking with Bishop Nigel of Ely, Henry learned the reasons for preserving a proper relationship between kingdom and Church and the role of the sovereign. During his two years in England, the young prince also learned the importance of maintaining the superiority of royal power over the barons to avoid open conflict.

While Empress Matilda was occupied in England, Geoffrey began sending military forces across the border into Normandy to attack King Stephen's line of defensive fortifications. He slowly defeated the supporters of Stephen, moving deeper into the duchy. With the king battling the empress for control of the English kingdom and unable to personally defend his Norman lands, the Angevins seized the strategic towns of Bayeux, Caen and Falaise. In 1143, the citizens of Rouen opened the city's gates to Geoffrey after becoming disillusioned with Stephen. In the following year, the Count of Anjou summoned his son back to Angers to help legitimize the conquest of Normandy with his presence as the rightful heir to the duchy. The prince remained in France, helping his father enforce his sovereignty, while being provided with the opportunity to learn the skills of governing the duchy.

Empress Matilda's offensive against King Stephen had continued to struggle, and in late 1146 she again asked Geoffrey for support. Early the following year, he sent a small force of knights and foot-soldiers under the nominal command of Henry to reinforce his wife's war effort. Prior to the prince's landing, rumours spread in England that he was leading a powerful and well-financed military force, creating panic among Stephen's men. After reaching England, Henry tried to capitalize on the alarm by marching his band of soldiers to the castles at Cricklade and Purton in south-west England. The Plantagenet prince's force was largely made up of mercenaries, and after his assaults against the fortresses were repelled, they soon abandoned him, leaving his campaign in disarray. Henry appealed to his mother for money to pay the hired soldiers, but she was confronting a resurgent Stephen and had none to give. Requests for help from his uncle, Robert of Gloucester, met with similar results, and as a last resort he appealed to his other uncle, King Stephen, who sent him enough funds to return to Anjou. Henry's first attempt to seize his rightful inheritance had ended in failure, but his resolve to claim the throne remained unbroken.

During the civil war, Stephen slowly regained the allegiance of the English warlords, while the empress's momentum steadily declined. Matilda lost the support of one of her principle allies, Earl Ranulf of Chester, who was forced to pay homage and surrender strategic castles to regain the acceptance of the king. In the autumn of 1146, Robert of Gloucester's son, Philip, defected to Stephen as the empress's coalition of lords and bishops grew weaker. After Earl Robert died on 31 October 1147, Matilda crossed the Channel back to Normandy at the beginning of the new year, never returning to England and leaving King Stephen to celebrate his triumph. She established her residence near Rouen, and when Henry later became Duke of Normandy and King of England, she provided him with political advice, while also working with the Church until her death in 1167.

Henry remained with his father for two years, helping him govern Anjou and the newly won Duchy of Normandy, while learning the skills necessary to rule a feudal fiefdom. Despite the defeat of Empress Matilda, a political faction of barons and bishops in England still supported the succession of Henry as the rightful king. To retain the loyalty of his followers, in the spring of 1149 the prince returned to England, allegedly to be knighted by his great-uncle, David I, King of Scotland. He landed in Bristol in south-west England and made his way north to Carlisle, where King David received him with great honour and respect. On 22 May, Henry knelt before the Scottish monarch and was tapped on the shoulders as a knight. While at Carlisle, the prince was joined by many lords and churchmen opposed to Stephen's rule, who planned an attack against York. Henry united his allies with a large army of David I and set out to besiege York. As the coalition forces neared the city, their scouts reported the presence of Stephen with a formidable host. Confronted by the royal army, Henry was compelled to abandon his campaign and proceed towards south-west England, where he had many loyal supporters. With a small contingent of mounted men-at-arms, he avoided capture and safely reached the haven of Hereford. Stephen was soon notified of the prince's arrival and sent his son and heir, Eustace, to seize him. Henry was warned of Eustace's approach, escaping to Devon.

After reaching Devon, the Plantagenet prince continued his offensive against the royalists, and with the help of the earls of Gloucester and Hereford led his men in an attack against the enemy held castle at Bridport, overrunning the garrison and gaining his first military victory. He then ravaged the countryside, leaving a wide path of destruction before learning from his spies that Eustace was advancing against the anti-royalist forces in Wiltshire. The prince sent a contingent of soldiers to reinforce Wiltshire's defences, but they arrived too late to prevent the king's son from plundering through the shire.

While Prince Henry had widespread support in the south-west of England, King Stephen still maintained the allegiance of many powerful barons and clergymen. In January 1150, Henry journeyed back to Anjou to raise a large army of Angevin and Norman troops to renew his quest for the English throne. Soon after his return, the 17-year-old Henry received the Duchy of Normandy from his father and took the title Duke of the Normans.

While Henry was in England, Count Geoffrey began besieging the rebel stronghold of Lord Rigauld Berlai at Montreuil-Bellay, who had repeatedly violated his pledges of fealty. As the siege wore on, Berlai sent a messenger to King Louis VII of France asking for his intervention. Meanwhile, the castle was stormed and destroyed by Geoffrey. During the assault, Lord Berlai was captured and placed in irons. In 1151, the French king invaded Normandy, and with the support of Prince Eustace and his household soldiers hurried to Arques, while Duke Henry, who had recently returned to Normandy, was at Torigny near Caen, attacking the castle of a dissident warlord. When news reached him of the French incursion, he quickly proceeded to Arques in north-west France, driving back the invaders. Geoffrey now appeared with his Angevin army, and with the intervention of churchmen serving as mediators a truce was arranged with the French.

In August 1151, Geoffrey and his son rode to Paris with their entourage of knights and churchmen to negotiate a settlement for Normandy. Henry needed peace in the duchy to free him for his planned conquest of England to enforce his inheritance of the crown. The populace of England was currently suffering from widespread crop failures and there was extensive instability and discontent. Looking to take advantage of the internal unrest, Henry was eager to reach an agreement with the French. Despite some initial delays in the talks, a treaty was signed, Henry pledging to cede his sections of the Norman Vexin to the king and offer homage for Normandy, while in return Louis VII recognized him as Duke of Normandy.

Following the agreement with the Capetian king, Henry and Geoffrey proceeded from Paris to Maine, where they parted, with the count going to Anjou and the prince to Normandy. During his journey in the hot summer weather, Geoffrey became ill and was taken to the Chateau Eure-et-Loire, where he died on 7 September 1151. Before his death, he made his magnates pledge not to bury him until Henry swore to abide by the provisions of his will without reading it. The prince wavered but was convinced to make the oath, after which Geoffrey was taken to Le Mans and buried in St Julian's Cathedral.

In the aftermath of the count's funeral, Henry Plantagenet read the provisions of the will, which bound him to immediately transfer three castles to his younger brother, Geoffrey. By the terms of the second stipulation, he was required to appoint his brother to the countships of Anjou and Maine following his conquest of England. Henry had no intention of complying with the second clause of the will, but for the moment gave his brother the three castles. Henry then travelled to Angers to receive the oaths of the lords and churchmen as the Count of Anjou. Count Henry remained in Anjou and Normandy during the winter, solidifying his rule, while preparing for the invasion of England and defeat of King Stephen.

In July 1137, King Louis VII of France had married Eleanor, Duchess of Aquitaine, in a political union to secure Capetian control over her duchy. Eleanor, described by contemporaries as a high spirited and sensuous woman, was ill-suited to the pious and monkish French monarch. In 1148, she accompanied Louis VII on the Second Crusade to the Levant, where rumours of her infidelity were widespread. Her alleged sexual relationship with her uncle, Raymond, Prince of Antioch, led to the end of her marriage. After their return to Paris from the crusade, in August 1151, the king decided to divorce his wife on grounds of their too-close blood relationship, despite losing possession of her strategic Duchy of Aquitaine. On 21 March 1152, the French Church granted the annulment at the request of Louis.

Following the dissolution of the marriage, Eleanor hastened to Poitiers, the capital of Aquitaine, and set about establishing her rule over the duchy's lords, churchmen and people. To provide security for her duchy, Eleanor needed a husband capable of defending her lands against foreign invasion and internal unrest. Henry of Normandy, eager to expand his demesne, made arrangements for his marital union with the duchess. Two months after Eleanor's return to Poitiers, she was married to Henry on 18 May 1152. With his marriage to Eleanor, Henry had extended his empire south to the border with Spain.

Soon after Louis VII learned of his ex-wife's marriage to Henry, he summoned his vassal to court to answer his disobedience. When the duke failed to appear, the French king formed a coalition with Henry's brother, Geoffrey, Theobald of Blois and several rebellious Angevin warlords. In response, the Norman duke quickly mobilized his men, advancing to relieve the stronghold at Neufmarche, 32 miles east of Rouen, which was under attack by Louis. After driving away the besieging forces, the prince's army made its way south, pillaging the Vexin as it marched. He then clashed with the troops of Louis VII, who had again invaded Normandy, at Pacy, 50 miles south of Rouen. When the Capetian king saw the size of the Norman army, he withdrew his forces east into France. Henry continued his pillaging campaign, burning the town of Moulins. The French made no additional attempts to attack Normandy, and after reinforcing his eastern frontier defences, Henry moved against his rebellious brother in Anjou. Advancing into the countship, he quickly defeated his brother's allies, capturing Geoffrey at the Battle of Montsoreau. Henry's victories in Anjou dissolved Louis VII's coalition and a truce was soon negotiated, again securing the borders of the duke's lands.

Henry spent the early winter of 1152 with Eleanor, travelling through her duchy and receiving pledges of loyalty from the lords, prelates and people. After establishing a stable regime, he journeyed to Barfleur in western Normandy to resume his preparations for the twice-delayed invasion of England. In early January 1153, the assembled Norman and Anjou army of over 3,000 men embarked on ships to sail across the Channel, landing in Dorset in western England, where the duke was met by William of Gloucester and Reginald of Cornwall, the leaders of his local allies. In February, Henry advanced against Stephen's strategic fortress at Malmesburg. After first capturing the town, his forces attacked the citadel, but were repeatedly repelled. When King Stephen learned of the siege, he hastened to reinforce its defenders. As he approached

Malmesburg, the king found the besiegers too strong for his forces, and unwilling to risk a pitched battle, he offered to negotiate a truce. The rivals for the crown agreed to destroy the fortification, but before the demolition was carried out, the garrison captain deserted the king and handed over the castle to Henry. Stephen then withdrew his forces to the north, while the Norman duke toured the western counties to shore up his supporters. After the Earl of Leicester, Robert Beaumont, abandoned the king and joined the invaders, Henry headed to Wallingford in Oxfordshire, on the River Thames, with a reinforced host of infantry, cavalry and archers. During the advance, he captured the royal strongholds at Tutbury, Warwick and Stanford, strengthening his hold on the Midlands. Stephen, learning of his nephew's approach, moved his forces to intercept him. In October 1153, the two armies came face to face, but fearing a pitched battle, Stephen rode out to negotiate a settlement with his nephew. They first arranged a truce and agreed to finalize a permanent peace at Winchester. On 6 November, Henry met his uncle and signed a peace treaty. Under the terms of the Winchester agreement, the civil war was ended and Stephen was to reign for the remainder of his life, while Henry was recognized as successor to the English crown. To preserve the peace, all castles constructed since 1135 were to be destroyed and the seized properties returned to their owners. The treaty was confirmed in London, and at a great council gathering on 13 January 1154, the English barons gave their oaths of homage to Henry Plantagenet as their next king.

As Henry was arranging his succession to the throne in England, Louis VII had resumed his cross-border raids into Normandy, encouraging the Norman barons to revolt against the duke. Despite the French regime's political and military campaign to weaken Henry's hold on Normandy, the barons and ecclesiastic lords continued to support the duke. In the spring of 1154, Henry sailed across the Channel to Normandy, securing his duchy and ensuring his laws were enforced. As he travelled through the duchy, a rebellion broke out in Aquitaine, which was quickly suppressed by the duke's loyal vassals. Henry then began negotiations with Louis VII to settle their border dispute. An agreement was reached to transfer the French-seized towns of Verneuil and Neufmarche to Henry, while Louis VII pledged to renounce his title as Duke of Aquitaine.

After restoring peace in his border lordships, Henry remained in Normandy enforcing his rule against the recalcitrant barons. As he was again besieging the rebel Lord Robert of Torigny, news reached him of the death of King Stephen at Faversham. After defeating and receiving the homage of Lord Robert, Henry rode to Barfleur in October to cross the Channel to his new kingdom. Due to contrary winds, Henry was delayed until 8 December before setting sail for England, accompanied by Eleanor and his two brothers, Geoffrey and William. After landing in England, Henry proceeded to London, where on 19 December 1154 he was crowned king in Westminster Abbey by the Archbishop of Canterbury, Theobald, in the presence of the kingdom's great lords and bishops. The 21-year-old Henry II of Plantagenet now ruled an empire that in size and military power had not been seen since the days of Charlemagne, reaching from the border with Scotland in the north, to the countship of Blois in the east and the Pyrenees in the south. In the aftermath of nineteen years of civil conflict, the English people hoped their new king would now bring peace and prosperity to England.

Shortly after the coronation, Henry II and Eleanor, along with their year-old son William, established their residence at Bernmondsey Palace to the south of London. While in London, the queen gave birth to her second son, Henry, in February 1155. Shortly after taking the reins of government, the king began the implementation of a central ruling council. For the post of chancellor, he appointed Thomas Becket, who was highly recommended by Archbishop Theobald. Other high barons and churchmen were named to the royal administration, who had consistently demonstrated their loyalty and abilities during the civil war against Stephen. Following his assumption of power, Henry II frequently travelled about his new realm, securing the loyalty of the nobles, churchmen and people. Under the reign of Stephen, royal revenue had fallen dramatically and relations with the English Church remained hostile following the crown's battle with the Archbishop of Canterbury over the jurisdiction rights of the government. Meanwhile, in northern England, the frontier counties with Scotland were now governed by the Scots, and the Welsh had seized many of the western border castles built to protect the English towns from pillaging raids. The new sovereign began his rule by rectifying the failings of Stephen's reign, voiding every transfer of property made since 1135 and cancelling earldoms issued after the rule of Henry I. Henry made it clear that all lordships now came from his regime. All illegal castles were ordered demolished and mercenary soldiers, a source of widespread death and destruction, were banished from the kingdom. To end the threat of rebellion against the crown by the great magnates, they were deprived of their wealth and powerbase, while those deemed loyal were reissued their properties after making their pledges of loyalty to the king. There was little resistance to Henry's succession to the throne as he continued to recover the lands and rights of the monarchy usurped by the English barons and border realms during Stephen's weak reign.

While Henry was enforcing his supremacy over the nobility, the English lords along the Welsh border stubbornly resisted the new monarchy and fought for their continued independence. They considered themselves largely autonomous of the king's rule, refusing to abide by his laws. Possession of the strategic castles along the Welsh frontier was vital to the security of his kingdom, compelling Henry to seize them by force. Roger of Hereford, who had supported the Plantagenet king during the civil war, now rejected the transfer of his strongholds at Hereford and Gloucester to the crown's control. He was finally convinced by the Bishop of Hereford to comply with Henry's orders and received new lands in exchange. Hugh of Mortimer refused to obey the throne's orders and prepared his fortresses for a siege by vassals loyal to the monarch. In May 1155, Henry II mounted attacks against three of Lord Hugh's castles in the Midlands at Bridgnorth, Cleobury and Wigmore. Lord Mortimer was unable to withstand the royalists' assaults, and in May, after Cleobury was destroyed, he submitted at the Council of Bridgnorth. Hugh was allowed to keep his castles at Wigmore and Stratfield, while the king reclaimed Bridgnorth. During the siege at Bridgnorth, Henry narrowly escaped death when an arrow aimed at him hit a nearby knight from his bodyguard.

Henry II spent the summer of 1155 peacefully in southern England, governing his kingdom and hunting in the vast forestlands. He travelled to London for the Christmas season, where news reached him of his brother's revolt in Anjou. Geoffrey, who demanded possession of Anjou and Maine in accordance with his father's will, had begun promoting rebellion against his older brother. To protect his countships, in early January 1156, Henry II sailed from Dover, landing near Caen in Normandy and hastening to Rouen to prepare his opposition to Geoffrey. Henry had no intention of surrendering the countships, which strategically separated Normandy from Aquitaine. Meeting with his rebel brother, Henry disavowed the terms of Count Geoffrey's will, claiming their father had been forced to agree to it under threats from the Anjou magnates. His brother Geoffrey then appealed to Louis VII for armed intervention, but received only encouragement to oppose his elder brother. As the brothers prepared for war, Empress Matilda intervened with attempts to negotiate a settlement. Under the recommendation of their mother, in mid-February Henry II conferred with Geoffrey on the French border but failed to agree on a resolution.

While in Rouen assembling his force of mercenaries to attack Geoffrey, Henry II met Count Thierry of Flanders, who persuaded him to act as warden for his countship while he was on a pilgrimage to the Levant. During the meeting with Thierry, Henry received the armed services of 1,000 soldiers in either England or Normandy, or 500 men in Anjou in exchange for an annual remuneration. When Geoffrey led his troops against his brother's lands in Anjou, Henry II sent his knights and Flemish mercenaries south to defend the countship. The king's army laid siege to the rebel-occupied castles at Chinon and Mirabeau, while blocking reinforcements from the French realm. The two castles held out until May before surrendering. Geoffrey was compelled to abandon his pursuit for an independent realm and accept his brother's offer of an annual annuity, but no properties were tendered. Later in the year, the citizens of the Breton city of Nantes overthrew their ruler, Hoel, and petitioned Geoffrey to assume the title of Duke of Brittany, giving Henry's brother a domain of his own, which satisfied his quest for Aquitaine and Maine.

The barons of Aquitaine still had not rendered homage to the Plantagenet king. To secure the loyalty of the lords, the king pledged his fealty to Louis VII as his overlord for the duchy. The French monarch had earlier renounced his suzerainty over Aquitaine in favour of Henry II, but he remained popular with the ducal warlords. With Henry's relationship established with the French throne, the Aquitaine warlords agreed to give him their fidelity. Following the peaceful settlement with Geoffrey, in October the English king – accompanied by Eleanor and their two children, Henry and the recently born Matilda, William having died earlier in the year – travelled south to Aquitaine to receive oaths of fealty. In the autumn of 1156, most of the region's lords gathered in Poitiers to give their pledges of allegiance to Henry II, but a few barons still refused to attend the ceremony and stayed loyal to Louis VII, including Count Raymond V of Toulouse, whose independence would later challenge the king's quest to expand his empire to the Mediterranean coast. After remaining away from England for over a year, in

April 1157 Henry II sailed back across the Channel with the wife and children to personally lead a campaign to consolidate his reign over the recalcitrant barons.

Shortly after his arrival in England, Henry II organized a campaign to recover his rule against rebellious barons in the east, where Stephen had been highly popular. He mobilized his army, first marching against the Earl of Norfolk, Hugh Bigod. The earl had repeatedly refused to surrender his castles or offer homage to the Plantagenet throne, while ignoring the royal decree requiring monetary payments in lieu of military service. Henry advanced his forces against Hugh, compelling him to relinquish his fortifications to the king. After occupying the Earl of Norfolk's strongholds with mercenary troops and gaining his pledge of fealty, the king moved to eliminate the disobedience of King Stephen's young son, William. Meeting with William, Henry persuaded him to surrender his fortifications in England and Normandy. The king kept control of the seized crown fortresses that had been given to William by his father, but returned others after receiving his pledge of fealty.

As Henry continued his offensive to unify the kingdom under his authority, he next moved against the Scots, who had occupied northern England during the turmoil of Stephen's reign. He sent envoys to King Malcolm IV demanding the return of the lordships of Northumberland, Westmorland and Cumberland. To resolve their differences, he met Malcolm at Chester, where, under threat of attack, the Scots agreed to surrender the border counties. The Earldom of Huntingdon was ceded to Scotland to secure peace along the northern frontier, with the border established along the line of the River Tweed.

After reasserting his monarchy in the north, Henry II announced to his barons at a grand council meeting at Northampton in July 1157 that his army was preparing to invade Wales to regain the lands and suzerainty lost during Stephen's impotent kingship. The Welsh princes had taken advantage of Stephen's preoccupation with the civil war to violate their oaths of homage and expand their territorial holdings into western England. The Plantagenet king summoned his knights and their retainers, while those not called to service were required to make cash payments to fund the military operation. The Welsh prince, Owain, had enlarged his Gwynedd princedom and now controlled most of northern Wales, while the southern region was ruled by Prince Rhys. The English army assembled at Chester and advanced against Gwynedd, with the support of the Welsh princes Madog ap Maredudd of Powys and Cadwaladr, brother of Owain, while Rhys remained neutral in the south. The king's men marched into eastern Gwynedd, ravaging the towns and farmlands and leaving a broad path of destruction. The army then proceeded up the west coast toward the Welsh stronghold at Rhuddlan. Owain deployed his men at the castle of Basingwerk to block the English route. As Henry II approached the Welsh, he divided his army and personally led a small contingent through the woods of Ewloe to outflank the enemy at Basingwerk. Learning of the presence of the invading forces, the Welsh prince sent troops to ambush them. In the ensuing battle, Henry II's men were routed and driven back. During the fighting, the king was nearly killed by the charging Welsh, but the Earl of Hereford, Robert, intervened to rescue him. Believing the Plantagenet monarch had been killed, his standard bearer dropped the royal banner and fled the battlefield, creating panic among his comrades. Only the sudden reappearance of

Henry II averted disaster. He quickly reformed his army and resumed the battle against Owain's soldiers, forcing them to retreat after a violent fight. The English pursued the Welsh, capturing their castle at Rhuddlan and compelling Owain to flee into the safety of the mountains. The Welsh prince now sued for peace, offering fealty to the monarch for his principality. The Welsh fortresses at Rhuddlan and Basingwerk were garrisoned with English troops to enforce Henry's sovereignty. Shortly after the submission of Owain, the prince of the southern portion of Wales, Rhys, also tendered his allegiance.

Henry II spent the following year journeying through his kingdom, holding court, issuing charters and imposing his justice and law. At the beginning of 1158, he was in northern England inspecting the fortifications recently acquired from the Scots. He then travelled south through Yorkshire, touring the towns and defensive works of the castles. Eleanor joined her husband in the spring at Worcester, celebrating the Easter season with him following the birth of her fourth child, Richard.

The English king, having spent over sixteen months eliminating obstacles to his reign in England, returned to Normandy in August 1158 to quell simmering disorder in the duchy. Henry was determined to regain the Norman Vexin, which had been ceded to the French six years earlier. The English chancellor, Thomas Becket, led a preliminary diplomatic mission to Paris to arrange the marital union of the king's heir, Henry, to Louis VII's daughter, Margaret, with a dowry of the Norman Vexin. On 21 August, Henry II met the Capetian monarch at Neufmarche to finalize the agreement. Under the terms of the treaty, the French agreed to the marriage between Henry the Younger and Princess Margaret when they came of age, while the Vexin castles at Gisors, Neaufle and Neufchael were entrusted to the Knights Templar until the nuptial ceremony took place. In September, King Henry travelled to Paris to sign the treaty and take possession of Margaret, who would now be raised at the English court.

In July 1158, Count Geoffrey of Nantes had died and his strategic countship was immediately contested by Conan IV of Brittany. During their meeting in Paris in August, Henry II had convinced Louis VII to grant him the title of seneschal – a term meaning steward or governor – for France, and under the authority of this office he now had a mandate to overthrow Conan IV. Returning to Anjou, the English king ordered his Angevin forces mobilized at Avranches and prepared to besiege Nantes. When Conan IV learned of Henry's planned invasion, he went to Avranches to submit and offer fealty. Conan IV's oath was accepted by the English king, who confirmed his title as Duke of Brittany. Through this political manoeuvre, the Plantagenet king gained control of Brittany as overlord.

After securing the overlordship of the Bretons, Henry II returned to Normandy and spent the following months touring the churches and castles ensuring his suzerainty over the barons and ecclesiastic lords. He visited Mont-Saint-Michel Abbey, attending a special Mass of Thanksgiving and later spending time with the monks. From the abbey, he proceeded south to inspect his newly won city of Nantes and confer with Conan IV to discuss his rule over the duchy. From Brittany, the king continued on to Le Mans, where he met Louis VII. The two sovereigns travelled north together to Mont-Saint-Michel and then to Rouen, from where the Capetian king returned to Paris. The journey from Le Mans solidified Henry's friendship with Louis, stabilizing his hold on his continental lands.

Since his assumption of power in England, King Henry had forced the submission of the Scots, Welsh and Bretons, and he now turned to the southern countship of Toulouse ruled by Count Raymond V. Through his marriage to Eleanor, he had a claim to Toulouse, which had been under the suzerainty of his wife's grandfather. During the king's absence from England, Eleanor had served as regent, but during the Christmas season she joined her husband at Cherbourg. After the holiday celebrations, he began preparations for the invasion of Toulouse, despite Louis VII's disapproval. To fund the war, he required his knights and lords to pay a fee to avoid service in a foreign land, using the money to hire mercenary soldiers. On 22 March 1159, a summons was issued for the army to assemble, and three months later the troops gathered at Poitiers in the County of Poitou. On 24 June, the soldiers departed from Poitiers and marched south-east, with contingents of English knights, Scots led by Malcolm IV, men from Normandy and Anjou and a large force of mercenaries. When the invading army moved into the countship of Toulouse, they stormed their way forward, pushing aside Count Raymond V's defenders. In early July, the coalition host reached the city of Toulouse, establishing an encampment and laying siege to the fortress. While the siege continued, Thomas Becket was sent with a contingent of knights and infantrymen to plunder the surrounding countryside and occupy Raymond's castles scattered about the lordship. Louis VII had reached Toulouse with reinforcements for his ally Raymond before Henry II's arrival, and with the encouragement of the French, the Count of Toulouse repulsed the besiegers' repeated assaults. The English king's campaign was hampered by its long lines of communications, and when an epidemic erupted, he decided to abandon the invasion. The royalists withdrew north, with Becket in command of the rearguard.

When the royal army returned to Normandy in October, Henry II learned that the French, during his absence, had unleashed raids across the frontier, ravaging his Norman towns and farmlands. The English king responded by leading his soldiers into France, laying waste to the land and capturing several castles. After the French monarch returned to his kingdom from Toulouse, a ceasefire was soon negotiated. During the following peace, Henry II toured Normandy inspecting his fortifications and towns, while personally imposing his laws and justice and enforcing his fealty over the recalcitrant barons. Before the end of the truce, both kings desired a permanent peace, agreeing to terms in the spring of 1160 which restored all seized properties to their former lords. The agreement was confirmed in October, bringing a period of peace to Henry II's lands in continental Europe.

In the summer of 1160, Louis VII's second wife, Constance, died without delivering a male heir. The French king, impatient for a successor, quickly arranged his marriage to Adela, sister of the Count of Blois, Theobald V. If Adela gave birth to a male successor, Prince Henry the Younger's chances of receiving his dowry or inheriting a portion of his father-in-law Louis' domain would be greatly reduced. To protect his son's endowment, Henry II acted quickly, convincing a papal legate to perform the marriage ceremony between the 5-year-old Henry and 3-year-old Margaret, despite their young ages. The Norman Vexin held by the Knights Templar was now occupied by royal troops and under the suzerainty of the English regime. When the Capetian king was informed of the marriage, he united with his brother-in-law, Count Theobald V, to unleash plundering raids into Normandy. The Plantagenet regime responded by sending its army across the border into Theobald V's countship, seizing his castle at Chaumont on the River Loire. With winter now approaching, Henry II withdrew to Le Mans after reinforcing his Norman castles and preparing Anjou for the expected French invasion. In the spring of 1161, only minor skirmishes were fought, and peace negotiations were begun in October at Freteval, Louis VII agreeing to accept the loss of Vexin. The Plantagenet king spent the following year in Normandy and Anjou, governing his lands and consolidating his sovereignty.

While Henry II and the French were occupied with the border conflict, in England the Archbishop of Canterbury, Theobald, had died in mid-April 1161 at his palace in Canterbury. The archbishop served as the highest-ranking ecclesiastic lord in the kingdom, who historically had worked closely with the monarch in the administration of the realm. Henry II desired to have Prince Henry crowned as English king-designate and needed an archbishop who would willingly support his wishes. He considered his candidates closely and chose his chancellor, Thomas Becket, for the office. Becket had served the king faithfully as chancellor and had performed his administrative duties well. To ensure the election of Becket, Henry sent him and Richard of Luci from Normandy to Canterbury in May 1162 to meet with the electors. In a speech before the assembled prelates, the wishes of the king were announced by Richard of Luci. He told the delegates: 'If the king and archbishop be joined together in a bond of affection and cherish each other in friendship, there is no doubt that times will be happy and the church will preserve her estate in joy and tranquillity.' Despite the opposition of some who argued against Becket on personal grounds and others who resented the regime's interference in ecclesiastic affairs, the sovereign's choice for archbishop was duly elected. On 2 June, Becket was ordained a priest and the following day consecrated archbishop at the cathedral in Canterbury.

Thomas Becket, having not been educated for the priesthood, felt ill-suited for his new office. As archbishop, he was disliked by his bishops and abbots, being considered an outsider for his close association with the royal court. Henry II had placed Becket in the position expecting his cooperation in furthering his throne's policies, but the archbishop, feeling the need to exert his independence, now began to move away from the Plantagenet regime. Becket started to aggressively defend the Church's rights, opposing the crown's attempts to limit its influence. In January 1163, Henry returned to England to personally deal with the new obstacle to his rule.

When the king disembarked at Southampton, he was met by Archbishop Becket and his heir, Prince Henry. At first, relations between Henry and the archbishop remained cordial, but when the king began implementing a new set of legal and governmental reforms, later known as the 'Constitutions of Clarendon', the two former friends grew apart. The decrees were issued to draw a clear separation between the Church's jurisdiction and royal authority. The English king now demanded that clergymen who committed crimes be punished in secular courts, instead of under the more lenient ecclesiastic canons. Archbishop Becket strongly opposed the loss of Church jurisdiction and refused to abide by the decree. Relations deteriorated further after Henry II ordered that the Church's annual payment to the sheriffs for their peacekeeping duties be sent directly to the royal exchequer. Becket spoke out against the reform, writing to the king: 'It does not become your excellence to defend something that belongs to another to your use.' The monarch was infuriated by his archbishop's response, telling him: 'By God's eyes, it shall be given as revenue and entered in the royal rolls.' Despite Henry's reply, Becket refused to pay the tax to the crown. As affairs between the throne and Church grew increasingly hostile, in early October 1163 Henry summoned the ecclesiastic lords to a council meeting at Westminster, where he demanded they obey his laws. Led by the archbishop, the prelates answered that they retained the right to observe canon law over secular. The king abruptly departed from the conference, leaving the issue unresolved.

As the question of the Church's jurisdiction remained unanswered, Pope Alexander III and the English cardinals now urged Thomas Becket to cooperate with the crown. Finally swayed by the advice of the prelates, he agreed to submit to the regime. After he complied privately to Henry II at Oxford, a great council meeting of the barons and bishops was called to Clarendon in late January 1164, where Archbishop Becket pledged to obey the laws of the throne. After receiving the archbishop's oath, the king issued the 'Constitutions of Clarendon', which listed sixteen laws where the royal jurisdiction was superior, including limitations on appeals to the pope and the supremacy of the monarchy's courts over the Church.

The issuance of the decree left Becket in a state of depression and torment. He withdrew from his duties as archbishop and attempted unsuccessfully to flee to the French court. At this point, the monarch issued charges against Becket for embezzlement during his tenure as chancellor, summoning the archbishop before a royal court to answer the accusations. When Becket was found guilty, he was sentenced to the forfeiture of his properties. Following his conviction, the disgraced Becket fled to Lincoln and then to Sandwich before crossing the Channel in early November 1164, disembarking in Flanders and making his way to seek refuge at the court of Louis VII. While Becket remained safe in the Capetian realm, the English king sent his envoys to Pope Alexander III and the French king to present his case against the deposed archbishop.

During Henry II's four-year absence from England, the Welsh princes had again broken their pledges of fealty and renewed their attacks against the western English shires. In 1164, the ruler of northern Wales, Owain, formed a coalition with Prince Rhys of the southern princedoms, and together they moved against the Plantagenet regime. After meeting with his council, the king decided to mount a large military campaign to subjugate the Welsh. With money from the great lords, Henry's formidable army of mounted knights and lightly armed infantrymen set out in May 1165. With the king at the head of the host, the Englishmen and their mercenaries advanced toward the fortress at Rhuddlan, but discovered their enemy had withdrawn south. After buttressing his stronghold at Basingwerk, Henry II fell back to Shrewsbury to reinforce his army before attacking the Welsh along the Clwyde valley. The march south was beset with steady rains, which turned the roadways into quagmires. With his lines of communications to England broken and supplies dwindling, the king ordered his men to retreat to Chester, where he was compelled to cancel the invasion, defeated by the severe weather.

While Henry II was suffering through the rainy weather in Wales, Louis VII's third wife, Adela, gave birth to the long-awaited male heir, Philip, ending any chances of Prince Henry's wife inheriting the French kingdom and assuring future conflict with the English. Louis VII thereafter returned to his long-delayed campaign to challenge Henry II for possession of his lands in western France.

In the aftermath of the birth of the heir to the Capetian throne, Henry II began preparations to return to his continental lands. In March 1166, he crossed over to Normandy to make arrangements for the expected renewal of the border war with the French. During his absence in England, Eleanor had ruled as regent for her husband, but from distant Poitiers in Aquitaine she had little success in preventing the rise of widespread dissent. In Brittany, numerous barons formed a coalition with insurgent warlords from Maine to gain their independence from Henry's overlordship. They soon allied themselves with Louis VII, who pledged to support their uprising. Shortly after arriving in Normandy, the English king summoned his knights and infantrymen and hired mercenaries from his domains, advancing south to quell the growing unrest. After reaching the Breton–Maine border, he attacked the nearby fortress at Fourgers, whose warlord, Ralph, was the leader of the rebellion to replace the Plantagenet-appointed Duke of Brittany, Conan IV, with Eudo of Porhoet. The allied troops of King Henry besieged the fortress, launching sorties against the defensive works for two weeks before the garrison submitted. Henry's forces then proceeded into Brittany and moved against Rennes, plundering the lands of Lord Eudo as they pressed on. Without any support from the French crown, the rebel lords abandoned the fight, surrendering to Henry II. To further tighten his hold on Brittany, Henry arranged the marriage of his 8-year-old son, Geoffrey, to the 4-year-old daughter of Conan IV and forced the unpopular duke to transfer the duchy to Geoffrey. Soon after the collapse of their resistance, the rebel barons gathered at Thouars, 40 miles south of Angers, to offer their fealty, solidifying Henry's authority over Brittany.

After quelling the rebellion in Brittany, Henry II returned to Normandy in the autumn to challenge the escalating threat from the French throne. The neighbouring fiefdoms of Boulogne, Blois and Flanders had formed an alliance with Louis VII to recapture their lands earlier seized by Henry's soldiers and were threating to attack the border defences. The English king sent emissaries to the barons offering an annual pension for their loyalty, and at little cost thus deflated the war effort of the Capetian monarchy.

Thomas Becket had remained in France and was residing at the Cistercian Abbey of Pontigny. In the autumn of 1166, Henry II resumed his campaign of harassment against the archbishop. Becket's patrons were from the Order of Cistercians, which was becoming a powerful ecclesiastic house in England. Henry threatened to banish the order from his kingdom unless the churchmen stopped sheltering the archbishop. In danger of being expelled from England, the Cistercians were forced to end their relationship with Becket, asking him to leave the abbey. Determined to keep the archbishop in his kingdom, Louis VII arranged for him to reside at the Abbey of St Columba in central France, where he remained for the following four years, serving as a clergyman and sending repeated appeals to Pope Alexander III to gain his support against Henry II.

In early 1167, Henry pressed his political initiative to degrade Thomas Becket while continuing his diplomatic campaign to gain the support of the rulers from his neighbouring fiefdoms against the renewal of cross-border attacks by the French crown. In March, after subduing a revolt in southern Aquitaine, the Plantagenet king received homage from Count Raymond V of Toulouse, who had grown increasingly embittered with the French. As the count's overlord, Henry II had expanded the territory under his control to the Mediterranean Sea. Following the loss of Toulouse, Louis VII sent his army into the Vexin in June in retaliation, pillaging and burning the border towns and farms. The Plantagenets responded by destroying the French stronghold at Chaumont and ravaging the surrounding area. Plundering raids by both kingdoms continued through the summer months until late August, when a truce was negotiated. In early 1168, hostilities resumed after renewed peace talks failed to find a settlement. After another year of sporadic cross-border attacks, a peace agreement was approved at Montmirail in north-east France at the beginning of 1169. Under the terms of the Treaty of Montmirail, Henry II pledged his fealty to Louis VII for his European mainland possessions and arranged the disposition of these lands after his death. The 14-year-old Prince Henry was given Maine, Anjou and Brittany, and Richard was ceded Aquitaine, while the 10-year-old Geoffrey received the Duchy of Brittany as vassal to his eldest brother. The treaty was signed with the pledge of Richard's marriage to the French king's daughter, Alice. During the talks at Montmirail, Henry II met with Thomas Becket, who had been invited to the summit by papal legates to forge a reconciliation with the English regime. Anxious to return to England, Becket agreed to seek the crown's mercy but ended his plea with the words 'Save God's honour', which implied his unwillingness to accept the superiority of the king.

In the wake of the unsuccessful meeting at Montmirail with Thomas Becket, Henry II assembled his army of knights and mercenary troops in March 1169, advancing into Gascony to quell a festering rebellion of the local warlords. As the Plantagenet king remained in the south, Becket issued a decree again excommunicating the English barons instrumental in his disgrace. After the failure of the Montmirail meeting, Pope Alexander III again sent legates to resolve the dispute. The king and Becket agreed to confer and attempt to reach a resolution to their differences. The adversaries met in November at Montmartre, where King Henry became more conciliatory and lessened his demands, allowing near total freedom for the Church in England. Despite the appearance of a resolution, when Becket asked the king to give him the kiss of peace, which implied permanence to the agreement, the king refused, thereby ending their negotiations.

Soon after the failed negotiations, Henry II spent the Christmas season with his son, Geoffrey, in Nantes. After the holiday celebrations, he travelled through Brittany inspecting the defensive works of the castles and receiving pledges of allegiance from the Breton warlords. During his tour, he seized the lands of Eudo of Porhoet, lessening the danger of revolt against Geoffrey's rule. Following his short visit to Brittany, Henry crossed the Channel to England after an absence of four years. During the voyage, the small fleet was struck by a violent storm, one vessel sinking with the loss of over 400 men. The monarch's ship made its way alone to England, landing at Portsmouth the next day.

Henry II proceeded to London and summoned a meeting of the grand council. During the king's absence on the European mainland, his appointed sheriffs had repeatedly violated their oaths of office by engaging in numerous acts of abuse. A detailed audit into the behaviour of the sheriffs was ordered to be presented in June. When the report was rendered in mid-June, it described massive abuses by the appointed loyal officials, who had repeatedly increased the taxes but kept the extra revenue, while also accepting bribes from the guilty in exchange for lighter sentences. After receiving the inquiry, fifteen officers were replaced with royal agents and the regime maintained a closer watch on the sheriffs.

While the king waited on the inquiry into the sheriffs, he made arrangements for the coronation of his heir, Prince Henry, as king-designate. Traditionally, the crowning ceremony was performed by the Archbishop of Canterbury, but with the dispute with Thomas Becket making his presence impossible, the Archbishop of York was appointed to anoint the prince. Becket, not wishing to allow the challenge to his authority to go unanswered, ordered the Archbishop of York, Roger de L'Eveque, and the English bishops not to perform the coronation ceremony. The prelates ignored Becket's wishes, and Prince Henry was crowned at Westminster Abbey on 14 June 1170 in the presence of the great magnates and bishops. Prince Henry's wife, Margaret, was absent from the ceremony, the affront giving cause for Louis VII to resume his conflict with the Plantagenets.

When Pope Alexander III was informed of the coronation, he ordered his legates to issue an interdiction against Henry II's European mainland fiefdoms if the dispute with the archbishop was not resolved. Under the threat of the papal decree, the English king agreed to meet with Becket and Louis VII at Freteval in mid-July. On 22 July, the terms of the Montmartre Treaty were offered and accepted by Becket, with no mention of the kiss of peace. After six years of conflict, peace was finally established between the two former friends. As Henry and his archbishop rode together from Freteval, the king told him: 'My lord archbishop, let us return to our old friendship and each show the other what good he can and let us forget our hatred completely.'

Following the signing of the treaty, work began on the restoration of the relationship between the royal government and Church. Henry II remained in Normandy, where he became seriously ill, which delayed the process of reuniting the two institutions. Letters were obtained from the papacy threating the king with excommunication unless the settlement was quickly concluded. On 12 October 1170, the recovered King Henry met with Becket at Amboise, where the reconciliation took place. When Becket approached the subject of the kiss of peace, the monarch evaded the issue and two days later departed from him at Chaumont. From the castle, Becket left for England and Henry hastened to Argentan to prepare his invasion of Berry in response to the growing hostility of the French throne. While at Argentan, Henry received reports of Becket's excommunication of the prelates who had participated in Prince Henry's coronation. The decree weakened the validity of the ceremony. to the dismay of the sovereign. He summoned a council meeting of his magnates asking for their advice at his Christmas court in Argentan. During the fiery discussions, a baron yelled out: 'My lord, while Thomas lives, you will have no peace, no quiet nor prosperity.' The enraged Henry replied to his barons: 'What idle and miserable men I have encouraged and promoted in my household, faithless to their lord, who let me be ridiculed by a low-born clerk.' After the king's demeaning outcry, four knights rode to the coast and crossed over to England, making their way to Canterbury. On 26 December, the soldiers broke open the door to the cathedral and confronted Becket. They demanded the withdrawal of the order for the excommunication of the bishops and attempted to arrest the archbishop, but when he resisted, the knights cut him down with their swords. Upon hearing the news of Becket's death, Henry was distraught, withdrawing to his rooms alone for three days.

As reports of Thomas Becket's killing spread in the European courts, Henry II was deemed the cause of the brutal assassination. Louis VII dispatched envoys to Pope Alexander III, urging him to excommunicate the Plantagenet king. Henry was compelled to send his personal delegation of bishops to Rome to protect him from possible hostile actions by the papacy.

Alexander III delayed issuing the excommunication order but continued to consider decreeing an interdiction against the king's lands. While Henry waited for the pope's decision, he continued his diplomatic campaign to strengthen his fiefdoms against a renewal of the war with the French regime and its allies. In 1171, although Henry II ruled a powerful empire not seen in Europe since the era of Charlemagne nearly 300 years earlier, he was constantly under threat of rebellion from many barons who were seeking independence. In the spring, he initiated negotiations to shore up his southern mainland border defences by forming a coalition with the Count of Savoy, Humbert. The alliance gave Henry the opportunity to spread his power into Italy and gain a supporter in his continuing confrontation with the papacy.

Remaining in lower Normandy, the English king summoned his magnates and prelates to a council meeting at Argentan to announce his plans to cross the Irish Sea and invade south-eastern Ireland. The expedition to Ireland had a secondary benefit, allowing him to avoid contact with the newly arrived papal legates, thus delaying any interdiction. On 1 August, Henry II sailed from Normandy to England, spending a month preparing his army for the Irish expedition. He then made his way to southern Wales for the sea crossing to Ireland. While waiting for favourable weather to set sail for Ireland, the king arranged a meeting with the Welsh prince, Rhys, granting him custody of territories in south Wales in exchange for men and supplies to be used in the coming campaign. It was not until mid-October that the royal army was finally able to sail to Ireland, landing near Waterford. Henry disembarked with 400 knights and a force of 4,000 mounted warriors, infantrymen and archers. Soon after his arrival, he received the homage of the Irish kings of Cork and Limerick to gain a foothold on the island. The English host and its Welsh mercenaries proceeded north and in mid-November reached Dublin, where the southern Irish rulers submitted to the crown. With the surrender of the kings, Henry now held suzerainty over three-quarters of Ireland. The papacy had long harboured desires to bring the Irish Church under its jurisdiction, and the Plantagenet king took measures to gain control of the native religious body to acquire the friendship of Pope Alexander III in his dispute over Becket. Henry summoned an ecclesiastic council at Cashel, which enacted laws to unite the Irish and English churches. A set of laws was introduced that brought the Irish Church in line with Rome's decrees. The council further established a new central government for the realm and arranged the division of the kingdoms among loyal English magnates. Richard, Earl of Pembroke, was named governor of the newly conquered territory in 1173. Richard had earlier sailed to Ireland in 1169 and seized control of Dublin and Waterford, establishing an English enclave with permission from Henry's regime. Henry II's introduction of English law and customs would last for nearly 700 years in southern Ireland, while the north remained more independent.

Henry stayed in Ireland for nearly six months, personally enforcing his supremacy before events in his continental domains forced him to make arrangements for his return to Normandy. He crossed the Irish Sea in April 1172, revisiting Prince Rhys to ensure his continued allegiance before pressing on to Winchester. After a brief stay ensuring his rule was enforced by his regime's officials as ordered and confirming his vassals retained their loyalty to him, he crossed the Channel to Barfleur. Landing in Normandy, he hastened to Gorron in Maine to meet with the papal legates to finally resolve the festering dispute with the pope. Negotiations began on 17 May but were quickly ended, Henry refusing to compromise with the pope's representatives. Two days later, the discussions were renewed at Avranches in Brittany, where Henry changed his mind and agreed to comply with the pontiff's conditions for absolution. On 21 May, at the cathedral in Avranches, the Plantagenet overlord placed his hand on the Bible and swore that he had not ordered the death of Thomas Becket, which had caused him great grief. He willingly accepted the penance of the Church, pledging to send 200 knights to the Levant, withdraw the 'Clarendon Constitutions' and take an oath of homage to the pope. At the doorway to the cathedral, he knelt to receive absolution.

Shortly after his settlement with Pope Alexander III, the Plantagenet king met with Louis VII to regain his friendship. Following Henry II's appeasement with the Church, the French king was willing to make peace. His principal grievance remained the refusal of Henry to have his daughter-in-law, Margaret, crowned as queen. The English monarch agreed to the nuptial ceremony, and on 27 August 1172 at Westminster Abbey, Margaret was anointed by the papal legate as Queen of England.

While Henry II was in Ireland, his eldest son and heir, Prince Henry the Younger, had been growing increasingly dissatisfied with his lack of authority as king-designate for England and Normandy. Prior to departing on his Irish expedition, the English monarch had instructed his son and daughter-in-law to return to Normandy, and soon after arriving they proceeded to meet with Louis VII at Gisors. Henry the Younger was advised by his father-in-law to demand the sovereignty of either England or Normandy, which further elevated his festering ambition for independent rule. Prince Henry was now approaching his 18th birthday and had the titles and honours of a mighty king, but was continually denied any real power. His father had been 16 when the Duchy of Normandy was ceded to him, and Henry the Younger grew increasingly determined to rule his own lands.

After spending Christmas 1172 with Queen Eleanor at Mirebeau in Anjou, Henry II, accompanied by his heir, travelled to Montferrat in early January 1173 to meet Humbert of Savoy to arrange the marriage of his youngest son, Prince John, to the count's daughter. While at Montferrat, King Henry was asked to arbitrate in the dispute between the King of Aragon and the Count of Toulouse, Raymond V. Under the guidance of Henry, the quarrel between the two magnates was soon resolved, after which the English king met privately with Humbert to finalize the terms of the marriage contract. As part of the agreement, John was to be ceded three castles – Chinon, Mirebeau and Loudin – by his father. The fortifications had earlier been given to Henry the Younger, who was encouraged by his mother, Queen Eleanor, and many barons in England and Normandy to retain authority over them. A bitter argument thus erupted between King Henry and his son. The king refused to grant Prince Henry control of any lordships, while the Plantagenet heir demanded possession of either England or Normandy, which was supported by Louis VII and the majority of nobles.

As Henry the Younger's discontent grew stronger, his father ordered several of his son's influential friends to leave court to quell his anger. Learning of the king's actions, Prince Henry quietly departed from Chinon and made his way to the fiefdom of Louis VII's brother, Robert I, in the Countship of Dreux, seeking French support against his father. Robert I was an experienced soldier, having participated in the Second Crusade and conflict against Henry II in the border wars, and he encouraged the young prince to press his demands from the French court in Paris. The English king was enraged at the parting of his son from Chinon, sending emissaries to Louis VII demanding his return. Shortly after hearing of his son's departure, Henry II rode to Gisors, ordering reinforcements to the defensive works in preparation for the renewal of the war with Louis VII. While remaining at Gisors, the king was informed that numerous barons had now joined forces with Henry the Younger, including his sons, Richard and Geoffrey, in opposition to the repression of their independence. As the rebellion escalated, Queen Eleanor attempted to reach her children in France but was intercepted by royal guards and detained. Fearing her influence over their sons, Henry ordered her confined at Chinon and later in England.

Meanwhile, at the Capetian court, Louis VII threw his support behind the Plantagenet heir, and under his influence his French magnates pledged to recognize him as king. To strengthen his rebellion against his father, Prince Henry issued grants of properties to the lords of the border fiefs. Count Matthew of Boulogne was given Mortain, Theobald V, Count of Blois, was ceded Amboise, William I of Scotland was allotted Northumberland south to the River Tyne to secure England's northern frontier, while the Flemish count, Philip, received lands in England. In return, Prince Henry received their pledges of homage and promise of military aid. While the prince was securing allies from the neighbouring fiefdoms, he also needed the support of the barons in his father's lordships of Normandy, Anjou, Brittany and Aquitaine. The revolt against Henry II was predominantly concentrated in Aquitaine, Maine and along the Breton borderlands with Normandy, where the Plantagenet monarchy's policy of centralized government had been implemented and the warlords were in opposition to the loss of their independence. In the Midlands of England, several earls also rallied to Prince Henry's call to arms.

As Henry the Younger's rebellion strengthened, King Henry waited for his son to make the first move, while reinforcing his castles and preparing for an attack. In May 1173, Prince Henry the Younger led his army into Normandy, attacking Gouray and Pacy 40 miles south-east of Rouen in probing raids. The following month, Flemish forces under Count Philip crossed the border into Normandy, capturing the stronghold at Aumale, while Louis VII invaded from the south, besieging the castle at Verneuil with the support of Earl Robert of Leicester. At the Breton border, rebels advanced against Avranches, reinforced by Hugh, Fifth Earl of Chester. Hugh was a powerful and wealthy English warlord with large properties in western England and mainland Europe. When the earl had assumed control of his lands in 1161, he acknowledged the rule of Henry II, but in 1173 he abandoned the Plantagenet crown to join the revolt of the king's three sons.

With his domains under attack, Henry II boarded a ship and made a quick voyage to England, riding to Westminster to raid the royal treasury for more money to hire additional mercenaries from Brabant. Prince Henry's invasion of Normandy made little progress, and after the brother of Count Philip of Flanders, Matthew, was killed during the fighting, Philip abandoned the campaign and returned to Flanders. After the withdrawal of the Flemish troops, King Henry mobilized his army and proceeded to attack the French army at Verneuil. As Henry's forces neared the French siege, Louis VII sent a reconnaissance patrol to locate the advancing enemy. Informed that Henry II was at the head of a formidable army and ready to attack, Louis broke off his siege and retreated back to France. During the hasty withdrawal, his rearguard was virtually destroyed by the Plantagenet soldiers.

With the French army in retreat, Henry II hastened east to seize Damville before moving to Rouen to reorganize his army, while sending a strong force of mercenary troops west to engage the Bretons. When the Bretons were attacked, they retreated to Dol after suffering heavy casualties. The mercenary troops from Brabant pursued the Bretons, besieging them at Dol. When Henry II was informed of the siege, he rode to Dol with reinforcements, tightening the encirclement of the stronghold. Surrounded by royal forces, the rebels surrendered on 20 August. The leaders of the Breton army, Earl Hugh of Chester and Ralph de Fourgeres, were captured and imprisoned. Hugh soon made his peace with King Henry and his lands were later restored to him, but his castles remained garrisoned with royal soldiers.

Having suffered several defeats, the insurrection of Henry the Younger and his rebel allies was in disarray in western France. To regain the initiative, Robert de Beaumont, Third Earl of Leicester, was sent by Henry the Younger with a force of Flemish knights and foot-soldiers to launch a diversionary attack in England. On 29 September 1173, they landed at Walton in Suffolk and united with local supporters led by Hugh Bigod, First Earl of Norfolk. The two earls hastened west across the Midlands to relieve the royalist siege of de Beaumont's fortress at Leicester. When Robert's forces arrived in England, the royal army under Robert de Lucy was in the north, fending off an invasion by the Scottish king, William I, who had penetrated south into Northumberland, ravaging towns and farmlands. After beating the Scots back across the border, de Lucy proceeded south, intercepting the rebel army at Fordham. On 17 October, the king's cavalry unleashed a fierce charge against the rebel horsemen. The mounted knights surged forward at full gallop on their warhorses, overpowering their opponents, Earl Robert's Flemish infantry also being shattered during the fighting. The rebel soldiers scattered in disarray into the countryside, where they were slaughtered by the local peasants with their pitchforks. The earl, his wife and many household knights were taken prisoner. While Robert de Beaumont remained in captivity, Henry II confiscated his lands and titles. In the wake of the rout of Robert's invasion, King Henry's supporters checked the rebellion of the Earl of Norfolk. The rebels then sued for peace, and a truce lasting until early July 1174 was quickly negotiated. With southern England now under the control of the king's loyal vassals, preparations were begun for a renewal of the Scottish war in the north and potential flare-ups in the Midlands.

At the beginning of winter, the Norman and French regimes arranged a ceasefire lasting until the end of March 1174, while a similar truce was negotiated in England by the Bishop of Durham with the Scots. During the winter months, Henry II remained in Normandy preparing for the renewal of hostilities. At his Norman court, he met with the papal envoy of Alexander III, who had been sent to orchestrate a peace treaty. The French crown resisted any attempt to settle the conflict and the pope's diplomatic mission failed.

In the spring of 1174, William I of Scotland, with support from northern dissident nobles, resumed his attacks across the English frontier, attacking the fortification at Wark, where his sorties were repelled. William abandoned his quest for Wark and resumed his campaign of devastation by pressing on to besiege the castle at Carlisle. Leaving a force of Scottish soldiers to take the stronghold, William led a large contingent of his troops along the borderlands, capturing several castles, while laying waste to the countryside and villages. He returned to the siege at Carlisle and met with the English garrison captain, who pledged to surrender if reinforcements did not arrive by late September. Leaving men to monitor the English, the Scottish king proceeded to Prudhoe, where he besieged the citadel. Meanwhile, the loyal northern English warlords mustered an army and advanced against the Scots at Prudhoe, forcing William to withdraw. Following his retreat, he moved against Alnwick, laying siege to the castle there. As the Scottish investment continued, an army of Henry II's supporters was mustered in Yorkshire and marched north against the Scots. At dawn on 13 July, a strong reconnaissance force of over 400 English knights broke into the Scottish camp, catching King William and his troops by surprise. The Scottish monarch was captured and most of his nobles either killed or taken prisoner.

Count Philip of Flanders had pledged his support to Henry the Younger, and with the rebels' war effort having stalled, issued orders for his men to assemble for a campaign against Normandy. While Henry the Younger and his Flemish allies attacked the royalists in Normandy to aid the failing barons' revolt in England, Philip sent an army of Flemish knights and infantrymen to buttress the army of Hugh Bigod of Norfolk. After receiving the Flemish reinforcements, Bigod led his forces to Norwich, compelling the royalists to submit. After fighting against Henry II's rule in Normandy, in June 1177 Count Philip travelled to Jerusalem as a pilgrim to seek remission of his sins. In the holy city, he met his cousin, King Baldwin IV of Jerusalem, who was dying from leprosy, and was offered the regency of his kingdom. Philip refused to accept the kingship, saying he was there only as a pilgrim. Before returning to Flanders, he took part in a campaign against the Saracens in the Antioch Principality.

While the English rebels were challenging the royalists for possession of northern England, in Aquitaine, Henry II led his troops in a plundering sweep around Chinon, ravaging three dissident strongholds and occupying the town of Poitiers. With his demesne under attack, the king's second son, Richard, marched his army into the duchy, besieging his father's loyal fortress at La Rochelle, but the defenders repelled his repeated assaults. Richard then advanced against the castle at Saintes, and in May 1174 his troops took the town by storm. While Richard remained in Aquitaine defending his lands, King Henry resumed his Poitou campaign, attacking Saintes and overrunning its defences. After reoccupying the fortress, he moved against Ancenis in Anjou, destroying the town in June, as Prince Henry's rebellion against his father continued to lose momentum.

After receiving reports of his English supporters' defeat at Norwich and the escalating threat from the barons, the king decided to return to his kingdom. He sailed from Barfleur in early July after ensuring his Norman defences were prepared for any attack. Landing at Southampton, he first went to Canterbury, offering prayers at the shrine of Thomas Becket, who had been canonized in 1173 by Pope Alexander III. He then proceeded to London and established his residence at Westminster Palace, where news reached him of William I's capture. With the danger of invasion from Scotland eliminated, the king hastened north, laying siege to Huntingdon and forcing the garrison captain to submit. The royalists continued their offensive to Northampton, which quickly surrendered. As the king continued to attack the dissident barons, the rebellion in support of Henry the Younger wavered and then collapsed. Henry II now summoned the remaining rebel warlords to secure their submission.

Shortly before Henry II had sailed from Barfleur, Prince Henry and Philip of Flanders joined their forces with Louis VII for a joint invasion of Normandy. Encountering only scattered resistance, the Franco-Flemish army encamped outside the walls of Rouen and besieged the fortress. With his suzerainty over England confirmed, King Henry recrossed the Channel on 8 August, landing at Barfleur and pressing on towards Rouen. The coalition troops had not fully encircled the town's defensive works, allowing supplies to still enter the ducal capital as the defenders remained defiant in support of Henry II. On 10 August, Louis VII ordered an assault against the walls, but his men were repulsed in bloody fighting, suffering heavy casualties. The following day, King Henry and his mercenaries from Brabant and Wales reached Rouen, entering the city through a break in the enemy's lines. Soon after arriving at his Norman capital, he sent his Welsh mercenaries to harass the French lines of communications. Hiding in the woodlands, the Welsh attacked the French supply lines, and within two days Louis VII's food supplies began running low, forcing him to abandon the siege. Soon after the withdrawal from Rouen, Prince Henry sued for peace. The rebels' failure to take Rouen marked the end of the revolt on the European mainland and the resurgence of Henry II's power.

Following his retreat, Louis VII sent his representatives to the Plantagenet king to propose a meeting between them to set the terms for a lasting peace. Henry II agreed to the summit, but delayed its start so he could first force the submission of Richard in Aquitaine. The royalists proceeded south, reaching Aquitaine and steadily pushing back Richard's forces, taking castle after castle without a fight. Finally, on 23 September, the rebel son met his father at Poitiers, falling to his knees begging for a pardon.

At the end of summer, King Henry, his eldest son and Louis VII met at Tours to negotiate the terms of a peace treaty. Under the resulting Tours settlement, Henry II granted his sons a pardon, while they pledged their fealty to him. Prince Henry received two fortifications in Normandy and an annual pension of 4,000 pounds, while the other rebellious brothers received similar bequests. The youngest son, John, was given rich properties in England and Normandy, which elevated him to an equal status with his brothers, much to their disapproval. The citadels of the English lords who had rebelled against the throne were destroyed, while King William I of Scotland was forced to abandon his occupation of northern England and give homage to Henry II and his heir as overlord.

With peace restored to his lands, Henry II remained in Normandy dealing with his eldest son, resolving the problems created during the two-year civil war. He travelled throughout his demesne, ensuring his laws and justice were obeyed and reorganizing his disorderly government, while securing the fealty of the nobles who had fought against him in support of Henry the Younger. King Henry met with his third surviving son, Geoffrey, giving him instructions for the administration of his lands to best advance the policies of the Plantagenet crown. On 8 May 1175, Henry II and Henry the Younger sailed to England to reimpose Plantagenet rule over the increasingly unruly barons, landing at Portsmouth. The king's initiative to suppress the rebellious warlords on the European mainland and maintain peace in England depended on the continued flow of revenue from his English subjects. To sustain the collection of taxes, the king and his son began a campaign to strengthen the economy. They travelled to Westminster to hold a council of ecclesiastic lords to re-establish the relationship between the Church and kingdom and deal with the practice of priests marrying, which was opposed by large segments of the clergy. Henry II departed the council on 28 May to make a second pilgrimage to

Canterbury, giving thanks to St Thomas Becket for his recent defeat of the rebel coalition. After his journey to Canterbury, King Henry and his successor-designate summoned the Welsh princes and border warlords to a council at Gloucester in late June. The English barons, with martial support from the Welsh, had been engaged in private wars against each other to expand their influence and princedoms, but the king ordered them to end their hostilities to secure his frontier lands. Henry II and Prince Henry held another gathering of magnates and churchmen at Woodstock, issuing decrees to bring peace to England and end the rampart lawlessness that developed during their absence on the European mainland. On 10 August, King Henry and his heir met William I of Scotland at York to implement the terms of the peace treaty signed in Normandy. At the meeting, the Scottish king and his high lords and churchmen pledged their allegiance to the English crown, securing peace on the kingdom's northern border. The royal court continued its campaign to regain firm control of England, and on 25 January 1176 Henry II announced to an assembled council at Northampton the creation of a permanent office of travelling justices responsible for hearing criminal and civil cases to supplement the workload of the normal county courts. The king and his son held further meetings with local government officials and prelates throughout the realm to ensuring their English rule was unchallenged, enacting laws to create a prosperous kingdom after years of ineffective government by royal surrogates.

While Henry II and his successor-designate reimposed Plantagenet rule in England and reorganized the government, Richard was in Aquitaine subduing the remaining pockets of rebellious barons. In May 1176, he led his mercenary soldiers against the dissident warlords Vulgrin of Angouleme and Aimar of Limoges, overpowering them and occupying their lands. In June, the king sent Henry the Younger to join Richard, and they campaigned together in Aquitaine. Unlike his father, Henry the Younger had little interest in leading his men in battle, soon deserting his brother to take part in his favourite activity of tournament jousting. Richard resumed his campaign of subjugation, and by the end of 1176 had enforced the rule of the Plantagenets in the north of the duchy. During the following spring, he led his forces south, capturing more rebel fortresses and gaining oaths of allegiance to his father's throne. The reign of the Plantagenets was now secure throughout western France, from Normandy in the north to the Spanish border in the south, but the political status quo with France was thrown into disarray in 1180 with the death of Louis VII and the succession of his son, Philip II.

Unlike Louis VII, his successor was ambitious and determined to regain the prestige and western French lands lost under the reign of his father. The three sons of Henry II viewed the new monarch as a friend, who could bolster their quest to secure independent fiefdoms from their father. Henry the Younger persistently demanded his own lands, but the English king stubbornly refused, driving his son ever closer to the Capetian regime. In early 1182, Henry II sailed to the European mainland in an attempt to regain the loyalty of his sons. At his Christmas court at Caen, he ordered Richard and Geoffrey of Nantes to pledge their allegiance to his oldest son as his successor, but they refused the command. Richard swiftly left the court and returned to Poitou. Prince Henry was ordered by the king to return his brother to Caen, but instead he rode to Poitou to join forces with Richard's enemies. The family dispute between the two brothers soon became a widespread conflict, Philip II of France and Geoffrey of Nantes uniting with Henry the Younger against Richard. In danger of losing Aquitaine, Henry II mobilized his army and advanced south against his eldest son and his allies, besieging them at Limoges.

During the siege, Henry the Younger, who had left the city to raise money and reinforcements, was stricken with dysentery and died at the fortress of Martel on 11 June. Following the death of the Plantagenet prince, the alliance against Richard disbanded; as the eldest surviving son, he was recognized as heir to his father's demesne. Henry II's lands were again at peace following the surrender of Limoges.

In September 1183, King Henry summoned his remaining three sons to Angers to arrange the redistribution of their inheritances. As the oldest son, Richard was now acknowledged as king-designate for England, with Geoffrey holding Nantes and John ruling in Aquitaine as vassals of their older brother. After fighting for possession of Aquitaine for over eight years and spending his youth in the duchy, Richard refused to transfer the fiefdom to Prince John. He quickly left the royal court to defend Aquitaine. Unable to convince his heir to comply with his wishes, King Henry sent John to seize the duchy by force of arms, with support from Geoffrey and his soldiers. The fighting was inconclusive, and Henry II, who had returned to England in the summer of 1184, ordered his three sons to join him to resolve the Aquitaine dispute. Meeting at Westminster Palace, a tense peace was eventually negotiated.

Henry II then remained in England, while Richard and John returned to their fiefdoms on the European mainland. Under the recent initiatives of the king, the independence of the English lords had been crushed and his proclamations had brought prosperity and an end to lawlessness. His appointments of qualified and loyal governmental officials triggered the enforcement of his laws and justice, and resulted in a peaceful kingdom. The king's rule over England was now respected by the barons, prelates and populace, unlike his mainland European fiefdoms, where rebellion remained widespread.

Henry made several attempts to dislodge Richard from Aquitaine, but failed to convince him to transfer the duchy to John. In April 1185, the king crossed the Channel to Normandy and brought Queen Eleanor to his court. The king now demanded his heir surrender Aquitaine to his mother. Richard reluctantly obeyed his father, turning over the duchy to her. While Richard stayed at his father's court, Count Raymond V of Toulouse launched brutal pillaging raids into southern Aquitaine in an attempt to regain his independence from the rule of the Plantagenets. To reimpose his power, Henry II sent his oldest son with an army of mercenaries to end the forays and punish Raymond. While Richard hammered Raymond with ruthless sorties, in April 1186 the political picture was again altered by the unexpected death of Geoffrey of Nantes, who was killed in Paris during a martial tournament, leaving Henry II with just two sons to succeed to his conglomerate of fiefdoms.

Following his elevation to the throne of France in 1180, Philip II had been occupied suppressing the revolt of his vassals, so it was in his best interests to remain on cordial terms with the Plantagenet regime. After spending six years securing his reign, in 1186 King Philip began launching probing attacks into the Norman Vexin lordship on the border between the two realms to regain the disputed area. The Vexin was the dowry for Philip's half-sister Alice's marriage to Duke Richard, but the English king would not allow the wedding to take place and the Capetian monarchy demanded the return of the county. While the French crown continued its demands for the Vexin, Philip claimed the guardianship for the three children of Count Geoffrey of Nantes, which would give him control over the strategic county with its border with Brittany. With war again looming between the two thrones, Henry II and the French king agreed to a temporary ceasefire. After the truce expired in the summer of 1187, Philip II ordered his army into the contested region of Berry. As the fighting threatened to spread, a two-year truce was negotiated by the papal legate sent by Pope Clement III. This ceasefire was soon broken by the French when the Capetian monarch again sent his army into Berry in an inconclusive campaign. In August 1187, the Plantagenets retaliated by advancing toward Mantes, 30 miles west of Paris, laying waste to the region. As the war continued, the two kings and Richard met at Bonsmoutin to try to reach a settlement. After failing to find an understanding, the Capetian king and Richard met privately to negotiate a compromise, but when it was presented to Henry II, he refused to accept the treaty.

Philip II then resumed his ravaging forays, sending his Breton allies to batter numerous Plantagenet-held castles and towns. During the prior meetings between the two regimes, Henry II had repeatedly refused to recognize Richard as his king-designate and approve his marriage to Alice. It was in the best interests of Philip II to have his half-sister as Queen of England, which gave him greater influence with the English court, while Richard's acknowledgement as king solidified his rights to the throne. When the two sovereigns met again in the spring of 1189 to discuss a peace treaty, Richard and Philip met secretly and thrashed out terms, but their demands were again quickly rejected by King Henry. Unable to secure his succession to his father's crown, Richard joined forces with the French, attacking Henry II's domains in Maine. Earlier in the year, the English king had been ill and remained weak with fever. As his lands were steadily overrun by his son and his French allies, he agreed to discuss peace terms with the Capetian king and Richard on 4 July 1189, south of the city of Tours at the fortress of Colombiers, current-day Chateau Villandry. Under the subsequent Treaty of Colombiers, Henry II pledged to recognize Richard as his heir and arrange his son's marriage to Alice. As the frail king departed from Richard, he whispered: 'God grant that I not die until I have my revenge on you.' Too weak to ride to Chinon, Henry was carried on a litter. During the night, his illness worsened, and King Henry II died on the morning of 6 July at the age of 56. Several days later, his body was taken down the River Vienne by barge to the Abbey of Fontevraud and buried by the nuns there. As the eldest surviving son, Richard succeeded to his father's crown and ruled as Richard I – known as the Lionheart for his reputation as a military leader – for the next ten years. He had earlier taken the cross of a crusader, and after ensuring the fealty of his vassals, departed for the Levant to take part in the Third Crusade. In June 1191, Richard joined the crusaders at the ongoing siege of Acre. The fortified city submitted on 12 July, after which the English king began his quest to capture Jerusalem, which ended in failure. After agreeing to a truce with the Muslims holding Jerusalem and establishing Christian control over a coastal strip of land, King Richard began his long journey home, but was captured in Austria and held prisoner until February 1194. Richard spent the remainder of his reign fighting for Normandy and his continental lands against Philip II of France. Richard I died on 6 April 1199 from a wound suffered during the siege of Chalus in Aquitaine, and was succeeded by his brother John, who continued the rule of the Plantagenets.

Selected Sources

Ackroyd, Peter, *Foundation – The History of England from its Earliest Beginnings to the Tudors* (Thomas Dunne Books, 2011).

Ault, Warren O., *Europe in the Middle Ages* (D.C. Heath, 1937).

Barber, Richard, *Henry Plantagenet, 1133–1189* (Barnes and Noble Books, 1964).

Barber, Richard, *The Devil's Crown – A History of Henry II and His Sons* (BBC, 1978).

Barratt, Nick, *The Restless Kings – Henry II, His Sons and the Wars for the Plantagenet Crown* (Faber & Faber, 2018).

Bingham, Caroline, *The Crowned Lions – The Early Plantagenet Kings* (Rowman and Littlefield, 1978).

Brooke, Christopher, *From Alfred to Henry III, 871–1272* (W.W. Norton, 1961).

Brooke, Christopher, *The Saxon and Norman Kings* (Fontana and Collins, 1967).

Carpenter, David, *The Struggle for Mastery – Britain 1066–1284* (Oxford University Press, 2003).

Gillingham, John, 'Henry II', in Fraser, Antonia, *The Lives of the Kings and Queens of England* (Alfred A Knopf, 1975).

Hallam, Elizabeth M., *Capetian France, 987–1328* (Pearson Education Ltd, 1980).

Jones, Dan, *The Plantagenets – The Warrior Kings and Queens Who Made England* (Viking, 2013).

Schlight, John, *Henry II Plantagenet* (Twayne Publishers, 1973).

Warren, W.L., *Henry II* (University of California Press, 1973).

Henry III

On 28 October 1216, the 9-year-old Henry III was anointed King of England in Gloucester Abbey by the papal legate of Pope Honorius III and inherited the once-powerful Plantagenet Empire, which had been fragmented during the rule of his father, John. The eastern region of England, including London, now accepted the French dauphin, Louis, as its overlord, while the northern lordships were occupied by rebellious barons, who defied the succession of Henry III as their monarch. The English king could claim the allegiance of just the Midlands and south-western nobles, Church and populace. At its summit, the Plantagenet regime had held control over England and lands in western France that reached from Normandy in the north to Toulouse in the south, but by the end of John's kingship only the French Duchy of Gascony remained loyal to the English monarchy. Henry III governed England for fifty-six years and was occupied with the suppression of the recalcitrant English nobles, who after two bloody and destructive civil wars were forced to recognize him as king. At the end of his reign in 1272, Henry III bequeathed to his successor, Edward I, a united and prosperous kingdom, but had failed to regain the lost Plantagenet possessions in France.

Henry Plantagenet, the oldest son of King John and Queen Isabella of Angouleme, was born on 1 October 1207 at Winchester Castle. At the time of Prince Henry's birth, the English regime was struggling against rebellious barons in the north and endeavouring to regain its lost possessions in western France. Adding to the despair, Pope Innocent III had imposed an interdiction on the kingdom to secure the submission of the English king to the Holy See. As the English monarchy continued to defy the pope, in 1209 John demanded his English subjects take an oath of fealty to his son to ensure his succession to the throne. Henry spent his early years in the household of the queen, cared for by several servants. At the age of 5, he was placed under the custody of the Bishop of Winchester, Peter des Roches, who provided his education and guardianship. Henry had four legitimate siblings – Richard, born in 1209, and three sisters, Joan, Isabella and Eleanor. The royal children lived in the south of England, away from the mayhem of their father's reign.

While Prince Henry remained isolated from his father's court, in 1212 – to regain the obedience of the insolent English monarchy – Pope Innocent III excommunicated King John, declaring him dethroned. With the crown of England legally vacant by papal decree, several magnates plotted against the king, planning to murder him and force his family from the realm. After discovering the conspiracy, Henry was placed under heavy guard and remained isolated. Attempts to assassinate King John failed, but Henry was now directly exposed to the dangers of his father's reign.

Confronted by the threats of rebellion by his barons, uprisings by the Welsh princes and the mobilization of the French army by King Philip II to invade England, John arranged to meet the papal legate, Pandulf, at Dover to settle the dispute with the Holy See. He agreed to submit to Innocent III and accept the authority of the papacy. On 15 May, before his gathered nobles, John formally ceded England to the See of Rome as a fiefdom. Under the agreement, the papacy was to receive an annual tribute of 1,000 marks, while in return the pope pledged to forbid Philip II from launching his attack against England.

With the danger of a French invasion eliminated, John assembled his army to recover his lost lands in western France. As the royal army mobilized, many warlords refused to answer the call to arms, but with a large treasury to hire mercenaries and a contingent of loyal English troops, the king set sail to La Rochelle in February 1214. John had negotiated an alliance with the German emperor, Otto IV, and the dukes of Flanders and Boulogne for a two-pronged simultaneous attack against the French from the north and south. After landing in France, John quickly overran the local Count of La Marche, Hugh IX, forcing his submission, while Otto IV and his allies from Lorraine, Brabant and Flanders moved into northern France. Reinforced with soldiers from La Marche, the English king marched north into Anjou but was compelled to withdraw by the presence of Prince Louis of France with a formidable host. While John returned to La Rochelle, on 27 July the northern allied army of over 9,000 knights and foot-soldiers clashed against the 7,000 Frenchmen of King Philip II at Bouvines. The Capetian heavy cavalry launched the first charge, slamming into the left flank of the Flemish forces to break through their line in a bloody and fierce onslaught. Meanwhile, in the centre, Otto IV's knights and infantrymen repelled the first French attack but were unable to hold their front when a second cavalry charge was initiated under the command of Philip II. As the allied line began to collapse, the French renewed their assaults against the still-defiant right wing, finally driving the enemy from the battlefield. After the defeat of his allies, John sent emissaries to the Capetian monarchy in September, negotiating a five-year truce. The failure of John's French campaign shattered his support from the English barons, rendering Prince Henry's future succession to the crown in jeopardy.

While the English king was battling the French, in England the barons gathered at Bury St Edmunds in Suffolk, threatening to take arms against the Plantagenet crown unless John agreed to grant a Charter of Liberties. The victory of the Capetian forces at Bouvines seriously weakened John's hold on the monarchy and emboldened his magnates to press their demands for greater participation in the government of the land. In January 1215, the monarch met the disgruntled warlords to resolve their dispute, but no agreement was made. During the spring of the same year, the English lords wrote to Innocent III asking him to force their king to accept the Charter of Liberties issued by Henry I over 100 years earlier, while John sent envoys to Rome pressing the papacy to forbid the nobles from revolting. When Innocent III gave his support to the monarch and told the warlords to cease making demands on the Plantagenet crown, an alliance of rebels renounced their oaths of fealty on 5 May, igniting the First Barons' War.

A force of dissident barons and their troops occupied London on 17 May as rebellion spread throughout England. From the capital, they sent messages to earls, lords and knights around the realm, calling for them to join the growing revolt. With the rebels holding London, John established his court at nearby Windsor and began communicating with the leaders of the uprising. A preliminary settlement was approved in mid-June. After several more days of bargaining, a final charter was approved by both parties on 18 June. The next day, at Runnymede on the banks of the Thames, the barons renewed their oaths of fealty to the Plantagenet monarchy, pledging to obey the agreement, while John swore to accept the charter known as the *Magna Carta*. The principal clauses of the charter set out the limits to the king's powers and called upon the lords to make war on him if the treaty was violated.

However, the newly negotiated peace between the king and his barons lasted less than two months. When John received an annulment of the charter from the pope, the royalists reformed their troops and resumed the war against the rebel lords. As the fighting escalated, Philip II began preparations with his dauphin, Louis, to invade England at the invitation of the English warlords. On 14 May 1216, a French army led by Prince Louis landed in Kent and proceeded to London, where it was welcomed by the citizens. As the Capetians expanded the lands under their control in the east, John travelled about the rest of the kingdom with his army, attacking his enemies and laying siege to their fortifications. During the sovereign's campaign to retain his rule, he became increasingly ill with dysentery and fever. King John died on 19 October 1216 at Newark Castle and was buried in Worcester Cathedral.

Following the funeral of his father, Henry Plantagenet was taken from his residence in the south-west of England to the castle at Devizes, while preparations for his coronation were made in Gloucester under orders from William Marshal, the Earl of Pembroke. Marshal, a renowned knight and loyal counsellor, had faithfully served four previous Plantagenet kings. He was born into a minor noble family and rose to prominence through his martial skills in battle and during jousting tournaments. Through his marriage in 1189 to Isabella de Clare, he acquired possession of large estates in England, Wales, Normandy and Ireland, along with the title Earl of Pembroke.

On 28 October 1216, beneath the great nave of Gloucester Abbey, a small gathering of ecclesiastic lords and loyal barons watched anxiously as the 9-year-old Henry was carried to the main altar. The anointing of the king was traditionally performed by the Archbishop of Canterbury but in his absence, Peter des Roches, Bishop of Winchester, carried out the coronation ceremony, placing a circlet of gold from the queen on the head of King Henry III. The customary royal crown, sceptre and other regalia were missing from the ritual, remaining in Westminster Abbey due to the French army's control of London. Henry III stood in the abbey and recited the oath of office, pledging to observe peace, honour and offer reverence to God, and give his people justice and good laws. After swearing fealty to the pope as his overlord, he was knighted by William of Pembroke.

While Henry III was pledging to provide good government to his subjects, over half of his kingdom had sworn allegiance to rebel barons or the French invaders.

Garrisons of French knights and foot-soldiers occupied castles spread across the eastern part of the realm, while to the north, the recalcitrant nobles controlled large areas. Before his death, King John appointed William Marshal as his son's guardian and regent, and to him fell the task of reuniting the kingdom in the name of the boy-king. In his quest for solidity, Marshal was aided by the papal legate, Cardinal Guala Bicchieeri, whose presence provided legitimacy to Henry III's succession to the English throne, and chief minister Hubert de Burgh, giving the new regime continuity. Cardinal Bicchieeri was from a prominent northern Italian family and entered the priesthood after studying law. He was named cardinal by Pope Innocent III in 1205, and later served him as legate to France and afterward to England in 1216.

Shortly after Henry III's coronation, a great council was summoned to meet at Bristol. However, the meeting was attended by only four earls, along with numerous barons from the heartland of the throne's support in the south-west and eleven bishops. On 11 November, William Marshal was confirmed as regent and a new ruling council was formed. A modified Charter of Liberties was reissued by Marshal and Cardinal Bicchieeri in the king's name, giving the barons the assurance the new monarchy would respect their rights and privileges. To weaken the French campaign of conquest in the realm, the papal legate excommunicated Prince Louis and his English allies, giving the war against the rebels the lustre of a holy crusade. While William Marshal and the papal legate formed the new government and attempted to restore order, Henry III resumed his education under the tutelage of Philip of Albini. Remaining at Bristol, the sovereign celebrated the Christmas season with Bicchieeri and the regent.

As Henry III's regime continued its campaign to regain the fealty of the barons, Prince Louis of France remained active in the south-east, gaining the allegiance of numerous lords and control over their castles through siege warfare and negotiated submissions. At the end of 1216, Louis had consolidated his rule over most of the south-eastern lordships and west into Wiltshire, while the loyalists retained power in the Midlands. The Capetians had begun laying siege to the stronghold at Dover before the death of King John, and despite the recent offer of great riches from the French, the garrison governor refused to surrender. While the French continued the siege at Dover, the Capetian dauphin mustered a formidable force and advanced against the royalists at Hertford Castle. He brought up his siege engines and bombarded the defences with large boulders. Although the English defenders put up an energetic resistance, William Marshal agreed to surrender the fortification along with the fortress at Berkhamsted in return for a general ceasefire, which was accepted by the dauphin. When the peace expired, another truce was negotiated for the transfer of additional castles to Louis. Several similar agreements were arranged, the French and their English allies gaining possession of nearly all of eastern England. The occupation of the newly acquired strongholds limited the rebels' ability to both garrison them and expand their campaign of conquest, forcing the dauphin's return to France to collect reinforcements. He sailed from Dover in late February, leaving Enguerrand de Coucy in command of his army.

In the wake of the dauphin's departure, the English regent sent his son, William the Younger, and the Earl of Salisbury, William Longspee, to lay siege to the

French at Winchester, while he moved on Farnham. Taking command of the troops, Marshal proceeded to Farnham, occupying the rebel town and besieging the citadel for a week before the Anglo-French defenders agreed to submit. After the castle was garrisoned, Marshal rejoined the royalist forces at Winchester. He took charge of the siege there, sending his son and the Earl of Salisbury on a sweep to the south to attack the fortifications at Southampton and Odiham in Hampshire and Marlborough in Wiltshire. After seizing Southampton, the king's men advanced against Odiham, forcing the thirteen defenders there to surrender on 9 July. The loyalists then hastened to besiege the castle at Marlborough, and after a week the garrison captain submitted. While Marshal's men were expanding Henry III's rule, other royal warlords were enforcing the English regime's authority at Portchester and Chichester in the south-east of the kingdom.

In late April 1217, the Capetian dauphin recrossed the Channel with a small force of knights and foot-soldiers to reinforce his quest for the English throne. On 23 April, he attempted to land at Dover but learned his besieging forces had been driven back by Marshal's men. After disembarking at Sandwich, he set out for Winchester, but en route discovered it had fallen to the loyalists. After William Marshal received reports of the dauphin's return, he ordered the recently captured castles abandoned and destroyed to prevent his soldiers from becoming tied down by prolonged sieges.

The French had begun siege operations against the royalist garrison at Lincoln in February, and after initially advancing toward Winchester, the dauphin changed his mind and proceeded to the ongoing siege at Lincoln with reinforcements to press the attack. Marshal, who was at Northampton when he learned of Louis' arrival at Lincoln, ordered his army to assemble at Newark, his forces being enlarged by the garrison troops from the recently demolished fortresses. Lincoln was a strategically important fortification in the Midlands and the only castle still loyal to Henry III in the region. The capture of the stronghold would be a major loss to the king's campaign against the rebel barons and French.

After mobilizing his forces, Marshal moved north to relieve the siege at Lincoln. The French had already occupied the city, but the fortress continued to hold out against the besiegers. Marshal's troops approached Lincoln from the north-west, hastening to attack the city's defensive works at the northern gate. The Anglo-French army at Lincoln, comprising over 1,600 soldiers commanded by the Count of Perche, was opposed by 700 English knights and approximately 800 infantrymen and crossbowmen. The French and their English allies had blocked the northern gate, and to clear the obstacles, the regent sent his crossbowmen under Falkes de Breaute to occupy the castle's walls and unleash volleys of deadly bolts on the enemy. The English foot-soldiers, led by Ranulf, Earl of Chester, then stormed forward, breaking through the obstructions at the gate to gain access to the town. Perche's men were driven back to the city's cathedral, where he attempted to rally them. The English knights and infantrymen pushed ahead, driving the Anglo-French back through the narrow and bloody streets. As the fighting continued, an English knight rushed forward, striking the Count of Perche with his sword and killing him. The surviving Anglo-French troops fled after six hours of fierce and ruthless fighting. Many rebel English nobles were captured, including Robert FitzWalter and the Saer of Quincy. After the battle, which became known as the Lincoln Fair, the loyalists looted the city.

In the aftermath of the great English victory at Lincoln, Prince Louis left the siege at Dover, returning to London with his advisors to rethink his campaign. The royalists, now at Chertsey, sent messages to the Londoners offering the reconfirmation of their liberties and privileges to entice their pledges of loyalty to Henry III. To prevent the inhabitants from abandoning him, Prince Louis ordered the gates of London closed and the renewal of their fealty to him. Remaining in London, he was forced to send raiding parties into East Anglia to collect food and supplies, while his wife, Blanche of Castile, began raising reinforcements in France.

As the French quest for the English throne faltered, the earls of Arundel and Warren abandoned Prince Louis, pledging their allegiance to the boy-king. On 6 August, the regent summoned his council to Oxford, where he agreed to divide the royal army, deploying Cardinal Guala Bicchieeri – accompanied by Henry III – toward London with part of the host, while Hubert de Burgh and the regent led the remainder south to prepare for the expected landing of French reinforcements sent by Blanche of Castile. At Dover, Marshal ordered the crown's fleet to assemble at Sandwich and the royal justiciar, Hubert de Burgh, was appointed commander of the naval forces, with preparations for the ships' departure being intensified.

With his hold on England disintegrating, Louis of France employed the well-known pirate, Eustace the Monk, to bring the 100 knights, several hundred infantrymen and many tons of supplies collected by his wife from Calais to reinforce his English war effort. On 23 August 1217, Eustace set sail with eighty vessels, including ten warships, heading toward the mouth of the River Thames. As Eustace's ships approached the English coastline, Hubert de Burgh followed the enemy fleet from a distance. With the coastline under the control of the king's supporters, Eustace was compelled to sail up the Thames to reach Louis with the reinforcements. In the shallow waters of the river, Eustace's flagship was difficult to steer, allowing the justiciar to pull alongside and board it. In the ensuing fight on the deck, many French sailors and lords were killed, while Eustace was captured and executed for his crimes as a pirate. As de Burgh was siezing the flagship, his fleet slammed into the enemy ships, firing crossbows at the French sailors and forcing them back to Calais.

Following the two recent disastrous defeats for the French, Cardinal Bicchieeri advanced his troops to retake London for Henry. Seeking refuge in the Tower of London, Louis asked for a conference with Marshal to discuss peace terms. Before meeting the dauphin in London, the regent blockaded the Thames and joined his army with Bicchieeri's forces to bottle-up the remaining Anglo-French supporters. With his soldiers now trapped, Louis agreed to the terms offered by Marshal. Under the Treaty of Kingston, all prisoners were to be freed, rebel Englishmen were to offer fealty to Henry III, all seized lands were to be restored to their former owners and the French prince was to receive a large cash payment of 10,000 marks. At Kingston on 12 September, in the presence of King Henry, the French pledged to honour the treaty, while the English agreed to return the occupied lands to the rebel barons. On 28 September, Louis and his Frenchmen sailed from Dover, thereby ending the First Barons' War and securing Henry III's rights to the English crown.

On 29 October, Henry III entered London for the first time, accompanied by William Marshal, and was received by the residents with respect and homage. Under the guidance of the regent, the king's education continued and he became increasingly exposed to the governance of his realm, routinely meeting with the barons and prelates at court. Soon after entering the capital, the Earl of Pembroke summoned his ruling council and held discussions to establish a stable regime. To affirm the hard-won peace, a new revision of the *Great Charter* was issued in November 1217, providing for the enforcement of the king's laws and authority, while allowing the magnates a voice in the government. The charter dealing with forest lands was liberalized by the council, giving the people greater access to pastures, wood for fuel and supplies of food. During the civil war, the office of exchequer had ceased to function and taxes remained uncollected. Under the Earl of Pembroke's government, the sheriffs were ordered to begin the collection of the revenue due the king. The throne's rights to require barons to pay a fee in lieu of military service were reaffirmed by the regency administration. With the strong hand of William Marshal on the reins of government, Henry III's kingdom remained at peace, the once-rebel barons now honouring their vows of homage.

During the civil war and its resulting disruption of the royal government, Alexander II of Scotland had taken advantage of the internal turmoil to cross the border and seize possession of Carlisle. Following the withdrawal of the French, the Earl of Pembroke sent envoys to the Scottish court demanding Alexander II withdraw his forces from England, but his ultimatum was ignored. When the Plantagenet regime threatened to void the Scottish rights to the English Earldom of Huntingdon, Alexander II agreed to meet with Henry III in mid-December at Northampton to resolve the conflict. To retain the earldom, the Scots were compelled to abandon Carlisle and return to their lands, while offering homage for Huntingdon to the English monarch. As the king's council continued to secure the royal borders, Henry III received the fealty of King Ragnald IV for the Isle of Man and the Orkney Islands in September 1219 and pledged to aid him against threats to his English kingdom, while in return the Plantagenet crown received his protection for its interests in the Irish Sea region. In 1219, the royal justiciar for Ireland, Geoffrey de Marsh, went to England to swear his allegiance to the young king, further binding the Irish to Henry III's throne.

As William Marshal and his governing council continued to settle border issues with the neighbouring realms, Henry III's regime moved to resolve the dispute with the Welsh princes, who had taken advantage of the war with Prince Louis to expand their influence and enlarge the territory under their control. During the Anglo-French distraction, Cardinal Bicchieeri had placed the Welsh under interdiction to force their pledges of allegiance to King Henry, but the princes continued to defy the English crown. Despite the cardinal's failure, Marshal began to negotiate with the Welsh lords to secure their oaths of peace. In February 1218, the Welsh prince Llewellyn agreed to meet the king at Worcester, and after their conference pledged his fealty. In late May that year at Woodstock, other princes offered their homage to Henry III, thus restoring peace to large areas of the Welsh frontier.

In early February 1219, William Marshal became seriously ill while visiting the town and castle at Marlborough. After returning to London, he took up residence at the Tower and carried on his governmental duties. In mid-March, as his health continued to deteriorate, Marshal was forced to move to his manor at Caversham, where he was frequently visited by the king and the council members. Bicchieeri had recently resigned his position as papal legate and was replaced by Cardinal Pandulf Verraccio, who took his seat on the English ruling council. As his death became imminent, Marshal named Verraccio as the new guardian for Henry III. The appointment of the legate was strongly opposed by the king's tutor, Peter des Roches, Bishop of Winchester, who pressed his candidacy for the position. On 14 May 1219, William Marshal died with his family and friends at his bedside, and he was interred with great honours in London at the Temple Church.

In the aftermath of the death of Marshal, the papal legate became the dominant advisor on the regency council of the king, while des Roches and Hubert de Burgh took minor roles. The political powers formerly held by Marshal and Bicchieeri were now united under Verraccio. The triumvirate of Verraccio, Bishop Peter des Roches and Hubert de Burgh resumed Marshal's programmes to strengthen the powers of the central government and the recovery of Henry III's rights as overlord. King Henry was now 12 years old and was routinely consulted by the regency council on governmental issues, expanding his involvement in the administration of the kingdom. The maintenance of peace with France was vital to the continued recovery of the throne's authority over England, and with the five-year truce with the Capetian crown nearing its expiration date, Pope Honorius III – acting through Pandulf Verraccio – negotiated a one-year extension. The peace treaty was later extended to four years.

To magnify and glorify the reign of Henry III, the royal council voted to hold a second coronation in London. On 17 May 1220, a large number of richly dressed magnates and prelates gathered at Westminster Abbey to witness the crowning of the king. Attired in his royal ceremonial robes, Henry III stood at the high altar and recited the coronation oath. The Archbishop of Canterbury then placed the crown of Edward the Confessor on the king's head, to the acclaim of those in attendance.

Meanwhile, Pope Honorius III continued to intervene in English policies to strengthen the rights of Henry III, corresponding with Verraccio and ordering him to limit the barons to possession of only two castles at a time to weaken their military power. This measure was favoured by de Burgh but opposed by des Roches, which served to further the dissension between them. During the summer of 1220, the Plantagenet king, accompanied by his council members, travelled about England to reclaim castles from the barons and restore the crown's authority. In mid-June, Henry met Alexander II at York to negotiate the marriage of his sister, Joan, to the Scottish king, binding the two realms closer together.

As Henry III and his regency council continued to impose their authority, Lord William of Aumale refused to surrender his fortifications, compelling the king to order their seizure by force of arms. The castle at Rockingham was besieged and forced to submit, while the stronghold at Sanney was taken later in June. After gaining control of the strongholds, the monarch proceeded to Canterbury in early July, attending a ceremony transferring the tomb of St Thomas Becket to the cathedral. The royal court celebrated the Christmas season at Oxford, where William of Aumale spoke out strongly against the seizure of his castles. He stormed out of the king's presence, hastening to Lincolnshire to protect his fortress at Bytham from seizure by the crown. He then ravaged the neighbouring towns and destroyed numerous churches in protest against the regime. As the lord continued his plundering attacks, Pandulf Verraccio ordered his excommunication and assembled an army to restore the throne's peace. In early January 1221, Henry III, accompanied by the papal legate and the Sixth Earl of Chester, Ranulf de Blondeville – who had recently returned to England after serving in Egypt during the Fifth Crusade – marched against Bytham, laying siege after the garrison refused to surrender. The rebels held out against the attacks of the king's troops for six days before submitting. Lord William of Aumale had earlier sought sanctuary at Fountains Abbey, but following the loss of his fortification he yielded to Henry III. When William later took the cross of a crusader, the Plantagenet monarch pardoned him and welcomed him back to court.

Cardinal Verraccio had aggressively pursued his duties as the head of the triumvirate regency, alienating many powerful nobles and churchmen. In mid-1221, the Archbishop of Canterbury, Stephen Langton, travelled to Rome to complain to the pope about the cardinal's relentless interference in governmental affairs. To placate the archbishop, Pope Honorius III recalled his legate and agreed to leave the post vacant. Hubert de Burgh and Bishop des Roches now served as the king's counsellors.

While Langton was in Rome, Henry III met Alexander II again at York during the summer while attending the marriage ceremony of his sister, Joan, to the Scottish king. At the time of the wedding, the Scottish king was 23 years old and Princess Joan was not yet 11. The marital union with the Scottish regime further enhanced the peace between the two kingdoms. Shortly after the English sovereign returned to his court in London, a riot broke out between the city's followers of Prince Louis of France and the supporters of the Plantagenets in the surrounding towns. In late July, as the violence escalated, the previous sheriff of London, Constantine FitzAthulf, collected a small army and led his men into Westminster, attacking the residents and pillaging. To quell the escalating violence, Hubert de Burgh, acting as justiciar, sent Falkes de Breaute with a large contingent of troops to arrest Constantine and force the submission of the Londoners. The former sheriff was seized and quickly hanged without trial. When London's mayor was later deposed for his involvement in the revolt, Henry III took possession of the city. He spent Christmas 1221 at Winchester, ending the year with the fragile peace in his kingdom still in place.

As the English barons continued to honour their oaths of allegiance to the Plantagenet crown, William Marshal the Younger, son of the deceased regent, began attacking the Welsh princedoms to expand his lands. He advanced his soldiers into the territory of Prince Llewellyn, ravaging his princedom of Gwynedd. The Welsh prince responded by attacking Marshal's fiefdoms, as violence escalated along the frontier. In 1222, Marshal forced the prince to abandon his strongholds at Cardigan and Carmarthen, thereby regaining the initiative. In October 1223, Llewellyn was excommunicated by the Archbishop of York in a bid to quell the hostilities, but the Welsh ignored the decree. As the border conflict spread along the frontier,

Henry III – with the justiciar at his side – summoned the great council to Worcester to announce the regime's intervention against the Welsh. The royal army was mobilized at Gloucester, and in late 1223 the English advanced to relieve the siege of Builth in mid-Wales. After compelling the surrender of the garrison troops, the king moved against Montgomery, securing the submission of the Welsh defenders. As the might of the English pressed forward, the Welsh were forced to accept a peace agreement that ended the hostilities along the western borderlands of Henry's kingdom.

During the Plantagenet regime's incursion into Wales, the king's men continued the campaign in England to reclaim the royal castles from the barons, in compliance with the papacy's decree. The occupation of the fortresses was not without opposition, as the Earl of Chester, Bishop des Roches and Lord William of Aumale openly resisted the loss of their castles. In early December, Henry III reclaimed ownership of Colchester Castle, while the defiance of the barons grew increasingly hostile. As war with the nobles loomed, Archbishop Langton threatened the dissidents with excommunication, compelling them to accept the transfer of their properties to the crown. Langton's intervention against the barons led to the surrender of most of the remaining fortifications and further strengthened Henry III's hold on the throne, while reinforcing his status as king of England.

On 14 July 1223, the reigning French king, Philip II, died and was succeeded by his son, who became Louis VIII. Following the coronation of the new Capetian monarch, Henry III sent emissaries to Paris demanding the French regime restore Normandy to England's possession. Louis VIII refused to return the duchy, and in opposition to the Plantagenet crown began preparations to invade the English-held lands in the Duchy of Gascony. In February 1224, Pope Honorius III wrote to Louis VIII, pressuring him to remain at peace with the English kingdom, but the demand was ignored. King Henry met with his council at Northampton in June, informing them that France was threatening to invade his lordship in Gascony after Louis VIII announced his claims to the lands were just and the English had lost their rights to rule the region. In reply to the French belligerence, Henry refused to recognize Louis VIII's rightful assumption of the Capetian throne.

In late 1224, the French army assembled at Tours and proceeded against the English-occupied seaport at La Rochelle. The town was encircled and siege engines were brought forward to batter the defensive works. La Rochelle's townspeople offered little resistance and quickly surrendered. The loss of the port eliminated a vital Plantagenet enclave on the coastline of mainland Europe that served as a major trading centre for English merchants. As King Louis consolidated his control over his recent acquisitions, the Count of La Marche, Hugh X, negotiated an alliance with him and marched his army into English-occupied Gascony. He soon overran Henry III's defences and took possession of nearly the entire duchy, leaving only Bordeaux and a few small coastal towns under Plantagenet rule.

Henry III and his chief advisor, Hubert de Burgh, were determined to recover the lost French lands to rebuild the empire of Henry II, but the barons had little interest in fighting in what they considered a foreign war. To gain the support of the magnates and prelates, the justiciar spread rumours that Louis VIII was preparing to invade England, giving the nobles cause to rally to the king's defence. To finance the Plantagenet army for the Gascony expedition, the monarch offered to increase the liberties of the barons and churchmen in exchange for a tax on personal property of one-fifteenth. In January 1225, a great council was summoned and the 17-year-old Henry III granted a new *Magna Carta* to the people of England, which incorporated the new laws.

In February 1225, the order to implement the new property tax was sent to the county sheriffs to fund the Gascony expedition, and the collection of revenues began. The amount of money gathered far exceeded the expectations of the government, allowing Henry to field a large and well-equipped army. The king's brother, Richard, was appointed commander of the royal forces, with William II Longspee, Earl of Salisbury, serving as his military advisor. William was an experienced veteran, who was later killed in Egypt during the Seventh Crusade. Before leaving England for the Gascony campaign, King Henry knighted his brother and ceded the Earldom of Cornwall to him. Richard was the only brother of Henry III, and in 1225 was heir to the Plantagenet crown. He later took part in the Seventh Crusade against the Muslims in Outremer, gaining a reputation as a skilled soldier. In 1252, Richard was elected Emperor of the Holy Roman Empire at Aachen, but resigned the office seven years later, returning to serve with his brother in the conflict against the barons.

After preparations were completed for the Gascony expedition, the English army embarked on 23 March and sailed across the Channel, landing at Bordeaux to the wild cheers of the townspeople. With Richard at the head of the English host, the soldiers proceeded against the French at St Macaire, overpowering the defenders and capturing the stronghold. The Plantagenets next moved to Bazas, taking the citadel after a brief fight. Richard then turned his forces to the north-east, besieging the town of La Reole, which repelled his repeated sorties and withstood the bombardment of his siege engines. While part of the army continued the siege, the remaining troops cleared the French from Henry III's lands in Gascony. On 13 November, La Reole finally fell to the Plantagenets and Richard prepared to resume his offensive by attacking the County of Poitou in Aquitaine. However, the Earl of Salisbury advised the prince that Poitou was too well-defended for the English forces to seize. The campaign thus ended with the capture of La Reole, creating an English enclave that would last for the next two centuries.

With the Duchy of Gascony once again under the rule of the English, Richard sent envoys to the neighbouring fiefdoms, negotiating alliances with them against future incursions by the French king. The Duke of Brittany, counts of Auvergne and Toulouse and other enemies of Louis VIII agreed to join the coalition to end the attacks of the Capetians into their lands. In December, Pope Honorius III wrote to Louis VIII, admonishing him for his invasion of Gascony. As the Holy See continued its political initiative in support of Henry III's monarchy, in early January 1226 the pope sent a letter to Hugh X of Lusignan, expressing his anger at his alliance with the French and his campaign into English-claimed Gascony, threatening to excommunicate him.

In early November 1226, King Louis VIII of France died from a high fever and dysentery at Montpensier, the Capetian crown being taken by his 12-year-old son as Louis IX. Before his death, the French king appointed his wife, Blanche of Castile, as guardian and regent for his heir. The French barons perceived an opportunity to regain their lost independence, motivating the Duke of Brittany and Count of La Marche to begin plotting against the regent, making contact with the English and encouraging their intervention. Richard of Cornwall had remained in occupied France negotiating the king's alliances with the dissident French lords. Many nobles, who had recently forced Henry III's soldiers out of Poitou, abandoned their French overlord and joined the league with the Plantagenets.

Since the death of William Marshal in May 1219, Henry III had increasingly assumed the reins of independent power, his relationship with Hubert de Burgh growing strained. On 8 January 1227, the king met with his council at Oxford to declare his self-rule and relieve his counsellors of their offices. In mid-March that year, Honorius III died and was succeeded as pope by Gregory IX, who the following month decreed the 19-year-old Henry III was of age to govern his realm autonomously. Meanwhile, at the French court, Queen Blanche sent the royal army into south-western France to quell the threatened rebellion and secure the barons' pledges of homage to her son, ending any immediate opportunity for Henry to recover more of his lost lordships. With the war in the south of France now at a stalemate, the adversaries agreed to a truce.

While the peace treaty negotiated by Louis IX's regency government continued to be honoured, back in England unrest with the Welsh flared up along the borderlands in August 1228. Prince Llewellyn mobilized an army and led it in an attack against the English castle at Montgomery. After learning of the siege, the royal army was assembled and Henry III hastened to defend the fortress. At the approach of the English, the Welsh prince abandoned his positions, retiring without a fight. The Plantagenet monarch resumed his campaign of subjugation, advancing west into the Princedom of Powys and razing the town of Kerry. Many of the Welsh princes now united under Llewellyn, harassing the king's towns and creating havoc along the frontier. After failing to suppress the Welsh, King Henry made peace with the princes and in October returned to his English court.

The Christmas court of 1228 was held at Oxford, where the sovereign received letters from the warlords of Normandy and Poitou seeking the intervention of the English in their struggle for independence from France. While preparations were made for the cross-Channel incursion, the Archbishop of Canterbury, Stephen Langton, died. When the monks elected their candidate to fill the vacant office, Henry III nominated Richard le Grant in opposition. Plantagenet envoys were dispatched to Rome to secure Gregory IX's approval, offering the proceeds from a new levy on England's properties. In need of money to fund his war against Emperor Frederick II, the pontiff agreed to le Grant's appointment.

The Plantagenet government kept in contact with the French rebels while the army prepared for the campaign against Louis IX. As the assembled army waited in harbour, the fleet began to arrive, but even after several days of delay not enough ships to transport the troops reached Portsmouth and the expedition was therefore cancelled.

Henry III spent the Christmas of 1229 at York with Alexander II of Scotland, renewing their friendship, while preparations for the campaign against the Capetian regime were renewed. Finally, on 30 April 1230, King Henry and his ships – loaded with knights, foot-soldiers and archers – sailed out of Portsmouth and crossed to St Malo, where they were greeted by Peter of Brittany and his Breton troops. The united army marched south against the local French supporters of Louis IX in Poitou, while Queen Blanche mobilized her army to defend the lands of her son. As Henry III and Peter advanced into Poitou, the local warlords remained loyal to Louis IX and made plans to attack the approaching English and Breton invaders. Following some initial victories over the French lords in Poitou, the English king was compelled to withdraw after encountering the massed army of Louis IX and his allies, ending his expedition to regain his occupied French lands.

After returning to England, Henry met with his council in January 1232 at Westminster to request a special tax to pay for the recent campaign against the French. When he issued letters guaranteeing the privileges and exemptions of the churchmen, Archbishop-elect John Sittingbourne withdrew his opposition and the funds were granted. While the king continued to rule his kingdom and his barons remained at peace, in the spring Prince Llewellyn again broke the truce agreement and began pillaging the English towns and farms along the Welsh frontier. When the king attempted to raise funds to finance his intervention against the Welsh, the barons refused aid for the expedition and Llewellyn remained unchecked. As his rule was increasingly opposed by the nobles, in late July Henry III blamed de Burgh for the festering rebellion, discharging him from his office as justiciar and naming Stephen Seagrave as his replacement. De Burgh was charged with numerous crimes – from murder to witchcraft – and placed under guard by four knights at Devizes Castle. With Hubert de Burgh out of the government, the formerly discredited Bishop des Roches of Winchester took charge of important offices in the royal regime, with the permission of Henry's throne. Later in the year, the royal council was summoned to Oxford but the majority of the magnates refused to attend in protest against the replacement of English governmental officials with men from Poitou by order of des Roches, who had close-ties with the French countship. To enforce the allegiance of the nobles, the king required them to provide hostages to guarantee their peace, while the Bishop of Winchester pressed the continued advancement of his countrymen at court.

On 29 September 1233, Hubert de Burgh arranged his escape from Devizes after learning his sworn enemy, Peter des Roches, was now custodian for the castle. Despte seeking sanctuary in a nearby church, he was recaptured by supporters of the bishop. When the Bishop of Salisbury, Robert Bingham, heard the Holy See's sanctuary law had been violated, he ordered de Burgh returned to the church, but the guards refused to obey his instructions. The bishop then presented his case before the monarch, who ruled in favour of de Burgh's return to the church at Devizes. While de Burgh remained under the protection of sanctuary, a small group of men rescued him, taking the former justiciar to safety in Wales.

During the summer of 1233, the English barons rose up once more over the increasing influence of Bishop des Roches and the influx of his Poitou governmental officials. The king summoned his lords to meet in early July to resolve their disputes, but again they refused to answer the call. A third gathering at Westminster was announced for 1 August, with those barons not attending labelled as traitors. Most of the magnates finally came to the assembly and made peace with Henry after either being threatened with attacks or received monetary rewards.

As Richard Marshal, who had inherited the Pembroke lands of his deceased brother, rode to the Westminster council meeting, he received information that Bishop des Roches planned to take him captive. Fearing for his life, he fled to safety in Wales. After the flight of the Earl of Pembroke, the rebel barons gave their support to him and withdrew their allegiance from the Plantagenet regime. As the threat of rebellion escalated again, Henry III hired mercenary soldiers from Flanders and prepared to advance against the rebels. Marshal was declared a traitor and his properties were confiscated by the crown. King Henry's loyal troops and mercenaries mustered at Hereford and moved against Marshal's castle at Usk, overrunning it in September. The king agreed to return the fortress to Marshal if he would give guarantees of his fealty. By 8 September, Henry had accepted the earl's assurances, but when Marshal disappeared, the Plantagenets seized his properties and destroyed several of his castles.

The English lords then rose up against the king and his hated advisor, des Roches. In opposition to the crown, the rebels joined forces with Prince Llewellyn of Wales. Richard, Earl of Pembroke, and Llewellyn sent their troops into Glamorgan, pillaging the lands of des Roches' Gloucester lordship. As the dissidents intensified their attacks, Henry mustered his army in early November, and after marching through Marshal's lands in Gwent he made camp at Grosmont. During the night of 11 November, the anti-royalists launched a surprise assault, catching Henry's men unprepared and forcing their withdrawal. While the king was falling back toward his kingdom, the two forces clashed again near Monmouth Castle. During the melee, Richard was captured, but when his men counterattacked he managed to escape. He rallied his soldiers, defeating the king's troops in a bloody onslaught and taking possession of Monmouth Castle. In the wake of his victory, Richard joined his men with the Welsh of Llewellyn and unleashed an attack against the town of Shrewsbury. On 22 December, Henry III offered terms, but the Earl of Pembroke refused to negotiate, continuing the fight. In January, Shrewsbury fell to the rebels and was burned. After the loss of the town, the monarch retreated to the south-east, holding a council meeting in early February 1234 with his bishops and barons at Westminster. The bishops warned the king about the corrupt influence of des Roches, while advising him to negotiate peace with Marshal. Henry III heeded the advice of his churchmen and talks were begun with the Earl of Pembroke and the Welsh princes in late February, ending with an agreement for a truce.

The Archbishop of Canterbury had died over two years before and his vacant post was finally filled by Edmund Rich in April 1234 after three previous choices for the post were rejected by Pope Gregory IX. Soon after taking his office, the new archbishop met with King Henry, threatening to excommunicate him unless he dismissed Bishop des Roches and his Poitevins from his government. With the realm at war with the barons and famine and disorder rampant, the monarch duly relieved des Roches and his Poitevin supporters from their posts. The justiciar, Stephen Seagrave, was also dismissed and his position left open, as the king now ruled his kingdom alone.

In mid-April, Richard Marshal died and his properties were inherited by his younger brother, Gilbert. At the 28 May Gloucester council, the transfer of the earldom to Gilbert was confirmed. Following the meeting, the Archbishop of Canterbury arranged a truce with the Welsh princes, while the English barons came to terms with the Plantagenet throne, bringing a period of peace to the kingdom.

In 1235, Henry III was nearly 28 years old and had not yet married. With his kingdom at peace, he turned his diplomatic initiatives toward finding a wife. He sent representatives to the County of Poitou to discuss his marriage to Joan, daughter of the count. The matrimonial union with Poitou would give Henry a formidable presence in south-western France and enhance his claim to Gascony. However, Louis IX opposed the wedding, using his influence to convince the pope to disallow it. After negotiations with the Count of Poitou ended, Henry wrote to Raymond IV, Count of Provence, proposing marriage to his daughter, Eleanor. A marital union with Eleanor offered the English monarch a strong influence in the south of France and an association with the Capetian kingdom, whose king was married to the count's eldest daughter, Margaret. When Henry III's envoys returned from Provence, they brought news of the acceptance of the marriage. In January 1236, Eleanor arrived in England and the wedding ceremony was soon after held at Canterbury. On 19 January, she was crowned Queen of England at Westminster Abbey. During their long marriage, they developed a happy and loving relationship. Through her influence with the English sovereign and her large entourage of French followers, she became highly unpopular with the barons. Eleanor gave birth to a son in 1239, the future Edward I, and in the following years had four additional surviving children.

Henry III had persistently agreed to govern by the terms of the *Great Charter*, but after the dismissal of the justiciar his reign largely ignored its provisions. Governing with only the aid of his clerks, the king's personal authority over the kingdom had been strengthened but at the expense of alienating the barons. Henry's marriage had resulted in the influx of many office-seekers from his wife's homeland, and their presence at court brought strong opposition from the magnates. To quell the mounting threat of revolt, the king recalled Justice Seagrave to his regime and appointed new sheriffs to end corruption in the collection of taxes and enforcement of law. Despite the crown's attempts to ease the growing unrest, the nobles continued to object to the high taxes and their increasing lack of participation in the administration of the realm.

As the danger of rebellion continued, in January 1237 King Henry assembled his council to resolve the kingdom's festering financial problems. The Plantagenet regime proposed a new tax on a thirtieth of all personal property in exchange for greater freedom for the barons and the election of three nobles to serve as advisors to the crown. The barons agreed to the proposal, resulting in the easing of the throne's lack of money, but the king's frequent gifts to the Church and the demands of Queen Eleanor's family continued to put a strain on the treasury. To appease his lords, Henry requested the pope send a papal legate to England to intercede with the protesters. At the end of June, Cardinal Otto arrived, and during the following months he met with the rebels to placate their demands. In further support of their protests, Henry was later given a large list of grievances from the Church and was threatened with excommunication for violating the *Great Charter*.

In the summer of 1237, Henry III and his court travelled to York, meeting with King Alexander II to resolve the Scottish claim to Northumberland. The Scots agreed to renounce their rights to the northern lordship in return for several castles in Northumberland and Cumberland. The meeting with Alexander II reconfirmed the friendship between the two kingdoms and returned a northern district to English sovereignty. While in York, Alexander II renewed his oaths of fealty for his English lands.

Early in 1238, Henry arranged the marriage of his sister, Eleanor – widow of the younger William Marshal – to the French magnate, Simon de Montfort, Earl of Leicester. Since the king's other sisters had married the Scottish king and the emperor of the Holy Roman Empire, the English lords considered the French earl an unsuitable husband for a Plantagenet princess, vocally opposing the marriage. Despite loud outcries from the barons, the wedding ceremony was performed in January. De Montfort had come to England seven years earlier and was established at court as a favourite of the king. Through his mother, he had inherited the English Earldom of Leicester.

Under the banner of Earl Richard of Cornwall, the barons displeased with the marital choice for a princess of the realm rebuked the king for not consulting with them. As the dissidents mobilized their troops at Kingston under the command of Richard, Henry III took refuge in the Tower of London. As the danger of rebellion grew, the warlords agreed to a meeting with the king in early February to reduce tensions, at which Henry pledged to reform his regime in favour of the rebels, satisfying their outrage.

Henry spent the following three years ruling his kingdom and keeping the barons in check. In 1239, his queen delivered their first child, a son named Edward, after the Anglo-Saxon King Edward the Confessor. The birth was celebrated cheerfully and enthusiastically throughout England. Cardinal Otto performed the baptism, with Richard of Cornwall and Simon de Montfort serving as godparents. Nevertheless, the crown's relations with the lords remained contentious as foreigners continually crossed the Channel seeking positions in the royal government, while relatives of the queen continued to arrive from Provence and were given prime offices and rich estates. While the Plantagenet regime was attempting to appease the nobles, Pope Gregory IX and Emperor Frederick II were involved in a war of words over a new crusade to the Levant, each petitioning Henry III for his support and intervention. As a papal vassal, Henry was obligated to obey the pope, but he attempted to maintain friendly relations with the emperor by remaining neutral.

The peace agreement with the Welsh had been honoured under the rule of Prince Llewellyn for several years, but in April 1240 he died, creating friction between his two sons. Before his death, Llewellyn named his second son, Dafydd, as his successor, disregarding the rights of his eldest child, Gruffydd. Soon after taking the reins of power, Dafydd arrested his brother and imprisoned him to secure his reign. The supporters of Gruffydd then rallied to his cause and civil war broke out. With the Welsh distracted by their internal conflict, the English border counties remained at peace. In the following year, Henry III was petitioned by the Bishop of Bangor to arrange the release of Gruffydd. The king received a message from Gruffydd promising to conquer his brother's lands and hold them as the vassal of the English regime. Henry responded by mustering his army at Gloucester and proceeding along the borderlands, threatening to invade Wales. Confronted by the might of the Plantagenet host, Dafydd agreed to terms and released Gruffydd. In October, Dafydd went to London to give fealty to the English sovereign for his lands in Wales.

In August 1241, Pope Gregory IX died, and with Rome under the danger of attack by the army of Emperor Frederick II, no election for a new pope could be held. Without the restraining interventions of the pontiff, relations between Henry III's realm and Louis IX of France quickly deteriorated. Hugh X of Lusignan sent envoys to King Henry, telling him his former countship of Poitou was ready to rebel against the Capetians and accept English rule. The Plantagenet king quickly called the royal council to London, pressing the barons for money to invade Poitou. Despite Henry's appeal for funds, the nobles refused to grant the necessary money or take part in the foreign campaign.

Despite the lack of participation by his barons in the Poitou campaign, Henry assembled his loyal magnates and knights in May 1242 and set sail across the Channel, landing at Royan in Gascony to regain his inheritance. The king's brother, Richard of Cornwall, who had recently returned to England from the crusade in the Levant, joined the expeditionary force, bringing several hundred knights with him. Learning of the English army's arrival, Louis IX mobilized his troops, advancing against Hugh X of Lusignan's lands and quickly capturing numerous castles in a lightning attack. On 19 July, the English clashed with the French at the stone bridge in Taillebourg. Louis IX's soldiers charged into the English and their Lusignan allies, pushing them back to the village of Saintes. Two days later, as the French approached Saintes, their advance guard skirmished with Henry's men; hearing the sounds of battle, both armies rushed forward, leading to a melee of bloody and fierce fighting. When the heavy French infantrymen armed with swords, maces, pikes and axes charged into the invaders, Henry panicked and withdrew from the battlefield.

In the wake of the defeat at Saintes, Count Hugh X deserted his English ally, negotiating a settlement with King Louis as Henry fell back to Bordeaux with his battered army. Remaining in Gascony, the Plantagenet king arranged a five-year truce with the Capetian realm before returning to England, with his Poitevin lords now swearing allegiance to the French monarch. The expedition's failure only added to the financial troubles of the regime, resulting in a loss of prominence and esteem for the king.

Following a nineteen-month delay, Innocent IV was elected pontiff of the Holy See in June 1243. After Henry III's return from France, he was confronted by the pope for his continued interference in Church affairs. During the prolonged lack of a pope, the English ecclesiastic lords had kept much of the money routinely sent to the Roman Church, and soon after taking office, Innocent IV wrote to Henry complaining about the treatment of his representatives sent to collect the funds. When the Archbishopric of Canterbury became vacant, Boniface of Savoy was named to fill it in September 1243. Boniface was the queen's uncle, and his appointment by the crown ignored the long-established Church procedure for the election of officials. In defence of the Holy See's rights, Innocent IV sent a letter to Henry asking him not to interfere in Church elections.

Henry III's reign then remained peaceful for several years, but his barons continued to oppose any new taxes, placing a strain on the regime's ability to meet the repeated demands from the papacy for money to fund its crusade and the requirements to abide by the laws of the *Great Charter*. In 1247, Dafydd of Wales died without leaving a direct heir, creating a potential succession crisis in the princedom. As the danger of civil war loomed, the Welsh lords recognized Dafydd's two nephews, Owain and Llewellyn, as the successors to a now divided throne. Seeking to capitalize on a weakened Wales, the English border barons began threatening to cross the frontier and pillage Welsh lands. In April 1247, with their territory in danger of attack, the two brothers agreed to give homage to Henry for his acknowledgement of them as ruling princes.

In the aftermath of Henry III's departure from Gascony in 1243, the appointed governors had increasingly failed to enforce the Plantagenet crown's rule and the duchy became fragmented into pockets of resistance. The Gascon lords then ignored their feudal oaths of allegiance to the English regime and began attacking rival fiefdoms. Gascony was the last remaining lordship of King Henry on the European mainland and he was determined to retain his inherited land. To impose his sovereignty, Henry appointed Simon de Montfort as seneschal, with wide-ranging powers to govern. After reaching Gascony, de Montfort negotiated an extension of the truce with Louis IX, and without fear of intervention from the French steadily regained royal authority over the Gascons through diplomacy and military might. When he returned to the English court in early 1249, the duchy was firmly under the control of the Plantagenet crown, despite repeated complaints by the barons against his harsh rule.

In March 1250, Henry III took the cross of a crusader, pledging to take part in the war to reclaim Jerusalem from the Saracens. He later received a message from Pope Innocent IV granting him permission to take one-tenth of ecclesiastic funds in his realm for three years in return for his participation in the new crusade to Outremer. The collected funds were used to pay off some of the throne's pressing expenses, instead of funding the sovereign's journey to the Latin East. While Henry continued to struggle with the barons over his lack of revenue and the demands from Innocent IV for additional donations, in Gascony the nobles complained about de Montfort's over-zealous government as revolt began to simmer. In 1251, de Montfort was forced out of Gascony by the rebellious warlords. Gascony was now in open revolt and the barons were threatening to disavow their allegiance to England. Simon de Montfort returned to court, meeting with the king and requesting soldiers and money to regain control of Gascony. Despite his depleted treasury, Henry granted de Montfort his appeal and he crossed back over the Channel to put down the uprising.

Arriving in Gascony with his reinforcements and supplies, de Montfort renewed his campaign to enforce Henry's kingship, but his initiatives failed to suppress the recalcitrant nobles and he was recalled to the English court. Meeting with the king, de Montfort was threatened with arrest for his persistent misgovernment.

During the discussions, de Montfort was called a traitor by Henry III, at which he erupted into a rage, telling the monarch: 'Were thou not my king it would be an ill hour for thou.' As tempers simmered, de Montfort was sent back to Gascony, but the rebels continued to defy Plantagenet rule. In April 1252, de Montfort's men clashed with a force of rebels and put them to flight after a fierce and barbaric fight. Despite their defeat, the Gascon rebels, led by Gaston de Bearn, refused to submit, resuming their fight against the English and steadily gaining control. In September, Simon de Montfort was removed as governor of Gascony and left the service of the Plantagenets, making his way through France. As English sovereignty over the duchy continued to weaken, de Bearn began talks with Alphonse X of Castile to create an alliance of mutual support.

When Henry III learned of Gaston de Bearn's offer to the Castilians, he opened his own negotiations with them to form a bond of friendship through the marriage of his heir, Edward, to Alphonso's half-sister, Eleanor. As the talks slowly proceeded, the impatient king mobilized his army at Portsmouth in August 1253, sailing across the Channel and moving his troops to Bordeaux, from where the English set out to regain Gascony by force of arms. Henry advanced to Benauges, taking the stronghold by storm before marching against the fortress at La Reole, which was overrun and occupied. Shortly after these initial victories, the campaign lost momentum and the Gascon rebels remained in defiance of the Plantagenet regime. Meanwhile, Henry III negotiated the continuance of the truce with the French and shored up his relations with the neighbouring warlords to discourage their intervention against him. To the south, his representatives met with Alphonso X, arranging a truce with him to strengthen his border with Castile. Henry remained at Bazas during Christmas, continuing his campaign of pacification in Gascony and advancing the areas under his authority. When Simon de Montfort rejoined the English court after a reconciliation with the king, the duchy was soon brought under Plantagenet control.

While the English had been struggling to maintain control over Gascony, in April 1252 Henry III announced the departure date for his crusade to the Holy Land as 24 June 1256 and began collecting money for the expedition. At a meeting of the London council, he met with his prelates, demanding they pay for part of his campaign's expenses. The bishops immediately refused the king's order. When he later reduced the amount of aid requested, the churchmen agreed to the new terms. As Henry prepared for the crusade, he wrote to Louis IX beseeching him to restore his inherited European mainland properties to hasten his ability to leave England for the Levant, but the French had no interest in negotiating the return of Normandy and Aquitaine. While King Henry struggled to raise the funds for the expedition to the Holy Land, Pope Innocent IV sent him letters encouraging him to leave for Outremer. Henry had been granted ecclesiastic revenue by the pope, but the king wrote to him complaining that the papal collectors were not sending all the money due. At the April 1253 parliament, Henry again pressed the barons for increased taxes. The assembly ended with the king receiving a pledge from the churchmen and magnates to pay the papal decree.

In 1254, Henry III was again in Gascony enforcing his rule. While he was in the duchy, the terms for the marriage of Prince Edward to Eleanor were finalized with the crown of Castile. Henry then sent for the queen and his two sons to meet him at the Gascon court. In May 1254, they crossed the Channel and joined the king in Bordeaux. The wedding ceremony was held on 1 November at the Cistercian monastery of La Huelgas in Burgos, northern Spain. Following the marriage, King Alphonso X renounced his rights to the Gascony duchy in favour of Edward. As a wedding present, Henry gave Edward his Aquitaine and Gascony duchies, along with most of Ireland. While in Gascony, King Henry sent envoys to the French court to arrange a meeting with Louis IX to reinforce their ongoing truce. Having recently returned to France following his defeat in Egypt during the Seventh Crusade, the Capetian monarch quickly agreed to a conference with Henry. The two kings met at Chartres and travelled together to Paris, passing through towns where they were greeted by large cheering crowds. In Paris, the English king and his entourage were royally entertained by Louis, with lavish royal banquets and city tours. Louis personally escorted his guests through Sainte Chapelle, the French king's royal chapel, viewing the many holy relics he had collected. Over the following days, Henry III and Queen Eleanor continued their tours of the city, marvelling at the magnificent churches and palaces. During their stay in Paris, they distributed alms to the poor, while offering prayers at numerous religious sites. At the end of the visit, Henry and his court travelled to Boulogne, where they boarded ships for the crossing to England.

Returning to London, the king was welcomed back into the city by cheering crowds. Early in 1255, Henry III received a gift from Louis IX, who arranged for an elephant to be sent to him. Henry added the elephant to his large menagerie of various exotic animals. The Londoners were amazed at the strange-looking beast, flocking to view it. The victorious campaign to reclaim Gascony and the royal visit to the French court had depleted the Plantagenet treasury, and at a meeting of parliament in April, King Henry petitioned the barons for more tax money to defray the expenses, but his request was rejected. Parliament did, however, offer to fund the Gascony expedition in exchange for the creation of a commission of elected ministers to oversee the government and its expenditure. The monarch refused to accept the conditions, so his quest for money remained at an impasse.

During the reign of the German emperor, Henry VI, and his successors, the Kingdom of Sicily was united with the Hohenstaufen Empire, threatening the papacy for dominance over Italy. To enforce his rule over Italy, Pope Innocent IV had offered the Sicilian crown to Henry III's second son, Edmund, in 1254 as a papal fief of the Holy See. In May 1255, the Plantagenet king announced to his parliament that he had accepted the pontiff's Sicilian proposal and had pledged to fund an entire expeditionary force heading for Sicily. The barons were astonished to learn he planned to pay for the army and its advance across France into southern Italy to launch an amphibious invasion of Sicily. After listening to Henry's appeal, his request for funds was quickly voted down.

Following the death of Innocent IV in 1254, the new pontiff, Alexander IV, reaffirmed the Sicilian agreement with King Henry. In the autumn of 1255, the pope ordered three bishops to England to invest Prince Edmund with his Sicilian kingdom. After arriving in London, the papal prelates summoned the bishops to meet with them to discuss payment for part of the Sicilian campaign. The bishops spoke out against the undertaking, refusing to provide money to the king. Five days later, Edmund was granted the crown of Sicily by the papal churchmen, despite the lack of money to fund the expedition and strong opposition from the English lords and clerics.

As Henry III struggled to fund his son's quest for the Sicilian crown, in February 1256 the pontiff wrote to him demanding full payment of his debts incurred by the Holy See for the Italian campaign. Henry summoned his parliament asking for new taxes but was unable to secure any money. After explaining his difficulties with the nobles to Pope Alexander, the king was granted the proceeds from the vacant English ecclesiastic offices and deferred payment for his papal debt to a later date.

When the Prince of Gwynedd died in 1254, his two sons, Owain and Llewellyn, had divided the princedom and each ruled his separate fiefdom. In the following year, war erupted between the brothers and Llewellyn overpowered Owain, uniting the princedom once again. Llewellyn began pillaging the Welsh lands occupied by English barons, ravaging towns and burning farmlands. As the Welsh continued to drive out the English, Henry III mustered an army and proceeded to the border. He demonstrated along the Conway River basin before withdrawing, lacking the funds to resume the campaign. The next year, a truce was negotiated, with the English conceding the occupied territory to Llewellyn. To meet the cost of the expeditionary force, Henry forced the nobles not taking part in the campaign to pay a tax in lieu of their military service. During the Welsh conflict, the king received a message from Pope Alexander IV threatening him with excommunication if his debts for Sicily were not finally paid.

In 1257, King Henry's brother, Richard of Cornwall, was elected King of the Germans, gaining authority over Germany and northern Italy. With his brother on the German throne, Henry III gained a powerful ally in Europe for his containment of France, but in England his rule was weakened by his continuing pursuit for money to claim Sicily and Llewellyn's rise to power along the Welsh border. Later in the year, the Welsh threat intensified after the prince sent envoys to Scotland and the English shires seeking allies against the Plantagenet crown.

By the end of 1257, the Hohenstaufen king, Manfred, had seized the Sicilian crown, leaving Henry III with a huge debt payable to the Holy See. In early April 1258, Henry met his hostile barons in parliament to ask for additional taxes. His request was again denied, as the wrath of the warlords intensified. The king now had few supporters, and those he had were in danger of attack by the rebel barons. The brewing hostilities led to the formation of a party in opposition to the regime, with the earls of Gloucester, Norfolk and Simon de Montfort of Leicester taking a strong stand against Henry's continued disregard for the *Great Charter* and his irresponsible spending of tax money.

When the next parliament met in June at Oxford, the united barons put forth their demands for changes to the government, which became known as the *Oxford Provisions*. During the assembly, a council comprised of twenty-four members – half chosen by the crown and half by the barons – was created to serve as a check on the king's rule. The twenty-four counsellors swore an oath on the Bible, devoting themselves to the oversight of the reigning sovereign. Under their direction, the Council of Fifteen was established, made up of seven earls, five barons, two prelates and a royal clerk, to serve as the king's permanent commission of advisors. Simon de Montfort was a leading advocate of the opposition party, and under his orders the barons moved to strengthen their hold on the English crown and pushed for the acceptance of the *Oxford Provisions*. Henry III was now required to consult with the fifteen counsellors regarding all affairs of the kingdom, while the offices of chancellor, justiciar and treasurer were to be appointed by council members in consultation with the crown. It was further agreed that parliament would meet three times a year, in October, February and June.

With virtual control of the government, the English lords moved against the royal castles held by the king's foreign favourites to eliminate further sources of potential support for the regime. Henry III's family members from the countship of La Marche in Gascony rejected the calls for the abandonment of their English lands and castles received as gifts from Henry. When de Montfort made clear the magnates' intention of seizing the castles, the Lusignan allies of the king fled to the safety of the diocese of Winchester. The barons then mustered their troops and advanced against the bishop. King Henry was with the army at the siege of Winchester and witnessed the submission of the Lusignans on 5 July. The defenders were allowed to retain their properties but were forced to leave England.

Henry III was now a king without a kingdom and was forced to observe the *Provisions of Oxford*. In October 1258, parliament met again and the sovereign affirmed the twenty-four-member council. Acting under the provisions of the Oxford agreement, four knights from each shire appeared before the barons to present the grievances of the people against the sheriffs, as required under the new reforms. Henry gave his approval to the removal of the guilty sheriffs and approved the appointment of their replacements. In actuality, the council of magnates was now ruling the realm without the consent of the monarch.

While Simon de Montfort and the magnates solidified their hold over England, peace negotiations were being held with the French court. On 9 February 1259, the ruling council comprised of de Montfort and key barons gathered in London to finalize the agreement with Paris. Under the terms of the Treaty of Paris, Henry III pledged to relinquish his rights to Normandy and Aquitaine, while the French confirmed his claim to Gascony. In mid-November, the Plantagenet king, accompanied by Queen Eleanor, sailed across the Channel and arrived at the Capetian court in Paris ten days later to formally ratify the treaty. The settlement with the Capetians reinforced the friendship between Henry III and Louis IX, ending years of conflict between the two kingdoms. The king and queen accompanied by their entourage remained in France for nearly four months before returning to England in April 1260.

During Henry III's absence in France, Prince Edward had formed a friendship and alliance with his uncle, Simon de Montfort, threatening the reign of his father. In response to the festering rebellion, after reaching England from Paris, the king marshalled his army of local men-at-arms and soldiers at St Paul's, preparing for an attack from the recalcitrant barons, while the prince and de Montfort stood ready for war in the Clerkenwell district of London with their armed supporters. The standoff lasted for two weeks before the sovereign and his son were reconciled. Charges of treason were then brought against de Montfort, as both factions prepared for war.

To regain his usurped authority over England, Henry III sent emissaries to Rome in 1261 to arrange his release from the *Provisions of Oxford*. While his representatives negotiated with the papacy, the king called the barons to meet in parliament, but they refused to attend. In violation of the Oxford provisions, he dismissed the lords' chosen justiciar and appointed his own nobleman. As he continued to expand his self-rule, in April Pope Alexander IV issued a bull cancelling the *Provisions of Oxford*, freeing the monarch from any of its conditions. Now residing in the secure Tower of London, Henry III began forcing the surrender of the royal castles taken by the rebel lords and replaced the newly appointed sheriffs as the barons' rebellion began to lose momentum. With the king now reigning autonomously, negotiations between the warring parties were started in October to resolve their dispute. Pope Alexander had died earlier in the year, and when Henry received confirmation from the new pontiff, Urban IV, that the bull annulling the provisions was valid, he presented it to parliament, claiming there were no restrictions to his rule.

In July 1262, Henry III and Queen Eleanor returned to France to strengthen their alliance with the French regime. Shortly after arriving, the king became ill with a high fever, which became life-threatening. Over the next four months, he slowly regained his health, and in November made a pilgrimage to Rheims Cathedral to give thanks for his recovery. Henry returned to his kingdom the following month without gaining additional assistance from the French monarchy.

During the king's absence in France, the rebel barons renewed their quest for power and expanded their hold on the government, forcing Henry III to abide by the *Oxford Provisions* to keep the peace. To regain his independence from de Montfort and his supporters, in March 1263 the king announced a pledge of allegiance to Prince Edward as his successor would be required from the nobles and churchmen. The barons replied by demanding the prince swear to agree to the Oxford provisions. After hearing of the lords' response, the king sought safety in the Tower, fearing an attack. Simon de Montfort responded by declaring war on those who refused to honour the provisions, while Urban IV ordered the Archbishop of Canterbury to use his office to oppose the document, in support of the crown. By the summer of 1263, the anti-royalist nobles under de Montfort had raised armies, preparing for war. While Henry III and his wife remained secure in the Tower, Prince Edward positioned his troops at Windsor and Isleworth to protect the approaches to London. During the summer, the rebels moved east from Bristol and Gloucester, outmanoeuvring the prince and quickly taking control of London. As the two armies stood ready to attack, Richard of Cornwall intervened, negotiating a truce between the rival parties. Henry again agreed to abide by the *Provisions of Oxford* and the appointment of a new justiciar.

As the uneasy peace remained in force, parliament met in September, when Henry III was granted permission by the barons to travel to France to seek the mediation of Louis IX. On 22 September, the English king and Simon de Montfort met Louis at Boulogne. The negotiations ended without any final settlement, and Henry recrossed the Channel to England in early October. After the king's return, relations between him and de Montfort grew more hostile. In mid-December, it was agreed that the French king should again attempt to arbitrate a resolution to the

1. Henry I: British Library, Henry I – Cotton Claudius D, i i f 45v.

2. Henry II.

3. The coronation of
King Henry III.

4. An illuminated
illustration of Henry IV.

5. Henry V of England.

6. King Henry VI crowned as King of France.

7. Young Henry VII.

8. Henry VIII of England by Joos Van Cleve.

9. Westminster Abbey.

Above: 10. The coffin of Henry II at Fontevraud Abbey, France.

Below: 11. The battle of Agincourt.

12. *The Field of the Cloth of Gold*, oil painting circa 1545, housed in the Royal Collection at Hampton Court Palace. Henry VIII, on horseback, approaches at bottom left.

implementation of the Oxford provisions. Meeting with Henry and representatives of the barons at Amiens in northern France, the *Provisions of Oxford* were declared void by Louis IX, reinforcing the earlier proclamation of the papacy. The decision returned all royal castles to the regime, crown officials were to be appointed by the court, employment of foreigners was permitted and the king was to rule according to the Charter of Liberties granted by King Henry I in 1100. This ruling by King Louis ignited the Second Barons' War.

Anticipating the English lords would challenge the Amiens accord, Henry III returned to his kingdom and raised a large force of troops. When the Londoners learned the terms of the ruling by the French monarch, they rose up and marched against Richard of Cornwall's manor at Isleworth, burning it to the ground, while in defence of Louis IX's ruling, the king's son took Gloucester from the rebels. As the royalists pillaged the lands of the insurgent lords, King Henry marched on Northampton, which was held by de Montfort's son, Simon the Younger. The castle fell after a brief siege and the surrounding countryside was laid to waste.

While the loyalists were active in the north against the anti-royalist lords, the rebel army of de Montfort was welcomed by the citizens of London. After securing control of the city, he resumed his campaign into the Cinque Ports region along the south-east coast of England to besiege the royalists' stronghold at Rochester. The defenders, led by the Earl of Warenne, repulsed the rebels' repeated assaults, giving the king time to hasten south to relieve the siege. The royalists then took Tonbridge on 1 May. With their provisions now nearly exhausted, the forces of King Henry moved to Lewes to resupply, encamping at the Priory of St Pancras, while Prince Edward occupied Lewes Castle with the heavy cavalry.

Simon de Montfort followed the royal army south, camping 9 miles from Lewes. To avoid the uncertainty of a pitched battle, he sent messengers to the king offering a large sum of money in exchange for his agreement to accept the *Provisions of Oxford*. Henry III quickly rejected the proposal and prepared to attack. In the early morning of 14 May 1264, the rebel army of 500 horsemen and 4,500 infantry moved south, deploying on the high ground at Offham Hill overlooking the priory. The royal force of over 10,000 men was formed for battle under the standard of the Plantagenets, with Richard of Cornwall on the left flank, Prince Edward with his cavalry on the right and the king commanding the foot-soldiers in the centre. The battle began with the charge of Prince Edward's heavy cavalry into the London volunteers holding the rebels' left flank, shredding their ranks and pushing them back. The prince continued his attack, forcing his opponents back several miles across the Sussex countryside, while Henry III led his foot-soldiers forward up the hill under their multi-coloured standards, with armour glistening in the bright sun, ploughing into de Montfort's defenders. The baronial troops held their line and began driving Henry's forces down the hill. When Edward returned to the battlefield, his father had taken refuge behind the walls of the Priory and Richard of Cornwall was trapped in the windmill. With his army shattered, King Henry was compelled to surrender and accept a humiliating peace treaty. Under the agreement, he was permitted to remain free and serve as titular king, with Edward held as hostage to ensure his collaboration. The terms of the Oxford provisions were again confirmed, but Simon de Montfort was now the power behind the throne, Henry III merely acting as his pawn.

Shortly after signing the agreement of submission, Henry III was taken to London, arriving on 27 May and taking residence in St Paul's. While the Earl of Leicester ruled in the name of the Plantagenets, in late June he summoned parliament to meet, and under his direction a new council of nine counsellors was created to advise the sovereign. Queen Eleanor had earlier escaped to France, and in support of her husband began raising an army, threatening to invade England. When de Montfort learned of the forces mustering in France, he ordered the king to send messengers to the queen to abandon the attack. After the queen duly gave up her efforts, the papal legate issued an interdiction against the citizens of London and the towns in the Cinque Ports region, warning de Montfort's allies to renounce him or face excommunication. In late December, the king was directed to summon the parliament to Westminster, where the magnates and bishops – along with two elected knights and burgesses from each of the kingdom's large towns – met to give their approval to de Montfort's decisions on policy matters, which established a precedent for the development of the future House of Commons.

As de Montfort continued to hold the reins of power, he negotiated an alliance with Prince Edward, but his relationships with Gilbert, Earl of Gloucester, and Roger Mortimer, First Baron of Mortimer, were increasingly strained. Edward remained under guard, but escaped while hunting on 28 May, meeting Mortimer in the forest and hastening to safety at Wigmore Castle. After Edward pledged to uphold the *Great Charter*, within a few days many earls and barons abandoned de Montfort and joined forces with the prince. Edward thus became the new leader of the fight to regain the monarchy for his father. With many of his powerful allies now deserting him, the Earl of Leicester negotiated an alliance with Prince Llewellyn of Wales for his military support.

Under the command of Prince Edward, the royalist army assembled and advanced against de Montfort. After skirmishing with Edward's forces during the early summer months in several inconclusive battles, on 4 August de Montfort – with the king under guard close by his side – led his troops to Evesham, where his scouts reported the royalist soldiers were assembled. Edward's army of over 12,000 knights and foot-soldiers approached from the west, occupying the high ground at Greenhill, with the prince holding the centre, Gilbert of Gloucester on the right flank and Roger Mortimer on the left. Following a violent early morning thunderstorm, Prince Edward, wearing a white garment with the red cross of St George across the front, rode onto the battlefield around 9.00 am and prepared for battle.

Outnumbered by his enemy, de Montfort ordered his cavalry and infantry to concentrate their attack on the centre of the prince's line. With his Welsh foot-soldiers and English horsemen at the front, de Montfort led his men forward, the sounds of their war cries echoing across the battlefield. As the two armies clashed, the royalists were initially pushed back in a melee of bloody fighting. Despite de Montfort's early success, when the soldiers of Gloucester and Mortimer entered the onslaught from the flanks, the rebel forces were surrounded. De Montfort formed his men into a defensive circle, but confronted by the larger army of the prince, they wavered and then broke in widespread panic. Fighting valiantly during the battle, de Montfort was unhorsed and killed by Roger Mortimer, with his head severed and body mutilated. No quarter was given or hostages taken by the loyalists, the majority of the rebels being slain. Henry III had been forced to remain at de Montfort's side during the battle and was nearly killed by his son's men. He called out at the top of his voice, 'I am Henry of Winchester, your king', and only after receiving several blows to the body was he recognized and taken to safety.

After reuniting with his son, Henry III was escorted to Marlborough, where on 7 August he issued a proclamation decreeing his return to power and the cancellation of the writs issued during his captivity. He later met with his advisors at Winchester, announcing the forfeiture of the rebels' properties, while a second council meeting was held at Windsor on 29 September, attended by the magnates and prelates, where the Londoners were ordered to peacefully submit and pay a fee for their participation in the revolt. Meanwhile, in Rome, the new pope, Clement IV, issued a bull recognizing Henry III's assumption of power and directing the supporters of Simon de Montfort to swear fealty to the king or be excommunicated.

In the wake of their disastrous defeat at Evesham, the surviving rebels fled England, while others took refuge in their castles, but the kingdom was now firmly under the king's control. On 13 October, Henry met with parliament in London, formally divesting the warlords who had fought against him of their properties. As a reward for his sons' support, Prince Edward was ceded the Earldom of Chester and Edmund received Simon's Leicester earldom.

While Henry III's rule was widely acknowledged, rebel factions continued to resist the Plantagenet regime. In early April 1266, Prince Edward led the royal army against the dissidents in the Cinque Ports region, overpowering them and imposing his father's sovereignty. When the Earl of Derby raised a revolt, he was overrun by the king's allies at Chesterfield. As the monarch's lords renewed their campaign against the rebels, another parliament was summoned to Kenilworth in August, where the sovereign was granted a levy of a tenth of the Church's revenue and the Dictum of Kenilworth was approved, which provided the recalcitrant barons with the opportunity to gain forgiveness and possession of their forfeited lands. When Prince Edward forced the submission of the rebel lords at Ely through force of arms and negotiations in late 1267, the last remaining pocket of resistance was eliminated, ending the Second Barons' War. To enhance the loyalty of the lords, at the 1267 parliament at Marlborough, the king reaffirmed the provisions of the charters, while regaining the right to appoint his own government officials and sheriffs.

During Henry III's campaign to enforce his rule over the recalcitrant barons, Prince Llewellyn had expanded his control over most of mid-Wales and into the English lands along the border. Worn out from the conflict with Simon de Montfort and his allies, in September 1267 the king, Edward and the newly arrived papal legate, Ottoboni, negotiated a peace settlement with Llewellyn, ceding his recent conquests to him. While the legate remained in England, in 1268 he encouraged the knights and lords to take the cross and organize a new crusade to the Levant. In midsummer at Northampton, Prince Edward agreed to take part in the expedition and began wearing the white cross of a crusader on his outer garment. Henry continued to reign over

England unopposed, periodically summoning parliaments while enacting new laws and dealing with foreign governments. The assembly at Westminster on 13 October was attended not only by the magnates and prelates, but also knights and officials from the larger cities in a carryover from de Montfort's rule. When the assembly of representatives gathered in April 1270, the delegates voted to aid Prince Edward's expedition to the Holy Land, and in August he departed for Jerusalem from Dover.

In the winter of 1271, Henry became ill at Westminster Palace, but by April his health had improved. Despite the lingering illness, he continued to rule and was unchallenged by the barons. In August 1272, he journeyed to Norwich to oversee the settlement of a riot by its citizens, which depleted his strength. As the monarch prepared for the Christmas season at Westminster, he became increasingly ill, dying on 16 November at the age of 65 after a reign of 56 years. On 20 November, King Henry III was buried at Westminster Abbey next to the tomb of the Saxon king, Edward the Confessor.

When the king died, Prince Edward was in Outremer honouring his vows as a crusader, only learning of his father's death while returning to England. Despite his absence, immediately after the death of the king, the prince was recognized as successor to the throne by the once-recalcitrant barons and the kingdom was ruled peacefully in his name. Edward I reigned over England for the next thirty-five years, gaining the fealty of the Welsh, expanding English power over Scotland and securing the French regime's recognition of his rights to the Duchy of Gascony, while maintaining the unchallenged support of his nobles, churchmen and subjects.

Selected Sources

Ackroyd, Peter, *Foundation – The History of England from its Earliest Beginnings to the Tudors* (Thomas Dunne Books, 2011).

Ashley, Mike, *British Kings and Queens* (Carroll and Graf, 2004).

Ault, Warren O., *Europe in the Middle Ages* (D.C. Heath, 1937).

Brooke, Christopher, *From Alfred to Henry III* (W.W. Norton, 1961).

Carpenter, David, *The Struggle for Mastery – Britain 1066–1284* (Oxford University Press, 2003).

Church, Stephen, *Henry III* (Allen Lane, 2017).

Davis, John Paul, *The Gothic King* (Peter Owen, 2013).

Earle, Peter, 'Henry III', in Fraser, Antonia, *The Lives of the Kings and Queens of England* (Alfred A. Knopf, 1975).

Hallam, Elizabeth, *Capetian France, 987–1328* (Pearson Education Ltd, 1980).

Hallam, Elizabeth, *Four Gothic Kings* (Weidenfeld and Nicolson, 1987).

Harvey, John, *The Plantagenets* (Franklin Watts, 1948).

Jones, Dan, *The Plantagenets* (Viking, 2013).

Lewis, Matthew, *Henry III – The Son of Magna Carta* (Amberley Publishing, 2016).

Roberts, Clayton and Roberts, David, *A History of England – Volume 1* (Prentice Hall, 1991).

Smith, Goldwin, *A History of England* (Charles Scribner's Sons, 1957).

Henry IV

In late 1397, the future Henry IV was expelled from England by the reigning king, Richard II, for alleged treasonable acts, taking refuge at the French court in Paris. While Henry of Bolingbroke remained in exile in France, his father died the following year and the English king seized his inheritance and extended his banishment to life. Richard II then governed England with a tyrannical hand and was feared by the barons, prompting Henry to orchestrate the overthrow of the regime by claiming a right to the throne through his mother's lineage. By July, he had marshalled a small army of 300 men and boarded three ships, sailing across the Channel and disembarking in Yorkshire. At the time of Henry's landing, King Richard was in Ireland with his army to enforce his rule, and without the threat of immediate royal intervention numerous English lords broke their pledges of allegiance to the crown and joined the rebels. When Richard learned of Henry's invasion, he hastened back to England, but soon discovered most of the nobles were now part of the revolt. Without the support of his barons, Richard withdrew to Conway Castle, where he agreed to meet with Bolingbroke to resolve the conflict. As the monarch approached Henry, he was seized and held in the Tower of London under armed guard. When parliament recognized Henry as king, Richard II signed a letter of abdication, thereby ending the long reign of the Plantagenets. On 13 October 1399, Henry IV was crowned King of England at Westminster Abbey, swearing before the gathered magnates and prelates to protect the laws and rightful customs of the kingdom and defend them with all his might.

Henry IV was born in April 1366 at Bolingbroke Castle in Lincolnshire, the only surviving son of John of Gaunt and Blanche of Lancaster. John of Gaunt was the fourth son of King Edward III and uncle to the heir of the English throne, Richard. He was a powerful and wealthy magnate, possessing large estates with over thirty castles, while his wife was the daughter of the Duke of Lancaster and great-great-granddaughter of Henry III. Soon after his birth, Henry was taken from his mother and cared for by a lady from the ducal court at Bourne Castle with his two younger sisters. When Henry of Bolingbroke was 2 years old, his mother died from the plague and he continued to be raised by his guardian. In 1374, Henry began his academic education with the appointment of a governor by his father. Bolingbroke excelled in his studies of reading, writing, Latin, French and religion, while also learning the social graces of etiquette, singing and dancing. He developed a special interest in music and was taught to play the flute. The following year he began his martial training, acquiring the skills of fighting with the sword, axe and mace of a knight. Under the tutelage of his instructors, he learned how to charge into an adversary's formation on horseback with his lance and how to lay siege to castles.

In April 1377, the 10-year-old Henry Bolingbroke made his way to Windsor Castle to be knighted by the monarch and receive the Order of the Garter, a chivalry order founded by King Edward III in 1348 and dedicated to St George, England's patron saint. On 23 April, he entered the Chapel of St George with his cousin, Richard Plantagenet, and ten other young lords for the knighting ceremony. Kneeling before the frail and aged Edward III, Henry of Bolingbroke swore his oath and was tapped on his shoulders, rising as a knight. Following the ritual, Henry and Richard were received into the Order of the Garter.

On 21 June 1377, Edward III died after a reign of fifty years and the English crown passed to his young grandson, Richard II. Henry was present at the king's funeral service at Westminster Abbey on 5 July as part of his father's entourage, and later in the month attended the coronation of Richard II. Bolingbroke played a prominent role during part of the ceremony, carrying the sword of mercy. Following the anointment of the new king, John of Gaunt – who had also become Duke of Lancaster following the death of his first wife in 1368 – assigned his Earldom of Derby to Henry, anxious to elevate his standing at court among the young lords.

At the time of his assumption to the English throne, Richard II was only 10 years old and not yet at the age of majority, necessitating the appointment of a regency council to govern the kingdom. The council members soon began to quarrel among each other as they sought to dominate the government and enrich themselves. Seeking to take advantage of the political turmoil, the French regime of King Charles V sent its forces to attack the Duchy of Gascony and the southern English seaports, while the Scots pillaged into northern England. As the English throne remained unresponsive under the weak rule of the council, Richard II lacked the will or desire to intercede. While the monarch had little interest in warfare, Henry of Derby – under the guidance of his military tutors – enthusiastically learned the skills of a knight. In January 1382, he participated in his first jousting tournament.

Following Richard II's coronation, Henry remained at court for several years, continuing his academic and military education before rejoining his father's household. During his stay at the royal court, he maintained a polite relationship with the monarch but they never developed a close friendship. When Henry departed from Richard II's court, they did so as subject and sovereign-lord.

Soon after Henry returned to his father, in early February 1381 he was married to Mary Bohun at Rochford Hall. Mary, who was just 11 years old, was the younger daughter of the Earl of Hereford, Humphrey de Bohun. The marital relationship was arranged by the families to benefit their political and economic interests. John of Gaunt had earlier paid 5,000 marks to the king for the right of his son to marry Mary. The Earl of Hereford had died in 1373, leaving his vast estates and great wealth to his two daughters, which was divided between them. With her marriage to Henry, Mary brought her rich properties to her husband's family.

The wedding ceremony took place at the residence of the bride's mother and was a place of great merriment. Companies of minstrels were sent by the king and John of Gaunt's brother, Edmund of Langley, and they performed throughout the day, while a lavish banquet was provided. The guests were also entertained by comedy performances by actors and numerous games. Mary was initially too young to reside with Henry and remained with her mother for a short period. The couple shared a common interest in music, and Henry would play the flute while Mary sang in a pleasant voice. They also developed an interest in chess, spending many evenings playing the game. She frequently accompanied Henry as he attended court, met with parliament and looked after the family's properties. During their thirteen years of marriage, Mary gave birth to five sons and two daughters before her death in 1394 at the age of 26.

In the summer of 1381, the Peasants' Revolt erupted in England against the unpopular policies of the government, growing economic discontent and the imposition of a poll tax, prompting the Londoners to riot in the streets, while in the countryside the peasants rebelled in defiance of the crown. When the revolt broke out, Henry was in London and was forced to take refuge in the Tower with the king and most of the court. In mid-June, arrangements were made for Richard to meet with the organizers of the uprising to resolve their dispute. He made his way to Mile End in east London to negotiate with the rebels, who demanded the surrender of the hated royal ministers and abolishment of serfdom. While the king was at Mile End, the enraged mob gathered around the Tower of London, breaking down the doors and attacking the royal officials. The king's chancellor and other court representatives were murdered in the bloody onslaught. As the rampage intensified, Henry was rescued by a loyal guard, John of Ferrour, barely escaping the slaughter. During the mayhem, Duke John's great palace of Savoy in London was destroyed by the rioters. Meeting with the rebel leaders, the king agreed to end serfdom and bring justice to his guilty officials. Despite the regime's pledge to act, the rebellion continued unabated. King Richard then appointed several barons to restore order and more than 4,000 soldiers were assembled in London. After securing the capital, troops were sent into the countryside to round up the rebel leaders and re-establish peace.

After the revolt was suppressed, Henry resumed his life as a nobleman, frequently travelling from castle to castle with his own household and council. As he became older, Henry increasingly attended parliament and regularly appeared at the king's court. Through the influence of his father, in January 1383 he was appointed to a royal commission charged with the negotiation of a military agreement with the Flemish. The mission to Calais was the Earl of Derby's first journey across the Channel, enabling him to learn the skills of diplomacy. In the following year, he took part in John of Gaunt's expedition against the Scots along the northern border, gaining his first combat experience and exposure to the organization, preparation and command of an army during a campaign.

Three years after the first wife of John of Gaunt and mother of Henry of Bolingbroke died in 1368, John married Costanza of Castile, who gave him a claim to the Kingdom of Spain. In July 1386, he set sail to Spain from Plymouth, determined to lead an army and assert his rights to the Spanish realm. John was accompanied by his wife and family, while Henry remained in England to manage their lands. Gaunt had served as a moderating force in the royal council, but during his absence the king's uncle, Thomas of Woodstock, Duke of Gloucester, became the dominant magnate in parliament. Thomas led a political faction that was determined to control Richard II and rule the kingdom. When what became known as the Wonderful Parliament met at Westminster in October 1386, King Richard provoked his opponents by appointing his favourite, Robert de Vere, as the new Duke of Ireland. The Duke of Gloucester and his followers then demanded the removal of the crown's treasurer and chancellor, which the monarch reluctantly sanctioned. After enforcing his will over the regime, Gloucester arranged for parliament to establish an executive council to govern the realm for one year. Richard then withdrew from London, and after receiving a ruling from the court judges abolishing the new rebel council, ordered Gloucester and his ally, Thomas Arundel, Bishop of Ely, to meet with him. When the rebels met Richard, they accused Robert de Vere and four of his friends of treasonous acts against the kingdom, worsening the discord between the two warring factions.

When de Vere learned of the charges against him, he fled to Chester, raising an army against his enemies. Confronted by de Vere's mustering forces, Thomas of Woodstock formed an alliance known as the Lords Appellants with four magnates, including Henry of Derby. As de Vere set out for London, his troops were blocked by Henry at Radcot Bridge near Oxford on 19 December 1387 with a strong contingent of knights and archers. Upon reaching the Thames crossing, de Vere attempted to force his way across, but was beaten back by Henry's soldiers. As the fighting continued, the Duke of Gloucester arrived with his army in the enemy's rear, prompting de Vere to flee the battle and join Richard II at Windsor. Threatened by the rebels, they sought refuge in the Tower of London. Gloucester and his men followed the king to London, with Henry in the vanguard of the army. By late December, the forces of the Lords Appellants were encamped less than a mile from the Tower, cutting off the king's escape. Surrounded, King Richard was compelled to negotiate a settlement. During the meeting, the Appellants deposed Richard, while de Vere went into exile abroad. However, after failing to decide on either Henry of Derby or Thomas of Gloucester as the new sovereign lord, the Appellants agreed to reinstate the king. Despite the decision to restore him to the throne, Richard had been defeated and was under the power of the Lords Appellants, forced to sanction their rule. At the next parliament, the king's supporters were declared guilty of treason and condemned to death as the Appellants strengthened their hold on the monarchy. A new ruling council was created by the legislative assembly, with Thomas of Gloucester appointed to lead the government. Henry of Derby participated in the parliament, endorsing the new Gloucester administration while serving on the governing commission.

The Lords Appellants ruled over England in the name of Richard II during the following year, but their policies were ineffective and the economy continued to struggle, while their requests for new taxes met with widespread opposition. By April 1389, Gloucester's regime had lost the support of the barons and Church, prompting Richard II to reassert his sovereignty. At a council meeting on 3 May at Westminster Palace, Richard announced his personal assumption of the throne and the establishment of a new advisory body, with officials chosen by him. Gloucester and Arundel were removed from their posts, while Henry of Derby was named to the council to maintain cordial relations with his powerful family.

After retaking the reins of power, the king sent envoys to Paris to resolve the continuing war with France. After a truce was quickly arranged, in celebration of the new peace a French knight challenged the English and other European courts to defend their honour at a jousting tournament. The English knights were anxious to flaunt their battle skills, and Henry, as a warrior renowned for his numerous victories in tournaments, agreed to participate in the competition with more than thirty other knights. The tournament was held in Flanders in May 1390, at St Inglevert near Calais, where the Earl of Derby played a prominent part. During the event, Henry met a French crusader and discussed the war of the Teutonic Knights against the pagans in Prussia. Henry was anxious to spend time away from court, with the king still brooding over his involvement with the Lords Appellants and the resulting exile of Robert de Vere, his favourite baron.

Shortly after returning home, preparations for the military expedition to Prussia were started and men and supplies were assembled, with travel arrangements being made. After making an offering at Lincoln Cathedral for protection during the campaign and visiting his wife and children at Hereford Castle, Henry met his knights and soldiers at Boston for the passage to Prussia. Three ships were hired, with supplies and troops loaded. Henry was accompanied by eleven knights, a small contingent of archers, household staff and personal servants. On 19 July, they set sail across the North Sea and around Denmark into the Baltic Sea, reaching the Prussian coastline on 8 August. Henry and his men disembarked at Rozwie and proceeded overland to Gdansk in modern-day northern Poland. Additional horses, supplies and wagons were then purchased, and the Earl of Derby continued his journey to the camp of the Teutonic Knights at Ragnit.

The English received a cordial welcome from the Teutonic Knights, along with gifts of peacocks, horses and sheep from the marshal of the military order, Engelhard Rabe, and his men. Soon after the English force arrived at the encampment, Rabe received reports that the pagans, led by Skirgal, were near the River Vilnia at its junction with the Memel. The army was assembled and advanced through a dense forest to attack the heathen warriors. On 28 August, the English troops commanded by Henry took part in a major battle, crashing into the enemy soldiers with Rabe's men and compelling them to flee. The allied army resumed its campaign, and on 4 September attacked Vilnius, the capital of Lithuania. Henry and his English knights participated in the assault against the outer defensive works, seizing control of them in bloody and fierce fighting. The crusader army next moved against the two forts defending the hilltop city, besieging them. The pagans repelled repeated sorties by the allies, and after five weeks the siege was abandoned as provisions and supplies became depleted.

The allied army was now dispersed, with Henry and his men setting out for Konigsberg, reaching the Baltic port-city on 20 October. The Englishmen remained in Konigsberg through the winter, occupied with hunting deer and boar in the woodlands, martial games and hawking. During the long cold winter nights,

Henry was entertained by minstrels and played games of chess and dice. In mid-February, the crusaders departed for Danzig, where they spent six weeks. During the Easter season, Henry made pilgrimages to several churches, presenting gifts and offering prayers. With the arrival of warmer weather, Henry planned his return to England, hiring two ships and purchasing provisions and stores. In late March, the vessels were loaded and the crusaders headed into the Baltic Sea, sailing westward toward home. Henry reached Boston in late April, making his way from the coast to Bolingbroke Castle. To give thanks for his safe return, he made a pilgrimage to the church at Bridlington. In October, Henry visited his wife Mary at her residence in Peterborough, and in November he attended parliament.

While Earl Henry continued to manage his sizable estates and participate in martial tournaments, in February 1392 he joined his father on a diplomatic mission to the French court to transfer the earlier-arranged truce into a permanent peace. The English party landed at Calais and travelled overland to Amiens, where they waited for the arrival of Louis VI. On 25 March, the French king made his grand entry into Amiens, accompanied by his lords and knights in a great processional parade. The English were royally entertained by Louis at a magnificent banquet in the archbishop's palace. When Henry and his advisors met with Louis VI's representatives, both parties' demands were too extreme and no permanent resolution was possible. Although no progress was made during the talks, the truce was extended for another year. In April, the English sailed back home and reported the failure of the negotiations to the king.

Meanwhile, the Teutonic Knights in Prussia had resumed their war against the pagans, and Henry was resolved to rejoin the fighting. In July 1392, he collected money from his father for another expedition, and provisions and supplies were purchased in London and King's Lynn. On 24 July, the earl set sail across the North Sea with nearly 200 knights, squires and servants. The fleet landed at Danzig on 10 August and the expeditionary force set out overland, reaching the Teutonic Knights at Konigsberg on 2 September. Shortly after his arrival, Henry met with the leaders of the martial order, where he was told they were not currently involved in a campaign against the heathens and his services were not required. The Englishmen remained in the city for several days before returning to Danzig. During the journey to Danzig, Henry decided to make a pilgrimage to the Levant.

Before Henry departed for the Holy Land, the size of the expeditionary force was reduced and one ship was sent to England with over half of the men. On 22 September, Henry departed from Danzig, travelling overland and reaching Frankfurt in early October. By November, they had arrived in Vienna, where Henry was the guest of the Duke of Austria, Albert of Habsburg. Upon the intervention of the Austrian duke, arrangements were made with the Senate of Venice for a galley to transport Henry and his soldiers to Jaffa in the Levant. After a short stay, their journey was renewed, and on 1 December the pilgrims entered the Republic of Venice. On the day of his arrival, the Venetians gave Henry a grand public reception. During his stay, he was received by Doge Antonio Venier and made offerings with him at St Mark's Basilica. In Venice, preparations were made for the voyage to the Holy Land, with provisions, stores and wine being purchased. On 22 December, the

Englishmen set sail, making their way to Rhodes, the headquarters of the Knights Hospitaller. Fresh provisions were purchased on the island and repairs made to their vessel. During his short stay on Rhodes, Henry visited the Grand Master of the Military Order at his palace and was received with honours. Following a brief stop, their journey continued as Henry and the pilgrims sailed east to Jaffa. The port town was 30 miles from Jerusalem, the Englishmen making the passage on foot. In the Holy City, Henry travelled to the sites of many biblical events and visited the Church of the Holy Sepulchre and Mount of Olives, making offerings and praying before the holy relics.

Following a short stay in Jerusalem, Henry and his entourage returned to Jaffa and soon after sailed to Famagusta on the eastern coast of Cyprus. Henry sent envoys to the palace of the King of Cyprus and titular King of Jerusalem, James I of Lusignan, establishing a friendly relationship with him, while fresh provisions and wine were purchased locally. The sea passage was soon resumed, the Englishmen making their way back to Rhodes, where offerings for a safe journey were again made by the earl at several churches. From Rhodes, they continued westward, following the same route as the outward voyage. In mid-March, Henry reached Venice and again made prayers at various churches, while beginning preparations for the long overland expedition to Calais. Horses and carts were hired, with food and other supplies purchased. The pilgrims set out on 28 April, and by mid-May arrived in Milan, where Henry was entertained by the city's duke. After remaining for a week, the English soldiers travelled through the Alps into France, and after a brief stay in Paris reached England in late June to complete a journey of nearly a year. During his long absence from England, Henry had developed friendships with many formidable European rulers and enhanced his renown with the English barons and churchmen.

Henry of Derby soon returned to public life, attending parliament in January 1394 and serving on the ruling council as a member of his father's political faction. In the autumn, Richard II travelled to Ireland to pacify the restless natives and his recalcitrant nobles, while Henry remained at home, having not been fully reconciled with the monarchy. John of Gaunt had been lobbying the government for his appointment to the rich lands of Gascony in western France, but the Gascons opposed the grant and the council supported their wishes. Henry was disappointed with the decision, which ended his opportunity to inherit the lordship. While Henry continued to support the regime of Richard II, in October 1396 he accompanied the king and his court to Calais to attend a ceremonial meeting with the French monarch, Charles VI, for the signing of a new truce. The agreement was signed at Ardres in a field decorated with large ornate tents overflowing with exchanged gifts of friendship. King Richard had earlier sent envoys to Paris to negotiate a permanent peace with the French government, but they could only arrange a four-year extension of the treaty and his marriage to Charles VI's 7-year-old daughter, Isabel, to solidify their friendship.

The subjugation of the Irish rebels, extension of the French truce and widespread prosperity in the kingdom had made the reign of Richard increasingly popular. With the support of the barons and churchmen, he began to quietly eliminate his opposition and strengthen his support base, ruling in an increasingly dictatorial manner. At the January 1397 parliament, the king openly spoke out against his uncle, Thomas of Woodstock, Earl of Gloucester, who had opposed his negotiations with the French. Relations with members of parliament deteriorated further when the king's request for money to aid the French invasion of Milan was denied. By July, the crown's association with the three founders of the Lords Appellants became increasingly tense, compelling the barons to withdraw to the safety of their castles. On 10 July, Richard moved against them, to quell their suspicions first arranging to meet the Earl of Warwick, Thomas Beauchamp, in London for dinner. However, the king then ordered Beauchamp's arrest and imprisonment in the Tower of London. During the night, the king led an armed party to his uncle's castle at Pleshey, taking Thomas of Woodstock into custody. Under guard, the duke was taken to a ship and transported across the Channel to a prison in Calais. The third of the Appellants, Thomas of Arundel, surrendered to royal soldiers and was sent to the Isle of Wight. King Richard then issued a proclamation announcing the three lords had been arrested for new offences against the throne, but the declaration was widely disbelieved by the barons, bishops and common people.

During the period before the next parliament in September, Richard II moved aggressively to eliminate his enemies, repealing the pardons granted to Gloucester, Warwick and Arundel and forcing the Archbishop of Canterbury into exile. When parliament met in September, John of Lancaster presided as lord high steward, using his prominent office to protect Henry from the revenge of the king. On 21 September, the Earl of Arundel appeared before the king and was accused of treason for his participation in the 1386 revolt. John of Gaunt pronounced him guilty and ordered his execution. He was taken from parliament to Tower Hill and beheaded with one stroke of a sword. King Richard continued his vengeance, ordering the Duke of Gloucester to be brought to parliament from Calais by Thomas Mowbray, Earl of Nottingham, who had earlier opposed the king as a member of the Lords Appellants. When the earl returned to London, he reported that Gloucester was dead. Unknown to the assembled barons and commons, the king had secretly ordered the death of Gloucester. On 28 September, the Earl of Warwick came before parliament to plead for mercy from the monarch. When several lords spoke out in his support, the earl was sentenced to life imprisonment on the Isle of Man. While the three founding Appellants had received their punishment, Henry of Derby and Thomas Mowbray were named dukes of Hereford and Norfolk respectively, and the monarch's favourites were granted earldoms. The September parliament ended late in the month, with Richard's rule over England now unchallenged.

Following the meeting of the September parliament, the relationship between Henry of Derby and Thomas Mowbray became increasingly hostile. Mowbray was part of a faction that had opposed the Lancastrians, viewing them with suspicion and jealousy. Charges of treason were made against Henry by the Duke of Norfolk, allegations which were strongly denied. The king was petitioned to decide the guilty nobleman and he chose to resolve the issue through trial by combat.

On the appointed day, Henry rode out to Gosford Green near Coventry on a large warhorse, dressed in armour and carrying a sword, dagger and silver shield decorated with the red cross of St George. Riding to the presiding constable, he announced he had come 'To prosecute my appeal in combating Thomas Mowbray, Duke of Norfolk, who is a traitor, false and recreant to God and King.' Henry next took his lance from his attendant and rode to await Mowbray. When the Duke of Norfolk arrived, he took his place in the lists ready for combat. As the two dukes prepared to charge, Richard II suddenly intervened, halting the joust. Following a two-hour delay, he made the decision to stop the duel and exiled Mowbray for life, while Henry was banished for ten years. Both former Appellants were compelled to make a pledge to live in separate realms and not meet abroad. With the enforcement of his pronouncement, Richard had taken his vengeance against the two remaining members of the Lords Appellants.

After leaving John of Gaunt at Eltham Castle in London, Duke Henry of Hereford departed in mid-October, making his way to the east coast and embarking on a ship to begin his ten-year banishment. Landing in France, he proceeded to Paris and was cordially received by King Charles VI, who arranged his residence at the Clisson Hotel. Away from the English court, Henry grew restless and began to consider taking part in a crusade against the pagans, but his plans were changed in February 1399 when he received news that John of Gaunt had died. While Henry mourned the death of his father in Paris, Richard II sought ways to deprive him of his birthright to the family's Lancastrian lands. It was determined by the king's counsellors that since the duke was a traitor, he could not inherit the vast Lancaster properties. On 18 March, a committee of the parliament declared John of Gaunt's estates had been forfeited to King Richard, with Henry's exile extended to life.

Thomas Arundel, Archbishop of Canterbury, had earlier also been exiled to France by Richard II for his involvement with the Appellants. He now arranged to meet with Henry in Paris to devise a plan to overthrow King Richard. To gauge the duke's support among the English barons and churchmen, Thomas Arundel secretly travelled to London and conferred with Henry's friends, who offered to aid his usurpation of the throne. After the return of the archbishop to Paris with the endorsements of the English lords, Henry carefully planned his seizure of Richard's crown. He corresponded with the dominant and influential barons in England, gaining their pledges of support, and negotiated an agreement of friendship with the French king's younger brother, Louis of Orleans, securing his approval for the undertaking to take the crown. Henry continued his quest for allies by riding from Paris to Nantes in south-west France, meeting with another loyal friend, John IV, Duke of Brittany and Earl of Richmond, who agreed to take part in the attempted overthrow of the king.

With his preparations completed, in early July 1399 Henry assembled his force of 300 knights and archers, sailing from Vannes in Brittany to Ravenspur in Yorkshire, where there were numerous Lancastrian castles garrisoned with loyal troops. As the rebels were preparing to invade England, Richard II had departed from his kingdom on 29 March with a formidable army to impose his reign over the Irish, who had rebelled once again and killed his favourite and designated heir, Roger Mortimer, at the Battle of Kells. Encountering little resistance upon their landing, Henry consolidated his position and moved inland, where many lords abandoned Richard and joined the growing army of the usurper. At Doncaster, Henry met the formidable Earl of Northumberland, Henry Percy, falsely swearing an oath to him that his campaign was only for the enforcement of his rightful inheritance to his father's properties. The addition of the earls of Northumberland and Westmoreland with their private levies greatly strengthened Henry's forces. He continued his campaign of mistruths, claiming the king was plotting to sell the Duchy of Gascony to raise money for his personal use and that he was the rightful successor to the throne, not Richard II. Numerous lies were told to further Henry's quest for the overthrow of the king.

As news of Henry's arrival spread across England, thousands of knights and squires rushed to join his growing army. The royal government left behind in London by the king was led by his uncle, Edmund Langley, Duke of York, and when he attempted to raise an army in support of his nephew, few men responded to his summons. Edmund advanced against the rebels, but after a brief skirmish he surrendered. In late July, Richard II returned to his kingdom, crossing the Irish Sea to land in Wales. He ordered his army to mobilize in south Wales, but learned that many of his knights had deserted him in favour of the Duke of Hereford. As his support quickly dissolved, in early August Richard hastened north, taking refuge in Conway Castle, one of the strongest fortifications in his kingdom. King Richard sat helpless there, only able to pray for God's intervention to save him from the wrath of his barons. While he remained isolated in north Wales, Henry continued his triumphant march across England. On 5 August, the king's base of support in Chester collapsed as Henry became the undisputed ruler over England. Henry then sent Henry Hotspur Percy of Northumberland, eldest son of the earl, and the Archbishop of Canterbury with a force of knights and archers to bring the monarch to meet him at Flint Castle in north Wales. Before entering Richard II's presence, Hotspur hid his troops in a forest to conceal his plot to capture him. When the envoys appeared before Richard in the chapel, they presented what they said were Henry's stipulations, which allowed the king to keep his crown if an independent parliament was established and the Duke of Hereford's inheritance was restored. However, Hotspur had concocted the terms in a bid to dupe the king and capture him. Believing he was to retain the throne, Richard agreed to talk to his cousin at Flint Castle to resolve the uprising. As Richard rode toward the castle, he was surrounded by Percy's armed men and taken to Flint as a prisoner. When Henry of Hereford and his men approached the castle in the early morning, the king watched from the ramparts, alarmed at the number of his former followers now supporting his cousin, and reportedly said: 'Now I see the end of my days coming.' Meeting with the king, Henry bowed deeply and acted respectfully, telling him: 'I have come to help you govern your kingdom, which you have not ruled well.' Richard II replied: 'Fair cousin, since it pleases you, then it pleases us well.'

At the end of August, King Richard was taken under guard to London and confined in apartments in the Tower of London. As Henry entered the city to the wild acclaim of the citizenry, Richard was alone, deprived of his friends and servants. While he remained isolated in the Tower, the great English magnates, prelates and town officials assembled on 30 September at Westminster Hall to debate his fate. In the presence of the vacant throne, covered with a gold cloth, the Bishop of St Asaph, Llywelyn de Bromfield, read the list of accusations against Richard II. He was charged with thirty-three allegations, the most serious being the murder of the Duke of Gloucester, breaking his coronation vows and causing the impoverishment of his subjects. After discussing the charges, the assembled delegates of the realm decided there was sufficient evidence to declare the deposition of Richard II from the sovereignty of the English kingdom.

Following the acclamation of those present, Henry declared that by virtue of his bloodline through King Henry III 'I have come to recover a realm on the point of being undone by bad government.' He was then led to the golden throne at the front of the hall by the Archbishop of Canterbury, Thomas Arundel, and halted, kneeling in prayer. After a few minutes, Henry was seated on the English throne by the archbishops of York and Canterbury, as the lords and commoners thundered their acclaim. By the approval of the people, England had deposed Richard II and elected Henry IV as their new monarch. The following day, Richard II was formally divested of his kingdom, after which Duke Henry of Hereford was anointed with the English crown.

On the afternoon of 12 October, Henry led a procession of over 2,000 lords, ladies, knights and servants from the Tower of London to Westminster Palace, through streets richly decorated for the coronation ceremony. Early on the morning of Monday, 13 October, Henry began the day by taking confession and hearing Mass. He was next purified with holy oil and incense by the archbishops of Canterbury and York, before proceeding to Westminster Abbey with his 13 year-old-son, Prince Henry of Wales, carrying the sword of justice and Henry Percy of Northumberland bearing the Lancaster sword. Upon entering the abbey, the king's party moved to the raised stage, which was wrapped with a crimson cloth. Henry stepped up onto the platform, sitting on the throne, again covered in gold cloth. The Archbishop of Canterbury, Thomas Arundel, then asked the congregation if they accepted Henry's accession to the crown, and they loudly replied in the affirmative. Archbishop Arundel turned to Henry and read the four articles of the coronation oath, which he swore to defend with all of his might. After swearing to protect the laws and rightful customs of the kingdom, Henry's upper body was anointed with holy oil, which was believed to have been given to St Thomas Becket by the Virgin Mary. The ceremony was followed by a banquet at Westminster Hall. During the celebrations, the king's champion, Sir Thomas Dymock, entered the great hall on horseback dressed in armour, challenging to battle anyone who disputed Henry IV's right to the English monarchy. Henry responded to his champion's call, telling him: 'If necessary, I will defend my kingdom by my own person.'

On the day following the coronation ceremony, the English parliament assembled at the request of the king. Summons for the members had been sent earlier, and sixty-three lords, clergymen and burgesses gathered at Westminster. The usual tax on wool exports was granted to Henry for three years, but no additional levies were approved, as following his recent overthrow of Richard II, the new monarch's hold on the kingdom was still tenuous and his regime too weak to demand additional tax money. The decrees passed by Richard II's 1397 parliament were voided and the king's oldest son, Henry, was officially acknowledged as successor-designate and named Prince of Wales, Duke of Cornwall and Earl of Chester. On 23 October, it was agreed that the deposed king would remain in the custody of the monarchy and be denied visits by his former advisors and servants. To further secure his control over the former sovereign, Henry appeared before parliament to announce his banishment of Richard II for life. Soon afterwards, the exiled king was secretly taken at night from the Tower to Henry IV's fortress in Yorkshire at Pontefract. Henry next moved against the ex-king's principal supporters, depriving them of their lands granted during the reign of Richard II.

Shortly after seizing the reins of power in England, Henry IV began corresponding with neighbouring realms to gain their recognition of his kingship. He wrote to the Scottish king, Robert III, encouraging him to renegotiate the extension of the truce between the two crowns that was due to expire on 29 September. He maintained friendly relations with the French court, and in November sent envoys to Paris to renew the ceasefire with King Charles VI. The English king also wrote to the Doge of Venice, renewing their cordial relationship that had been established during his pilgrimage to the Levant. With his sister, Philippa of Lancaster, being married to the Portuguese King John I, and his half-sister, Catherine, being the Queen of Castile, Henry IV retained favourable rapports with the two kingdoms. In mid-October, the trading privileges of the Hanseatic League were confirmed by the new regime, ensuring that English merchants received similar commercial privileges from the league's member towns in Central and Northern Europe.

After voting on numerous petitions, Henry IV's first parliament dissolved on 19 November. With his reign seemingly secure, more than half of the royal army was released, and in early December the king left Westminster for Windsor to spend Christmas with his family and courtiers. While King Henry remained at Windsor, on 17 December the Abbot of Westminster, William Colchester, held a meeting in his abbey with a faction of disgruntled earls and barons to plot the murder of the monarch and restoration of Richard II in what became known as the Epiphany Rising. As the plotters solidified their assassination plans, an informant betrayed details of the conspiracy to friends of the crown. When Henry was informed of the plot, he took his sons with an armed escort from Windsor and hastened to London. Upon reaching the city, he called on the citizens for their support. Meanwhile, the band of conspirators stormed into Windsor searching for the king. Learning he had escaped, they rode to Sonning, taking control of Richard II's wife, Isabel, while Henry collected an army of Londoners and advanced against Colchester's men to defend his fledgling rule. After the rebels were informed of the approaching royal army, they withdrew from the town, making their way to Cirencester. During their journey, a supporter of the king, Sir Walter Hungerford, was captured by the plotters and forced to accompany them. Upon reaching Cirencester, Hungerford managed to escape, telling the townspeople of the threat against Henry IV. The citizens then rose up attacking the rebels, beheading several earls. Over eighty insurgents were seized and later brought to trial in Oxford in the presence of the king. Following the court's verdict, more than twenty-five rebels were executed, while others were imprisoned and several released. Those plotters who had escaped from Cirencester were soon rounded up and tried in London. The Abbot of Westminster and several others were confined for a short period to the Tower of London, while some were put to death. Although the revolt of the earls was short-lived, it vividly revealed to Henry the weakness of his regime and the continued threat of Richard II. The Epiphany Rising convinced Henry that his usurpation of the crown was still not secure, and to prevent another rebellion under the banner of Richard II, he ordered the former king's assassination. The death of King Richard II was announced on 14 February 1400. His body was taken from Pontefract Castle and put on display in St Paul's Cathedral before burial at King's Langley Priory in Herefordshire, 28 miles north of London.

In the aftermath of the suppression of the rebellion, Henry IV set out on a punitive campaign against the Scots to display the power of his regime to his potential enemies, both internal and foreign. To raise the money needed for the expedition, he had summoned a great council of magnates and ecclesiastic lords to meet at Westminster on 9 February. Nineteen barons and thirteen prelates were present for the council meeting, which agreed to support Henry's venture. The churchmen granted a tenth of their revenue to the king, while the lords agreed to take part in the martial operation without any compensation. A total of over 1,750 mounted knights and 11,000 footmen assembled for the invasion of Scotland. The king's two eldest sons, Henry and Thomas, travelled with the army as part of their military training. The English forces also included a unit of artillery armed with fourteen cannons, relatively new weapons which would later prove decisive in one of Henry's campaigns. When King Robert III of Scotland learned of the strength of the approaching army, envoys were sent to Henry IV to negotiate a resolution. Henry agreed to the talks, but the Scots had not been truly interested in a peace treaty, only sending the emissaries to delay the advance of the English troops. While the discussions dragged on without resolution, Henry's supplies and money were becoming depleted. The English king was compelled to ask the bishops and the ecclesiastic lords for a loan to keep his army in the field. With the negotiations faltering, he gave orders to advance north to force the submission of Robert III.

On 14 August, the English crossed the Scottish border and marched on Edinburgh. As they hastened toward the city, the Scots withdrew, drawing their enemy deeper into a barren land void of provisions and supplies. With his money and food again nearly depleted, Henry IV was compelled to agree to talks. During the negotiations, Henry pressed his demands for the Scottish king to render homage to him for his kingdom, but Robert III continued to delay a response. When the Scots finally pledged their willingness to comply to a future summons from the English throne, Henry ordered his army to withdraw, the incursion having achieving little.

As the crown's forces returned south into England, Henry received reports of a new uprising in Wales led by the charismatic Owen Glendower, who had claimed the title Prince of Wales in defiance of the English regime. Glendower, who was likely born around 1354, was a descendent of Llewellyn, Prince of Wales. He was educated in London and studied law at the Inns of Court. In 1384, he served in the English army on the Scottish border, performing garrison duties, and the following year was assigned to the forces of John of Gaunt along the northern frontier. In 1387, he fought with Henry of Hereford at the Battle of Radcot Bridge, afterwards returning to his estates in Wales to live the life of a wealthy landowner.

The rebellion of Glendower erupted after parliament rejected his petition for the return of his lands forcibly seized by the English nobleman, Lord Grey of Ruthyn. In retaliation for the loss of his estates, Glendower unleashed an attack against the town of Ruthyn in north Wales, destroying many buildings and disrupting commerce. He then moved against the English-held coastal town of Flint, pillaging the villages and countryside as his army advanced. By 23 September he was proceeding south, attacking Powis Castle and sacking the town of Welshpool in the Powis earldom. As the Welsh revolt spread, Henry IV mustered a large army on 22 September at Shrewsbury and hastened against the rebellious Welshmen, plundering their lands in revenge for their attacks. Owen Glendower engaged in a campaign of small raids, ambushes and skirmishes, avoiding a pitched battle and thereby keeping the royal troops in check.

The war dragged on into 1401, Glendower still defiantly resisting the English incursion. The Welsh uprising put pressure on Henry IV to fund his campaign, as parliament repeatedly refused to grant his requests for money. In June, the Welsh army of several hundred men was attacked in the Hyddgen valley by 1,500 royalists, but Glendower rallied his troops and drove off his enemies. In the aftermath of the defeat of his forces, King Henry mustered an army of knights and footmen, advancing into central Wales and plundering the towns and countryside, while Glendower assailed his flanks and rearguard, refusing to fight a pitched battle. When the English reached the abbey at Strata Florida in central Wales, the soldiers partially destroyed the church in revenge for the monks' support of the rebels. After sacking the abbey, Henry's forces withdrew to Worcester without having managed to weaken the war effort of the Welsh. The fighting in 1401 ended with the inconclusive Battle at Tuthill near Caernarfon, after which Henry's forces were compelled to retreat to England after failing to suppress the Welsh revolt.

As Henry IV continued to struggle against the attacks of Glendower, in April 1402 Lord Grey of Ruthyn was captured in an ambush, further weakening the war effort against the Welsh rebels. While Grey remained in captivity, an English army led by Sir Edmund Mortimer clashed with the Welsh on 22 June at Bryn Glas in central Wales, near the town of Knighton. As Mortimer's men neared, Glendower divided his forces, sending his archers to hide in a nearby ravine while the remaining troops – with a contingent of bowmen – occupied the slopes of an adjacent hill. Upon reaching the enemy's position, Mortimer's infantrymen swept up the hill under the heavy fire of Glendower's archers. As the royalists surged forward, the Welsh rebels hidden in the ravine charged into their rear and flanks. While the battle raged, the Welsh archers in Mortimer's army deserted, joining the rebels and helping them overwhelm the king's soldiers. As the decimated troops of Mortimer retreated, the Welsh women followed them, killing many wounded English soldiers in revenge for their earlier plundering and raping.

While the war against the Welsh continued, Henry IV was married by proxy on 3 April 1402 to Joanna of Navarre, whom he had earlier met at the court of the French king. Joanna was the daughter of the King of Navarre and widow of Duke John IV of Brittany. The official wedding ceremony was held at Winchester Cathedral on 7 February 1403, with King Henry's half-brother, Henry Beaufort, Bishop of Lincoln, officiating. On 26 February, Joanna was anointed Queen of England at Westminster Abbey. Their marriage was part of a political agreement, bringing the English support against the French monarchy, while providing Brittany with an ally against the incursions of the Valois King of France, Charles VI. She was described by contemporaries as well-educated and a lady of grace and charm. Joanna had earlier served as regent for Brittany and used her governing experience to aid her husband. The marriage to Joanna resulted in no children.

Henry IV's incursions against Glendower had failed to enforce his sovereignty over Wales, and in late 1402 the Scots – under the command of Archibald, Fourth Earl of Douglas – invaded England in support of the Welsh. After pillaging towns and burning farmland in Northumberland, the Scots withdrew toward their homeland. When the First Earl of Northumberland, Henry Percy, and his son, Harry Hotspur Percy, learned of the Scottish incursion, they assembled an army and hastened against the enemy. Moving rapidly, the Northumberland forces intercepted Douglas at Homildon Hill on 14 September. At the approach of the English, Douglas deployed his men into schiltron formations of large squares. However, this left the Scots as tempting targets for the English archers, and they were decimated by their volleys of arrows. When Douglas ordered his army to charge, it was routed by Percy's men. Numerous Scottish soldiers were taken prisoner, including Archibald Douglas.

Shortly after the victory over the Scots, relations between the English crown and the Percy family rapidly deteriorated, Henry IV having refused to allow the earl to ransom his prisoners from the Battle of Homildon Hill or reimburse him for the cost of his campaign. To press his family's claims, in late autumn Hotspur Percy went to London to personally demand payment. When the king again rejected the petition, Percy withdrew from court, severing his fealty to the monarchy. After returning north, the Earl of Northumberland and his son raised their banner of revolt on 10 July 1403 and agreed to join forces with the Welsh.

Henry IV was at Burton-on-Trent when reports of the Percy rebellion reached him. To counter the threat against his regime, he ordered his army to assemble, more than 12,500 men rushing to his standard. The king hastened to Shrewsbury with his forces to join his son, Prince Henry, who had been leading raiding parties into northern Wales. Reinforced with the prince's men, the king set out to strike Hotspur before his troops from the north united with the Welsh. As the Percys moved toward Shrewsbury, Hotspur's uncle, Thomas Percy, First Earl of Worcester, broke his allegiance to the crown, joining his soldiers with his nephew's army. Hotspur was further reinforced when contingents of over 1,000 renowned Cheshire longbowmen arrived at his encampment. Henry IV reached Shrewsbury first, forcing Hotspur to withdraw to nearby Berwick Field, 2 miles from the town. As Hotspur established his camp for the night, scouts were sent to search for the approaching forces of Glendower.

Meanwhile, King Henry left Shrewsbury with the royal army and encamped at Haughmond Abbey to force Hotspur into battle. In the early morning of 21 July, the crown's scouts reported that Hotspur's army of over 10,000 men was deployed on a nearby hilltop. After hearing Mass, Henry ordered his troops to advance against the enemy. The royal army was divided into three divisions, the king commanding the main body on the right flank, while Prince Henry's royalists were deployed to the left and the Edmund, Earl of Stafford, led the soldiers in the centre. Before the battle, three loyalist knights were dressed in replicas of the king's armour in an attempt to confuse the enemy. As the royalists aligned to attack, Hotspur's men were positioned on a small ridgeline, forcing Henry's troops to move up the slopes of the hill into range of their foes' deadly archers. To avoid a bloody battle, the king sent the Abbot of Shrewsbury, Thomas Prestbury, with a message to Hotspur offering to discuss his grievances. Hotspur refused to meet the king, but sent his uncle, the Earl of Worcester, to confer with Henry. When the earl met Henry, their discussions soon turned hostile after the king was accused of ordering Richard II's death and unlawfully seizing the throne. The negotiations quickly ended and both armies prepared for battle.

In the early morning, before the battle, Henry IV walked among his men, telling them to fight well and that victory would be for the common good of the realm. As the sun rose higher in the hot summer sky, the blasts of trumpets and battle cries of the soldiers echoed across the battlefield, the royalists shouting 'Saint George and upon them', while the rebels responded with 'Esperance Percy'. King Henry ordered the vanguard, predominately archers, to move up the hill, led by the Earl of Stafford. The earl valiantly led his men forward under the withering waves of arrows from their enemy's longbowmen. The front ranks of the royal troops were cut down, but Stafford pressed his attack on up the hill. Although the Cheshire longbowmen had killed many royalists, their supply of arrows began to run out, allowing the king's soldiers to engage their opponents in hand-to-hand fighting with sword, axe and spear. During the bloody melee, Edmund of Stafford was killed, the royalists being driven down the hill and Hotspur's troops renewing their charge into the king's centre.

With his vanguard falling back under the rebels' assaults, Henry sent a message to his son on the left flank, telling him to attack, and ordered his trumpeters to give the signal for the main body of men to move forward. The royalists, led by the king, then clashed with the rebels in bloody and savage fighting. To disrupt the loyalists' attack, the Cheshire archers aimed their remaining arrows at Henry IV, while on the left flank they fired at Prince Henry. While the Prince of Wales had the visor of his helmet raised, he was struck by an arrow in the face below his left eye, but continued forward, leading his soldiers into the fray. As the battle raged into the afternoon, King Henry's men began to overwhelm their foe. Sensing defeat, Hotspur mounted a desperate charge against the king. He collected over thirty knights and fought through the melee toward the banner of Henry. The Earl of Dunbar saw the approaching Hotspur forces and convinced the monarch to withdraw. As the rebel knights charged, however, they were slain by the crown's men-at-arms and footmen. During the onslaught, Sir Walter Blount, who wore the livery of Henry IV's armour, was killed and there were loud shouts that the king had been slain. King Henry then raised his visor and yelled: 'Harry Percy is dead.' Seeing the sovereign alive and Hotspur dead, the rebels fled the battlefield, leaving their wounded to be slaughtered by the royalists. During the three-hour Battle of Shrewsbury, the Percy forces sustained over 5,000 casualties, while 1,600 loyalists were killed and some 4,000 wounded. The body of Hotspur was first taken to his family's chapel at Whitchurch and then to Shrewsbury to be exhibited in the marketplace. To assure any sceptics about his death, his head was cut off and mounted on a gate in York for all to see.

Shortly following his defeat of Hotspur, Henry IV headed north to capture the Earl of Northumberland and hold him for trial on charges of treason. Henry Percy had taken refuge in Warkworth Castle, where he received a message from the king ordering him to travel to York and make his submission to the English crown. In an attempt to save his life, the earl rode to York, entering the city through the gate where his son's head was fixed to a pike. Meeting with Henry, he swore his innocence of conspiracy against the regime, claiming that Hotspur pursued the revolt without consulting him. After listening to the earl's pleadings, the king told him he would be allowed to defend himself before the next parliament. Henry then took Percy to his castle at Pontefract, where the earl was forced to send letters to his vassals ordering them to swear fealty to the throne. The Earl of Northumberland was then sent to Baginton near Warwick to await the meeting of the parliament.

While at Pontefract, Henry IV ordered his army to muster for another incursion into Wales after the subjugation of the Percys. Before leading his forces against Glendower, the king was compelled to hasten to Herefordshire to prevent an uprising of the local lords and knights. He reinforced his fortresses in the region and arranged for provisions and arms to be delivered to his soldiers. In mid-September, the king finally led his troops across the border into south-west Wales to renew his war against Glendower.

The English army made its way to Michaelchurch in Herefordshire before advancing into Carmarthen in south-west Wales, solidifying the throne's rule over the area. Henry established his headquarters in the stronghold and set about reinforcing the royal castles in the region. He ordered the fortresses' walls repaired and strengthened, while arranging for the provisioning of the garrisons. Following a brief campaign to ensure his uninterrupted control over the Welsh in the area, the king returned with his forces across the border to England.

As Henry IV was suppressing Hotspur Percy's revolt and intervening in Wales with his army, English pirates in the service of the French crown had been attacking royal shipping. The king responded by encouraging English privateers to seize French vessels to disrupt their trade. The sea war escalated in August 1403 when Plymouth was sacked by pirates. In October that year, a force of French troops landed on the coast of south Wales in support of Glendower's war of independence and began attacking English-held castles, while in November the Count of St Poe attacked the Isle of Wight, presenting further challenges to the King of England.

The English parliament was summoned to meet in London on 14 January 1404, where Henry IV again planned to press his demands for increased tax revenue.

Before the legislative assembly gathered, he met with his council to discuss new taxes. Meeting with his counsellors, he proposed a levy of one shilling on every pound of income, while those without lands were to pay 5 per cent on the value of their personal goods. The parliament opened with a speech by the king's half-brother, Henry Beaufort, who presented the regime's reasons for increasing taxes, stressing the continued threat in Wales, the escalating conflict with France and hostile Scottish activities on the northern border. Despite the list of dangers to the realm, the parliament, led by the Commons, refused, arguing that the crown already had sufficient income to manage its affairs. Following his rebuke, Henry left parliament to modify his strategy. Several days later, he returned to argue for the money needed to protect the kingdom, but the Commons continued to resist his arguments.

During the parliamentary meeting, the revolt of Henry Percy, Earl of Northumberland, was discussed, the representatives declaring him guilty of trespass against the throne but not treason. After Percy formally submitted to the king, he was permitted to retain his earldom but was fined the forfeiture of part of his lands. The sovereign accepted his renewed allegiance and forgave the fine. After settling Percy's rebellion, the national assembly returned to the request for new taxes, and after King Henry agreed to numerous concessions, the Lords and Commons granted the revenue. The parliament finally disbanded on 18 March.

During the session of parliament, a letter arrived from Scotland proclaiming to be from King Richard II. An imposter had assumed the role of the deceased English king and was accepted as such by many lords and commoners in England and Scotland. The Scottish court supported his claim to weaken the kingship of Henry IV. The certainty of his identity remained unresolved and the legality of Henry IV's reign continued to be questioned, despite the crown's counterclaims.

Lacking money, soldiers and supplies, the war against the Welsh continued to go badly for King Henry throughout 1404 and into the following year. On 20 August 1404, Glendower's troops overran the town of Kidwelly, leaving it in ruins. As the Welsh prince continued to capture fortresses, the French landed an expeditionary force at Milford Haven, joining the Welsh rebels and proceeding toward Worcester, taking possession of several castles as Glendower expanded the lands recognizing him as prince. Under Glendower's charismatic leadership, his war of independence gained momentum, Welsh archers and men-at-arms in the English army deserting the throne and joining the rebels. As the size and strength of Glendower's army grew, the great castle at Harlech was occupied by his men when its small garrison surrendered after defiantly holding out. After Aberystwyth Castle also fell to the Welsh, most of north Wales was under the control of Glendower. As Henry IV's lack of money continued to prevent his intervention into Wales, Glendower was formally crowned Prince of Wales during the summer of 1404 in the presence of envoys from France, Castile and Scotland. After the coronation, the French king, Charles VI, negotiated an alliance with Glendower, agreeing never to sign a separate peace with King Henry.

As Glendower pressed his war of independence in Wales, King Henry was forced to remain in his kingdom, lacking the money to field an army. With the

Welsh still a threat to his monarchy, Henry summoned parliament to meet in October at Coventry to discuss sources of new revenue for his regime. Shortly after the legislative assembly opened, the Common members proposed compelling the clergy to relinquish a portion of their secular income for the kingdom, but the prelates convinced them to abandon the proposition in favour of reclaiming the lands, castles and titles previously granted by the crown since the reign of Edward III. Henry IV readily agreed to the proposal. Gaining the support of the throne, the Commons voted to renew the wool tax and passed a 5 per cent levy on incomes over 333 pounds in a gesture aimed at shoring up the finances of the monarchy. Three weeks later, the high churchmen met at Canterbury, agreeing to a large subsidy for the king's war effort in a new era of cooperation between the monarchy, Church and Commons.

When Henry IV usurped the English monarchy in 1399, the two young heirs to the Mortimer family, Edmund and Roger, had possessed a claim to the kingdom that was superior to his, and were thus a threat to his continued reign. After his assumption of the throne, Henry had the Mortimer brothers placed in the care of Lady Constance Despenser and kept under guard at Windsor. In mid-February 1405, Lady Despenser arranged the escape of the Morimers. The widow of Thomas de Despenser, who had been involved in the Epiphany Rising to assassinate King Henry, she intended to make a counterclaim to the English crown by taking the two boys to their uncle, Sir Edmund Mortimer, who was a supporter of Glendower's Welsh revolt. Constance fled with the two brothers, riding from Windsor to Abingdon before proceeding to friends in southern Wales. On 14 February, Henry IV was informed of the brothers' disappearance and quickly ordered his half-brother, John Beaufort, to take a small force of soldiers and hasten after them, while he prepared to join them. Pushing their horses hard, Beaufort's party caught Lady Constance at Cheltenham. Several of her men were killed and the rest fled. She was arrested, and Edmund and Roger Mortimer were taken into custody.

Shortly after his failed attempt to gain control of the Mortimer brothers, their uncle, Edmund Mortimer, formed an agreement with Henry Percy, Earl of Northumberland, and Owen Glendower to overthrow the regime of Henry IV and partition his kingdom between themselves. Under the terms of the Triple Convention, Percy was promised the twelve English counties in the north, while Mortimer would receive all of southern England and the Welsh prince would be given Wales and most of the Midlands. While the rebel alliance prepared for war against the English realm, Henry was informed of the new threat to his kingdom and in March 1405 announced to his council his intention to lead a new military expedition into Wales to defend his lands. He planned a two-pronged attack, sending his son, Prince Henry of Wales, with a force of 3,500 soldiers into north Wales, while he led 500 men-at-arms and 3,000 infantrymen, plus a large contingent of longbowmen, into south Wales. Before launching his campaign, he ordered 2,000 men to reinforce his remaining Welsh strongholds.

The English army was ordered to muster at Worcester in early May and prepare to counter the threat to the regime. On 10 May, the king led his men into Hereford, intending to move into Wales against Glendower. While the English delayed their advance in Hereford, the Welsh, led by the son of Glendower, Gruffydd, attacked the royal castle at Usk. The garrison had recently been augmented with additional troops, and with the arrival of Prince Henry with reinforcements, the enemy was compelled to retreat after a bloody and savage clash. During the fighting, Gruffydd was captured and taken in chains to Henry IV, while Tudor, the brother of Glendower, was killed.

While Henry IV continued his preparations for the Welsh campaign, he received intelligence from his council that Lord Thomas Bardolph, who was a close supporter of the Earl of Northumberland, had suddenly left Westminster and joined Henry Percy in the north. With the two rebels conspiring to renew their rebellion against him, Henry was compelled to cancel his Welsh invasion and move north to counter the growing danger. On 26 May, the king began his journey north with his army of knights, men-at-arms, archers and infantrymen. When he arrived at Derby, news reached him that Lord Bardolph and the earls of Northumberland and Norfolk had raised an army against him. While the king was making his way to Nottingham, rebellion erupted in the northern lordships. In York, Archbishop Richard Scrope led an armed mob of citizens to Shipton Moor, 5 miles north of the city, joining the growing insurgency in protest against Henry's assumption of power. The Earl of Norfolk, Thomas Mowdray, united his armed men with the insurgents, and a total of almost 10,000 men now gathered at Shipton Moor.

As the Yorkish rebels assembled on Shipton Moor, Henry Percy and Thomas Bardolph mustered their forces at Topcliffe, but were quickly defeated and captured by the king's second son, John, and Ralph Nevill, Earl of Westmoreland. After dispersing the rebel forces, Nevill and Prince John advanced against the conspirators led by the Archbishop of York. To avoid an attack against the poorly armed and trained York militiamen, Nevill and the king's son sent a messenger to the archbishop offering to present his grievances to the king. When Scope met with Nevill to further discuss the terms of the agreement, he was arrested and without their leader the northern uprising soon abated. Henry IV had proceeded north to Pontefract Castle, where Scrope and the Earl of Norfolk were brought to him. The monarch took the two prisoners to the archbishop's castle at Bishopthorpe, where on 8 June they were beheaded, despite the pleas of the Archbishop of Canterbury, who warned of a popular uprising in support of Scrope.

After enforcing his rule over the Yorkshire region, Henry IV set out to end the rebellion of Henry Percy. During the journey to Northumberland, he and his entourage were hit by a fierce thunderstorm and forced to take refuge at Green Hammerton. The royal party remained at the manor house, and during the night the king's sleep was interrupted as he cried out: 'Traitors, traitors, you have thrown fire over me.' When his servants reached him, they saw his skin covered in red abscesses. News of his illness spread quickly throughout the kingdom, where it was considered God's revenge for the killing of Archbishop Scrope. Henry was moved to Ripon, where he recovered from the illness within a few days.

Shortly after recovering from his illness, King Henry resumed his journey north to contend with the growing Percy revolt, receiving reports of his supporters capturing three Welsh castles at Haverfordwest, Tenby and Carmarthen. Heartened by this news, the royalists pressed on with their campaign, attacking Percy's stronghold at Warkworth. After the king's cannons blasted large holes in the walls of the Earl of Northumberland's great fortress, the garrison surrendered following a brief resistance. Several days later, Berwick Castle was attacked by the royal forces. Small cannons were fired at the fortification, demolishing a section of the walls before a large artillery piece destroyed a defensive tower, forcing the defenders to submit. After garrisoning the two castles with his troops, Henry IV proceeded down the coastal road to Alnwick Castle. As the royal army appeared before the castle, the Earl of Northumberland's grandson agreed to surrender. During the two months of Henry Percy's rebellion, Henry's aggressive campaign gained possession of all the earl's fortifications and the king was able to impose his rule over the northern rebels.

While the king divided the spoils of war among his allies and supporters and sought additional revenue for his war, in Wales, Owen Glendower strengthened his army with new volunteers and in early April was joined by a French force of men-at-arms and infantry. Glendower then launched a new offensive, attacking and burning English-controlled towns in south-west Wales. He continued his campaign by advancing east toward Worcester, as Henry IV hastened to defend the town. The king gathered his local troops and moved quickly against the Franco-Welsh army, meeting them at Woodbury. After an eight-day stand-off, both armies withdrew, neither willing to risk a pitched battle.

Henry returned to Hereford, establishing his headquarters and sending messengers to his troops ordering them to assemble. On 10 September, he set off to relieve the Welsh siege of Coity Castle in Glamorgan. Reaching the fortress, he drove away the besiegers and reinforced the garrison before returning to England. During the journey, the army was hit by a flash flood, losing part of its large supply train. Henry's fifth incursion into Wales thus ended in similar fashion to all the others, with only minimal success and Glendower remaining defiantly unconquered and a constant threat.

Henry IV spent the remainder of 1405 in England, meeting with his counsellors and administering his government, while searching for new sources of revenue to fund his regime. In December, letters were sent to the Lords and Commons of the parliament announcing the next meeting of the assembly in March. He spent Christmas at Eltham Palace with the queen, his children and friends.

The so-called Long Parliament assembled on 1 March 1406 at Westminster, only ending on 22 December. During its sitting, King Henry was frequently absent due to recurring outbreaks of his skin condition. With the king's prolonged absence, parliament passed new measures to clarify the succession rights of Prince Henry and subjected Henry IV's powers to the review of a council of advisory lords, which had the effect of limiting his independent rule. Without the king present to defend his sovereignty, the legislative assembly acquired new powers over the expenditures of the regime and its royal appointments. Throughout the session, the people's representatives spoke out aggressively against King Henry and his administration.

In early April, parliament adjourned and the king travelled to Eltham for the Easter celebrations. He had continued to struggle with ill-health, and during the spring his condition worsened. He was now unable to ride a horse and was forced to travel by barge or litter. When parliament reopened in late April, King Henry was absent due to his illness. The monarch communicated with the Lords and Commons through letters, but on 22 May appeared in parliament to personally present a bill to be relieved of some of his royal duties. On 7 June, he met with the assembled lords and the people's representatives to witness the formal recognition of his heir, Prince Henry of Wales, as his successor. Henry IV had summoned the parliament to grant increased taxes, but the Commons still defiantly refused, providing only a shilling increase on duties from foreign merchants' goods in a symbolic gesture. Following the contentious session, the assembly was suspended for the remainder of the summer and into autumn.

Parliament was scheduled to return in October, but the opening was delayed by French attacks against Calais, which were dealt with by the crown's council, the king remaining too ill to intervene against the incursions. When parliament finally reopened on 18 November, the bitter dispute between Henry IV and the Commons quickly resumed. Members of the Commons were displeased with the composition of the royal council, which comprised the king's relatives and friends. He was compelled to replace many of his allies with lords approved by the people's representatives. The commoners pressed their attacks against Henry, forcing him to sign the Thirty-One Articles, which severely limited his powers to govern the kingdom. After enforcing their will, the Commons voted a small increase in the taxes for the monarchy.

Weakened by his continuing illness and despondent at his loss of power, Henry IV spent Christmas with the queen and friends at Westminster, and on 30 January gave his great seal to Archbishop Thomas Arundel, who now acted as the virtual head of state. The archbishop was head of the royal council, and together with Prince Henry of Wales ruled the realm in the name of the monarch. King Henry spent most of the first half of the year in the Thames valley, receiving periodic reports from the council, while the archbishop governed the kingdom. He travelled to his castles in the north during the summer months, before returning in October 1407 for the next parliamentary meeting at Gloucester Abbey. The king attended the legislative assembly on the second day but refrained from speaking to the representatives.

As the royal council led by the Archbishop of Canterbury continued to rule the realm, on 14 November the Commons asked for the creation of a committee of lords to discuss state affairs. Arundel quickly appointed six magnates to the new committee and planned a meeting with them. When they met, the archbishop wanted to know what rate of taxation was needed to defend the realm. The lords agreed that half of one tenth equal parts and one fifteenth of fifteen equal parts, in addition to the wool subsidy, were required. Arundel then held a conference with the committee appointed by the Commons to present his conclusions. The representatives were outraged at the large amount of revenue required, but were forced to comply to avoid being held politically responsible for the inadequate defence of England. Through the political manoeuvring of Arundel, Henry IV would finally have the funds needed to protect his kingdom.

While King Henry remained at Gloucester during the parliament, in France, Duke Louis of Orleans was assassinated. He had been the primary exponent of war against the English, and with his death a renewal of the truce talks with France was again possible. Louis had also supported the Welsh revolt of Glendower and had offered to assist the Earl of Northumberland, while he had personally led an army into English-held Gascony to attack its castles and towns. Representatives from Henry's government soon met with the Valois ambassador, and an agreement was signed on 7 December to temporarily end French interference in English affairs.

In the aftermath of his defeat by the loyalists, Henry Percy had fled first to Scotland for protection and later to Wales. Finding little assistance for the rejuvenation of his rebellion in the north, he hastened to the French court seeking a sympathetic supporter. His hopes for support against the English crown were dashed following the renewal of the truce between Henry IV and King Charles VI, forcing Percy and Lord Bardolph to leave France and return to England in January 1408 to raise the flag of revolt. When Henry IV learned of Percy's arrival, orders were sent for the royal army to mobilize. As the king set out to the north, news reached him that Percy's rebels had already been defeated. Sir Thomas Rokeby, High Sheriff of Yorkshire, had mustered his levies and advanced against the insurgents, intercepting them at Bramham Moor on 19 February. After volleys of arrows from his longbowmen decimated the ranks of the rebels, Rokeby sent his men charging into the enemy forces under the flag of St George. In a fierce and bloody melee, the royalists broke through Percy's line, driving his men from the battlefield. Lord Bardolph fled but was soon chased down and killed. Percy was also later slain while leading the rearguard against the pursuing loyalists.

Henry IV was on his way to Nottingham when reports of the victory at Bramham Moor reached him. Despite his illness, he decided to continue north, and he reached Wheel Hall on 26 March. He remained in the town for eleven days overseeing the punishment of the rebel leaders, while rewarding Rokeby and his men for their triumph. The severed head of Henry Percy was later placed on a spike on London Bridge, and other parts of his body were sent to several towns as a warning against future rebellion.

In the wake of the suppression of Percy's rebellion, the king slowly travelled to his castle at Pontefract, where he remained through the Easter period. Henry continued to suffer from his illness, which further weakened his strength. In late April 1408, he set out for London, moving by litter and boat. Upon reaching the city, he met with Archbishop Arundel, and after discussions followed him to his manor house at Mortlake. Arriving at the manor completely worn-out by the journey, Henry IV fell into a coma. During the past two years, his health had grown progressively worse, and he now suffered from a festering of the flesh and rupture of organs. He regained consciousness after several hours, remained at Mortlake for a few weeks recuperating. After making a pilgrimage to Waltham Abbey seeking a divine cure, he spent the remainder of the year at private homes of family and friends, staying away from court. Prince Henry now stayed with his father, expecting his death at any time, ready to assume the monarchy as acknowledged heir and successor.

As Henry IV had been suppressing the revolt of the Percy faction and struggling witht his deteriorating health, his eldest son and heir, Prince Henry, had been pressing his father's war against Owen Glendower in Wales. In 1408, the English army unleashed an attack against Harlech Castle, overwhelming the garrison and recapturing the fortification after a long siege. The prince next moved his forces against the fortress at Aberystwyth, besieging it and forcing the defenders to surrender. Prince Henry resumed his campaign of conquest, relentless pressure compelling Glendower to retreat to the safety of the mountains of Snowdonia, shattering his quest for Welsh independence.

In March 1409, Henry IV's health surprisingly improved a little, enabling him to once again play a role in the governing of his kingdom. He began writing letters to his council, regularly dealing with routine affairs of state. In July, the king was well enough to attend a martial tournament at Smithfield, while during the late summer he made a tour of pilgrimage, visiting several abbeys.

While Henry IV's kingdom was being ruled by the council, relations between Arundel and Prince Henry deteriorated as the king's heir sought to assume greater control of the government. On 11 December 1409, the Archbishop of Canterbury resigned from the council after losing the support of several members, leaving Prince Henry to administer the realm. Under the Prince of Wales, the council's size was reduced to his loyal friends and the meetings were regularly held at his residence. Henry IV remained absent from the committee, staying with the Archbishop of Canterbury, his powers to govern seemingly having been usurped by his eldest son. When parliament met in April 1410, the prince further asserted his authority over his father, gaining the right to approve his decisions. By the time the parliament closed, Prince Henry had greatly strengthened his position as head of the government. The king then withdrew to the north, spending the remainder of the year travelling from castle to castle.

Despite the strong position of Prince Henry, the king refused to surrender all his powers to him, and in March 1411 summoned a great council to meet at Lambeth. The Prince of Wales' small ruling council was present, but was outnumbered by the high magnates and ecclesiastic lords invited by Henry IV. The council had been assembled to discuss the finances of the kingdom, and under the king's leadership the lords and churchmen successfully demonstrated to parliament that its current allotment was inadequate to fund the defences of the realm and royal household expenses. Through this personal intervention of the monarch, the budget was increased at the next parliamentary session.

Henry IV spent the next several months travelling about his kingdom, while the council governed the regime. He had earlier been approached for military support by the Duke of Burgundy, who was seeking English assistance against the repeated attacks of the dukes of Orleans and Berry against his ducal lands. In August 1411, the king decided to back Burgundy in his struggle, ordering his army to muster on 23 September to defend the area around Calais. As the troops prepared for the expedition, King Henry unexpectedly cancelled the campaign and summoned parliament to meet after Prince Henry of Wales attempted to force his father's abdication. Parliament met at Westminster in early November.

After handling routine business, the king summoned the royal council to his throne and thanked them for their service, but made no announcement of their reappointment, effectively relieving them of their committee seats. On the final day of the session, King Henry announced the annulment of the decree limiting his powers to rule. In late December, he formed his new government, appointing Archbishop Arundel as his chancellor. Only two members of his son's committee were reappointed.

While Henry IV was regaining control of the English government, civil war had erupted again in France between the Duke of Burgundy, John, and the Orleans faction led by Bernard VII, Count of Armagnac. The Burgundians were supported by the French monarchy of King Charles VI, and it was in the best interests of King Henry to associate his realm with the party in opposition. While in power, Prince Henry had begun talks with the Burgundians, but the king decided instead on an alliance with the Armagnacs, signing an agreement on 6 April with Bernard VII. Henry IV then announced his intention to lead an expeditionary force to Gascony in support of his new ally. Realizing he was too ill to command the army, the king passed over Prince Henry and named his second son, Thomas, Duke of Clarence, as head of the invasion force, further alienating relations with his eldest son. In frustration, Prince Henry left court on 1 June and headed for Coventry; he remained absent from court until September, when he was reunited with his father and knelt before him pledging his loyalty.

Meanwhile, the Duke of Clarence was preparing for the expedition to France. An army of 1,000 men-at-arms and 3,000 archers was assembled at Southampton to support the Armagnacs. As the English sailed across the Channel, the warring French factions were reconciled and the invaders were now recognized as their mutual enemy. On 16 September, Duke Thomas sent a message to the Armagnacs, refusing to recognize their peace settlement and declaring war. Three days later, he marched into their ducal lands, pillaging the town of Meung and leading his army across the River Loire into the realm of the Duke of Berry, continuing his campaign of destruction. While the English troops plundered the French kingdom, Henry IV was again growing increasingly ill in England. As he remained bed-bound at Merton Priory, the royal council met at Westminster on 20 October, sending him a list of issues for his decision. He replied with letters to his advisors addressing their concerns. On 1 December, parliament assembled to discuss a tax increase to adequately fund the needs of the realm, but Henry was still too weak to attend.

Henry IV spent the Christmas of 1412 at Eltham Palace with Queen Joanna and his friends. Early in the new year, he slowly made his way to London for the opening of parliament, but again was too weak to attend. The king was not able to speak and had frequent periods of unconsciousness. As he lay dying at Westminster Palace, the governing of the regime came to a halt as the lords and prelates waited for the reign of Henry V. On 20 March 1413, King Henry was carried by litter to Westminster Abbey to pray before the shrine of St Edward the Confessor. As he pleaded for remission of his sins, he lost consciousness and was carried by his servants to the nearby Jerusalem Chamber of the abbot. After regaining awareness, the king was told he had been brought to the Jerusalem Chamber. In a weak voice, Henry IV said: 'Praise be to the Father, for it was foretold long ago that I would die in Jerusalem.' The king died later that day while in great pain; he was aged 46 and had reigned for 13 years. His body was embalmed and laid in state at Westminster before burial in Trinity Chapel at Canterbury Cathedral, as per his wishes.

Selected Sources

Ackroyd, Peter, *Foundation – The History of England from its Earliest Beginnings to the Tudors* (Thomas Dunne Books, 2011).

Ault, Warren O., *Europe in the Middle Ages* (D.C. Heath, 1937).

Bevan, Bryan, *Henry IV* (St Martin's Press, 1994).

Cheetham, Anthony, 'Henry IV', in Fraser, Antonia, *The Lives of the Kings and Queens of England* (Alfred A. Knopf, 1975).

Harvey, John. *The Plantagenets* (Franklin Watts, 1948).

Kirby, J.L., *Henry IV of England* (Archon Books, 1971).

Mortimer, Ian, *The Fears of Henry IV – The Life of England's Self-Made King* (Jonathan Cape, 2007).

Roberts, Clayton and Roberts, David, *A History of England – Volume 1* (Prentice Hall, 1991).

Smith, Goldwin, *A History of England* (Charles Scribner's Sons, 1957).

Henry V

In 1413, Prince Henry of Wales was invested with the English throne after the death of his father, King Henry IV, and with justice, nobility and determination governed his realm for the following ten years. With his kingdom free of internal strife, he directed his rule toward the reacquisition of the lost English lands in western France. In August 1415, he crossed the Channel with his army and following the seizure of the port of Harfleur, set out for his enclave at Calais. During the march north, the English forces clashed with the French army at Agincourt on 25 October. Henry V positioned his men carefully to take advantage of the power of his English and Welsh longbowmen, deploying them on a recently ploughed field surrounded on either side by dense forestlands. As the French heavy cavalry and footmen charged, their ranks were shredded by a storm of arrows from King Henry's archers. When the decimated French troops reached the English defensive line, a bloody and savage melee ensued, Henry V leading his men in the hand-to-hand fighting. The Battle of Agincourt ended in less than an hour with the French in full retreat. Under the skilful leadership of Henry, his small army of 7,000 soldiers defeated the French force of over 20,000 men, marking the beginning of his campaign that secured northern France for his crown. In the aftermath of his victories, Henry V negotiated the Treaty of Troyes with the Valois regime of King Charles VI and rode into Paris recognized as regent and successor to the French throne, having reached the summit of his power.

The victor of Agincourt was an unrivalled ruler, whose military exploits secured his standing as one of the great warrior kings of the Medieval ages. Henry was born in mid-September 1386 at Monmouth Castle in Wales, near the border with England, the first child of Henry, Earl of Derby, and his wife, Mary de Bohun. While Henry of Monmouth was born into the noble house of Lancaster, he was not in the direct line of succession to the English crown. The young lord's father held extensive estates and castles in England and Wales, and as the eldest son, Henry was acknowledged as his heir. During his early years, he saw little of Henry of Derby, who was involved in the Appellants Uprising against the Plantagenet regime. He remained in the household of his mother under the care of a nurse and later a guardian. When Mary de Bohun died in 1394, Henry, along with his three brothers and two sisters, was raised at Bytham in Lincolnshire by his maternal grandmother, Joan of Hereford. The young Henry spent part of his childhood visiting the many properties of his father, mainly at Tutbury, Kenilworth and Leicester. Henry's uncle, Henry Beaufort, became his principal tutor, and under his instruction the young lord studied the English, French and Latin languages, literature, religion and court etiquette. Like his father and mother, he was fond of music, learning to play the harp. Renowned masters of arms were appointed for his martial training, and Henry acquired the skills of a knight by practicing fighting with the lance, sword, spear and mace from a charging warhorse. He spent his leisure hours fishing, riding and hunting with falcons. Henry was devoted to the Church of Rome and possessed a deep sense of piety, which grew stronger as he matured. He attended Mass routinely and engaged in regular acts of charity for the poor and sick.

In late 1398, Henry's father was banished from England by the monarchy for his involvement in the plot to depose King Richard II. At the departure of Henry of Derby, his 12-year-old son was summoned to court by King Richard, who treated Henry well and granted him a stipend of 500 pounds. It was likely that the king wanted to keep the young lord close to him to ensure his continued loyalty. While Henry remained with the royal court, in early February 1399 his grandfather, John of Gaunt, died and Henry of Derby inherited his vast estates in England. Soon after John's death, King Richard revoked the earl's rights to his Lancastrian inheritance, after which Henry of Derby began preparations to return to England with an army to overthrow the king.

While Henry of Derby made ready for his English invasion, the recalcitrant Irish had rebelled against Richard II, forcing him to muster his forces and sail to Ireland to reimpose his rule. The young Lord Henry participated in the campaign against the Irish and was knighted by the king for his martial services. While Richard II was enforcing his acceptance by the Irish rebels, he was informed of the Earl of Derby's presence in England, compelling him to forgo his offensive and return to his kingdom to defend his sovereignty. Despite his friendly relationship with Henry, he ordered him imprisoned in Trim Castle, north of Dublin. At the end of July, the monarch crossed the Irish Sea and landed in south Wales, hastening north to confront the rebel earl and leaving Henry under guard in Ireland.

As Richard II moved north, many of his supporters deserted him and joined Henry of Derby's army. Despite the loss of most of his troops, the king continued to make his way to Conway Castle in north Wales, where he was contacted by the father of Lord Henry. Richard II agreed to meet with the earl, but after leaving the security of the castle was seized by soldiers loyal to Henry of Derby. He was taken to London and imprisoned in the Tower. While Richard II remained under guard, the young Henry was brought from Trim Castle to join his father in London. In late September, parliament met in London at Westminster Hall, declaring Henry of Derby as King of England and acknowledging his son as successor to the throne. On 13 October 1399, Lord Henry participated in the coronation of his father, carrying the sword of justice. The following day, the newly crowned king named his eldest son Prince of Wales, Duke of Cornwall and Earl of Chester. Ten days later, the Archbishop of Canterbury officially invested Henry with his titles and lands. During the ceremony, the prince approached the king seated on his throne and was presented the symbols of his investments.

When parliament disbanded in mid-November, Henry IV and his family travelled to the royal castle at Windsor to spend the Christmas season. While the English court stayed at Windsor, the deposed king remained imprisoned at

Pontefract Castle. A faction of Richard's supporters then conspired to restore him to the English throne by capturing Henry IV and his sons. When Henry IV learned of the plot, he organized a force of soldiers, including Prince Henry, and moved against the rebels at Cirencester in defence of his family and crown. As the royalists approached the town, the inhabitants rose-up against the conspirators, ending the revolt to restore Richard II to the throne. The 12-year-old Prince Henry of Wales took part in his father's defence of his throne and was exposed to the dangers and brutality of rebellion, which would affect his later decisions as king.

Shortly after the suppression of the Epiphany Rising, the Scots intensified their pillaging raids into northern England, burning towns and destroying crops. In the summer of 1400, Henry IV responded to the repeated forays by mustering his royal army, and with the young Prince of Wales at his side advanced north to force the Scots back across the border. In Northumberland, he joined forces with the local Percy family to attack the Scots. Led by the king and Prince of Wales, the English attacked along the border but the Scots withdrew, refusing to give battle. The English proceeded deeper into Scotland toward Edinburgh, but were drawn into a barren land and with provisions depleted, were compelled to fall back. Following several fruitless weeks in the north, the royalists returned to London. The expedition to Scotland served as Prince Henry's introduction to leading an army in battle and exposed him to the organization, preparations and command of troops during a military campaign.

During the return journey from Scotland, the king and his son received reports of a new Welsh rebellion against English rule. While the young Henry had been granted the Principality of Wales, the lands under his immediate control were limited to a small region in the west, while the remainder was ruled by numerous English marcher lords. The Welsh uprising was sparked by a dispute over the ownership of properties claimed by the English Lord Grey of Ruthin and Owen Glendower. As their quarrel escalated, Glendower led his Welshmen into Grey's domains, plundering his villages and farmlands. The rebellion quickly spread, the red dragon banner of Welsh unity being raised across Wales against the English occupiers. With his lands in revolt, in September 1400 Henry IV raised an army and with the 13-year-old Prince Henry advanced into north-west Wales, plundering to the Menai Straits. Glendower and his rebels disappeared into the peaks of Snowdonia, refusing to fight the English invaders.

Leaving the Welshmen in the mountains, the king returned to London, while Prince Henry was sent to Chester to keep watch on the rebels and enforce his rule in the principality. Before travelling to his court, Henry IV created an advisory council for his son, naming Harry Hotspur Percy as chief counsellor. The Welsh revolt slowly gained momentum, as students at Oxford and Cambridge, along with many labourers, streamed towards Wales to join Owen Glendower's uprising. Prince Henry stayed in Chester, and under the guidance of Hotspur complained to his father about the lack of men and money to confront Glendower, while his castle garrisons remained undermanned and in danger of seizure by the insurgents. In 1401, Harry Percy resigned his Welsh position in protest at the lack of royal support, and when his replacement soon died, the office was left open, forcing young Prince Henry to struggle against the rebel forces alone. Glendower grew stronger during 1401, attacking English towns and castles and expanding the territory under his control. In January 1402, the Welsh rebels defeated Lord Grey, who three months later was captured during a second battle, while Glendower's forces continued to overrun royalist strongholds and destroy their crops. Despite Glendower's victories, there was no decisive victory in battle for the Welsh, and Prince Henry persistently maintained an English presence in Wales.

As Glendower and his Welshmen remained undefeated, Henry IV mustered an army in August 1402 and marched into Wales with a large force of mounted soldiers, archers and footmen. The expeditionary force was divided into three contingents, with the king, Prince Henry and the Earl of Arundel, John FitzAlan, each leading a division of men. As the English advanced into Wales, Glendower withdrew his soldiers into the mountains, refusing to engage the invaders in a pitched battle. When the royalists' provisions became depleted and the weather turned wet, Henry IV was compelled to abandon the invasion. Prince Henry stayed in Wales, renewing his pillaging raids against Glendower's followers and continuing his education in the art of war.

Glendower had earlier sent envoys to the Scottish regime, seeking its alliance against the English. In late 1402, the Scottish Earl of Douglas, Archibald, launched an invasion into northern England, attacking the earldom of Henry Percy and his son, Harry Hotspur. During the Battle of Homildon Hill, Archibald of Douglas was captured and held for ransom. When Henry IV demanded possession of the Scottish prisoner, Henry Percy refused, claiming the right to ransom Douglas to defray the expenses of his recent campaign. Hotspur Percy then prepared for war against the king, advancing to Chester with his troops to secure reinforcements from the Cheshire archers and Welsh volunteers. While Hotspur was at Chester, the Prince of Wales collected his forces and hastened to Shrewsbury to await the king's arrival for a combined attack against the rebels. Henry IV pressed his soldiers toward his waiting son, reaching Shrewsbury before Hotspur's army.

The opposing armies clashed on 21 July 1403. Percy's forces of over 10,000 men deployed along a hilltop, while the king's host of 12,500 was divided into three divisions, with the 16-year-old Prince Henry leading the left flank. As the rebels waited in their entrenched position, Henry IV ordered his troops in the centre, under the command of Earl Edmund of Stafford, to advance. At the sound of the trumpets, the royalists moved up the gentle slope of the hill into a murderous barrages of arrows from Hotspur's longbowmen. Pushing forward, the depleted forces of the earl made contact with the front line of the rebels. During the ensuing melee, Edmund Stafford was killed, and with his vanguard destroyed the remaining soldiers began to fall back. As his assault faltered, King Henry sent a messenger to his son with instructions for him to move forward. Prince Henry hastened up the left side of the narrow hill with his men and was soon struck by the enemy's storms of arrows. As he encouraged his troops forward, an arrow hit him in the face below the left eye. Despite the painful wound, the prince refused to abandon the battle; he broke off the shaft of the arrow close to the surface of his face and remained in the fray, engaging the rebels in hand-to-hand fighting. While he battled the Percys on the left, the loyalists on the opposite flank, led by the king, were driving the rebels back. With his men fleeing the onslaught in increasing numbers, Hotspur made a desperate charge at Henry IV but was cut down and killed. The surviving rebel troops then fled, securing the victory for the royalists.

In the wake of the victory at Shrewsbury, the wounded Prince Henry was taken to Kenilworth and treated by John Bradmore, a local metalworker and physician. Several royal surgeons had earlier attempted to remove the arrowhead embedded 6 inches deep in his face but had failed, leaving the point in the skull. Before his surgery, the prince's wound was treated with a mixture of honey, flour and barley to fight infection. Using his metalworking skills, Bradmore fashioned an instrument to slowly pull the arrowhead out. Bradmore then poured alcohol into the wound to prevent infection. Following the skilled surgery of Bradmore, Prince Henry slowly recovered, spending most of the following year in Worcestershire and Gloucestershire recuperating, and was not directly involved in the war against Glendower. During this time, he made a pilgrimage to Canterbury and Walsingham to give thanks to God for his recovery.

While Prince Henry was away from the war against Glendower, the Welsh rebels continued to overrun English-occupied towns and castles, expanding their presence into south-west Wales. In 1404, Prince Henry attended parliament, where he was given oversight of the Welsh campaign in a vote of confidence by the representatives. Thomas, Earl of Arundel, was appointed to lead the English offensive in the north of the principality, and Edward, Duke of York, directed the royal troops in the south, under the overall command of the king's eldest son. In July, the prince was in Hereford to keep the Welsh in check, and later in the year he led a relief force to the castle at Coety, beating back the enemy soldiers besieging the garrison. He spent early 1405 in south Wales, guarding against an attack by Glendower's supporters. In March, Henry's forces defeated the rebels at Grosmont, driving them out of the area and securing the king's authority. Later, he led his troops against the Welsh near the castle of Usk, again defeating them, while capturing Glendower's son, Gruffydd, and killing his brother, Tudor. In late April, Prince Henry moved northward, establishing his headquarters at Chester in anticipation of a new offensive by the Welsh. Under the command of Thomas of Arundel, the English had made few gains in the north against Glendower, and the prince – in conjunction with the king – planned a major campaign to regain the initiative. As the royal forces prepared to leave Chester, Henry IV received reports of an uprising in the north, headed by the Earl of Northumberland, Henry Percy, compelling the cancellation of the Welsh expeditionary force.

Glendower had previously sent envoys to the French court of Charles VI, seeking its intervention against the English. In the autumn of 1405, a force of 800 French men-at-arms, 600 crossbowmen and over 1,200 infantrymen landed at Milford Haven in west Wales in support of the Welsh. Glendower united his army with the French, launching an attack into south-west England and pillaging towns and farmlands as far east as Worcestershire. The French troops remained with the Welsh until the spring of 1406 before returning home, dissatisfied with the lack of booty and ransom opportunities, weakening the pressure against

Prince Henry's defence of English rule. In April, the English parliament appointed Henry commander of the Welsh war with the title of Lieutenant of Wales.

Glendower had captured the king's great stronghold at Aberystwyth in south-west Wales in 1404, making it his headquarters. As Prince Henry regained the initiative in Wales, in 1407 he marched his army of 600 men-at-arms and 1,800 archers against the castle. He sent six large cannons by ship to the castle, while smaller artillery pieces were brought overland along with a large stock of gunpowder and supplies in preparation for a long siege. At the approach of the royalists, the commander of the castle's garrison, Rhys the Black, moved his men into the fortifications, preparing for the English attack. Upon reaching Aberystwyth, the prince's troops encircled it to cut off any reinforcements and began bombarding the defensive works with the cannons. Despite the pounding from the guns and sorties against the walls and gates, the Welsh continued to defiantly resist the English. Finally, in September, Rhys agreed to surrender if not relieved by 1 November. As the siege dragged on into October, Glendower led a small relief force with supplies past the English lines, slipping into the fortress. The reinforced Welsh defenders held out through the winter into summer 1408, when Rhys the Black was finally compelled to submit, his provisions having been depleted. The loss of Aberystwyth was a major defeat for the Welsh, and when the fortress at Harlech was also forced to submit the following year, Glendower's fight for the independence of Wales was virtually over. He withdrew to the mountains with a small band of loyal followers, continuing to launch raids against English settlements until 1412, when he fell silent. A belief thereafter spread among the fiercely independent Welsh that Owen Glendower and his soldiers were asleep in a mystic mountain cave, awaiting another time to fight for their freedom. His actual fate remains a mystery.

While Prince Henry was leading the campaign to suppress the Welsh rebellion of Glendower, he became increasingly active in political affairs. In 1406, he was appointed to his father's council, serving as an advisor. As the Welsh war slowly wound down, the Prince of Wales attended the council meetings more frequently, taking a major role in the decisions presented to the king, and by 1409 began to dominate the committee along with the Archbishop of Canterbury, Thomas Arundel. King Henry IV had suffered a severe illness in 1405, which drained his strength and forced him to be routinely absent from council meetings and parliament, allowing the prince to increasingly advance his power and influence in governmental affairs. When fighting the war against the Welsh, he constantly lacked the money to pay his soldiers and purchase supplies. Now serving on the royal council, he was able to personally press parliament for the necessary funds. He became allied with the Archbishop of Canterbury, and together they lobbied their demands before the king and parliament.

The health of Henry IV had grown steadily worse, and by 1409 he seemed near death. During this period, the royal council assumed an increasingly independent role in the decision-making and policies of the royal government. As the recognized successor to the crown, Prince Henry played a major part in the administration of the kingdom. He now moved away from Thomas Arundel and arranged the appointment of his three Beaufort half-brothers – John of Somerset, Henry, Bishop of Winchester, and Thomas, Duke of Exeter – to the ruling council. Prince Henry used his growing influence with parliament to secure the election of Thomas Chaucer, a close relative of the Beaufort family, as speaker of the parliament. Allied with the Beauforts and his supporters in the legislative assembly, Henry possessed the power by 1410 to influence throne policies in the absence of his father. On 21 December 1410, Archbishop Arundel was forced out of the council, and Thomas Beaufort of Exeter was shortly after named chancellor, expanding the rule of Prince Henry. With the support of his allies, the prince held the reins of power for most of the following year.

In October 1411, the king's health partially recovered and he again took part in the ruling of his kingdom. Henry IV was now well enough to attend parliament, and during the November session he removed the Prince of Wales and his supporters from the royal council, naming his own allies and friends as their replacements. The affinity between the king and his eldest son deteriorated further when Prince Henry's brother, Thomas of Clarence, was placed in command of an expeditionary force to France to support the Armagnac faction in its fight against the Burgundians for control of the realm. The prince had earlier recognized the Burgundians as the ruling government in France and had begun negotiations to aid them. The repudiation of Prince Henry's plans increased the dissent between the king and his heir. As the relationship degenerated further, a faction of nobles and ecclesiastic lords loyal to the prince began preparations to force the king to abdicate in favour of his acknowledged successor. Prince Henry started actively raising armed followers in the Midlands and was rumoured to be preparing to march on London to seize the kingdom. The supporters of the king retaliated by levelling charges against his son of misappropriating money from his Calais garrison. To defend his honour, Prince Henry rode to London and met the king in his privy chambers at Westminster in July 1412. Approaching his father, it was said that the prince fell on his knees and said he knew very well that the king would punish anyone within the realm whom he should fear. Taking his dagger, Prince Henry told the king to ease his mind of all suspicions of him and to plunge the dagger into his heart, for his life was not as dear to him that he wished to live one day with his father's displeasure. Henry IV, it was reported, rose from his throne with tears in his eyes, embracing his son and telling him he would not now hold him in mistrust.

During the late autumn of 1412, Henry IV's illness grew worse, and when parliament met in December he was bed-bound and too weak to attend. The king spent Christmas at Eltham Palace in south-east London with his family, suffering frequent bouts of unconsciousness. In March 1413, with the king slowly dying, the Prince of Wales was summoned to his presence. When the heir entered the chamber, he saw the king laying on his bed with his face covered by a white cloth, and believing him dead took his crown from a nearby table. However, King Henry soon awoke and noticed the missing crown, asking his attendants where it was located. They answered that the prince had taken it. Prince Henry was called back to his father's bedside, explaining that he thought the king dead, so as the rightful heir had taken the crown as his inheritance right. When the king, in a feeble voice, replied, 'What right I had to it only God knows', the prince responded, 'If you die king, I will have the laurels and conviction to keep it with the sword against all enemies as you have done.' Shortly after their meeting, King Henry IV died on 20 March and his son succeeded to the throne of England unchallenged as Henry V, inheriting a kingdom free of internal rebellion and respected by the realms of continental Europe.

The day before his assumption of the English throne, Henry V attended Mass in the morning before riding through the streets of London in splendid regalia and spending the night at Westminster Palace in prayer. The coronation ceremony of Henry V was held at Westminster Abbey on 9 April 1413, amid great splendour and symbolism. Similar to his father's investment ritual, during the service the new sovereign-lord was anointed with sacred oil said to have been given to St Thomas Becket by the Virgin Mary. It was widely believed that a king thus crowned would recover the previously lost lands in France, while Normandy would be the first region regained by the English. Taking the reins of power, Henry first moved to establish his new government with his loyal supporters. His father's chancellor, the Archbishop of Canterbury, Thomas Arundel, was replaced by Henry Beaufort, Bishop of Winchester, and many of the king's trusted followers were appointed to high offices in the new administration. At the time of his crowning, the king was described by contemporaries as having a reddish complexion and dark brown hair cut in a circle around his head in a popular military style. He was unusually tall at over 6 feet and possessed a robust health hardened by his years of fighting against the Welsh.

Over ten years after King Richard II was said to have died, there were still factions of Englishmen who believed he had escaped captivity and was living at the Scottish court. To dispel such rumours, Henry V ordered the deposed king's remains removed from the plain grave site at King's Langley and reburied at Westminster Abbey. In a lavish ceremony, Richard II was reinterred in the abbey in an ornate tomb decorated with effigies of him and his first queen. Following the religious service at Westminster, the rumours of Richard II's presence in Scotland slowly died away. To further solidify his monarchy, Henry returned the titles and properties of the magnates confiscated during the reign of his father.

While the king was ensuring the allegiance of the barons, he also gained the support of the Church by following a policy of royal patronage. He undertook the reconstruction of Westminster Abbey and the completion of its nave. Under the sponsorship of his regime, a new monastery for Augustinian nuns and monks was built at Twickenham in south-west London, and the king founded and endowed the House of Jesus of Bethlehem at Sheen Manor for the Bridgettine Order. The monastery at Llanfaes, which had been severely damaged by Henry IV's troops, was restored and bequeathed with royal gifts. A new Carthusian monastery was planned for Bethlehem and arrangements made for the perpetual offering of daily prayers for Henry V and his father. While part of the motivation for his support of the Church was his personal piety, Henry V also undertook the projects to atone for the sins of his father, who had ordered the death of an archbishop and was responsible for the murder of Richard II. He made rich endowments to churches, created new monastic orders and made provisions for the care of the poor.

While his decrees had secured the loyalty of the nobility and support of the ecclesiastic lords, Henry V was compelled to suppress the religious order known as the Lollards. The Lollard faction opposed many of the current practices of the Church of Rome and sought to reform its doctrines. The principals of the Lollards believed the current Church was too involved in secular affairs, considered the pope an anti-Christ, attacked the privileges of the priesthood and proposed more simplistic rituals. In England, the movement was founded by John Wycliffe, who was dismissed from his teaching position at Oxford University for advocating ecclesiastic changes and in 1384 published an English version of the Bible in opposition to the teachings of the Holt See. Under the command of Thomas Arundel, Archbishop of Canterbury, the orthodox churchmen pressed the king for the suppression of the rebel sect, which was led by Sir John Oldcastle, Baron of Cobham. He was a comrade-in-arms of Henry V, having served with him in the military campaigns in Scotland and Wales, but was a passionate follower of the Lollards, placing him in opposition to his king.

Henry V met with Sir John of Cobham and attempted to persuade him to renounce his Lollard doctrine, pointing out the beneficial consequences of such a rejection. Oldcastle refused to answer, withdrawing to his castle at Cooling in Kent and defying the writs of the regime and Church. As Sir John stayed isolated at Cooling, he was excommunicated but remained defiant. When he received a royal writ ordering his arrest, the Lollard supporter submitted and was removed to the Tower. On 23 September 1413, he appeared before an ecclesiastic court, presenting his religious beliefs in generalities. When asked by the judges if he believed in the sacrament of the Mass and that confession to a priest was required for forgiveness, Oldcastle remained silent. Two days later, he appeared before the court and stated that the Church's doctrine was wrong. John Oldcastle was then declared a heretic and sentenced to death by burning. When King Henry was informed of the court's verdict, he sent representatives to the Tower to convince the Lollard to recant, but he again refused, claiming his beliefs were the way to Heaven. While the Baron of Cobham awaited execution, on the night of 19 October his supporters arranged his escape. The English Lollards then rallied to Oldcastle, issuing a call for their followers to rendezvous in London and march against Henry V. Their objectives were to proclaim Oldcastle regent of England, assassinate the king and seize the wealth of the Church.

While the monarch was spending Christmas at Eltham Palace, he was informed by Lollard defectors and his spies that the sect was planning to move against London. He immediately departed for London, ordering the gates closed and preparing to defend the city. Henry V collected an armed force and hastened to St Giles' Fields. The rebels arrived in the city piecemeal, with little organization, and were quickly subdued and imprisoned by the royalists. A commission was appointed to judge the Lollards and carry out out their executions. By the end of January1414, the rebellion had been crushed and the survivors were forced to flee. Sir John Oldcastle evaded arrest until late 1417, when he was captured and later hanged at St Giles' Fields. The Lollard movement in England was now in retreat, with King Henry considered the protector of the Christian faith as practiced by Rome, giving him new influence over the English ecclesiastic lords.

The swift suppression of the Lollards' revolt propelled King Henry V to new heights of power, securing his reign over England. With his monarchy now respected by the barons, churchmen and commons, Henry was free to pursue his hereditary rights to western France through his great-great-grandmother, Isabella of Capet, daughter of King Philip IV. While the English throne was suppressing the Lollard uprising, France was beset with internal strife between the warring Armagnac party of Charles of Orleans and the Burgundians led by Duke John II. In 1414, the Armagnacs gained control of the insane King Charles VI and attempted to govern the realm in his name. Driven out of Paris and the government, John II began preparations for a martial campaign to regain the French crown and plotted to open negotiations with the English for an alliance. The English still retained small enclaves in Gacony in south-west France and Calais, but by the beginning of the fifteenth century had lost Normandy, Anjou and Aquitaine to the Valois throne. Henry V, having been exposed to stories of his ancestors' military exploits on the battlefields of France, was determined to add his name to the roster of heroes by reclaiming western France by force of arms.

King Henry sent envoys to the Burgundians to negotiate a treaty of friendship and quickly came to terms with Duke John II. Under their agreement, Henry pledged to participate in the war against Charles of Orleans, while John II agreed to recognize him at the rightful king of France if the Armagnacs were defeated. After securing the alliance with Duke John, the English sent emissaries to the Armagnacs, making outrageous demands that were sure to be rejected, giving just cause for war. Henry V demanded the lands of the former Angevin Empire, the Duchy of Normandy, the unpaid ransom of King John and his marriage to Charles VI's daughter, Catherine. Despite the Armagnac negotiators attempts to modify the English terms, no settlement was possible and Henry now felt justified in preparing for war against the Valois crown.

During the early months of 1415, Henry V was in southern England occupied with preparations for the French expeditionary force. He sent agents to the Low Countries to hire ships to supplement his navy, while the throne's warlords and knights were ordered to confirm the number of soldiers they could provide for the royal army. The selected captains signed an indenture binding them to service in the king's army for a stated period. The men were responsible for their horses, equipment and arms. Orders were delivered to the mayor of London and county sheriffs to find agents who could deliver all manner of food, clothing, armour and arms to the port of Southampton to augment the supplies brought by the troops. To provide the money for the invasion, parliament and the Church agreed to extra taxation of the kingdom's lands and commerce, and the king also utilized the income from his extensive estates. To supplement his treasury, he borrowed funds secured with pledges of the monarchy's jewels and other assets.

By late July, Henry V's preparations were nearing completion. While the king was distracted by plans for the French invasion, Richard, Earl of Cambridge, began plotting the assassination of Henry and his brothers and the assumption of the crown by Edmund Mortimer, Earl of March, as the rightful English king. Mortimer's claim to the throne was through his descent from King Edward III as his great-great grandson. During the reign of Richard II, Mortimer was heir presumptive. Following the usurpation of the crown by Henry IV in 1399, Edmund was seized and imprisoned at Windsor Castle. In 1413, he was pardoned and his estates returned. Under Earl Richard of Cambridge's plan to gain control over the kingdom, Harry Hotspur's son was to invade northern England with his Scottish allies in support of Mortimer and provoke rebellion, while Sir John Oldcastle and his Lollards would incite an uprising in the West Country and the followers of Owen Glendower would attack from Wales. When Mortimer was informed of the conspiracy, he betrayed the plot to King Henry at Porchester Castle. The king ordered the arrest of the leaders of the conspiracy; they were quickly declared guilty by the assembled jury, with the sentence of death by beheading. The Earl of March was cleared of any involvement in the Southampton Plot and later served the king during the campaigns in France, fighting alongside Henry during the siege at Harfleur and the battles in Normandy.

Henry V formally declared war on the Valois crown on 6 July 1415, claiming it was the fault of Charles VI for not rendering justice to the appeal for his inherited French lands. By early August, an army of over 10,000 men had assembled at Southampton, ready to invade France. The fighting force comprised 2,000 men-at-arms, with 8,000 archers and footmen recruited from all parts of England and Wales. The English knights were clad in protective armour of overlapping plate and were armed with swords and long daggers, while the bowmen were armed with their powerful 6-foot Welsh bows, along with swords, axes and clubs for hand-to-hand fighting. The army included a large array of specialist troops, including miners, gunners, engineers and surgeons. A large contingent of Henry's soldiers was from Wales, who served in the royal army as opportunists looking for plunder.

During the afternoon of Sunday, 11 August, the English fleet set sail, with the king on board the *Trinity Royal*, bound for France. The royal fleet crossed the Channel, reaching the French shoreline on 13 August and anchoring at Chef de Caux, 3 miles from Harfleur. During the next three days, the men, horses, equipment and supplies were unloaded and an encampment established close to the French-occupied port. The English then moved against Harfleur, and by 19 August had surrounded the town, which was protected by a formidable 2½-mile moated wall, twenty-six towers and a determined garrison. Despite the ominous defensive works, Henry V was determined to seize Harfleur as his first French conquest in the quest for his inheritance, ordering his men to besiege the town.

The king ordered his sappers to tunnel under the defensive works and mine the walls. In response, the French dug counter-tunnels, attacking the miners and forcing them to abandon their digging. After the failure of the miners to force a way into the town, King Henry brought up his siege cannons and began bombarding the walls day and night. The monarch personally supervised the bombardment, spending many hours with the front-line troops. Large holes were blown in the defences, but the French quickly made repairs.

While the siege dragged on in the hot summer weather, dysentery broke out in the English camps, induced by soured wine, unsanitary encampment conditions and contaminated foods. Thousands suffered the dreadful effects of the illness, with more than 2,000 dying, while many others were forced to return to England. Among the sick were Edmund Mortimer, Earl of March, and Thomas, Duke of

Clarence. However, King Henry refused to abort the siege, in spite of the heavy losses in manpower.

Henry V then concentrated his attack against the defensive works to the south-west, continuing to unleash a relentless bombardment against the bastions, while the miners dug tunnels under the walls and set fire to the wooden underpinnings that supported the defensive structures. By mid-September, the defences along the south-western walls were in ruins, compelling the defenders to abandon them to the English. The besiegers intensified their assaults, bringing siege towers and scaling ladders forward for a sortie. Inside the town, food supplies were now nearly exhausted and dysentery erupted, seriously weakening the French ability to protect Harfleur. As Henry prepared for an attack against the weakened defences, the garrison commander, Jean II d' Estouteville, sent envoys to discuss submission terms on 18 September. Jean was Lord of Estouteville and Governor of Harfleur, and later lost his family's lands in Normandy during Henry's conquest of the region. An agreement was soon reached, with the defenders pledging to abandon the town if no relief army arrived by 22 September. When no reinforcements appeared, d' Estouteville knelt before the king and surrendered Harfleur to him, with the cross of St George being raised over the gates. The following day, Henry entered the town and went to the half-destroyed Church of St Martin, offering thanksgiving to God for his victory. He considered Harfleur his birthright and set out to turn it into another Calais enclave. The captured French knights were held for ransom, while the soldiers and most of the inhabitants were expelled from the town. To make Harfleur an English town, the royal regime offered merchants and artisans houses and money to resettle there. The victory at Harfleur was costly to Henry V, with over a third of his army either dead or disabled through the fighting or disease. The king had planned a march on Paris, but due to the heavy cost of his victory and the approaching winter, the troops were ordered instead to advance to the security of Calais.

After repairing the damaged fortifications and garrisoning Harfleur with a strong force of soldiers commanded by his uncle, Thomas Beaufort of Exeter, Henry V set out for Calais on 6 October with approximately 1,000 men-at-arms and over 5,000 foot-soldiers and bowmen. The army was formed into three divisions, with scouts positioned on the flanks. The king was anxious to reach Calais quickly, and travelled without artillery or supply train. He intended to advance north to the River Somme, crossing at Blanche-Taque and then heading straight to Calais. As the men proceeded, they ravaged the towns and farmlands, leaving a path of destruction. When they reached Blanche-Taque, the ford was blocked by over 6,000 Valois troops, forcing Henry's men to resume their march to the east in search of an unguarded passageway over the river. Finally, on 19 October, two unprotected fords were found. The causeways had been partially destroyed by the French, but Henry's engineers managed to repair them, allowing the army to cross to the northern side of the Somme.

As the English army pushed on toward Calais, three French heralds arrived from the commander of the enemy forces, Charles d'Albret, Constable of France, with a message for Henry V. Kneeling before the king, they told him:

'Many of our lords are assembled to defend their rights and they inform you through us that before you come to Calais, they will meet you to fight with you and be revenged of your conduct.' Henry replied that he was headed for Calais, and that if their enemies attempted to stop them, it would be at their peril. The messengers were sent back to the French army as the English prepared for the attack by d'Albret's forces.

When the French forces failed to attack in the morning, the English resumed their advance, expecting battle at any time. For three days, they moved north without sighting the enemy. Finally, on 24 October, the English encountered the French blocking their march near the village of Agincourt. Surveying the well-positioned Valois host, Henry V sent envoys to the constable, offering to pay for the damages of his army and abandon Harfleur in exchange for safe passage to Calais. The French, sensing a quick and easy victory, refused the offer and prepared to attack their enemy in the morning.

The English spent a fearful night in their camps under a heavy pouring rain, confessing their sins to the priests, while the French passed the time drinking abundant wine and gambling for the rich lords they expected to capture for ransom. During the night, King Henry made his way through the encampments, giving words of encouragement to his troops. He rose before dawn on 25 October, the Feast of St Crispin's Day, hearing Mass and taking communion. He dressed for battle wearing full armour with a surcoat embroidered with the three leopards of England and three golden fleur-de-lis of France. He arrayed his force of 1,000 knights and over 6,000 infantrymen and archers across the road to Calais in three divisions, with the dismounted men-at-arms in the centre flanked by archers in the woods, aligned in a wedge formation. Every bowman carried a 6-foot stake sharpened at each end, which was planted into the soil to provide a defensive barrier against the charging French cavalry. The centre of the formation was led by the king, while the Duke of York, Edward of Norwich, commanded the right wing and Lord Thomas Camoys was positioned on the left. The French host outnumbered the English with approximately 12,000 men and were expecting reinforcements during the day.

In the early morning, the French troops were formed into three battle lines in a muddy cornfield, with forestland on both flanks. They were aligned with the dismounted men-at-arms in the centre, carrying their swords and short lances, while two divisions of heavy cavalry occupied the flanks. D'Albret's plan was to send his dismounted knights forward while the cavalry attacked the enemy's archers on the wings. Constable d'Albret took his place in the front row with his soldiers, leading them into battle.

Before the fighting erupted, the English soldiers knelt and kissed the ground as a sign they might return to the earth before the fighting was over. The two armies faced-off against each other for three hours, exchanging taunts and insults to provoke an attack, before Henry V sent his archers forward and gave the command to the infantry: 'Banners advance, in the name of Jesus, Mary and St George.' As the pipes and drums sounded, the English moved forward, their battle cries of 'St George' echoing across the muddy fields. When the Englishmen came into longbow range of the French, at some 300 yards, King Henry gave the order to halt. Parties of bowmen and knights then rushed through the trees to attack the French flanks, while the archers began firing volley after volley of arrows at their opponents. As the arrows decimated their front, the French foot-soldiers began to advance forward, their cavalry charging the English flanks. The English longbowmen fired their arrows into the cavalry formation, breaking their charge and driving them into the front of the first French line of infantry, creating a mass of confusion on the narrow battlefield. In the centre, the dismounted heavily armoured French men-at-arms struggled forward through the deep mud under the deadly barrages of English arrows.

When Henry's bowmen exhausted their supply of arrows, they rushed forward against their adversary with billhooks, swords, axes and hatchets in a bloody and fierce melee. During the savage onslaught, the king fought alongside his men-at-arms, engaging the French in hand-to-hand fighting and receiving several sword blows to his helmet. When his brother, Prince Humphrey of Gloucester, was severely wounded, Henry V stood over him, fighting off the enemy footmen until the wounded prince was carried to the rear.

As the English slowly pushed forward, overrunning d'Albret's troops, the third French formation – led by the Duke of Brabant – prepared to charge. During the fighting, King Henry's men had so far captured over 3,000 enemy soldiers, sending them to the rear under guards. With the Duke of Brabant now threatening to attack, and fearing the prisoners might break free to rejoin the battle, Henry ordered them killed, threatening to hang anyone who refused to obey his command. More than 200 archers from his personal guard were sent to the rear to slaughter the captives, killing them with their daggers, axes and swords. The only prisoners spared were high-ranking noblemen, who could be held for ransom. The butchery continued until Henry ordered his bowmen to stop after realizing the third division of the enemy army was not going to charge, but was instead fleeing with the rest of the French survivors.

Henry only lost a small number of soldiers killed in the battle, the commander of his right flank, Edward of Norwich, Second Duke of York, and the Earl of Suffolk being the highest-ranking noblemen to die. The French losses were enormous, numbering over 8,000. Among those who fell were the army's commander, Charles d'Albret, the dukes of Brabant and Bar and over 1,500 knights. Henry had dealt the French army of King Charles VI a disastrous defeat, winning one of the greatest battles of medieval European history.

With the defeat of the French at Agincourt, King Henry's path to Calais was now clear, and after spending the remainder of the day stripping the dead of their valuables and burying them in large pits, the English set out to the north the following morning. Henry V reached Calais three days later with his troops and prisoners. He was anxious to renew the war against the French kingdom, but with his army depleted from the recent battle and many suffering from wounds and dysentery, he had little option but to return home. The troops remained at Calais until mid-November while passage to England was arranged.

Shortly after reaching Calais, the king sent a letter to his chancellor, Bishop Henry Beaufort, announcing his great triumph against the French. Bishop Beaufort read the letter to the gathered crowd in front of St Paul's Cathedral, and under orders from London's mayor, the bells of the city's churches rang out until sunset. The news of the French defeat spread quickly throughout England, to the loud acclaim of the people.

The English fleet landed at Dover on 16 November, the victorious soldiers being greeted by large cheering crowds. King Henry soon left his men, making his way to Canterbury Cathedral and offering prayers of thanksgiving to God for his victory at the shrine of St Thomas Becket. He remained at Canterbury for two days before travelling to London for the great festivities planned by the mayor. As the king approached Blackheath, he was greeted by the mayor and his aldermen, who escorted him into London to attend the gala celebrations. The city welcomed their sovereign-lord with an array of grand decorations celebrating his victory at Agincourt. Built on the top of London Bridge was a great effigy of two goliaths offering the keys of the city to the king. Situated in the middle of the bridge were two large pillars displaying the royal arms, while a choir dressed as angels sang songs of greeting from a nearby house. Proceeding onward toward St Paul's, Henry was greeted by a chorus of young girls with tambourines, singing songs of congratulation, hailing him as 'Henry V King of England and France'.

Continuing through the streets of the capital from London Bridge, the king saw images of a lion and antelope displaying the royal standards, while at the entrance to Cheapside were figures of twelve English kings and saints, along with the twelve apostles,. The streets were lined with wildly cheering spectators, eager to see the monarch with his French captives. At St Paul's Cathedral, the prelates greeted him with congratulations. Henry slowly proceeded through the church to the high altar, giving thanks to God for his triumph. After leaving the cathedral, he rode his horse to Westminster Abbey, leaving an offering before the shrine of Edward the Confessor. The king spent the night at Westminster Palace, and the following day attended a funeral service at St Paul's for both the English and French soldiers killed at Agincourt.

Despite the great triumph at Agincourt, Henry V's first military campaign against the French had added only Harfleur to his realm. To further his quest for the monarchy of France, he issued instructions for the muster of a new army to launch a second invasion against the Valois regime. While preparations for the expedition proceeded, he renewed his political campaign to ensure the conflict between the factions of Burgundians and Armagnacs continued its disruption of the French kingdom's administration. Meanwhile, Henry dispatched his envoys to the court of Emperor Sigismund, negotiating an alliance with the Holy Roman Empire against the King of France to further weaken his autonomy.

While Henry V pressed his claims to the French kingdom, sending envoys to European rulers seeking their support for his quest for the crown, in early 1416 the leader of the Armagnac party, Duke Bernard VII, besieged the English at their newly won port of Harfleur with his army and naval forces. The siege dragged-on for several months, threatening to starve the garrison into submission. In August, Henry V appointed his brother, John of Bedford, to launch a relief attack against the enemy. A fleet of English ships, led by Duke John on board the *Holy Ghost*, gathered in Southampton and other ports on the south coast and put to sea for Harfleur. On 16 August, the flotilla clashed with the French navy and their Genoese allies. As the warships manoeuvred closer together, the battle began with an exchange of arrows, crossbow bolts and stone missiles. The English captains moved nearer the French flotilla and began sending boarding parties onto the decks of the Armagnac and Genoese vessels, striking down many enemy sailors. The battle lasted for over six hours in the shallow waters off the Seine estuary. The English utilized their sailing experience and skills as seamen to outmanoeuvre and disperse the French fleet, while capturing four large vessels known as carracks. After the surviving enemy ships fled the battle, half of the English fleet landed at Harfleur, breaking the siege and bringing relief supplies to the garrison, while the other half returned home with Bedford, who had been severely wounded during the fighting. After Henry V learned of the great naval victory, he hurried to Canterbury Cathedral, ordering a Te Deum to be sung in thanksgiving.

After reaching his earlier agreement with Emperor Sigismund for his support against the regime of Charles VI, the English king and Habsburg emperor met with the leader of the Burgundian faction, Duke John II, at Calais to discuss a grand alliance. The Holy Roman Emperor played only a ceremonial role in the negotiations, as Henry and Duke John hammered out an understanding. Under their secret treaty, the Burgundian duke pledged to offer homage to Henry V if his English army conquered and occupied a large region of France. The arrangement with the duke ensured no separate peace treaty would be negotiated between the Burgundians and the court of Charles VI.

Meanwhile, the siege against Harfleur had demonstrated to King Henry that the French navy was a formidable obstacle to his conquest of the Valois monarchy, so he began building a larger fleet to protect his sea lanes across the Channel. By the summer of 1417, he had a fleet with eight large carracks with two masts and square sails, six smaller cogs and nine ballingers for use in shallow waters. Henry had also constructed three great carracks with three masts each: the *Jesus*, *Holy Ghost* and *Royal Trinity*. He continued his ship construction programme and eventually had a fleet of over thirty warships. This powerful flotilla patrolled the Channel protecting commercial trade with the European mainland, and was also available for use in the king's campaign against France. Henry V had become the first English monarch to create a royal fleet since the reign of Alfred in the ninth century.

King Henry needed a large treasury to pay for a second French invasion force, and aggressively sought new funds from parliament, Church and the commons. He borrowed money from Bishop Henry Beaufort, secured by a royal crown, while a jewelled collar was pledged for a loan from the city of London and smaller sums were obtained from the noblemen, high churchmen and cities of the realm. While the collection of money continued, the king began purchasing war supplies, sending them to large depots. The Duke of Bedford, John, was again appointed regent during Henry V's absence, being empowered to govern the kingdom and enforce the crown's laws. Recruitment for the royal army was now well underway, with the goal of fielding a force of over 10,000 soldiers. Royal messengers were sent to the shires with orders for those recruited by the throne's agents to be ready for the muster, outfitted with their armour, weapons, clothing and food, while a call for the warships to assemble at Southampton was also issued. As the date for departure neared, a force of Genoese ships began patrolling the region around Harfleur, and to keep the sea lanes open to his invasion fleet, Henry sent a detachment of warships to assault and drive away the Genoese vessels. The English naval force crossed the Channel and engaged the enemy ships on 29 June 1417, overwhelming them and capturing four large carracks for use in King Henry's navy.

With the Channel now safely under English control, a fleet of over 1,500 ships assembled, and during the final days of July some 12,000 soldiers and their supplies were loaded and set sail. Henry V was on board the newly constructed *Jesus*, which was distinguishable by its large purple mainsail. The crossing to France was made without incident, and on 1 August the English landed near Touques on the coast of Normandy. After securing his beachhead and driving off a small force of French cavalry, the king ordered two contingents of troops to capture the nearby fortifications at Bonneville and Auvillers, which surrendered without resistance. To begin his renewed quest for the French throne, Henry planned to first seize the Norman region south of the River Seine, moving initially against the city of Caen.

By 18 August, the English had reached Caen and laid siege to it, encircling the city. King Henry established his headquarters in a monastery and began bombarding the defensive works with his cannons. The guns fired large stones day and night, battering the fortifications and causing sections of the walls to crash down. From their ramparts, the French fired back with their smaller cannons, but this had little effect on the besiegers. While the bombardment continued, English miners dug tunnels under the walls, but were frequently driven off by French counter-miners. After breaches were made in the defences, the French troops and citizens used broken stones and timbers to reseal the gaps, meaning the siege wore on. When the Earl of March arrived with reinforcements in early September, Henry ordered an assault against the city. The Englishmen moved forward toward the walls, but were beaten back by waves of deadly bolts from crossbowmen and burning oil thrown from the ramparts. Following the failure of his first attack, the king sent forward a second and third wave. The English men-at-arms finally broke into the city through the hastily repaired walls, engaging the defenders in savage hand-to-hand fighting. While the English pressed forward, the king's brother, Thomas of Clarence, led an attack against the opposite side of the city. The duke's men battled their way to the centre of the city, where they were joined by the king and his troops. The reunited English army then charged into a surviving group of the French garrison, overwhelming them and forcing their surrender.

After gaining control of Caen, Henry V ordered the city's men, women and children to be collected and taken to the marketplace, where over 2,000 of them were brutally killed. After the slaughter was eventually halted by the king, the English troops were allowed to ravage the city, looting and raping without restraint. A force of French troops still remained in the old section of the city and in the citadel, but were soon forced to submit. Caen was now in the hands of the English crown. The capture of the city gave King Henry a secure base from which to conquer Lower

Normandy, the English brutality against the Normans having broken their resolve to resist the invaders.

While the English troops were besieging the French at Caen, the Earl of March, Edmund Mortimer, was sent to plunder the Cotentin area, with the Earl of Huntingdon capturing the towns of Creully and Villers-Bocage and the king's youngest brother, Prince Humphrey of Gloucester, occupying Bayeux. With the surrender of Caen, Henry advanced his army south, taking the formidable fortifications at Argentan and Alencon without a fight. Lower Normandy was now cut in two, with Brittany isolated. On 16 November, the monarch negotiated a truce with the Duke of Brittany ensuring the safety of his right flank and allowing Henry to proceed against the great fortress at Falaise in eastern Normandy.

In late November, Henry V led his army north-west to seize Falaise, which was considered impregnable. Falaise was defended by formidable walls and towers, while the citadel was located on a lofty hilltop. The city was duly surrounded and siege operations began on 1 December. To survive the cold winter weather, the English established their encampment nearby, building huts out of timber and turf and surrounding it with trenches and stockades to guard against sorties by the enemy. The artillery pieces were brought forward and guns bombarded the defensive works with large stone missiles night and day, destroying fortifications, houses and churches. The weather soon turned bitterly cold, the English soldiers struggling to maintain the siege lines. The king spent Christmas at Falaise with his men in their shabby camp. The cannons kept up their relentless fire on the town and finally, on 2 January 1418, the guns created a large breach in the defences, forcing the town's submission.

The French citadel was situated on a large cliff above the town and the garrison was under the command of celebrated soldier Olivier de Mauny, the standard bearer for King Charles VI. While the town had surrendered, the garrison in the fortress refused to submit. The citadel's elevation meant it was out of the range of the English cannons, forcing Henry V to construct sheltered approaches to the walls to allow his engineers to begin digging through the foundations and weaken their support of the walls. After several weeks of excavating, de Mauny realized the hopelessness of his situation and surrendered in mid-February. The fall of Falaise was a shattering blow to the Normans' resolve to resist the English, causing other castles and towns to submit to King Henry's troops, offering little resistance. By the spring, Henry had achieved his first objective, the conquest of Lower Normandy. The newly occupied territory was governed by four crown officials and the towns occupied with royal troops. Caen was named capital of Lower Normandy.

On 1 June, Henry V marched out of Caen with his army in an attempt to seize Upper Normandy and its principal city of Rouen. Following a week's march, he reached the fortified town of Louviers, which was defended by three large walls and great towers. When the garrison refused to surrender, the English began siege operations, battering the defensive works with artillery pieces and siege engines and breaking through the first line of walls. The troops continued their attack, and after two weeks of bombardment the town's defenders surrendered. During the siege, the king was nearly killed by an enemy stone missile. After the submission of Louviers, the French gunners responsible for firing at Henry V were seized and hanged on his orders.

Meanwhile, in May, the Armagnac faction had lost control of Paris to Duke John II of Burgundy, who quickly abandoned his agreement with the English, moving to protect France from Henry V's invasion. The duke strengthened his position by forming an alliance with Queen Isabella, who proclaimed herself regent for the insane French king. Duke John sent troops west to reinforce the Burgundian forces guarding the eastern bank of the Seine. King Henry planned to cross the river at Pont-de-l'Arche on his march to Rouen, but his way was now blocked. Other sections of the river were impassable, forcing the English to build pontoon bridges to make the crossings above and below the town. The separate wings of the English army then converged on the town of Pont-de-l'Arche, forcing its surrender on 20 July.

The road to Rouen was now clear, the English advancing on the city unmolested during the hot summer days. Henry V's men laid siege to the city, and by the end of July it was completely invested. The defences of Rouen were formidable, with 5 miles of strong walls, numerous towers and a large garrison of veteran troops. The French cannons were well positioned on the walls, keeping the English forces at bay. With Rouen's strong defensive works, it was impossible to take the city by storm, compelling Henry to try to starve the citizens and soldiers into submission.

While the siege dragged on, with the French showing no signs of succumbing, Henry sent troops to seize the remaining castles along the lower Seine and ensured he had sufficient food and supplies for his campaign. He remained at the front with his men, pressing the fight against the enemy, while directing counterattacks against the French forays from the city. The English cannons continually blasted Rouen's fortifications but could not force a breach. The French troops made repeated sorties, keeping the English away from the walls, while hoping for relief from the Duke of Burgundy. After four months of siege, Rouen's provisions were nearly exhausted and in early December the desperate municipal leaders ordered all old and sick men, women and children out of the city. When they first appeared beyond the walls, the English gave them food, but King Henry commanded his troops to turn the refugees away and they were forced to remain stranded between the English lines and the walls of Rouen, with thousands dying from exposure and starvation during the winter months.

With their provisions now exhausted and no relief army coming, the city officials of Rouen began negotiations for their submission. An agreement was reached on 13 January 1419, which levied a fine of 300,000 crowns on the city to be paid in yearly instalments of 80,000 crowns per year. The townspeople who pledged fealty to the English throne were allowed to stay in Rouen with their property, while those remaining loyal to the Burgundians were compelled to leave. Unlike at Caen, there was no ravaging of the city by the victorious English soldiers, and Henry took measures to end the starvation of Rouen's populace. He entered the desolate city on 20 January to attend a Mass of thanksgiving in the severely damaged cathedral.

Following the surrender of Rouen, Henry V remained there in his new Norman capital for the next two months, establishing his local government. The king appointed administrative representatives to govern the newly won territory, while he completed the subjugation of Normandy by leading his troops in the capture of the remaining isolated castles. By the summer, he could claim Normandy as part of his expanding realm and was able to implement the next stage of his quest for the capture of Paris.

During the six-month siege of Rouen, King Henry was holding peace talks with the Armagnacs, now known as the Dauphinists after the death of Duke Bernard VII. Led by the Earl of Salisbury, Thomas Montague, English envoys met with the French at Alencon to present their list of terms. Under orders from the king, the earl demanded the occupation of Maine, Touraine and Anjou, in addition to the already occupied lands of Normandy and Aquitaine. Montague also proposed the marriage of his king to the daughter of Charles VI, Catherine, to ensure peace, with the newly united Anglo-French joining together to defeat the Burgundians and place the dauphin, Charles, on the Valois throne in Paris. The negotiations continued for two weeks but ended without an agreement.

While the English embassy was holding talks with the Dauphinists, separate negotiations were begun with the Burgundians. The talks soon ended when Duke John II demanded 1,000,000 crowns as the dowry for Henry's marriage to Catherine, along with Normandy, Aquitaine and the remainder of western France. After the duke's excessive terms were rejected, the English representatives renewed their discussions with the Dauphinists, but were unable to reach a compromise. As the French political parties were holding talks with the English, they continued to unleash attacks against each other, while Henry steadily closed in on Paris

Despite the failure of his negotiations with the French, Henry renewed the talks with the Burgundians and Dauphinists. In early May 1419, the English secured an agreement with the Burgundians for a conference between King Henry and Duke John at Meulan. The meeting took place on 29 May, with talks lasting into June. Henry was willing to reduce his demands, now seeking sovereignty only over the lands already conquered and the remaining fiefdoms of the Angevin Empire of his great-grandfather. When the warrior-king agreed to give up his claim to the French throne, an understanding seemed possible. As the negotiations continued, the issue of the size of the dowry could not be resolved and the conference ended in a stalemate. During the negotiations at Meulan, John II of Burgundy was also holding secret talks with the French dauphin, Charles. On 11 July, Charles and the Duke of Burgundy signed a treaty pledging to unite against the English. Despite their promise to attack the invaders, Henry continued his campaign of conquest, the two French factions failing to coordinate their resistance and losing additional territory and towns to English attacks.

Soon after the failure of the talks at Meulan, Henry V renewed his campaign of conquest, sending his men to seize the castle at Pontoise. The English forces attacked in two divisions at dawn, taking the garrison by surprise and forcing their surrender. The capture of Pontoise gave King Henry an avenue of attack against Paris from the north. The king continued his campaign by sending the Duke of Clarence with a large force to raid close to the defences of the French capital. As the English moved nearer to Paris and securing control over France, the

Burgundians and Dauphinists agreed to meet on the bridge at Montereau, at the junction of the Yonne and Seine rivers, on 10 September to settle their differences and unite against the invaders. Dauphin Charles and Duke John II approached the centre of the bridge from opposite ends, each with their ten advisors armed with swords at their sides. Soon after the conference began, an unknown member of the dauphin's entourage drew his weapon and killed the duke. The duke's son, Philip III, was then recognized as leader of the Burgundians and issued a call for the French king, citizens of Paris and monarchy of England to unite and take revenge on the Dauphinists.

Following the murder of Duke John II, Henry V continued his campaign of conquest, adding the fortresses at Gisors, Meulan and the great stronghold at Gaillard to his realm, while monitoring the responses to the duke's death by the dauphin and Duke Philip III. Henry stayed in Rouen for the next three months, making arrangements for the civil administration of his new French territories. He appointed officials to govern his recent conquests and revived the local economy by bringing stability to the region, encouraging merchants from Paris and Flanders to return to Normandy, while also urging Englishmen to settle in the newly occupied French lands.

As Henry was in Normandy establishing his rule, the Dauphinists and Burgundians remained at odds, with Philip III renewing the civil war against the dauphin and resuming peace talks with the English. While Duke Philip and the Dauphinists resumed their struggle for dominance, Isabella and the Paris parliament acted independently, sending envoys to Henry V seeking terms for an alliance against the dauphin. The king received the delegation and presented his conditions for uniting with the French royalists, demanding his marriage to Princess Catherine and the French throne for himself after the death of King Charles VI, while pledging to aid the Burgundians in their revenge for Duke John's murder. In the interim, Henry was to reign over France as regent. Impatient to avenge the duke's death, the terms were quickly accepted by the French and a truce was arranged on 24 December.

During the spring of 1420, the combined English and Burgundian army carried the war to the dauphin, taking the towns of Roye and Compiegne, while negotiations for the formal treaty were finalized. By early April, the terms of the agreement were completed; Catherine's dowry was set at 40,000 crowns per year, and at the death of the French king, the crown would pass to Henry V and his heirs. The Burgundians further approved the appointment of King Henry as regent for the disabled Charles VI and his naming of French counsellors for his government, while the dauphin was disinherited. It was decided that King Henry would meet the Duke of Burgundy and the French king and queen at Troyes in mid-May to sign the accord. During the journey to Troyes, Henry passed through Paris, pausing long enough to visit St Denis to offer prayers to God for his success. He reached Troyes on 20 May and was presented to the French king, queen and Catherine. The following day, the Treaty of Troyes was signed in the cathedral, in accordance with the discussed terms. News of the treaty was carried to Paris and was affirmed by the parliament and city officials, while on 14 June the citizens of London celebrated the agreement with a solemn service at St Paul's. Twelve days after the signing of the peace treaty, Henry V was married to Catherine by the Archbishop of Sens in the church of St Jean. Catherine of Valois was born in Paris on 27 October 1401, the youngest daughter of Charles VI and Queen Isabella of Bavaria. She spent her early childhood in the royal household with nurses provided by the queen, and was later sent to be educated by nuns at the convent in Poissy. Catherine was described as a queen with great charm, intelligence and culture, and it was reported that when Henry first met her, he was struck by her beauty and elegance.

In the aftermath of the signing of the Treaty of Troyes and marriage ceremony, the allies left Troyes for Paris. As the 20,000-strong Anglo-Burgundian army headed west, Henry V ordered his troops to seize the remaining Dauphinist fortified towns surrounding the capital. The allied army first marched against Sens, forcing the garrison to surrender after a week-long siege. The forces of the king and Philip III then resumed their advance by moving against Montereau, where the duke's father had been murdered the prvious year. The defenders defiantly refused to submit and the Burgundians, driven by revenge, stormed and occupied the town on 24 June. While the dauphin's soldiers in the Montereau citadel continued to resist, Duke Philip III disinterred his father's body and placed it in a casket for reburial in the family crypt at Dijon. The garrison troops in the heavily fortified castle held out until 1 July, when the Dauphinists surrendered on terms which allowed them to peacefully abandon the town.

The Anglo-Burgundian army resumed its march down the Seine toward Paris. In mid-July, the allies reached the formidable fortress at Melun. The garrison of over 600 men led by Arnaud Guillaume refused to submit, and on 13 July Henry ordered the English and Burgundian forces to commence siege operations. During the investment, the allied troops were reinforced by 800 men-at-arms and 2,000 archers from England and a force of 700 German mercenaries. The French king, queen and Catherine had accompanied the army on the journey to Paris, and during the siege of Melun were housed nearby, where King Henry visited them frequently. While the Anglo-Burgundian guns pounded the defences, engineers began digging tunnels under the walls. Hearing the sounds of the excavation, the soldiers of the dauphin began digging countermines and frequently engaged in underground hand-to-hand combat, with Henry leading his men in the fighting. The allied cannons continued their bombardment, blowing breaches in the walls, but these were quickly repaired. The allies suffered large losses of troops due to the fighting at Melun and the effects of widespread diseases, but after a four-month siege, and facing starvation, Guillaume finally surrendered on 18 November.

With the seizure of Melun, the road to Paris was now open, the allies renewing their advance with Henry V riding side-by-side with Charles VI and Philip III. They entered the capital on 1 December, followed by a great procession of nobles and knights. The two kings and duke were greeted by large crowds of cheering people lining the streets. Despite the great welcome by the Paris citizens, Henry was only acknowledged as king by the northern French region of the kingdom, while the south remained loyal to Dauphin Charles. Henry remained in Paris establishing his French rule as regent for the incapacitated Charles VI. The Estates-General was summoned, and the deputies of the legislative assembly quickly approved the Troyes agreement. Under the regency of Henry V, taxes were reimposed and the coinage standardized. Restructuring measures were implemented to reform the government, but there was no attempt to Anglicize the Church. The Dauphinists were put on trial *in abstentia* for the murder of Duke John II, the dauphin being declared guilty and condemned to death for his involvement.

Following his visit to Paris, King Henry and his entourage travelled to Rouen to enforce his rule over the newly conquered territory. The king had been absent from England for more than three years, and in late January 1421 preparations began for his return to the kingdom. He remained in Rouen for a month before proceeding to Calais with Catherine for the sea voyage to England. They arrived at Dover on 1 February, where they were greeted by large enthusiastic crowds. The king and Catherine resumed their journey, stopping at Canterbury for a brief stay before riding on to London. They entered the city on 21 February, receiving a warm reception from thousands of spectators who had come to see the heroic conqueror of France. The streets were decorated with greenery and houses were covered with bright pennants, while choirs of young maidens sang songs of greeting. After spending the night in the royal palace, the French princess was escorted by the high magnates, churchmen and city officials to Westminster Abbey on 23 February, where she was anointed Queen of England by the archbishop. The religious ceremony was followed by a great banquet in Westminster Hall attended by the leading nobles, archbishops and abbots of the land.

In the wake of their joyous reception in London, Henry V and his queen made a royal progress across the kingdom. The royal couple were greeted by cheers of acclamation throughout the realm. The two-month tour allowed Henry to renew his bonds with the people following his long absence. The king had departed from France with his sovereignty only acknowledged in the north of the country, and needed more money and troops to enforce his rule over the followers of Prince Charles. As he travelled from town to town, royal commissioners followed behind securing loans from the barons, Church and towns and cities. The king's military victories in France had made him a national hero, meaning his requests for money were well received. By early May, King Henry was back in London attending parliament. During the legislative sessions, the representatives approved the Troyes agreement and voted new taxes for the continuation of the crown's war in France.

While Henry V was in England, he was occupied with civil affairs and preparations for his third French campaign. The Scots, meanwhile, had been actively supporting the Dauphinists by supplying arms and soldiers to supplement their resistance effort. Hearing of this, Henry sent agents north to prevent any future aid to Prince Charles. The Scottish monarchy was receptive to the king's initiative, agreeing to end their assistance and dispatching 200 knights and 200 archers to serve in the English army in France.

Before departing for England, Henry V had appointed his brother, Thomas of Clarence, to continue the war against the Dauphinists. From southern Normandy, Thomas launched forays across the border, pillaging the dauphin's towns in Anjou and Maine and destroying numerous castles. While in England, the king received news of his brother's death during a raid against the enemy at Bauge in the River Loire region. Prince Charles' victory over the English greatly enhanced his stature among the French lords, encouraging the Duke of Brittany, John V, to end his neutrality and declare his allegiance to the Dauphinists. With the Bretons now allied with Prince Charles, the English were attacked in their western lands of France, while the Dauphinists continued their offensive from the south. The leader of King Henry's forces in Normandy, Thomas Montague, Earl of Salisbury, was hard-pressed to defend his monarch's conquered territory, forcing Henry to return to France to remedy the situation. He put to sea from Dover for his third campaign on 10 June with reinforcements for his army.

Henry V landed in Calais with over 4,000 troops, marching his army to Montreuil to confer with Duke Philip III. During their meeting, the king agreed to send his soldiers to Chartres to relieve the siege against the Burgundians. Henry left his army, hastening to Paris with a small escort to deal with growing unrest in the city. The presence of the king calmed the Parisians and royal order was quickly restored. Remaining in Paris, Henry visited King Charles VI and the queen before attending Mass at Notre Dame. While Henry was in the French capital, Prince Charles' soldiers seized a chain of fortresses from the town of Dreux in the north to the Loire in the south, threatening to move against the capital. To defend his conquests, Henry rejoined his army and proceeded to attack the enemy at Dreux, 50 miles west of Paris. The town was besieged on 18 July, the English battering its defences with their guns and unleashing ferocious sorties. The defenders put up a strong resistance, but by 20 August were compelled to submit. The news of the surrender prompted many smaller castles to the north and west to open their gates to the English soldiers.

In the wake of securing the region around Paris, the English struck out to the south into the Loire valley to confront their enemy at Beaugency, downriver from Orleans. The town was stormed and put to the sword, but Prince Charles still refused to face the English in open battle, despite the slaughter of his men. The English and their allies resumed their campaign, moving east toward the town of Joigny. During the march, many English troops died or became severely ill from an outbreak of dysentery. Despite the losses in men, the king kept up his offensive, capturing Nemours and Villeneuve-Roy, then storming Rougemont in late September. At Rougemont, many of the defenders were seized after their surrender, and on orders from King Henry were drowned in the River Yonne as punishment for their continued resistance.

After clearing the Yonne region of Dauphinist fortifications, Henry V divided his small host of less than 2,500 battle-weary men into three divisions and proceeded toward Meaux, sweeping aside any remaining enemy troops en-route across a broad front. The army reunited at the great enemy fortress at Meaux, which was besieged on 6 October. The town was defended by a force of deserters and bandits under the command of Captain Guichard de Chissay. The capture of the town would advance Henry's campaign of conquest by removing a threat to Paris from the northeast, while encouraging many Dauphinist strongholds in the area to abandon their allegiance to Prince Charles. Expecting a long siege, the king brought up artillery pieces, munitions, food and supplies from Paris. Encampments were established and log huts built for the soldiers' dwellings, while trenches were dug for protection against forays by the garrison. The siege continued into the winter months, the men suffering from the cold and rainy weather, disease and food shortages. Dysentery was soon widespread among the besiegers, while the defenders launched repeated sorties from the town, wreaking havoc among the English. The king was frequently among his troops in the front lines, encouraging them to continue the fight. While Henry struggled to hold his army together, news reached him in December that Queen Catherine had given birth to their first son, Prince Henry, who became heir to the English and French crowns.

As the siege wore on, additional guns were brought to Meaux and a steady bombardment of the fortifications continued. When the French provisions were almost depleted, the garrison troops withdrew from the town into the citadel, taking the remaining supplies with them and leaving the residents to starve. With the absence of the French soldiers, the English quickly broke into the town and repositioned their artillery pieces nearer the castle, battering its walls from close range. At the end of April, with their provisions exhausted and the English steadily destroying the defensive works, the garrison finally surrendered after seven months of resistance. Following the capture of Meaux, many other Dauphinist strongholds submitted to the English, fearing the wrath of King Henry.

After occupying Prince Charles' fortifications in the Loire region, Henry V returned to Paris for a reunion with Catherine. They celebrated recent victories over the Dauphinists and the birth of Prince Henry with a great banquet in the Louvre Palace attended by the high dukes, magnates and churchmen of England and France. The king and queen established their residence in the Louvre for their short stay in Paris before moving to the citadel at Vincennes on the outskirts of the city. While Henry managed his rule of the occupied French territories, Dauphin Charles was active south-east of Orleans along the Loire at Sancerre and threatening Duke Philip III's capital at Dijon. When the prince's men began siege operations against the duke's town of Cosne, Henry and his allies made preparations to advance against them. The Duke of Burgundy assembled his troops and hurried south, while King Henry prepared to join him with his army. During the siege at Meaux, Henry had shown signs of being severely ill with dysentery. Nevertheless, on 7 July, the king moved his court to Vincennes, determined to lead his army to relieve the siege of Cosne. By now too weak to ride, Henry was carried by litter to Corbeil in the southern outskirts of Paris. He remained at Corbeil for two weeks, growing increasingly frail, and after learning the foe had withdrawn from Cosne, returned to Vincennes by barge down the Seine.

As King Henry V's health continued to deteriorate, and with his death apparently now approaching, he called his close advisors to his bed, telling them: 'I exhort you to resume these wars until peace is gained.' He provided for the government of his two kingdoms, naming John, Duke of Bedford, as guardian for his successor, the future King Henry VI, and Humphrey of Gloucester as Lord Protector. After the king's doctors informed him he had just hours to live, his priest was summoned to his bedside. The friar and Henry recited several psalms together before the king received communion. Around midnight on 31 August 1422, Henry V died peacefully age just 32. After his body was boiled in water to separate the flesh from the bones, the remains were placed in a lead casket and taken back to London for burial at Westminster Abbey on 7 November. Henry had died at the height of his power, leaving England and western France in jeopardy under the rule of a long regency government. Six weeks after the death of the English king, Charles VI also died and the 8-month-old reigning King of England, Henry VI, was recognized as sovereign of France.

Selected Sources

Ackroyd, Peter, *Foundation – The History of England from Its Earliest Beginnings to the Tudors* (Thomas Dunne Books, 2011).

Allmand, Christopher, *Henry V* (University of California Press, 1992).

Becker, Carl L., *A Survey of European Civilization* (Houghton Mifflin, 1936).

Cheetham, Anthony, 'Henry V', in Fraser, Antonia, *The Lives of the Kings and Queens of England* (Alfred A Knopf, 1975).

Earle, Peter, *The Life and Times of Henry V* (Weidenfeld and Nicolson, 1972).

Harvey, John, *The Plantagenets* (Franklin Watts, 1948).

Hutchison, Harold F., *King Henry V* (Dorset Press, 1967).

Roberts, Clayton and Roberts, David, *A History of England – Volume 1* (Prentice Hall, 1991).

Seward, Desmond, *Henry V – The Scourge of God* (Viking, 1998).

Smith, Goldwin, *A History of England* (Charles Scribner's Sons, 1957).

Henry VI

Henry V bequeathed to his son and heir, Henry of Windsor, a legacy of brilliant military triumphs on the battlefields of France, recognition of the House of Lancaster as ruler of France and the establishment of a peaceful and prosperous English kingdom. During the long and inept reign of Henry VI, the acquisitions in France were lost and England was beset by a bloody civil war between the supporters of the Yorkist faction and the Lancastrians known as the Wars of the Roses. Henry VI possessed little of his father's charisma, dynamic leadership or military skills, and was considered weak, timid and easily influenced. In 1455, when fighting erupted between warring factions for the English throne, the escalating stresses from the conflict propelled the king into long periods of depression and insanity, finally resulting in his dethronement. The Lancastrian monarch was briefly restored to the crown in 1470, but his rule was short and the following year he was overthrown again and murdered in the Tower of London.

Prince Henry was born at Windsor Castle on 6 December 1421, the only child of Henry V and Queen Catherine of Valois. On the following day, the mayor of London ordered all the city's church bells to ring out the joyful news, while Te Deums were sung in thanksgiving for the birth of the successor to the crown. Nine months after his birth, he was acknowledged as King of England following the death of Henry V in France, and seven weeks later, when King Charles VI of France died, was also proclaimed the French monarch, becoming the only English sovereign to rule both kingdoms. Shortly before his death, Henry V appointed his uncle, Thomas of Beaufort, as guardian for his infant son, with expressed authority to choose his servants. In his instructions to Beaufort, the dying Henry V named one of the queen's ladies, Elizabeth Ryman, as his principal caregiver, and she was responsible for Henry VI's health and wellbeing.

The king spent his early years in the royal household, making his first public appearance just before his second birthday when he attended parliament. He left Windsor Palace with his mother, and after a slow journey to London rode in state through the city's streets in a grand procession, amid the cheers of the spectators. On 18 November 1423, the king, accompanied by Queen Catherine, proceeded to parliament to be seen by the nobles and delegates and hear the address of the Speaker of the Commons. Henry's presence at parliament at such a young age was deemed necessary by his guardians to ensure the continued rule of the House of Lancaster after the attempted escape from the Tower of London by John Mortimer, who was believed to be plotting the overthrow of Henry VI and the assumption of the throne by his relative, Edmund Mortimer, Earl of March. The earl possessed a valid claim to the crown, having been heir presumptive to Richard II before he was deposed by Henry IV, so to eliminate any possibility of rebellion, John Mortimer was executed and the Earl of March was sent to Ireland as the king's first lieutenant, where he died six months later from the plague.

In 1424, Lady Alice Butler assumed the duties of governess for the young Henry VI, instructing him in the requirements of discipline, court etiquette and courtesy practiced by a monarch. A staff of six women was chosen to care for Henry under the guidance of the queen, who remained responsible for him until his seventh birthday. In 1428, Richard Beauchamp, Earl of Warwick, was made accountable for the academic studies of King Henry, who attended the court school with other children of the nobility. Under the guidance of Beauchamp, the king received instruction in reading, writing, languages, music and court etiquette. He was encouraged to play martial games to begin his training as a warrior-king, and was given a coat of armour and swords to practice the skills of a knight. However, unlike his father, Henry VI showed little interest in military activities and lacked the natural leadership of Henry V.

Until 1429, the monarch took part in only a limited number of public appearances, remaining under the protection of the queen and his tutors. Henry was present on the opening day of most parliaments to receive the acknowledgement of the delegates as king, and there were several special ceremonies he attended, but he was largely absent from governmental affairs. He remained in the south-east of England, travelling between his favourite residences at Windsor, Eltham and Westminster. In late 1429, at the age of 8, Henry's role in the administration of the regime became more secure with his coronation as king in Westminster Abbey. The ceremony began during the evening of 5 November, with Henry participating in the traditional creation of thirty-two new knights of the Bath. The following morning, he made his way from the Tower of London to Westminster Hall, acknowledging the loud cheers of the thousands of spectators along the route. Henry held a public audience in Westminster Hall before proceeding to Westminster Abbey for the coronation ritual. He walked slowly to the altar to begin the ceremony, which required repeated prostrations, disrobings and prayers. The articles of the coronation oath were read to the king, which he pledged to defend. The most solemn spectacle was the anointment of Henry VI by the Archbishop of Canterbury with holy oil, widely believed to have been given to St Thomas Becket by the Virgin Mary. Following the service in the abbey, the last act of the coronation was a large banquet held in Westminster Hall. The enthronement was specially adapted for Henry VI's dual kingships of England and France, with displays of St Edward the Confessor representing the English throne and St Louis IX the French, while another display showed the Virgin Mary with Jesus in her lap offering the kneeling Henry two crowns.

While Henry VI slowly assumed the duties of an English king, in France his uncle, John, Duke of Bedford, was opposing the army of the challenger to the French crown, Dauphin Charles of Valois. During his reign, Henry V had conquered and occupied most of western France. Before his death, he ordered his brother, John of Bedford, to carry the war to the French, and in December 1422 the English parliament had approved his appointment as regent. Bedford united his English army with the Burgundians of Duke Philip III and renewed the conflict against the dauphin, who controlled southern France and was acknowledged by many as the successor to the French throne. The allies advanced into the Loire valley in the name of Henry VI, steadily driving the enemy out of the region. As Duke John gained control of the area south of Paris, the dauphin negotiated an agreement with the Scottish crown and his depleted army was reinforced with over 6,000 Scottish soldiers. In mid-1424, with his forces strengthened, Dauphin Charles moved against the Anglo-Burgundian castles along the Normandy border, compelling the surrender of several fortified towns. When the French and their Scottish allies captured the town of Verneuil, the Duke of Bedford led his army against them and defeated them on 17 August in a fierce and bloody battle, securing a decisive victory with a magnificent counter-charge. Following this triumph, Duke John expanded his campaign, seizing and occupying much of the Loire region for Henry VI by early 1429, the French and Scots being repeatedly defeated and driven back.

Under the leadership of Bedford, the English throne reached the height of its power in France, but after 1429 the political and military situation changed significantly. Bedford now had to contend with the rise of Joan of Arc and the resulting revival of French resistance to the English, the desertion of Duke Philip III to the Valois monarchy and the thwarting of his efforts to defeat his enemies by the mounting government dissension in England led by his brother, Humphrey of Gloucester. Joan was a young peasant girl who claimed to have had visions from God telling her to lead the French army to the town of Orleans and break the English siege of the city. Meeting with the dauphin, she convinced him of her holy mission and was sent to Orleans with his army. On 7 May, Joan led the French forces to victory, continuing her campaign by reoccupying numerous towns and forcing Bedford to withdraw north-east toward Rheims. By the end of June, Rheims was once again occupied by the Dauphinists, allowing Charles to be anointed King of France at the traditional enthronement cathedral. Joan's triumphs and the crowning of Charles VII reawakened the French spirit of nationalism, and the English were compelled to retreat toward Paris. Charles VII's men, under the command of Joan, pursed the retreating English, but Bedford thwarted their attacks and forced them to abandon their offensive in the spring of 1430, thereby saving Paris for Henry VI.

To counter the growing threat from the reenergized Valois regime, John of Bedford urged the ruling council in London, led by Humphrey of Gloucester, to bring Henry VI to Paris for his coronation as French sovereign-lord. To protect Henry during his anointment expedition, an army of over 1,300 men-at-arms and nearly 5,600 archers was assembled, and in April 1430 the king set sail for the Pale of Calais, remaining for three months before heading toward Paris. However, he was forced to remain in Normandy for nearly a year, while his army cleared northern France of the resurgent Valois forces. Finally, in late November 1431, Henry VI set out for Paris, with his guardian, the Earl of Warwick, and the royal army protecting him against an attack by Charles VII's men. The king's party reached the outskirts of the city on 2 December without encountering any enemy troops. Henry was greeted by city officials and taken to St Denis Cathedral to give thanks for his safe journey and his French crown. Two days later he was officially welcomed to the city amid a grand celebration, with richly decorated streets and houses. All along the route there were large cheering crowds and numerous displays of French history and life. Henry briefly visited several churches, including Sainte Chapelle, viewing and kissing the many holy relics collected by King Louis IX. Henry remained in the city for the night at the Louvre Palace before moving to Vincennes to await the coronation. On Sunday, 16 December, the English monarch made his way to Notre Dame for the enthronement ceremony, accompanied by many ecclesiastic lords, nobles and city officials. He walked through the nave to the waiting Cardinal of Winchester, Henry Beaufort, who performed the anointment service. Beaufort approached the king, anointing him with holy oil and placing the crown of France upon his head. Following the rites, the cardinal sang the Mass in honour of the king. Shortly after the ritual, a great banquet was held at the royal palace to celebrate the new French king.

In the aftermath of his formal assumption of the French crown, Henry VI returned to Calais and soon sailed to Dover, landing on 9 February 1432. He then set out for his palace at Eltham, arriving on 14 February. He remained at the palace, resting from his Paris journey, before making his grand entrance into London on 21 February. The arrival of the king was greeted with a magnificent celebration arranged by the mayor. He was met by the city officials at Blackheath and personally conducted into London by the mayor. As Henry approached London Bridge, he could see the richly decorated arms of England and France hanging from the structure. On his way to St Paul's for a service of thanksgiving, he was greeted by a wide array of decorations symbolizing the numerous virtues, sciences and good government, as choirs of singers welcomed his return. At Cheapside, the king was presented with a precious stone royal castle replica, with a family tree displaying his ancestors since St Louis of France and St Edward the Confessor of England. Finally, at the Little Conduit, beside an illustration of the Trinity stood a gathering of 'angels' welcoming Henry VI home. Following the service at St Paul's, the monarch was escorted by the mayor to Westminster Abbey, where he viewed the relics of St Edward. The final ceremony of the day was the singing of a Te Deum before Henry was taken to Westminster Palace for the night.

As Henry of England and France resumed his preparations to govern as king, in the French kingdom his uncle, John of Bedford, continued the war against the forces of Charles VII, while his uncle, Humphrey of Gloucester, held the reins of English power. Humphrey possessed an abrasive personality and was widely disliked. Opposition to Humphrey's policies steadily increased, centred on the Bishop of Winchester, Henry Beaufort, who – allied with several supporters – openly confronted the Duke of Gloucester. During Henry VI's long absence in France, Humphrey attempted to eliminate Beaufort from the ruling council, charging him with treason. England was saved from civil war by the return from France of the king, whose advisors now utilized the power and prestige of his throne to arrange a settlement. Nevertheless, the hostile relationship between Gloucester and Henry Beaufort persisted and the kingdom remained at a stalemate.

Following his return from France, Henry VI remained removed from the governing of his realm, while Humphrey of Gloucester dominated the royal council. The king was, however, now more visible, attending special ceremonies and parliaments more regularly. In 1432, the Earl of Warwick reported Henry was becoming increasingly impatient with his limited involvement in the affairs of the ruling council. He was praised by the counsellors for his understanding of the government but cautioned he lacked adequate experience to rule alone. When Duke John of Bedford died in September 1435, King Henry became more directly occupied in the administration of the kingdom and began attending council meetings regularly. The duke had served Henry faithfully as his guardian and regent, and was replaced by the dukes of Warwick and Suffolk. By April 1436, the monarch was signing royal writs, signalling his participation in the routine affairs of the regime. Finally, in 1437, in his sixteenth year, Henry declared an end to his minority and his assumption to the throne. Nevertheless, he continued to rely on the advice of others, and it was most likely either Gloucester or Henry of Beaufort who encouraged him to make the decision to govern for himself. Following the announcement, the king embarked on a tour of his realm to present himself to his subjects. While he lacked a strong personality, he was a devout follower of the Church of Rome, attending Mass and refusing to conduct any governmental affairs on Sundays. He strongly disapproved of any lord who used profanity, his only dramatic remark being 'Forsooth, forsooth'.

Despite his attempts to rule independently, King Henry was still overshadowed by his powerful relatives, Gloucester and Henry Beaufort, which limited his opportunities to develop independent judgement. Henry lacked a forceful personality and was unable to dominate the policy decisions of his government, relying on his uncles and advisors, while his energies were directed toward his religious beliefs, ignoring his responsibilities as king.

After Henry's return from France in 1432, John of Bedford had continued to lead the army against the forces of Charles VII, but lacked troops and money to overwhelm his enemy. In 1433, Bedford returned to England to personally raise the necessary soldiers and funds. The following July, the duke sailed to Normandy with reinforcements and additional revenue, but was still unable to revive his campaign. With the French war at a stalemate, the duke arranged to hold peace talks with Charles VII's representatives. During the talks, in October 1435, Philip III of Burgundy abandoned his English allies, agreeing instead to support the Valois regime. The war effort against the Valois king was further damaged with the death of Bedford. Without the duke's martial skills, the English hold on western France quickly began to weaken. By April 1437, the Valois army had seized control of Paris and continued to drive the English back toward their stronghold in Normandy.

The English strengthened their defences in Normandy, slowing the advance of the French royalists. The conflict continued, with neither the English nor Valois armies possessing the troop strength or resources to force a conclusion. The loss of the Burgundians was a major setback to the English court, reducing the area of France under its sovereignty to only Normandy and parts of Maine and Gascony. The growing political unrest in London weakened the English war effort, and was compounded by the loss of John of Bedford. The English troops were now hard pressed to stop the advance of the Valois army, which steadily pushed into Normandy. Henry VI, however, had little interest in military affairs, and was devoted to his prayers and religious studies. The farther the French marched into Normandy, the more the king spoke out in favour of peace talks. When negotiations were arranged, they quickly ended in failure, both regimes refusing to make concessions. Later, the French offered to recognize English control over Normandy and Gascony, if Henry VI renounced his rights to the French crown. The inept English council was unable to make a decision and the war resumed.

The royal council of the monarch was dominated by Humphrey of Gloucester, Beaufort and Richard, Duke of York, who had recently been appointed to the government by Henry VI. Beaufort favoured a policy of negotiation and appeasement with the French, while Humphrey and Richard advocated a renewal of offensive operations. In the summer of 1443, an expeditionary force was sent to France, but it achieved little. After a humiliating encounter with the Valois army, Henry – at the encouragement of the peace party – dispatched an envoy, William de la Pole of Suffolk, to negotiate with Charles VII. Suffolk met with the French in the summer of 1444, negotiating a twenty-one-month truce with the promise of future talks and the marriage of Henry VI to Margaret of Anjou, the cousin of King Charles VII.

Under the terms of the Treaty of Tours, Margaret of Anjou crossed the Channel to England in 1445, accompanied by the Duke of Suffolk, with whom she was rumoured to be involved romantically. Margaret was the cousin of the French king and the second daughter of the Count of Anjou, René. Born on 23 March 1430, she was closely related to the reigning Valois family. Under the guidance of her mother, Isabella of Lorraine, she was well educated and versed in court intrigues. She was married to Henry VI on 23 April 1445 at Titchfield Abbey in Hampshire, and a week later was anointed Queen of England at Westminster Abbey. Queen Margaret possessed an outspokenly aggressive personality, quickly exerting her will over her submissive and indecisive husband. With the king exhibiting little interest in the ruling of the kingdom and the wars against the French, the queen took a major role in the formation of crown policies in the royal council, aided by her favourite at court, William of Suffolk.

Shortly after the marriage, the second round of peace talks with the French was held in London, with Henry VI personally participating in the discussions. While peace negotiations with the Valois regime were underway, Queen Margaret convinced Henry to cede Maine to the French to secure the favour of Charles VII. Maine was duly surrendered to the French court in return for a twenty-year truce, to come into effect after the signing of the final treaty. The yielding of Maine was widely rejected by the royal council, but was included in the preliminary agreement at the insistence of Queen Margaret.

In spite of several border flare-ups, the truce between the two kingdoms continued to be enforced. King Henry VI had little interest in the defence of his remaining French lands, allowing them to deteriorate and his troop strength to decline, while Charles VII aggressively rebuilt and reinforced his army. With the terms of the final settlement remaining unresolved, Henry wrote to King Charles in late December 1445 promising to withdraw from the County of Maine in March 1446 in an act of good faith to ensure peace. The English finally abandoned the county in March 1448 after long delays caused by local resistance to the order. With the loss of Maine before the twenty-year truce agreement was signed, the French now only agreed to a two-year extension of the peace. The English king's personal intervention in the negotiations greatly reduced the terms the Valois government had to pay for Maine, revealing his inexperience in foreign affairs.

After the English troops marched out of Maine, they were stationed in the south-west of Normandy along the border with Brittany. The Breton duke, Francis I, fearing an attack by Henry VI, appealed to Charles VII for his intervention. In the summer of 1449, the French army invaded Normandy, while Duke Francis attacked from the west. The English army, having been ignored by the government in London during the truce, was powerless to resist the invasion forces, which quickly overran northern Normandy. In April 1450, King Henry's government mustered a small relief army, sending the inexperienced troops to France to regain the lost lands. The Valois army, commanded by Constable Arthur de Richemont, clashed with the English near the town of Formigny, where a charge of the heavy French cavalry decimated their opponents. De Richemont resumed his campaign of conquest, and by August 1450 all of France – with the exception of the Pale of Calais and Gascony – was lost. England had been ill-prepared for the war, Henry's regime failing to secure the money and troops needed to oppose Charles VII. Unlike his father, Henry VI showed little inclination to lead his army into battle, remaining at his court in England.

The French continued the war against the English, and in the autumn of 1450 a formidable army invaded Gascony. On 29 June 1451, Bordeaux was seized, the city of Bayonne surrendering in late August. Henry VI's regime was slow to assemble a relief force, and it was not until late 1452 that 3,000 men sailed to Gascony. On 17 October, troops led by John Talbot, Earl of Shrewsbury, landed in Gascony and marched against Bordeaux. After 300 years of English rule, the townspeople considered themselves as subjects of the English crown, rebelling against the French garrison in support of Talbot's attack. The city was quickly back under English control, and by the end of the year western Gascony had been retaken. In the spring of 1453, Charles VII invaded Gascony with three armies, laying siege to the town of Castillon on 8 July. The French, led by Jean Bureau, set up an artillery park with 300 cannons, protected by a ditch and walls, and began bombarding the fortress. Talbot left Bordeaux with an army to relieve the siege, but as they approached the town his men were destroyed by the French artillery pieces and the charge of over 1,000 cavalrymen. Talbot was killed during the clash by a French infantryman with a battle axe, while leading his men in fierce and savage fighting. After the crushing defeat at Castillon, the French continued to attack the remaining English soldiers in the region, retaking Bordeaux. With the surrender of the capital, Henry VI's government had now lost Normandy and Gascony, retaining only Calais in France.

While the English were losing much of their French lands, in England, the king's principal minister, William de la Pole, Duke of Suffolk, was impeached by parliament for the loss of France and charged with treason against the crown. When additional allegations were brought against Suffolk by the House of Commons, Henry VI intervened, banishing him for five years to prevent his friend's conviction for treason. The lords of the kingdom, fearful of parliament gaining the power to try them for treason, had strongly encouraged the king to banish Suffolk. While Duke William was sailing from England into exile, his ship was boarded by rebel Kent sailors and he was executed after a mock trial. The murder of Suffolk by supporters of parliament was the spark for the revolt of Jack Cade.

During the French reconquest of western France, Henry VI's foreign policies had grown increasingly unpopular in parliament and with his English subjects. Meanwhile, the House of Commons pressured Henry to void his many grants of money and land to his court favourites. The expulsion of the English from Normandy negatively affected the maritime trade of Sussex and Kent with the western French region. Pirates from France, particularly Brittany, began raiding the coast of Kent and Sussex with impunity, disrupting the economy of the shires' towns and farmers. The struggling men of Kent gathered at Ashford in May 1450, choosing Jack Cade to lead them in protest to London. As they proceeded toward the capital, their numbers grew to over 3,000. On 11 June, the rebels were encamped at Blackheath, several miles from London. As the threat against his government escalated, King Henry sent an embassy to Cade demanding the end of his revolt. The order was quickly rebuffed, and led by Cade, the protesters attacked the royal envoys, hurling insults at the king and calling him a natural fool. They claimed Henry's policies had disrupted the welfare of his kingdom's subjects and wanted reforms to the government. While Cade and his followers increased their mutinous activities, on 13 June the monarch sent additional envoys to the insurgents' camp, ordering them to abandon London, while offering them pardons to peacefully end their uprising. Five days later, after they failed to disperse, the king advanced to their encampment with a force of soldiers, but the rebels had fled the previous night after receiving warnings from their local supporters. Several of the king's lords pursued Cade and his mutineers, but they were ambushed and killed. When news of the death of the nobles became widely known, a contingent of lords rode into Kent, killing several protesters in revenge. As the danger of open rebellion spread, Henry and his court fled the capital, hastening to safety in the Midlands, despite the pleas of the mayor of London to remain.

When Jack Cade heard of the king's flight, he reassembled his followers and returned to Blackheath, crossing London Bridge on 3 July and occupying the Guildhall. The rebels next attacked the Tower of London, overpowering the guards and executing several of the regime's counsellors who had sought shelter in the fortress. The Londoners, alarmed at the size of the growing uprising, mustered a force of citizens and confronted the protesters. Following a series of sporadic clashes, a truce was arranged by envoys from the Church and negotiations for a settlement were undertaken. It was agreed that the rebels would submit their list of demands to the king and then disperse after receiving their pardons. Most of Cade's men accepted the offer and returned to Kent and Sussex, but Cade himself refused and again raised the banner of rebellion. Cade fled south from London and was finally caught and arrested in a garden at Heathfield in Sussex, where he died. He had earlier been wounded during the fighting in London, and succumbed to his injures. With his death, the uprising was over, but not because of any personal actions taken by King Henry.

Shortly after the suppression of Jack Cade's revolt, Richard, Duke of York, returned to England from Ireland without the permission of his king. York had been sent to Ireland as lord lieutenant to limit his involvement in the London government. He was supported by many magnates and bishops, who lobbied for his reappointment to the royal council. With his natural charismatic personality, he attracted a large following and now posed a threat to Henry VI. Richard of York demanded reforms to the kingdom to advance his power at court. York's programmes of governmental restructuring were popular with the people, but were strongly opposed by many nobles. Instead of York assuming the role he sought of Henry's first minister, Edmund Beaufort of Somerset was named to the post. Somerset was personally blamed by many lords for the loss of France, but he was the friend of the king and used his influence to secure the position. With the support of Somerset, King Henry was exhorted to initiate reforms that restored peace. Unable to win approval for his proposals, Richard withdrew to his stronghold at Ludlow near the Welsh border.

The Duke of York was the great-grandson of King Edward III and heir to the English throne of the as-then childless Henry VI. In 1452, Richard began promoting himself as the recognized successor to the crown, putting before the king a petition demanding punishment for Edmund of Somerset for his loss of France, while emphasizing he was acting for the good of the realm. He marched against London with his armed supporters to enforce his ultimatums, but was refused entry. Forced to withdraw, the duke and his troops were confronted by the larger royal army east of London at Dartford and compelled to submit to the king. However, York was permitted to present his complaints to Henry after swearing an oath of allegiance at St Paul's Cathedral.

During the summer of 1452, Henry VI showed his first signs of mental illness, slipping into brief periods of unresponsiveness. He suffered a mental breakdown in August 1453, probably brought on by the news of his army's disastrous defeat at Castillon. For the next 18 months, the king was in a trance-like state, becoming unemotional and recognizing nobody. The illness was likely inherited from his maternal grandfather, King Charles VI of France. He could not walk without assistance and had no awareness of time. The royal council attempted to govern in his name, but was forced to summon a Great Council to choose a protector of the realm. Despite the opposition of Queen Margaret, who had given birth to a son and heir to the crown named Edward of Lancaster on 13 October 1453, the Duke of York, as the most senior nobleman, was appointed Lord Protector.

While Henry VI remained in his catatonic state, York assumed the reins of power and quickly moved against his principal enemy, ordering the Duke of Somerset imprisoned in the Tower for his loss of England's possessions in France. As protector and with his government's approval by the magnates and churchmen, the Duke of York dismissed Edmund of Somerset's allies on the royal council, replacing them with his supporters to solidify his administration. In spite of the uncertainty over how long York would rule, he provided England with a stable period of peace and economic growth during Henry's illness.

As Richard of York continued to rule over England as regent, King Henry remained in a depressive stupor, although there were brief periods where he seemed to be functioning normally. Henry appeared in public occasionally, performing his duties as king. In early September 1454, it was reported that Henry attended the formal submission ceremony of the Archbishop-elect of Canterbury, receiving his homage. While he looked to his subjects to be acting in a normal manner, his lack of attendance at parliament, council meetings and religious services continued to cast doubt on the king's mental stability, but by January 1455 Henry seemed to have made a complete recovery. Regaining his mental acuity, he ordered the release of Somerset and returned him to his favour. The Yorkist duke was deprived of his offices of protector and the captaincy of the Calais Pale. Edmund of Somerset slowly regained his former powers and offices as the head of the government, replacing the Duke of York. Taking no action to govern the kingdom, Henry VI was either still too incapacitated or allowed himself to be manipulated by Duke Edmund.

In May 1455, Duke Richard and Edmund of Somerset were summoned by the king to a great council at Leicester to resolve their differences. Believing himself threatened by the regime, York formed an alliance with Richard Neville, Earl of Salisbury, and his son, the Earl of Warwick, to defend against an attack by the royalists. On 21 May, Henry VI left London with a force of supporters, riding north to settle matters with the Duke of York and the Neville family. As the king advanced, Richard and the Nevilles assembled their followers to move against Henry's regime, while proclaiming their loyalty to the crown and demanding justice against Somerset. The royal army hastened north, stopping at the town of St Albans on the evening of 21 May to await reinforcements. While Henry's men delayed their march, Richard of York and the Nevilles arrived with their army of over 3,000 soldiers and set up their encampment to the east of the town at Key Field. Outnumbered by the rebels, King Henry sent the Duke of Buckingham to negotiate with the Yorkists. The talks quickly broke up without resolution, Duke Richard being unyielding on the surrender of Somerset for trial. In the mid-morning of 22 May, the Yorkists and Nevilles unleashed an attack against the loyalists in the town, marking the beginning of the thirty-year Wars of the Roses. The rebel footmen rushed into St Albans' Sopwell and Shropshine lanes, but after making repeated assaults were unable to break through the barricades constructed by the king's troops.

When the men of York and the Nevilles first charged into their opponents' barricades, Henry VI – dressed in full armour – withdrew to his tent on St Peter's Street and sat by his standard. He dreaded the sight of bloodshed and refused to lead his army into the fight, although during the night before the battle, while talking to his lords about the Yorkists, he had told them: 'I shall destroy them. They should be hanged and drawn and quartered.' Despite his bellicose statements, on the day of the battle, he remained sequestered in his quarters. When Warwick's reserves broke into the town, they charged down St Peter's Street, pushing the enemy back in a fierce melee and surrounding the king's tent. The rebel archers fired multiple volleys of arrows into the tent, slightly wounding Henry in the neck, as he quietly said to his attackers: 'Forsooth, forsooth.' The wound was attended to and he was removed to the house of a tanner to rest, later spending the night in the abbey. As Warwick's reserves swung the tide of battle, they had searched for Somerset and his ally, Henry Percy of Northumberland, both of whom were killed in the savage fighting. At the end of the battle, York and the Neville's declared they were King Henry's true liegemen, rather than Somerset. Having taken possession of the sovereign and eliminated his rivals, York was once again in control of the kingdom.

Following his victory at St Albans, Richard of York escorted the king back to London. With control of Henry VI, the duke summoned parliament during the summer, securing his pardon for the attack against the throne. Shortly after the fighting at St Albans, King Henry was again stricken by a mental collapse, caused by his defeat and capture. After a delay of several months, York was appointed protector, but under the influence of Queen Margaret, the king asked to be kept informed of the affairs of the new Yorkist government, fearing the loss of his sovereignty to the ambitious Duke Richard. With control of the regime, Richard dissolved the royal council, replacing Somerset's members with his own friends and supporters. When parliament met in early July, the protector used his office to solidify his growing powers. He pushed through reforms of the administration to improve the finances of the monarchy and to restore law and order, which had deteriorated into numerous local private wars between the lords. Before the legislative assembly reconvened, the great council met to decide if King Henry was mentally capable of ruling alone. The council members concluded that he was unable to govern without the support of the protector. . Under the terms of his appointment, York's protectorate would continue until the king personally appeared in parliament to assume his rule or until his heir, Edward of Lancaster, reached the age of majority.

During the months following his assumption of the protectorate, Richard attempted to revoke many of the grants of offices and lands made by Henry VI to his supporters. The Act of Resumption, if passed, would have negatively affected many powerful lords, including the king and queen, but the duke failed to garner enough support to pass it into law. In February 1456, as the king's mental stability improved and with the protector's actions detrimental to them, the high lords voted to end York's protectorate and the government fell back under the rule of King Henry and Queen Margaret.

In the wake of this loss of power, Richard of York was not dismissed from the royal government but continued to serve the king as an advisor. When the Scots crossed the border into England in May 1456, the monarch appointed York to lead the English army against the invaders. As York advanced north with a formidable force, the Scottish king abandoned his incursion, withdrawing back into his kingdom. Despite the duke's continued loyal service to the crown, in the autumn of 1456 he was summoned to the royal council and rebuked for his earlier attacks against the king at St Albans. As the king's supporters intensified their attacks on him, Richard was compelled to swear an oath of loyalty and pledge not to endanger the health of Henry VI.

In spite of having regained part of his mental capacities, King Henry remained weak-willed and easily influenced. Since their marriage, Queen Margaret of Anjou had significantly increased her sway over the king, and she now took a major role in the governing of the kingdom, acting in the name of her husband. She influenced the king's choices of high nobles for the council, which was now dominated by her friends. Henry participated in only a few council meetings, but was able to take part in public ceremonies performing the duties of king. As the Lancastrian party increased its verbal attacks against the Yorkists in 1458, the king and Queen Margaret travelled to the Midlands, where she had a large loyal following, and began preparations for war. In June 1459, the regime assembled a great council to meet at Coventry, which York and his Neville allies refused to attend, fearing for their lives. At the conference, Richard of York and the earls of Salisbury and Warwick were accused of treason.

After learning of their indictments, the rebel lords assembled their armies and hastened to unite their forces. As the Earl of Salisbury advanced from Middleham Castle in Yorkshire with 5,000 soldiers to link up with the Yorkist forces at Ludlow Castle, his troops were intercepted at Blore Heath in Staffordshire on 23 September by an army of 10,000 Lancastrians led by James Tucher, Lord of Audley. Positioning his troops on the barren heathland at Blore Heath, Audley ambushed the approaching Yorkists. When Salisbury's scouts spotted the enemy, he deployed his men into battle order. After an unsuccessful attempt to negotiate a settlement, the battle began with an ineffective archery exchange between the two forces. Salisbury then withdrew part of his middle line to the rear to encourage Audley to attack. With the Lancastrians believing the Yorkist soldiers were retreating, Audley ordered a cavalry charge across the muddy heath, but his horsemen were repulsed with heavy casualties in a fury of clashing swords, billhooks and spears. The king's troops regrouped and made a second attack against the Yorkist lines, Audley being struck down and killed in the violent and bloody fighting. The Lancastrian second in command, Lord Dudley, then ordered an advance by his 4,000 footmen, crashing into the Yorkists. When this assault was also beaten back, all Lancastrian resistance collapsed and the Earl of Salisbury counter-attacked, overwhelming his opponents. The rout continued into the night as the Yorkists pursued the fleeing royalist forces. Over 2,000 Lancastrians were killed at Blore Health, while Salisbury lost less than half that number.

In spite of his defeat at Blore Heath, Henry VI, under the influence of Queen Margaret, ordered his army to pursue the rebels to Ludlow Castle, where York and his allies had built a fortified encampment. The rebel dukes were reluctant to attack their king and risk being accused of treason, and when a large contingent of their men from Calais deserted, York and the Nevilles were forced to flee during the night, unwilling to risk battle with a weakened army. Richard of York fled to safety over the Irish Sea in Dublin, while the Nevilles sailed to the Pale of Calais. The lands and titles of the rebel lords were seized, and they were declared traitors by the crown. To regain royal sovereignty over Calais, the Duke of Somerset was named to the captaincy of the Pale by the throne. Somerset was sent to Sandwich to assemble a fleet and army to attack the rebel troops in Calais. However, as the ships gathered at Sandwich, the Earl of Warwick raided the harbour, disrupting the planned invasion force. The rebels captured the port, holding it as a bridgehead for a Yorkist invasion of England.

As Henry VI struggled to rule his realm, in the summer of 1460 Salisbury and his son, Richard Neville, Sixteenth Earl of Warwick, united their forces and launched an invasion from the Pale of Calais, landing in Kent. Richard Neville was the eldest son of the Earl of Salisbury and Alice Montagu, heiress of Thomas Montagu, Earl of Salisbury. Soon after his birth in November 1428, he was betrothed to Anne, daughter of Richard Beauchamp, Earl of Warwick. In 1449, through his wife's heritage, he assumed control over Warwick's large estates, becoming the premier English earl in both power and position.

Salisbury and Warwick landed at Sandwich on 26 June with an army of over 2,000 men. As they made their way west, their ranks were increased by thousands of volunteers from Kent. On 2 July, the Neville earls – now with 10,000 supporters – were welcomed to London, with only the Tower garrison remaining loyal to King Henry. They immediately went to St Paul's to give thanks to God for their friendly reception by the Londoners. Meeting with the city's officials, the earls professed their loyalty to the monarch and emphasized they only wanted to replace his evil counsellors and reform the corrupt government. The Londoners threw their support behind the Duke of York and the Nevilles, as did the populace of most of southeast England. With a strong base promoting their cause, Richard of Warwick took charge of part of the army and headed north in search of the king and his forces, while Salisbury remained with 2,000 men besieging the Tower of London. As the Lancastrians moved against the fortress, the loyalists opened fired with artillery pieces, keeping the earl's soldiers at bay. Salisbury responded by bringing up large cannons from the royal armoury to fire at the Tower, blasting holes in the curtain walls and – with help from the citizens of London – keeping the garrison bottled up.

While Salisbury pressed his siege against the Tower garrison, Warwick clashed with the king and his royalist forces at Northampton on 10 July. Henry VI's 5,000 soldiers were positioned in the grounds of Delapre Abbey, with a ditch in front of them and the River Nene at their rear. Following fruitless reconciliation talks in the morning, Warwick ordered an assault against the royalists during the rainy afternoon. With the rain blowing in their faces, the Yorkists moved forward into a barrage of arrows, but despite heavy losses they continued their advance. As they reached the king's lines, the left flank of the Lancastrians deserted the battle and Warwick's men rolled up their enemy's defences. The loyalists were overrun in less than an hour and Henry was taken prisoner in his tent, while his counsellors were slain on the instructions of Warwick. After his capture, the monarch was taken to London and installed as a puppet king under the rule of Richard of York. While the king had been seized by the rebels, Queen Margaret and her young son, Edward of Lancaster, remained free to lead a counter-revolt.

Ten weeks after the Lancastrian defeat at Northampton and the recapture of Henry VI, Duke Richard of York returned to London from Ireland and soon met with parliament, demanding to be recognized as king. The lords and judges refused his ultimatum, unwilling to risk later charges of treason, but agreed to a compromise. Under the settlement, King Henry retained his throne until his death, then Richard and his heirs would succeed to the English monarchy. When the king accepted the proposal, York was acknowledged as successor designate. In spite of the agreement, Queen Margaret refused to accept the arrangement, with her son's loss of his inheritance rights to the Lancastrian crown, and began preparations to overthrow York.

As Duke Richard was negotiating with parliament, Queen Margaret and Prince Edward fled west to Wales and on to Scotland, leaving her English retainers under the command of Jasper Tudor. At the Scottish court, she arranged for military aid in her fight against the Yorkists and negotiated the marriage of Prince Edward to a sister of King James III of Scotland. Meanwhile, in England, the queen's allies secured the allegiance of the great northern warlords in her quest for the throne. The supporters of Margaret of Anjou mustered their troops and at the end of 1460 set off south to meet the Londoners and warlords of the south-east who advocated Richard's claim to the monarchy. In defence of his rights to the crown, the Duke of York advanced north, reaching his fortress at Sandal near Wakefield on 21 December. During the day, he sent scouts to reconnoitre the loyalists, who had encamped at Pontefract 9 miles to the east. Unknown to the Yorkists, half of the queen's 10,000 men were hidden in forestland. Believing he was now facing an army no larger than his, Richard moved against them. The Yorkist soldiers unleashed their attack against the Lancastrians at the bottom of a hill below Sandal Castle. As Richard's troops slammed into their adversary, the queen's men hidden among the trees set upon them, quickly overwhelming the rebel troops. During the fighting, the Duke of York was killed and Salisbury was taken prisoner and later executed. The Yorkists were completely routed by the queen's forces, with over 2,000 killed, while the Lancastrians lost only some 200 soldiers. Following the death of Richard of York, his 18-year-old eldest son, Edward, claimed his lands and titles and resumed the war against the Lancastrians, while Henry VI remained in the custody of the rebels.

Shortly after taking command of the Yorkists, Edward of York advanced against the Lancastrians in defence of his inheritance rights to the English throne, as agreed under the settlement negotiated by his father. Jasper Tudor had earlier moved into Wales with Queen Margaret's troops, recruiting Welsh volunteers to augment her army. Edward now hastened west to prevent Tudor's forces from uniting with the queen's northern soldiers and Scottish allies, who were advancing against London. On 2 February 1461, the forces clashed at Mortimer's Crossing, where the Lancastrians were defeated and pushed back into Wales.

When Edward, Duke of York, learned of Queen Margaret's march against London, he took his men and hastened east to intercept her. During his advance, he met Richard, Earl of Warwick, in Oxfordshire, and together they advanced their armies toward London to occupy the capital and have Edward acknowledged as king. After reaching London, the Duke of York was welcomed by large cheering crowds as the new King of England. Henry VI was dethroned for not recognizing Edward as his heir under the earlier agreement negotiated with parliament.

Meanwhile, Queen Margaret marched south with her army of northern lords and Scottish allies to rescue her husband from captivity, plundering towns as they advanced toward the capital. The Earl of Warwick, in command of London's defences, hastened to intercept the queen, taking Henry VI with him. Warwick constructed a fortified encampment for his army north-east of St Albans and two outposts were reinforced. The queen's troops were led by Sir Andrew Trollope, a seasoned veteran soldier from Calais, who had earlier deserted Warwick's faction. The rebels were taken by surprise on 17 February after Trollope led his men in a night march on St Albans. Shortly after dawn, the Lancastrians stormed up the hill past the abbey to enter the town, where they were quickly repulsed by archers shooting from the windows of the houses. The queen's men-at-arms regrouped and attacked from a different direction up an unguarded street into the town. The Lancastrians now manoeuvred to the north, assaulting the rear of Richard of Warwick's line and overrunning his men in savage hand-to-hand fighting. After seizing the left flank, the royalists charged into Warwick's centre, rolling over the defenders and attacking their right wing, which was overwhelmed as Trollope secured a resounding victory for the Lancastrians. During the Second Battle of St Albans, Henry VI was rescued from his captors a mile away from the town, while sitting under a tree singing in a catatonic state.

Following the defeat of the Yorkist forces at St Albans, Edward returned to London for his crowning. On 4 March, Edward entered St Paul's Cathedral to offer prayers to God before proceeding to Westminster Abbey and his coronation. Henry VI was still alive and had not abdicated the throne, so with Edward IV's crowning England had two kings acknowledged as ruler by separate factions. King Edward now united his army with Warwick and left London in pursuit of Henry and Queen Margaret to secure his kingship. The Yorkists headed toward Nottingham, where Henry VI had been reportedly sighted. Edward IV hastened after the king's troops, first clashing with them on 27 March at Ferrybridge. The Yorkist vanguard, led by Richard of Warwick, attacked the Lancastrians at the bridge, forcing their way across. As Warwick moved forward the following morning, his advance guard was ambushed and compelled to fall back with heavy losses. After the Yorkists retreated, the Lancastrians destroyed the bridge, compelling Edward IV to cross the river upstream at Castleford before resuming his search for Henry VI's army. After fording the River Aire, the Yorkists bivouacked for the night near Castleford, while King Henry's forces encamped in the open countryside south of the small village of Towton. On the morning of 29 March, the two armies deployed into battle formation, facing each other on a plateau between the villages of Saxton and Towton. Henry VI was present with his army but took no part in the fighting, spending the day in prayer. The 35,000 Lancastrians were under the command of Henry Beaufort, Duke of Somerset, who organized his troops into three divisions, while the 28,000 Yorkists were led by Edward IV. Beaufort was positioned at the right of his line, with the soldiers of Henry Percy, Earl of Northumberland, on his left wing and the Duke of Exeter in the centre. King Edward divided his army into three groups, leading the left flank himself while Sir John Wenlock held the right wing and the Fourth Duke of Norfolk, John de Mowbray, commanded the rearguard.

Just before the battle began, it started to snow, with the strong prevailing wind blowing into the faces of the Lancastrians. Edward IV first ordered his longbowmen to fire into Henry Beaufort's men. As the Yorkists' arrows struck the front lines, the Lancastrian ranks were decimated. When the Lancastrian archers replied, their arrows fell short of the Yorkists due to the strong wind. With his casualties growing from the archers' attack, the Duke of Somerset sent his infantrymen charging across the open field through the snowstorm into the enemy ranks. After shooting a final volley, the Yorkist archers retired and their footmen rushed forward. As King Edward's infantry advanced, on the left flank the Yorkists came under a gallant attack from the Lancastrian cavalry, quickly falling into disorder with heavy casualties. During the bloody melee, the Lancastrians shouted taunts of 'King Henry, King Henry'. Seeing his left collapsing, Edward IV took command and rallied his men, encouraging them to stand their ground. Over on the right wing, the Earl of Northumberland's assaults against the Yorkists were beaten back, as King Edward's men continued to hold their position. Henry Beaufort continued to throw his troops into the left flank onslaught, forcing the Yorkists to fall back. Fierce fighting continued there, with Edward's men beginning to flee the battlefield, but the Duke of Norfolk then arrived with his cavalrymen, charging over a ridgeline into the infantry of the Duke of Somerset. Under the thundering assaults of the fresh horsemen, the Lancastrian attack broke and the soldiers fled the field after ten hours of savage combat, the forces of Edward IV pursuing them into the snowy night with their pathway illuminated by the glow of the nearly full moon. The chase was continued into the following day. Over 18,000 men were killed at Towton, including Sir Albert Trollope and John Neville, Earl of Northumberland. Henry VI took no part in the battle at all, staying isolated in his tent with his priest and servants.

In the wake of the defeat of their army at Towton, Henry VI, Margaret and the 7-year-old Prince Edward of Lancaster fled the kingdom, seeking shelter in Scotland. Upon crossing the border, the deranged King Henry was housed in Edinburgh with Dominican monks. While the king remained in the north, he served as the figurehead to his supporters in England, who continued his fight for the crown. Henry's mental condition rendered him incapable of ruling, so Margaret led the campaign to regain the English throne for the Lancastrians. The warlords of northern England retained their allegiance to the King Henry's cause, continuing to resist the regime of Edward IV. In June 1461, the Scots attacked the Yorkists at Ryton and Brancepeth in support of Henry VI's return to power, but were defeated. Later, the Earl of Oxford, his son and other followers of Henry VI were captured and executed by Edward IV's government for planning an armed landing in Essex. Meanwhile, in Northumberland, the Lancastrian fortresses at Alnwick, Dunstanburgh and Bamburgh were captured in 1464 by the army of the Yorkist king.

Queen Margaret remained at the centre of the campaign to defeat Edward IV, and in July 1461 she sent Duke Henry of Somerset to the French court of Charles VII seeking military aid. When the duke returned with empty promises, the queen crossed the Channel to Brittany with written authorization signed by Henry VI seeking martial help, with the offer of the Pale of Calais in return. She travelled to Touraine with her entourage and negotiated an agreement for armed support against Edward IV's regime. Margaret recrossed the Channel with a fleet of forty-three ships and 800 French soldiers, landing in Scotland. Following the arrival of the French reinforcements, who were led by Pierre de Breze, the Lancastrian king, Somerset and a contingent of Scottish troops joined the queen and her allies, sailing south and landing at Bamburgh in late October. The queen's forces set out inland, recapturing Alnwick Castle for their local followers. The anti-Yorkists won several skirmishes, but lacking money and troops, Henry VI, Margaret and de Breze were compelled to abandon their campaign. After reinforcing the remaining pro-Lancastrian fortifications and making their presence known to the Yorkists with pillaging raids, the queen's army put to sea for Scotland. During the voyage, the fleet was wrecked in a violent storm, Henry VI and Margaret only just managing to reach safety at Berwick on the north-east coast of England.

With her husband's quest for the English throne in shambles, Margaret and Prince Edward of Lancaster left Henry VI at Bamburgh in June 1463 and made their way to the Duchy of Bar in France, where her father, Rene of Anjou, gave his daughter, Edward and their small entourage a permanent residence. King Henry was taken back to Edinburgh under the care of the Bishop of St Andrews. While the king remained in Edinburgh in a state of mental confusion, the Scots negotiated a truce with Edward IV, increasing the risk of Henry's extradition to England as a traitor. In 1464, the Lancastrian king was forced to leave Scotland, returning to Bamburgh for his own safety. Henry's supporters then resumed their efforts to regain the English monarchy for him.

In April 1464, a Lancastrian force led by Henry Beaufort, Duke of Somerset, was defeated at Hedgeley Moor, and the following month the Yorkists won another battle in northern England near Hexham. The fall of the remaining Lancastrian fortresses soon followed, ending resistance to the reign of King Edward IV. Henry VI had been with the Lancastrian army as it advanced to Hexham, staying at Bywell Castle before the battle. After the Lancastrian defeat, he was taken by his remaining loyalists into Lancashire, moving from friendly house to friendly house to evade capture by the Yorkists. With the defeat of King Henry's allies, Edward IV was able to move to solidify his rule over England, securing the allegiance of the magnates, ecclesiastic lords and populace.

Following the defeat of his followers in northern England, Henry VI apparently wandered through the towns and countryside, frequently dressed as a monk, accompanied by two priests, a doctor and loyal squire. He travelled for nearly a year through Lancashire, western Yorkshire and Westmoreland until he was finally captured in June 1465 in woodlands near Clitheroe, some 30 miles north-west of Manchester. He was then taken to London on a horse, with his feet tied to the stirrups. The king was met on 24 July by the Earl of Warwick, Richard Neville, and paraded through the capital's streets to the Tower of London. While Edward IV was in Canterbury, he received news of his rival's capture, ordering a celebration in the cathedral with the singing of a Te Deum, followed by a sermon and a visit to the shrine of St Thomas Becket to give thanks.

The deposed King Henry VI spent more than five years confined to the Tower. He was provided with a staff drawn from Edward IV's household and given a small budget for his food and clothing needs. A priest was assigned to him, who met with the king daily for prayers. During his long confinement in the Tower, Henry received humane and largely lenient treatment from his captors. He welcomed occasional visitors, but normally spent his days sitting or walking quietly alone. From his lack of activity, the deposed king appeared to have been resolved to his fate.

With Henry VI secure in the Tower and no longer a threat to his reign, Edward IV was accepted as king throughout England, although pockets of Lancastrian support remained in the northern shires. With his kingship largely solidified, the Yorkist monarch turned to the recovery of the lost English lands in France. Before mounting his invasion across the Channel, he negotiated alliances with King James III of Scotland, the Danes and the Duke of Brittany. The Valois king, Louis XI, countered the danger by making contact with the Lancastrians and supporting their plots against the Yorkist regime. King Edward's chief advisor, Richard Neville, Earl of Warwick, continued to favour an alliance with France and began clandestine negotiations in 1464, proposing the marriage of Edward IV to Louis XI's daughter, Anne. When the Earl of Warwick discovered the king had secretly married Elizabeth Woodville, he was incensed and embarrassed at the loss of his prestige in the courts of Europe. Elizabeth Woodville, a widow with two children, was from a family of lower nobility. At a time when most kings married women of royal blood, the marital union with the Woodvilles was not popular among the nobles and churchmen. Elizabeth's father was a knight and her mother a widowed duchess, which brought little prestige to the Yorkist monarchy. The new queen's family was now in a dominant position at the royal court and posed a threat to Warwick's association with King Edward IV. Soon after the wedding, the king arranged a series of marriages for his wife's sisters and brothers, which further diminished the opportunities for other families to build a strong relationship with the Yorkist regime. The result of the unpopular marriage was the weakening of the once strong affiliation between Edward and the powerful northern English Nevilles.

The split between the king and Warwick grew deeper when Edward negotiated an accord with Burgundy and Brittany, while Earl Richard favoured an alliance of friendship with Louis XI. The Woodvilles were related to the ruling Breton family, while Warwick was receiving favours from the French crown. As the king continued to expand his connections with the Burgundian and Brittany magnates, Warwick withdrew to his lands in Yorkshire and began to conspire against the Yorkist regime, bringing the king's younger brother, George of Clarence, into his party of supporters. Rumours spread in the summer of 1467 that Warwick had fashioned an agreement with Queen Margaret of Anjou for a joint military campaign to overthrow Edward IV and place Henry VI back on the English throne.

In the summer of 1469, while Henry VI remained in the Tower under guard, Edward IV learned that the Duke of Clarence was about to marry Warwick's daughter. The king had earlier forbidden the marital union, and the defiance of his order was viewed as a clear act of insubordination. A messenger also reported that the ceremony was to take place in Calais and the rebel party was preparing to sail to the Pale. Warwick's deputy in Calais had earlier been involved in a plot against the Yorkists, and the earl considered the Pale a safe haven. After reaching Calais, Warwick issued a proclamation calling for a rebellion in the northern English shires, encouraging his supporters to join him in mid-July at Canterbury and march against the Yorkist regime.

Warwick crossed the Channel with a force of troops and made his way to London, where he was welcomed by the local government and citizenry. Following a brief stay, he hastened to Coventry, his followers continuing to join his army during the march. In Coventry, the earl united his troops with Sir John Conyers, who had also risen in revolt against the unpopular regime of King Edward. When the king's army challenged Warwick, the rebels launched a surprise attack, forcing the loyalists to withdraw.

Edward IV was on the road to join his army when he learned of his soldiers' defeat. The Yorkist king turned back toward London, but was seized by Warwick's men and confined to a rebel castle. During the revolt in the north, two members of the Woodville family – the queen's father and younger brother – were captured and beheaded on orders from Warwick. With possession of the Yorkist monarch, Earl Richard now had control of the government and attempted to set up his administration, but without the legitimacy of an anointed king he lacked the support to rule. Violence and rebellion erupted, the orders of Warwick being widely ignored. With unrest spreading, he was compelled to release the king from custody. To maintain peace in his kingdom, Edward IV invited his brother, Duke George, to meet Warwick to resolve their differences. George, who had actively supported Edward's claim to the English throne, was invested with the Duchy of Clarence by his brother in 1461 and named Lord Lieutenant of Ireland. With the backing of Duke George and Richard Neville, England was once again under the rule of an accepted king, but the Earl of Warwick still harboured desires for the throne, while Henry VI was isolated and beset with prolonged periods of mental instability in the Tower.

Despite his gestures of reconciliation, Warwick was again implicated in a rebellion in the spring of 1470, this time in Lincolnshire, where the rebels favoured the assumption of the English crown by George of Clarence. After hearing of the escalating threat of his brother and the Earl of Warwick, the Yorkist king mustered his forces and moved to put down the uprising. Marching into Lincolnshire, the rebellion was quickly suppressed, with Warwick and Clarence forced to flee to the European mainland. After the Duke of Burgundy refused to receive them, the two rebel lords were obliged to join arms with Louis XI. The French king offered to support their revolt if they agreed to reconcile with Queen Margaret and Prince Edward of Lancaster.

With the help of the French, Warwick landed in Devon in mid-September 1470 and proceeded toward his followers in London, while Edward IV was suppressing a revolt in Yorkshire. When Warwick reached Doncaster, he waited for his brother, John Neville of Montagu, who was advancing with a large army of reinforcements. After the Yorkist king learned of Montagu's desertion to his brother, he fled from England, making his way to sanctuary in Burgundy.

After the mayor of London and his alderman heard of the Yorkist king's flight from northern England, they took charge of the Tower, visiting the imprisoned Henry VI with the Bishop of Wainfleet. They removed the mentally deranged Lancastrian monarch from his captivity, taking him to the palace of the Bishop of London. When Warwick and Clarence arrived in the city on 5 October with a large armed force, Henry VI was moved to the Bishop of London's palace. Eight days later, he was taken in royal procession to St Paul's and recrowned King of England. Following the ceremony at the cathedral, the Lancastrian sovereign served as a figurehead ruler for Warwick's party. Henry VI remained in his palace for the next five months as the designated monarch, but the kingdom was governed by Warwick as Great Chamberlain and George of Clarence. As co-heads of state, they made appointments for the kingdom's many administrative offices, set foreign policy and summoned parliament. During their rule, a ten-year truce with France was negotiated and arrangements were finalized for Queen Margaret and Prince Edward's return to court from France.

In 1471, Louis IX resumed his quest to break the powers of the French feudal warlords, declaring war on the Duchy of Burgundy. The threat from the French crown gave the Burgundians just cause to finance Edward IV's restoration to the English throne to thwart the French king's alliance with the Warwick faction. On 11 March, the Yorkist king sailed from Flushing with an army of 1,200 English and Burgundian mercenaries. He landed in Yorkshire at Ravenspur, occupying York after the city officials surrendered and opened the gates. From York, the king hastened to Nottingham. After entering the town, he again declared his inheritance rights to the throne of England and prepared to advance to London to enforce his rule. After learning of the return of his rival, Warwick took refuge in the castle at Coventry and awaited the arrival of his brother, John Neville, Earl of Montagu, with his army. While Warwick was delayed at Coventry, his ally, Clarence, realized his future was better served with his brother, deserting the Lancastrians and joining forces with the Yorkist king at Banbury. The united Yorkist army continued south, reaching London without encountering Warwick. When Edward IV reached the capital, his supporters rallied to his cause and opened the gates. Following her earlier departure from the royal court during the overthrow of her husband, Queen Elizabeth Woodville had taken refuge in Westminster Abbey, but was now reunited with Edward. In the late afternoon of 11 April 1471, Edward IV entered the city unopposed. He went directly to St Paul's Cathedral to offer prayers and secure possession of Henry VI. When King Henry met Edward, he embraced him and reportedly said: 'Cousin of York, you are very welcome. I hold my life to be in no danger in your hands.' The Lancastrian monarch was kept close to King Edward and placed under guard.

While the Yorkists were reoccupying London, Warwick and his Lancastrian army of 10,000 men reached Barnet in Hertfordshire. After Edward IV had secured his possession of London, he moved north with Henry VI in his entourage to challenge Warwick for the crown of England. When his scouts reported the advance of the Yorkist army, the Earl of Warwick positioned his forces north of Barnet on a ridgeline near the road to London. The Lancastrians were deployed into three divisions, with the left wing under the command of John de Vere, Earl of Oxford, the right flank headed by Henry Holland, Duke of Exeter, and Warwick leading the infantry in the centre. The Lancastrian cavalry was placed on the two wings, while the archers were concentrated in the middle of Warwick's front.

The army of Edward IV, comprising approximately 8,000 soldiers, arrived near Barnet at sunset on 13 April. He formed his divisions in the dark to repel an expected attack in the early hours. When the Yorkist monarch departed London, he took Henry VI with him to prevent his rescue by Lancastrian supporters. Throughout the coming battle, the deposed king would remain in the centre of the Yorkist line, as usual taking no part in the fighting. During the night, King Edward's right flank, led by Duke Richard of Gloucester, was repositioned too far from the enemy's battle line, leaving the left wing of Lord William Hastings exposed to the Lancastrian troops. The soldiers of both armies spent a sleepless night awaiting the battle at dawn, while listening to the constant fire of the Lancastrian cannons.

As the sun slowly broke through the thick morning fog, the sounds of drums and trumpets called the men to arms. Around 5.00 am, the Yorkist footmen moved forward, while Warwick led his soldiers into the mist. When the opposing armies collided, Gloucester quickly realized there were no enemy troops on his front, so swung his forces to the right, ploughing into the flank of Exeter's men. Meanwhile, on the opposite wing, the Earl of Oxford attacked, pushing the Yorkists back in savage fighting. With no support on his flank, Hastings' men were quickly overwhelmed and fled the battlefield, pursued by the Lancastrians.

After defeating William Hastings' forces, Oxford returned to the battle, but in the still dense fog mistakenly attacked the centre formation of Warwick. Under assault by Oxford's men, the troops of Warwick believed their compatriots had deserted the Lancastrian cause, so unleashing a fierce counter-attack. As the Lancastrians thus began to waver, Edward IV sent his reserves into the fray, securing victory as Warwick's line collapsed and his soldiers fled. During the fighting, John Neville, Earl of Montagu, and his brother Richard, Earl of Warwick, were both killed, along with approximately 2,000 other Lancastrians, while 500 Yorkists fell.

In the wake of the Yorkist victory at Barnet, Henry VI was taken back to London under heavy guard and returned to the Tower. On the same day as the battle, Queen Margaret and her 18-year-old son, Prince Edward of Lancaster, landed at Weymouth in Dorset. The Lancastrians, compelled to abandon their plans to march on London after their defeat at Barnet, instead headed north to join their mustering supporters. They then travelled through the western counties, their followers rushing to join their growing army. At Exeter, the army of the queen and prince was merged with the forces of the Earl of Devon and the Third Duke of Somerset, Edmund Beaufort. Margaret and her allies planned to advance through the Severn valley to unite with the forces of Jasper Tudor and then move into the heartland of their Duchy of Lancaster, where more volunteers were waiting to join their army.

After Edward IV learned Margaret of Anjou had landed and was advancing toward the Lancashire heartlands with her army, he assembled his men and set out on 24 April to defend his rights to the English throne, while the deranged Henry VI remained imprisoned in the Tower. Late on 3 May, the Yorkists intercepted the

Lancastrians at Tewkesbury. King Edward established his encampment for the night 3 miles from his enemy and prepared for battle in the morning. Early the following day, he sent his scouts to reconnoitre his foe's position. At Tewkesbury, the Lancastrian army of 6,000 men was deployed with Prince Edward serving in the centre as the nominal commander-in-chief as the ranking nobleman. The left wing was commanded by the Fifteenth Earl of Devonshire, John Courtenay, and the right flank by Lord John of Wenlock. The Lancastrian centre was under the command of Edmund Beaufort of Somerset, with Prince Edward positioned near him.

During the middle of the morning, the Yorkist king formed his 5,000 infantrymen for battle. He took command of the troops in the centre and sent his brother, Richard of Gloucester, to lead the vanguard, while ordering Lord William Hastings to take charge of the rearguard. A contingent of 200 mounted spearmen was placed on the left flank to protect the exposed wing.

With his army in battle formation, Edward IV sent his men forward over rough terrain, hampered by ditches, hedges and rutted ground. Nearing the enemy, Gloucester halted his advance and fired at Edmund of Somerset's division with his artillery pieces and archers. Under heavy fire, Edmund Beaufort ordered Wenlock to support him from the right wing, and then launched a counter-attack against the Yorkist left. Gloucester responded by unleashing an assault on Somerset's men, his 200 mounted spearmen also charging into the enemy's ranks. Attacked on the front and right flank, Beaufort's division was decimated, the survivors of the bloody onslaught starting to flee the battlefield, leaving behind their dead and wounded. As the Lancastrian centre collapsed, their remaining divisions were overrun by the powerful assaults of Edward IV and Lord Hastings. Approximately 500 Yorkist soldiers were killed at Tewkesbury, while Lancastrian losses were over 2,000. During the fighting, Henry VI's son, Prince Edward of Lancaster, was killed, along with John Wenlock and John Courtenay of Devonshire. The Duke of Somerset and fifteen other noblemen escaped the battlefield, taking refuge in Tewkesbury Abbey. They were granted sanctuary by the priest, but King Edward disregarded the asylum and seized them. After a short trial, they were executed in the grounds of the church.

Two weeks after his victory at Tewkesbury, Edward IV returned to London in triumph. With the death of Prince Edward at Tewkesbury, Henry VI was the only direct surviving member of the Lancaster family. While the deposed monarch remained alive, he was a constant rallying point for revolt and a threat to the security of the Yorkist regime. During the night of his arrival in the capital, Edward ordered the assassination of King Henry. After the 49-year-old monarch was killed, his body was taken from the Tower and placed in St Paul's Cathedral, where it could be viewed by the populace. Following the funeral service at Blackfriars, Henry VI's remains were carried by barge to the Benedictine Abbey at Chertsey and buried in the Lady Chapel. Queen Margaret remained in the Tower for the next five years before her cousin, King Louis XI, paid her ransom. She then returned to France and spent the next six years living in Bar and Anjou, dependent on a pension from the French crown. The king's wife eventually died in August 1482 at the age of 52 and was buried in the cathedral at Angers.

In the aftermath of Henry VI's murder, Edward IV reigned over England for the next twelve years unchallenged. Upon his death in April 1483, the Yorkist throne was inherited by his young son, who became Edward V. At the time of his succession to the monarchy, he was only 12 years old and his uncle, Richard of Gloucester, was appointed Lord Protector of England, heading the government for his nephew. The Duke of Gloucester had aspirations for the crown of England, his supporters in the legislative assembly of Lords and Commons declaring Edward IV's children illegitimate and Richard their rightful king. On 6 July 1483, Gloucster ascended the throne as King Richard III. Soon after seizing the kingdom, Edward V and his younger brother, Richard of York, were taken to the Tower and killed, apparently on orders from their uncle. Richard III held the reins of power for the following two years before he was unhorsed and killed by Rhys ap Thomas at the Battle of Bosworth Field on 22 August 1485, with Henry Tudor thereafter taking the crown as Henry VII.

Selected Sources

Ackroyd, Peter, *Foundation – The History of England from Its Earliest Beginnings to the Tudors* (Thomas Dunne Books, 2011).

Cannon, John and Hargreaves, Anne, *The Kings and Queens of Britain* (Oxford University Press, 2001).

Cheetham, Anthony, 'Henry VI', in Fraser, Antonia, *The Lives of the Kings and Queens of England* (Alfred A. Knopf, 1975).

Griffiths, R.A., *The Reign of King Henry VI* (Sutton Publishing, 1998).

King, Edmund, *Medieval England – From Hastings to Bosworth* (Phaidon Press, 1988).

Ross, Charles, *Edward IV* (Methuen, 1974).

Seward, Desmond, *The Wars of the Roses* (Carroll and Graf Publishers, 2007).

Smith, Goldwin, *A History of England* (Charles Scribner's Sons, 1957).

Watts, John, *Henry VI and the Politics of Kingship* (Cambridge University Press, 1996).

Weir, Alison, *The Wars of the Roses* (Ballantine Books, 1995).

Wolffe, Bertram, *Henry VI* (Yale University Press, 1983).

Henry VII

On 21 May 1471, the deposed Lancastrian King of England, Henry VI, was murdered in the Tower of London on orders from the reigning Yorkist regime of Edward IV, casting Henry Tudor into the leadership of those opposed to his rule. Henry Tudor was forced to flee to safety in Brittany, fearing his position as the only surviving Lancaster claimant to the crown made it too dangerous for him to remain in England. During his years in exile, the bloody Wars of the Roses continued, but a strong faction loyal to the Lancastrians supported the return of Henry Tudor as king and the overthrow of Edward IV, and later his successor, Richard III. In the wake of the death of King Edward in 1483, Henry Tudor crossed the Channel and made an unsuccessful attempt to seize the English kingdom. He was compelled to return to France and wait another two years before landing in Wales with an armed force of English dissidents. As he hastened toward London, his small army amassed hundreds of volunteers, and on 22 August 1485 clashed with Richard III at Bosworth Field, winning a decisive victory. Henry VII was crowned King of England on the battlefield, becoming the first king of the Tudor dynasty.

Henry Tudor was the only son of Edmund Tudor, Earl of Richmond, and Lady Margaret Beaufort. Edmund Tudor and his brother, Jasper, were half-brothers of Henry VI, receiving their grants of land and titles from him. Henry was born at Pembroke Castle in Wales on 28 January 1457 and was acknowledged as heir to his father's properties and title of Earl of Richmond. Henry was a direct descendent of the Lancastrian lineage through his father and mother, who was a great-great-granddaughter of King Edward III. During the Wars of the Roses, Edmund Tudor was appointed guardian for the continued Lancastrian hegemony along the Welsh border, but while confronting enemy forces was captured and died in captivity in November 1456. With the death of her husband, Lady Margaret was compelled to seek support from her brother-in-law, Jasper Tudor.

After Henry's birth, he spent his first years at Pembroke under the protection of his uncle Jasper. In 1461, the infant Henry's life changed dramatically when Edward IV seized the English throne and granted Pembroke to Lord William Herbert, forcing Jasper Tudor to flee from Wales. Lord Herbert was named guardian for Henry Tudor and was responsible for his protection and upkeep. When Henry was aged 5, he moved with Herbert and his large family to Raglan Castle in south Wales and was raised in his household. Under the care of Herbert's wife, Anne, the young Tudor was well provided for and received a rounded education. Under the instruction of his tutors, Henry excelled in his studies of French, reading and writing, mathematics and religion. While at Raglan Castle, a local master of arms provided his military training, teaching him to fight with the sword, billhook, hammer and battle axe, while also learning the skills of horsemanship.

As Henry Tudor continued his education and military training at Raglan Castle, in late July 1469 Herbert of Pembroke led 5,000 Welsh and English troops at the Battle of Edgecote Moor against the 6,000 Yorkist archers and foot-soldiers of Robin of Redesdale, who were attempting to enforce the rule of Edward IV. Lacking a strong contingent of archers, Pembroke's infantrymen were driven back, but he rallied his men and regained the advantage. On the verge of victory, Yorkist reinforcements arrived and the Lancastrians broke and fled the field. During the retreat, Pembroke was captured, and on the following day he was executed. In the aftermath of the death of his guardian, Henry Tudor remained under the custody of Anne Herbert until the Lancastrians overthrew the monarchy of Edward IV and restored Henry VI to the English throne. With the Lancastrian party back in control of the realm, Jasper Tudor returned from his refuge and took back responsibility for his nephew. In 1470, Jasper travelled with Henry to the royal court in London to encourage the regime to restore the Earldom of Richmond to him. During his visit at court, Henry Tudor was presented to King Henry VI, who greeted him saying: 'This is he unto whom both we and our adversaries must yield and give over the dominion.' The king's prophecy came true the following year when Henry Tudor became the heir to the Lancastrian crown.

While Henry Tudor resided in Wales, moving from castle to castle, in England the Lancastrian king's return to power was short-lived. In 1471, his army was shattered at the Battle of Tewkesbury and Henry VI was soon after murdered in the Tower of London on orders from Edward IV. As the lone Lancastrian claimant to the English throne, it was no longer safe for Henry to stay in Wales as a threat to the Yorkist regime. To protect Henry, Jasper Tudor took his nephew to the Welsh coast with a small contingent of supporters. They were recognized in the town of Pembroke and imprisoned for a short period, before escaping to Tenby. They then boarded a ship to France, but during the voyage a storm drove them to Brest in Brittany. Henry Tudor and his uncle were received by Duke Francis II and granted asylum in his duchy. Francis II had become Duke of Brittany in 1458 and was occupied for most of his reign with the quest of the French monarchy for his duchy. In defence of his lands, he joined the League of Weal against Louis XI of France in 1465 and invaded Normandy. The duke later became an ally of Edward IV in their conflict against the French throne. When Francis II died in September 1488, he was succeeded by his daughter, Anne.

Henry Tudor resided in Brittany under the protection of Duke Francis II, who was continually pressed by Edward IV to return him to England to eliminate his threat to the English crown. As the duke of a small independent duchy, Francis used Henry as a pawn to his political advantage in his bargaining between Edward IV and the French king. At the Breton court, Henry was witness to the duke's diplomatic intrigues, playing the French against the English. During his stay in Brittany, Henry learned the skills of negotiations, while monitoring events at the English court. Henry Tudor and his uncle, along with part of his entourage, were later sent to the royal chateau at Suscinio, where they stayed for the next eleven years. To protect Henry and Jasper against an attempted kidnapping by the Yorkists, Francis II fortified the castle with his soldiers.

Henry Tudor remained in exile in Brittany for fourteen years. Meanwhile, in England, following the death of her first husband, Henry's mother Lady Margaret Beaufort had remarried twice, the second time to Lord Thomas Stanley, who was a trusted follower of the Yorkist king. In 1459, Thomas Stanley succeeded his father as Baron Stanley and Lord of Man, inheriting his father's vast estates and numerous titles, which gave him immense power across north-west England. He supported the Yorkist monarchy, and was appointed Steward of the Household and in 1483 Constable of England for his loyal services to the crown. During the short reign of Edward IV's son and successor, Edward V, Lord Stanley remained a faithful ally of the young monarch.

From the English court, Margaret Beaufort corresponded with her son Henry in Brittany and frequently suggested a marriage between him and a daughter of Edward IV to bind the two houses closer together, likely at the insistence of the Yorkist king. As Margaret urged her son to marry into the Yorkist dynasty, in 1476 Edward IV pressed Duke Francis II to return Henry Tudor to England to marry one of his daughters, hinting that the presence of his mother at court would ensure his security. The duke finally agreed and arranged for Henry to be sent to England. Envoys from Edward IV reached the Breton court and accompanied Henry Tudor to St Malo for the passage across the Channel. Fearing he was actually being taken to his death, Henry mimicked an illness en-route to the coast. He was able to escape Edward's envoys and obtain sanctuary in a monastery, thus being protected against seizure by the Yorkists. Following the failure of his envoys to return Henry Tudor to England, King Edward made no further attempts to capture his rival during his reign.

In the summer of 1483, Richard of Gloucester usurped the English crown after the death of Edward IV and the murder of his young nephew, Edward V. Richard III's seizure of the throne and his rumoured implication in the death of Edward V created widespread animosity to his reign. Henry Stafford, Duke of Buckingham, had supported Richard's assumption of the monarchy, but grew increasingly disenchanted with his tyrannical rule. In September, the duke secretly wrote to Henry Tudor in Brittany, assuring him of his loyalty and imploring him to land in England to end the autocratic reign of King Richard. Buckingham assembled an army of dissident Lancastrians in Wales, and in October 1483 began to march against the king in the name of Henry Tudor. Soon after the rebels set out, violent rain storms swept across Wales, overflowing rivers and washing out roads. With his route to England blocked by the stormy weather, Buckingham was forced to stay in Wales. As the storms continued unabated, many of his men deserted, forcing him to abandon the attempt to overthrow Richard's rule.

While Buckingham was struggling to advance against the Yorkist monarchy, in Brittany, Duke Francis II agreed to finance Henry Tudor's invasion of England, providing him with a fleet of transport vessels and an army of 5,000 soldiers. Henry and his expeditionary force set sail for the port of Poole in southern England in October. During the crossing, Henry's fleet was scattered by a violent storm and his ship reached the coastline at Plymouth with only one other vessel. As Henry Tudor approached the shore, there were soldiers claiming to be adherents of Buckingham and exhorting him to land. Henry became suspicious of the men, and fearing a trap quickly returned to his ship and escaped back to the European mainland. Without the presence of Buckingham or Henry Tudor, the rebellion against Richard III was crushed. Henry's ship landed in Normandy, and with permission from the new French king, Charles VIII, he set out for Vannes in Brittany. While the rebellion against the Yorkists had failed, a large number of Welsh and English fugitives crossed the Channel to join Henry and form the nucleus of his new army and government in exile.

When Richard III's parliament met at Westminster in January 1484, both Henry and Jasper Tudor were convicted of treason for their participation in the recent uprising. Many powerful English magnates then rallied to Henry, fleeing into exile in Brittany and joining the revolt in opposition to Richard's autocratic rule. Margaret Beaufort continued to correspond with her son, encouraging him to make war against the king and claim the throne for himself. Margaret's husband, Lord Stanley, remained an influential and dominating nobleman, whose presence at the English court was vital to limiting possible retaliations against Henry Tudor's mother. Although Lady Margaret was accused of high treason, the Yorkist regime took no action against her and she maintained communication with her son.

Richard III resumed his older brother's attempts to convince Duke Francis of Brittany to send Henry to him, but was repeatedly refused. In the summer of 1484, the Duke of Brittany became incapacitated by mental illness, and his ducal treasurer, Pierre Landois, temporarily led the Breton government in place of the duke's under-age daughter, Anne. Constantly in need of archers and men-at-arms to protect the duchy against probing incursions by the French, Landois agreed to surrender Henry for 3,000 bowmen. At the English court, Lord Stanley learned of the agreement during a council meeting and sent a messenger to Henry urging him to flee the duchy. When the Tudors were informed of the plot, Jasper and Henry escaped to the French kingdom, where they were welcomed and provided with financial resources by Charles VIII's government.

Henry Tudor remained in France organizing his campaign against Richard III. In the summer of 1485, he was joined by John de Vere, Earl of Oxford, who had recently escaped from imprisonment in Yorkist-controlled Calais. The earl was an experienced soldier whom Henry could utilize in the recruitment and organization of his expeditionary force. To enhance his claim for the English crown, Henry pledged to marry the eldest daughter of Edward IV, Elizabeth of York. The marriage would weaken the power of the king by buttressing the support of the Yorkists to his cause and unify the two families that had been fighting for the English throne for over twenty years. To bolster his campaign further against the usurper, Henry met the French king, Charles VIII, in Angers, seeking financial and military aid. Conferring with Charles, he claimed to be the rightful sovereign-lord of England and to have the recognition of the nobility. The French monarch replied that he was well informed about his pursuit of the throne but promised little help. In France at this time, the power behind the throne was Charles VIII's older sister, Anne of Beaujeu, who was more willing to subsidize Henry in his quest for the crown. She agreed to lend Henry a large sum of money, while his friends in England advanced additional funds. With this money, he recruited an army of over 3,000 mercenaries and prepared to invade England again. The Tudor's forces were augmented to over 5,000 men with a contingent of French soldiers and nearly 500 English and Welsh volunteers.

Henry chose to land in Wales, where his family had many allies who would rally to his fight against the Yorkists. Early on 1 August 1485, Henry Tudor set sail from Harfleur with his small fleet, making his way to Wales in favourable weather as a southern wind propelled his ships across the Channel to Mill Bay on the south-west coast of Wales. Upon landing late in the day on 7 August, Henry kissed the ground and recited a verse from the Bible, saying: 'Be thou my judge, O Lord, for I have come innocently.' He formed his troops into marching order and set out into central Wales, hoping to recruit additional forces. Henry had previously corresponded with the Welsh warlord, Rhys ap Thomas, and expected him to join his army, but the Welshman failed to appear as the invaders began to move across mountainous terrain. Finally, over a week later, he received the much-needed reinforcements from Rhys at Newport in east Wales. During his advance into England, Henry wrote to Lord Thomas Stanley notifying him of his arrival and seeking his support. On 17 August, he met Stanley at Stafford, asking for his aid, but Lord Thomas remained hesitant to join the rebellion.

As Henry proceeded down Watling Street, King Richard III, having expected the invasion during the summer, had moved his army to Leicester to be better positioned to defend his realm. After learning of his rival's movements, he hastened with his forces to intercept him on Watling Street. Shortly after his meeting with Henry Tudor at Stafford, Lord Stanley followed the Tudor army into England but remained noncommittal. On 19 August, the king rode with John Howard, Duke of Norfolk, and other loyal magnates from Nottingham to Leicester to join his mustering army. Richard III had received intelligence from his scouts that Lord Stanley and his 5,000 men were in the area, and now strongly suspected him of treachery. Henry Percy, Earl of Northumberland, was part of the royal army, but Richard also considered him untrustworthy. On the evening of 21 August, Richard encamped at Sutton Cheney, several miles from Bosworth, while Henry Tudor was at White Moors, about 15 miles away. During the night, the king sent a message to Lord Stanley ordering him to unite with his army, but received no reply. Early on the morning of 22 August, greatly outnumbered by his enemy, a despondent Henry Tudor also dispatched a messenger to Stanley urging him to come to his support. Henry received a confusing communication from Sir Thomas, stating he would come in 'Time convenient'.

Later that morning, the Tudor army deployed for battle at Bosworth Field, with Henry's 5,000 men awaiting orders. Lacking military experience, Henry Tudor named the veteran solider, John de Vere, Earl of Oxford, as commander of his army, while he took a position with the rearguard. At de Vere's recommendation, the troops were aligned into four sections, with Sir John Savage on the left flank, Sir Gilbert Talbot holding the right wing and the centre under de Vere, while

Henry was in reserve with a small force of cavalry, billmen and archers. John Savage was an early supporter of Henry Tudor, encouraging him to invade England and overthrow the Yorkist king. He had fought at Tewkesbury and became a close friend of Edward IV, but now opposed Richard III's oppressive rule. Gilbert Talbot was the second son of the Earl of Shrewsbury, and his leadership at Bosworth would contribute greatly to Henry Tudor's victory.

Richard III's soldiers were placed on the western slope of Ambion Hill, overlooking the rebels. He led an army of 12,000 men and appointed the Duke of Norfolk, John Howard, to command the vanguard, while Henry Percy of Northumberland was in charge of the rearguard of 3,000 northerners. In the front of the Yorkist soldiers were a strong contingent of archers. The king's vanguard was made up of billmen, archers, foot-soldiers and a detachment of artillery, which protected the flanks. Richard's field artillery comprised 150 cannons and a similar number of light pieces known as serpentines. The still uncommitted Lord Stanley deployed his men to the side of both armies in two formations, with the first division under his command and the second led by his younger brother, William Stanley.

The battle began when the Earl of Oxford ordered his infantrymen to advance uphill into the troops of the Duke of Norfolk. De Vere led his men around the marshy field and up the slopes into volleys of enemy arrows. As the Tudor assault staggered under this fire, Norfolk sent his foot-soldiers charging down the hill. Under a savage attack, Oxford rallied his men around their standards and formed them into a triangle formation, counter-charging uphill. During this bloody onslaught, Norfolk was killed by an arrow to his neck while engaging Oxford in hand-to-hand fighting. After the failure of the duke to penetrate Henry's line and now fearing Lord Stanley's betrayal, Richard III ordered Henry Percy to block his advance, but the message was ignored. As the tide of battle turned against him, the Yorkist king led his household knights and yeomen in a furious charge downhill toward the red dragon banner of Henry Tudor. Richard smashed into the Tudors, killing the standard bearer and several other men in a fury of slashing swords and billhooks. During the melee, Henry exchanged several blows with Richard. To protect Henry from the onrushing enemy troops, his bodyguards formed a circle around him, fending off the Yorkists.

As Henry Tudor fought for the English crown, less than half a mile away, Stanley was carefully observing the battle now turn in Richard's favour. He had to decide to either throw his support behind Henry or allow the Yorkists to win the day. Stanley, having made his decision, rode to the front of his men and led them in an attack against Richard's troops. The power of Stanley's charge quickly swept aside the Yorkists, who fled the battlefield, leaving behind many dead and wounded men. Richard III refused to surrender, continuing to fight by swinging his sword wildly, shouting 'Treason, treason!'. He fought on alone until the last Yorkist king was killed by Rhys ap Thomas. Soon after his victory at Bosworth Field, Henry Tudor was crowned King Henry VII of England by Lord Stanley as his men roared 'God save King Henry, God save King Henry!'. Richard's body was taken to Leicester for public display as proof of his death, and later buried in the local Church of Greyfriars. The remains of the Yorkist king were discovered in 2013 and reburied in Leicester Cathedral. An examination of the skeleton showed he had died a violent death, with ten wounds – eight to the head and two to the body.

Following his triumph at Bosworth, Henry VII's possession of the English throne was his by right of conquest, but his hereditary claim was inferior to that of Edward Plantagenet, Earl of Warwick. To further secure his hold on the crown, Henry sent a trusted servant to Sheriff Hutton Castle near York – the former seat of the Neville family, which had passed to Richard III after Richard Neville's death at the Battle of Barnet – to take custody of the 10-year-old Plantagenet, who was imprisoned in the Tower of London under guard.

After spending two days in Leicester after the battle, Henry set out for London. On 26 August, he was greeted by the mayor and aldermen, who escorted him into the city. He went to St Paul's Cathedral to offer prayers for his victory and succession to the throne. From the cathedral, the king was housed for several days at the palace of the Bishop of London, where he was reunited with his mother, Lady Margaret Beaufort, following a separation of many years. To solidify his rule, he ordered parliament to assemble on 7 November so he could receive the recognition of the Lords and Commons as their rightful king.

Shortly after establishing his court in London, Henry VII created the Yeomen of the King's Guard to serve as his personal bodyguard, which comprised fifty veteran soldiers. The Guard is the oldest military organization still in existence in England, with its sixty participants taken from retired members of the British armed services. It performs a purely ceremonial role for the monarch. To govern the kingdom, Henry organized his ruling council, appointing loyal supporters to high offices in his regime. He rewarded his allies by naming his uncle, Jasper Tudor, the Duke of Bedford, while Lord Thomas Stanley was given the Earldom of Derby along with several other royal offices. The Earl of Oxford, John de Vere, was honoured with high offices and the Admiralty of England and Ireland. Sir Rhys ap Thomas was appointed Chamberlain of South Wales, while other lesser lords were compensated with minor properties. The estates of his allies seized by the regime of Richard III were also now returned to their original owners.

At the time of Henry's assumption of the English throne, the kingdom had fewer than 3 million inhabitants. London was the centre of the kingdom's commercial activities, while Westminster was the seat of government. The majority of the Tudor monarchy's subjects made their living by farming the land, making agriculture the main industry. In 1485, the realm was far from being a united state, with loyalties to the powerful regional magnates still prevailing. Regional differences remained common, and during the reign of Henry VII the process of creating a unified England was started with the destruction of the territorial supremacy of the magnates and enforcement of the rule of the monarch.

Henry VII wanted his coronation ceremony to be held before parliament assembled to prevent the legislative members from claiming they had conferred the crown to him. The anointment was now scheduled for 30 October 1485 in Westminster Abbey. Following protocol, he spent the night before the ritual at the Tower of London in special apartments. While in the Tower, he appointed seven new knights, according to tradition. On the afternoon of 30 October, he departed from the Tower in a great procession, preceded by the mayor of London and the high magnates of the realm, through richly decorated streets to Westminster. Henry was dressed in a long purple gown edged with ermine, and rode on a great warhorse under a royal canopy supported by four knights on foot. He entered the abbey, and sitting on the coronation chair was anointed and crowned by the Archbishop of Canterbury. The honour of bearing the king's crown was given to Jasper Tudor, while the sword of state was carried by Lord Thomas Stanley. Following the anointment and taking of oaths, Henry VII, followed by his entourage, emerged from the abbey to show himself to the populace as the rightfully anointed King of England. The ritual was followed by a great banquet held at the Tower. During the dinner, the king's champion challenged all-comers to contend for the throne, following the custom of prior coronations.

As ordered by the king, parliament assembled on 7 November at Westminster, with Henry VII seated on his throne. The members of the Commons and Lords welcomed the new king and soon passed an act removing any doubt about the legality of his inheritance rights to the crown. To further consolidate his reign, the legislative assembly issued decrees of attainder against the enemy lords defeated at Bosworth. To fund his new administration, Henry was granted the revenue from the trade levies and the duchies of Lancaster and Cornwall were annexed to the royal regime. On 10 December, the Commons, acting through its speaker, beseeched the king to marry the daughter of Edward IV, Elizabeth of York, which was supported by the lords.

Soon after the Lords and Commons acknowledged Henry VII as king, his marriage to Elizabeth of York took place at Westminster Abbey. At the time of her wedding on 18 January 1486, Elizabeth was nearly 21 years old, while Henry was 29. She was described by contemporaries as a tall woman possessing beauty, charm and grace. At the Yorkist court, she had received a well-rounded education under the guidance of her father. While their marriage had been arranged for political reasons, they soon developed a relationship of deep mutual affection. As the daughter of Edward IV, who had been popular with the citizens of London, Elizabeth quickly developed a similar relationship. The wedding ceremony was performed without waiting for the required papal dispensation to eliminate further cause for rebellion in support of the Yorkists by joining together the two former rival families. Pope Innocent VIII's approval was necessary because Henry and Elizabeth were both descendants of John of Gaunt, making them related within the forbidden four degrees of relationship. The papal bull finally arrived in June 1486, clearing the last legal obstacle to the union between the Yorks and Tudors. As part of the Holy See' decree, Innocent VIII threatened to excommunicate any person who challenged Henry's right to rule over England, which served to further strengthen his sovereignty.

Assuming the government of the English people, Henry viewed the kingdoms of Europe in the traditional manner, considering France and Scotland as his historical enemies and the Low Countries as both economic friends and allies, while ignoring the Holy Roman Empire and Italy. In spite of only holding control of the Pale of Calais, England still regarded a large part of western France as its rightful possession, and its foreign policy was driven by a desire for the recovery of those lands. When Henry VII was crowned, it was as King of England and France, and he still subdivided his royal shield with the three English leopards and the lilies of France. In Henry's English kingdom, his subjects were induced by past history to favour any monarch that was hostile to the French, while an alliance with the Holy Roman Empire or Spain would receive popular support.

In the spring of 1486, Henry VII set out on a tour of the counties in the north-east, where support for the Yorkist faction remained strong. He travelled to Lincoln and into Yorkshire, meeting his local officials and churchmen, while presenting himself to his subjects in a show of royal pomp. While he was in Lincoln, the king heard that Lord Francis Lovell and the Stafford brothers, Humphrey and Thomas, who had fought for the Yorkists at Bosworth, had escaped from their sanctuary at Colchester and were now plotting revolt against the Tudor regime. Lovell had been a close associate of Richard III, and after the defeat at Bosworth continued to challenge the Tudor assumption of the throne. The Stafford brothers advanced into the West Country against Worcester, while Lovell and his supporters marched to seize control of the city of York. Henry swiftly ordered Jasper Tudor to assemble an army of 3,000 soldiers and move to destroy the rebels. As Jasper gathered his forces, the Tudor monarchy issued a decree pardoning all dissidents who immediately laid down their arms. The proclamation immediately led to the desertion of many insurgents and the collapse of the revolt. The Stafford brothers were again granted sanctuary by the Church, but Henry VII ignored the decree, arresting them and sending them to the Tower. Francis Lovell remained free and attempted to seize the king in York. After the failure of the York conspiracy, he also participated in Lambert Simnel's revolt against the Tudors in the following year.

King Henry, having been away from London for over three months, set out to rejoin Queen Elizabeth in the capital. In late summer, they proceeded to Winchester for the birth of their first child. Henry traced his heritage to the Saxon era and was resolved that his heir be born in the Saxon kingdom's capital to more closely associate his regime with the Britons. On 20 September, the queen gave birth to a son, who was named Arthur in honour of the Britons. There was great rejoicing by the king's subjects as news of the heir's birth spread across the realm.

In early 1487, rumours became widespread of a new plot against the Tudor monarchy. A priest from the town of Oxford had taught the 11-year-old son of an organ-maker, Lambert Simnel, to impersonate Edward, Earl of Warwick, who had remained a prisoner in the Tower of London. Warwick had been imprisoned in the Tower soon after Henry VII succeeded to the throne, and few could now remember how he looked and acted. Simnel, who was the same age and height as the earl, now claimed the kingship in place of Henry. As supporters began to rally to the pretender, the real Warwick was taken from the Tower to attend Mass at St Paul's, where he could be seen and thus dispel the rumours. After talking to Edward in the cathedral, the Earl of Lincoln, John de la Pole, recognized that the prisoner was the real Earl of Warwick but became convinced that by backing the imposter, Henry could be overthrown. De la Pole gained the patronage of Edward IV's sister,

Margaret of Burgundy, who remained an avid enemy of the Tudors, and with her financial aid formed an alliance with Francis Lovell. John de la Pole and Lovell hired 2,000 heavily armoured German mercenaries commanded by Colonel Martin Schwartz and sailed to Ireland, where they were welcomed by a large force of dissidents led by the Earl of Kildare, Gerald Fitzgerald. Simnel was brought to Dublin, and after securing Irish acceptance of his rights as the English monarch, he was crowned Edward VI in Dublin Cathedral.

With his army of Irish and German troops, the Earl of Lincoln crossed the Irish Sea with the imposter king, landing in Lancashire. The rebel army, now comprising 8,000 troops, marched toward Yorkshire, where the local populace was sympathetic to the Yorkist cause. During the rebels' advance, however, few Englishmen joined their ranks. After learning of Lincoln's arrival, Henry hastened to Kenilworth near Warwick with 12,000 soldiers, appointing Jasper Tudor and the Earl of Oxford, John de Vere, as his field commanders. As the king waited for the arrival of the enemy, the rebels turned south toward Newark. Henry then moved along the Fosse Way, intercepting the rebels on the slopes of Rampire Hill near Stoke Field. On the morning of 16 June, the Tudor forces were divided into three divisions, with John de Vere in command of the vanguard, Jasper Tudor leading the reserve and Henry VII in the rear. The Battle of Stoke Field began when the Earl of Oxford ordered his archers to fire volleys of arrows against their opponents' front. As the arrows struck, many of the lightly armoured English and Irish rebels were killed as they advanced. While Lambert Simnel's men struggled against Oxford, the Earl of Lincoln unleashed a supporting attack, sending his men against the royal vanguard. The hard-pressed loyalists held their line until reinforcements were sent by Henry, and after three hours of fierce fighting the front line of the pretender's army wavered and then broke, his soldiers fleeing with the forces of King Henry in close pursuit. During the battle, de la Pole, Colonel Schwartz and many followers of Gerald Fitzgerald were killed. An estimated 4,000 Yorkists and 1,000 loyalists died during the fighting at Stoke Field. Francis Lovell escaped from the battlefield but was drowned trying to cross the River Trent. Simnel also survived the battle but was taken prisoner, Henry VII assigning the pretender to duties in his kitchen and later making him royal falconer. The Earl of Kildare was pardoned after submitting to the king, and was later appointed Lord Deputy for Ireland. The fighting at Stoke Field finally brought to an end the Wars of the Roses after more than thirty years of brutal conflict, with the Tudor king securely on the throne of England.

In the aftermath of his triumph at Stoke Field, Henry remained in the north for several months before returning to London in early November. As he rode through the capital's gates, he received a rousing reception from his loyal subjects. The Tudor king then went to St Paul's to offer prayers for his victory at Stoke Field and his firm hold of the kingdom. On 9 November, Henry's second parliament, met with the Archbishop of Canterbury, John Morton, serving as Lord Chancellor. During the five-week legislative session, leaders of the Earl of Lincoln's uprising were condemned to death and lost their properties, hereditary titles and the right to pass them to their heirs under attainder. For her part in Lincoln's plot, parliament confirmed the forfeiture of Elizabeth Woodville's properties to the Tudor queen.

While parliament remained in session, Elizabeth of York was crowned queen on 25 November at Westminster Abbey. A choir of children sang songs of welcome as she entered the abbey and the coronation ceremony was performed by the Archbishop of Canterbury, with the king in attendance.

After thirty years of intermittent warfare for his kingdom, Henry VII required a prolonged period of peace to secure his sovereignty and end the period of stagnant economic growth. In October 1485, he arranged a truce with France for one year, which was later extended until January 1489. Henry continued his friendship with Francis II of Brittany and negotiated a commercial agreement with him in 1488. The Tudor crown also maintained friendly ties with the Scottish king, James III, who was occupied with rebellious barons. Relations with the Scots remained peaceful until James IV succeeded to the throne in 1488 and began pillaging raids across the English border. James was the first-born son of King James III and was acknowledged as heir to the Scottish monarchy. When the nobles revolted against his father, James supported the rebels and fought for them at the decisive Battle of Sauchieburn. James III was killed during the battle, with James IV recognized as his successor. James IV's later marriage to Margaret Tudor connected the houses of England and Scotland and led to the union of the two kingdoms in March 1603 when James IV's great grandson, James VI, became King James I of England.

Despite the unrelenting support of Henry VII, Brittany was invaded by the French, who had longstanding territorial ambitions in the duchy of Francis II. Henry feared the French takeover of Brittany would threaten his superiority in the English Channel and sent a force of volunteer bowmen to aid the Bretons. The 700 English archers were led by Edward Woodville, Lord of Scales. After crossing the Channel, he joined forces with the Breton army, advancing against the French. The allies met the host of King Charles VIII at St Aubin de Cormier in Brittany. During the ensuing battle on 28 July 1488, Scales commanded the vanguard of English and Breton troops and opened the fighting by shooting a storm of arrows into the ranks of the French, pushing them back. Scales then led a charge across the open field into the French front line. As the English and their allies fought the French and their mercenary troops, a gap opened in the Breton position and the enemy cavalry unleashed a fierce counter-charge, breaking through the line and routing Duke Francis and his English supporters. As the result of his defeat at the Battle of St Aubin du Cormier, Francis II was compelled to recognize Charles VIII as his overlord. In spite of the victory of the French army, the Tudor king continued to support the Bretons, and when parliament met he asked for more money to aid Duchess Anne, the recent successor to Francis. In 1489, Henry VII signed a treaty with Anne, pledging to send an army to reinforce her fight against Charles VIII.

During the English intervention in Brittany, Henry VII sent envoys to the European powers seeking allies against the French. He signed the Treaty of Medina with Queen Isabella and King Ferdinand of Spain in March 1489, restoring previous relations between the two realms. The agreement also included terms for expanding trade, which greatly benefitted English merchants. The bonds between the two kingdoms were solidified with the approval of the marriage of Henry's son, Prince Arthur, to Catherine of Aragon. Meanwhile, contacts with Archduke

Maximilian of Burgundy were resumed, and under the provisions of the Treaty of Dordrecht the realms' former accords were restored. The Tudor administration also sent agents into the Italian realms, seeking to increase commerce, while talks with the Hanseatic League reconfirmed the trade-related Treaty of Utrecht. The acknowledgement of King Henry's reign by the European states increased his prestige and popularity among his English subjects, while also expanding trade.

As Henry VII continued to bolster his hold on the English kingdom, he was again threatened by another claimant to his throne. In the autumn of 1491, a merchant from Brittany named Pregent Meno sailed into the port of Cork in Ireland with a cargo of silks and fine goods. Among the ship's crew was a young sailor, Perkin Warbeck, who had been hired by Meno to exhibit his goods to potential buyers. Warbeck was born in Flanders and was the son of a Flemish boatman. Dressed in the fine garments of a nobleman, the handsome Warbeck impressed the naïve inhabitants of Cork, who declared he was Richard, Duke of York, the younger brother of King Edward V. Despite Warbeck's continued denials, the Irishmen refused to believe him. Warbeck eventually agreed to impersonate the Duke of York and was taught to speak English and act like a nobleman. While the people of Cork supported his claim to the English crown, the Irish magnates refused to provide financial aid, so the plot to usurp the monarchy appeared over before it had really begun.

With Warbeck's future uncertain, news of the new pretender circulated across Europe. Relations between England and France had remained hostile, and Charles VIII invited Warbeck to his court to cast doubt on Henry's right to the throne. In the summer of 1492, the French king received the imposter and supported his claim as the English sovereign. Henry followed France's increasing aggression with concern, remembering Charles VIII's seizure of Brittany, and began preparations to defend his realm. He adopted a more aggressive foreign policy, making known his intention to assert his rights to the French crown. He summoned parliament to fund a formidable army and was voted two subsidies. An army of 15,000 men-at-arms, billmen and foot-soldiers, supplemented with cavalry, was mustered under the command of the Earl of Oxford, crossing the Channel in ships hired from Venice and landing at Calais. The earl hastened south to attack Boulogne, but the mobilization of the English army had taken too long and with the onset of winter fast approaching, King Henry was compelled to negotiate a peace treaty with Charles VIII. The French, also facing an invasion from northern Italy, quickly agreed to terms pledging to pay the English over 700,000 gold crowns in equal yearly instalments, while both kingdoms vowed not to aid the others' enemies. Realizing the Bretons had now permanently lost their independence, Henry VII agreed to the proposal, despite the strong opposition of his Lords and Commons, who continued to support Brittany.

In November 1492, the French signed the Treaty of Etaples with King Henry and were compelled to expel the pretender under its terms. Following his expulsion from the French regime, Perkin Warbeck found sanctuary in Burgundy at the court of Duchess Margaret of York, who acknowledged him as the rightful English monarch. At the ducal court, Warbeck became friends with the Burgundian

Duke Philip, who was the stepson of Margaret. In August 1493, Duke Philip and Warbeck travelled to Vienna and were received by the duke's father, Emperor Maximilian. At the Habsburg court, Warbeck was recognized as the successor to the English throne as King Richard IV. The pretender began issuing silver coins in his name and dressed his bodyguards in the colours of the Yorkists.

As Warbeck's quest for the English throne gained momentum at the European courts, in England the Yorkists' supporters began to conspire with him for his seizure of the crown. Henry VII felt increasingly threatened, sending ships to patrol the seas along the Suffolk coast and ordering reinforcements to buttress the defences of his ports. He made preparations to muster an army, calling on his nobles to provide men-at-arms. Henry, who had spies in Warbeck's entourage gathering intelligence, learned that in Calais and the shire of Suffolk, followers of the pretender were ready to rebel in support of him. Pro-Yorkist sympathizers, including Sir William Stanley, also made plans to aid Warbeck's English invasion.

With financial support from Margaret of York and her friends, the pretender raised an army and landed at Deal in Kent on 3 July 1495, expecting the locals to readily flock to his banner. He sent a scouting party ashore to gather intelligence on the loyalty of the populace, but the men of Kent had been warned of a possible invasion and challenged Warbeck's followers. Warbeck's campaign quickly fell apart, the Englishmen remaining loyal to Henry VII and mounting an attacked against his troops. In the ensuing battle, Warbeck's mercenary soldiers and volunteers were routed. During the clash, approximately 150 of his men were killed and most of the remainder were taken prisoner, with the foreigners to be held for ransom and the Englishmen hanged. After the defeat, the imposter and his remaining followers fled, putting to sea and heading for Ireland. He sailed into Waterford harbour with eleven ships, attacking the town by land and sea, anticipating the local Irish to rally to his quest for the English crown. However, once again he was repelled. The Irish resisted any attempt to enlist their support, and the imposter king wandered about Ireland for several months with a handful of supporters. With his pursuit of the English monarchy seemingly over, Warbeck received an unexpected invitation from the Scottish king, James IV, to visit his court at Stirling Castle. He reached the fortress in the winter of 1495 and received a friendly welcome from the Scots. With his relations problematic with the Tudor regime of Henry VII, King James IV used the pretender's presence to cast doubt on Henry's right to the English throne. The imposter king remained at the Scottish court for the next few months, being entertained by James IV. The king organized martial tournaments in his honour and arranged a marriage to his cousin, Lady Catherine Gordon. The longer Warbeck and his followers stayed in Scotland, the more his presence threatened to terminate the truce between the Scots and the English. As hostilities along the border intensified, in September 1496 the Scottish king assembled an army of 1,400 soldiers, and augmented with Warbeck's few Yorkists and mercenary troops advanced into northern England. Before unleashing their invasion, James IV, with Warbeck at his side, offered prayers at Holyrood Abbey for the success of their campaign. The allies crossed the frontier, pillaging the towns and farmlands of Northumberland before withdrawing to Scotland at the approach of a formidable

English army under Ralph Neville, Earl of Westmoreland. The king of the Scots had anticipated the northern English would rally to Warbeck's banner, but few volunteers joined his forces.

Still expecting an invasion of his northern shires from Scotland, Henry VII prepared to muster an army of 20,000 men to repel the Scots and Perkin Warbeck. He issued levies of taxes and forced loans to fund this force. The heavy taxes were highly unpopular, to the extent that in Cornwall the populace rebelled against the king's burdensome levy. As the Cornish rebels advanced unimpeded through the West Country toward London in opposition to the tax, they were joined by armed men from other regions. When the dissidents approached the capital, Henry VII took command of the troops at Henley Bridge and sent other loyal lords to defend the entrances to London. When the protesters reached Blackheath, close to London, they were opposed by the king's army and in the ensuing battle were defeated near the bridge at Deptford Strand, ending their revolt. After the rebels surrendered, Henry entered London to a hero's welcome. The leaders of the uprising were executed, but the king pardoned the remaining rebels after their payment of a fine. Following the suppression of the rebellion, the remaining Cornish protesters turned to Warbeck as their new champion.

Hostile relations continued along Henry's northern border, and following the destruction of the Cornish rebellion, envoys were sent to the Scottish court pressing James IV for a truce and the repatriation of the imposter Warbeck. Before the emissaries reached Scotland, the king of the Scots sent Warbeck to the English West Country with a small force to rally support against the Tudor king, while he launched an attack into northern England. James IV crossed into England and besieged the castle at Norham. As the loyal Englishmen continued to resist the assaults of the Scots, the Earl of Surrey hastened from Yorkshire with a relief army of 20,000 infantry and cavalry. King James was caught completely by surprise and forced to retreat north. After the withdrawal of his forces, James agreed to peace talks and a seven-year truce was signed at Ayrton Castle in the Scottish borders.

Meanwhile, on his way to the West Country, Perkin Warbeck stopped at Cork to muster the Irish Yorkists, but was forced to flee by the local royalists. The pretender's delay in Ireland gave Henry VII the opportunity to raise a powerful army to meet the rebels. Troops were mustered from south Wales by Rhys ap Thomas, while loyalists in Wilshire, Somerset and Dorset also rallied to defend the Tudor regime. Warbeck sailed to England with his small fleet, landing his men on the Cornish coastline at Whitesand Bay, near Land's End, on 7 September 1497 and proceeding toward Exeter. The pretender announced to the Cornish people that he would put an end to the exorbitant taxes levied to fight the Scottish, and was thus warmly received by the populace. At Bodmin, he was proclaimed the rightful King of England as Richard IV. As he advanced into Cornwall, more than 3,000 volunteers joined his army, despite the recent suppression of the Cornish rebellion. Following a ten-day march, the rebels reached the gates of Exeter. Warbeck ordered an assault against the walls and broke through the eastern gate. The defenders of Exeter rushed to the gate and beat back the enemy soldiers in fierce hand-to-hand fighting. Unable to take the town by storm, Warbeck abandoned his siege and made for

Taunton. During the march, he learned that a sizable royal army led by Henry VII was closing in on him, and during the night he deserted his forces and travelled to Southampton in an attempt to escape by ship. The coastline was heavily guarded by King Henry's naval forces, compelling Warbeck to seek sanctuary at Beaulieu Abbey in Hampshire with several loyal followers.

With his attempted usurpation of the crown in disarray, the pretender sent a representative to the king, offering to make a full confession in return for leniency. On 4 October the imposter was received by Henry VII and admitted his real name was Perkin Warbeck, while his father was a boatman from Flanders. With the imposter in custody, the remaining Cornish troops surrendered and the ringleaders were executed. Warbeck was taken to London in the royal entourage and paraded through the streets, amid the shouting and mockery of the city's populace, before being placed in the king's household under a light guard. After remaining in Westminster Palace for nearly six months, Warbeck escaped to Charterhouse in June 1498 but was soon recaptured. He was then placed under heavy guard and sent to the Tower of London. While in the confines of the Tower, Warbeck plotted his escape with Edward Plantagenet, Earl of Warwick, who had been a prisoner for over ten years. Their plans were quickly discovered and they were both executed for treason, eliminating the threat to Henry VII's throne.

In 1496, Henry VII signed the 'Great Agreement' with Philip IV of Burgundy to restore the wool trade between the two realms. England had become the dominant European trader in wool, and the Low Countries were its major export markets. The cloth industry comprised an important part of the English economy and the Burgundians relied heavily on trading in the commodity. In retaliation for Margaret of Burgundy's support for Perkin Warbeck, King Henry had earlier expelled the Flemish merchants and issued a trading embargo on the Burgundians, forcing the Merchant Adventurers, a trading company which maintained a monopoly in the Flemish wool trade, to relocate to the English enclave at Calais and abandon Antwerp. As the effects of the embargo stymied economic growth in both states, Henry and Philip agreed to end the restrictions and negotiated the 'Great Agreement'. The settlement instituted reciprocal trade privileges and established fixed duties. The results of the accord were highly favourable to the English, expanding wool exports and adding to the king's treasury.

While Henry VII's policies toward his European trading partners were largely driven by political motives, his relationship with the German Hanseatic League was mostly concerned with commercial issues. The Hanseatic League was a federation of merchant guilds and towns in north-west and central Europe, stretching from the Baltic Sea region to the North Sea. The Hanseatic League's members dominated trade for over 300 years, protecting their economic interest and political privileges. The League was centred on the German town of Lubeck. After securing his rule, King Henry moved to reduce the trading privileges previously granted to the League and expand English penetration into the markets of the Baltic Sea region. During the reign of Edward IV, his government had granted the League extraordinary rights in the 1474 Treaty of Utrecht, giving the German traders a reduction in the taxes and fees they paid to England. Reciprocal trade for the English merchants was given but not enforced in the German cities. King Henry introduced several measures to level the trading platform, but was forced to accept the current terms when members of the League threatened to offer financial support to the Yorkist Edward, Earl of Suffolk, who was a threat to the kingship of the Tudor monarch.

As the Tudor regime laboured to establish fair trade links with the Hanseatic League, Henry VII sent emissaries to the Danish court in Copenhagen to secure an economic agreement with King John for a treaty guaranteeing freedom of commerce in Denmark and its occupied zone in Norway. King Henry's representatives obtained a treaty guaranteeing open markets, promises of a trade depot in the town of Bergen and the right to fish in Icelandic waters. A new Anglo-French commercial accord was signed in 1498, removing obstacles placed on English merchants, and in 1505 the Tudor monarchy came to terms with Duke George of Saxony for friendly trading relations to counter the Yorkists' hopes of obtaining political and financial support from the duchy. Commercial relations with Spain were clouded by the matrimonial alliance between the two kingdoms, but Henry VII managed to reconfirm the trading privileges previously granted to Spanish merchants by Edward IV, which exempted them from duties paid by other nations and also applied to English traders in Spain.

In 1499, England was devastated by the plague, which killed thousands. To protect his family, Henry VII sent his children into the country, while he sailed to Calais with Queen Elizabeth. At the English enclave there, he met Archduke Philip IV of Burgundy and discussed possible marriages between the two royal families. During his stay in Calais, Henry staged martial tournaments, pageants and musical events to impress the European courts. Returning to England, King Henry and Elizabeth spent the summer months at Greenwich Palace with the royal court.

In October 1492, the Italian explorer Christopher Columbus, under license from the Spanish court, ignited the age of discovery and exploration in the New World by sailing west across the Atlantic Ocean, finding what was believed to be a sea route to the riches of China but was in fact the islands of the Caribbean. At the time of Columbus' journey, Genoese sea captain John Cabot was living in Bristol, making inquiries with bankers and merchants in London for an expedition of exploration to the west. Cabot's queries led to his introduction to the English king. Henry VII had earlier received the brother of Christopher Columbus, Bartholomew, who made a proposal for an expedition across the Atlantic Ocean. Henry showed little interest and missed the opportunity to share in the rich trade initiated by Columbus. To gain access to these markets, he agreed to sponsor Cabot's voyage.

On 5 March 1496, Henry VII issued letters patent to Cabot for his voyage to sail under the English flag and claim new lands in the name of the king. Cabot put to sea in early May 1497 on board the *Matthew*, reaching land on 24 June that was thought to be the coastline of China but most likely was present-day Newfoundland in Canada. He was rowed ashore holding the white English flag with the red cross of St George, claiming the territory for the regime of King Henry. Cabot's discoveries ignited the English quest for a colonial empire in the New World.

Following his return to England, Cabot was received by the king and granted an annual pension. Henry took special interest in the exploration of the west, and to challenge the Spanish for dominance in the New World he provided a manned and provisioned ship for Cabot's second voyage to 'China'. In May 1498, a fleet of five vessels sailed west from Bristol. During the crossing, the fleet was struck by a violent storm. One of the ships was damaged and forced to return home, but Cabot continued sailing west into the tempest. Cabot and the four remaining vessels were never seen again, most likely having been destroyed by the fierce winds and pounding seas.

The loss of Cabot's ships did not deter Henry VII from financing future voyages of exploration. In 1499, Bristol merchant William Weston led an expedition seeking passage west to the Orient with financial support from the Tudor king. He sailed across the Atlantic and continued down the coastline of current-day North America, claiming the territory for Henry's regime. In the following year, Hugh Eliot, with several other adventurers, purchased a ship with a share of the money provided by the king to search for new lands in the Far East. The son of John Cabot, Sebastian, with the sponsorship of the Tudor court, also embarked in two ships, sailing west to explore the shoreline of the present-day United States and Canada. The voyages of King Henry's sea captains, exploring under royal patronage, secured for England a lengthy extent of coastland in North America for future colonization, creating an overseas empire that reached from the Arctic Circle in the north to the Gulf of Mexico in the south.

King Henry enacted laws to expand the building of English ships for use in commercial and war endeavours. To encourage the construction of new vessels by his merchants, he published the Navigation Act of 1495, ordering all wine imports from Guyenne and Gascony to be transported only on English ships. Four years later, an additional navigation act was passed prohibiting the shipment of the dyers' plant woad from Toulouse in foreign vessels, when English ones were available. To boost the construction of large vessels that could be used as warships, the monarchy agreed to pay a subsidy to the builders.

The English navy had been rebuilt during the monarchy of King Edward IV and further expanded by Richard III. During the reign of Henry VI, the size of the royal fleet declined, and after the accession of Henry VII the rate of warship construction continued to fall. Richard III had a fleet of ten large warships, but by the end of the first Tudor's king's rule there were only five naval vessels remaining, including the 600-ton *Regent* with 225 cannons and the *Sovereign* with 141 guns. If needed in times of conflict, the Tudor regime could supplement its naval forces by employing merchant vessels and hiring Spanish ships. In 1495, Henry VII ordered the construction of the kingdom's first dry dock at Portsmouth and naval arsenals at Greenwich and Woolwich.

In the wake of his victory at Bosworth, Henry VII had taken the title of Lord of Ireland, but his rule was limited to only four Anglo-Irish counties and several towns, including Dublin. The larger part of the island was governed by the native princes. To enforce his sovereignty, Henry appointed Edward Proying as his Irish deputy. In early December 1494, Proying summoned an Irish parliament to meet in Drogheda to restore English authority. Under the Lord Deputy's leadership, laws were passed that protected the rights of the Tudor regime and a garrison of royal troops was established in the pro-English area to act in the king's interest. Despite Proying's enforcement of the king's laws, the cost of controlling Ireland from London proved too great and Henry was compelled to revert to the practice of depending on the Irish magnates to manage local affairs. To improve relations with the Irish, their uncrowned king, Gerald Fitzgerald, Earl of Kildare, was invited to London, where Henry established an amicable relationship with him. When Kildare returned to Ireland, he supported the Tudor crown and used his considerable influence to maintain peace with the English. In late March 1498, Kildare was authorized to assemble an Irish parliament to vote on local issues. He ruled Ireland with a tight rein in the name of the Tudor monarchy, suppressed a rebellion of the city of Cork in 1500 by hanging the mayor. When revolt erupted in Connacht in August 1504, Kildare raised an army and defeated the rebels at the Battle of Knockdoe. Following these events, Henry was respected as overlord for Ireland and established an era of peaceful relations.

In spite of his elimination of the threats from Warbeck and Edward Plantagenet, Earl of Warwick, King Henry remained uneasy about his English sovereignty. The Earl of Suffolk, Edmund de la Pole, who was now acknowledged by the Yorkist party as the rightful successor to the throne, began challenging Henry. Under risk of arrest by the royalists, Edmund fled across the Channel to the imperial court of Maximilian in July 1501. Meeting with the emperor, he sought his help in provoking a new rebellion to gain the crown of England. Henry VII was quickly informed of Edmund's treason and ordered the arrest of his brother, William, while other conspirators were also detained. Suffolk's attempts to win the support of the emperor failed and Edmund returned to Flanders under the protection of Archduke Philip of Burgundy. Henry made repeated attempts to secure custody of Edmund, but the archduke continued to give him safe haven.

The king remained on guard against new French aggression and was anxious to retain friendly relations with Archduke Philip to offset the hostilities of Charles VIII. As the archduke was sailing to the Spanish court in early January 1506, his fleet was struck by a violent storm. Philip's ship, battered by strong winds and waves, was forced ashore at Weymouth in Dorset. After learning of the archduke's unscheduled landing, Henry invited him to his court at Windsor. He treated his visitor with great courtesy, entertaining him with music and grand displays. They hunted deer together in the dense forestlands and enjoyed each other's company. During the Habsburg archduke's stay, the Treaty of Windsor was hammered out. Under the terms of the secret agreement, Henry pledged to support the Habsburg cause in Spain by recognizing Archduke Philip as the successor to Queen Isabella in Castile to undermine King Ferdinand, who was lobbying for the crown of his deceased wife. In return, the archduke promised to bring the Yorkist Edmund de la Pole, Earl of Suffolk, to Calais and turn him over to the English garrison. Suffolk was duly imprisoned in the Tower until 1513, when he was executed by the king's successor, Henry VIII. The imprisonment of the Yorkist claimant in 1506 ended the danger of a usurper uprising.

Following the imprisonment of Edmund de la Pole and the executions of Perkin Warbeck and the Earl of Warwick, the crown of England was now securely in the hands of Henry VII. Two Spanish envoys to the Tudor court had reported to Queen

Isabella and King Ferdinand in Madrid that King Henry 'Has established good order and keeps the people in such subjection as has never been the case before.' In spite of the lack of opposition, the king was still concerned about possible rebellions and sought astrologers and soothsayers, eager to hear their prophecies. Henry remained devout, attending daily Mass and praying for God's guidance.

While Henry had secured his assumption of the kingdom, the succession of his lineage grew increasingly questionable. He had married Elizabeth of York in January 1486 and they had eight children – four sons and four daughters – with only four living beyond infancy. The eldest son, Arthur, was born on 19 September 1486 and was acknowledged as heir to the throne. The second-born was Margaret, who was married to James IV of Scotland. Henry was the second son and became successor-designate following the death of his older brother. The last surviving child was Mary, who briefly became Queen of France when she married King Louis XII in 1514.

The Kingdom of Spain had been created by the union of Castile and Aragon, and to form an alliance with the new European power, Henry VII negotiated the marriage of his heir, Prince Arthur, to Princess Catherine of Aragon as a counter to the threat of France. In March 1489, Prince Arthur was officially betrothed to Catherine, but the monarchs of Spain continued to delay the ceremony and protect their daughter until all pretenders to the English throne were eliminated. After years of rearrangements in the terms of the marriage contract, the wedding finally took place on 14 November 1501 at St Paul's Cathedral in London.

Catherine had landed at Plymouth on 2 October after a perilous journey over stormy seas from Spain. The Spanish princess proceeded through the port city, where she was met by cheering crowds of well-wishers. The princess' entourage headed north to meet King Henry and Prince Arthur in Dogmerfield, near London. The king and his eldest son were escorted to Catherine's chamber and formally introduced to her. Following the meeting, Arthur wrote to his future father-in-law, Ferdinand, telling him 'He had never felt so much joy as when he beheld the sweet face of his bride'. When Catherine arrived in London for the wedding, she was greeted by trumpets and the sound of booming cannons. She rode through gaily decorated streets to the Bishop of London's palace. Several days later, the marital ceremony was held in St Paul's, with the Archbishop of Canterbury preforming the service. At the time of the wedding, Arthur was 15 years old and Catherine slightly older at 16. They were escorted down the aisle to the altar by his younger brother, Prince Henry. After the ceremony, ringing church bells echoed throughout the city. To celebrate the union between the two kingdoms, Henry VII ordered the spectacles of a jousting tournament, lavish banquets and performances of musical pageants. In the aftermath of the marital festivities, Arthur and Catherine resided at Ludlow Castle on the Welsh border. The union between the English and Spanish crowns was short–lived, however, as Prince Arthur died from consumption in April 1502.

After receiving the news of their son-in-law's death, Isabella and Ferdinand, wishing to retain their alliance with Henry VII, sent their ambassador to England to arrange the wedding of the widowed Catherine to Arthur's brother, Prince Henry. Negotiations dragged on over the payment of the remaining dowry. Finally, in early 1503, after the English agreed to accept a reduced dowry, the marital treaty was signed, conditional on Henry reaching the age of 15 and the securing of a papal dispensation for the marriage of Catherine to Prince Henry's brother. In spite of the agreement, the Spanish continued to delay the payment of the dowry, prompting King Henry to begin talks with the Duchy of Burgundy and the Holy Roman Empire for the marriage of Prince Henry. The question of the prince's wedding remained unresolved during the remaining few years of Henry VII's reign. During the negotiations for her marriage, Catherine stayed in England at the palace of the Bishop of Durham, her court becoming a centre for Spanish intrigue.

Less than a year after the death of Arthur, Queen Elizabeth of York died in London due to a post-partum infection. King Henry was grief stricken by her death, withdrawing to a private room and refusing to see anyone. After several days, the body of the queen was taken to the Tower of London and laid in state in the chapel for nine days, with six ladies of the court keeping a constant vigil. The queen was buried at Westminster Abbey on 23 February 1503 in the magnificent Lady Chapel, built by Henry VII.

Scotland had been an ally of France under the 'Auld Alliance' since 1295. To weaken the bond between the realms, Henry VII negotiated the marriage of his eldest daughter, Margaret, to the Scottish king, James IV. In January 1502, Princess Margaret was officially betrothed to the king of the Scots. Henry wanted to wait until his daughter was 18 years old before holding the marriage ceremony, but was pressed by the Scots to proceed with the marital union. In July 1503, on their way to Edinburgh, the king took Margaret to say farewell to her beloved grandmother, Margaret Tudor, at Collyweston. After travelling north, Margaret stayed in York, resting from the stresses of the journey and being entertained by the Earl of Northumberland. From York, the royal entourage continued northwards accompanied by Northumberland's supporters, who took the princess across the border, from where the Earl of Surrey escorted her to Edinburgh. The slow progression was planned by King Henry to show the wealth and glory of his kingdom. The wedding service was held in November at Holyrood Chapel. The matrimonial union with Scotland resulted in a period of peace between the two monarchies, as envisioned by the Tudor king.

After the death of Prince Arthur, only three of Henry VII's eight children remained alive, weakening the future of his dynasty. Several years after the death of Queen Elizabeth, he considered remarrying, and in 1505 he made contact with the Naples kingdom of Queen Giovanna for a matrimonial alliance. The king sent envoys to the Naples court to report on the queen and her prominence. He received favourable reports on Giovanna, but looked negatively on her financial position and future prospects, while there were also political concerns. Another possibility for marriage was the Duchess of Savoy, Margaret, but Henry showed little interest. He briefly considered marriage to Joanna of Castile in the hope of ruling her realm as regent for the reportedly mad queen. The Tudor king's marriage to Elizabeth of York had developed into an affectionate relationship, and her death rendered him more remote and melancholy in his contacts with others. Consequently, Henry chose to remain alone, never remarrying.

In the aftermath of his queen's death, Henry VII withdrew into his own private world, setting himself apart from his court bureaucrats. To ensure his privacy, a Privy Council was established and he selected only members who enjoyed his complete trust. The king resided and worked in private chambers, avoiding the more open reception rooms. The royal household was reorganized, being administered by loyal officials and servants known by the king. During his final years, Henry largely ruled without the consent of parliament, summoning only one legislative assembly during this time.

Despite maintaining sombre private living chambers, the king continued to keep a magnificent court. He spent freely to impress the monarchs of Europe and secure their acceptance of his assumption of English power. Martial tournaments and grand processions were routinely held, along with musical performances. Henry was entertained by dancers and acrobats, while curiosities were paraded for his courtiers' amusement. A large menagerie was maintained, with exotic animals purchased or given as gifts to the king. Henry hunted frequently and maintained a staff of five falconers for his enjoyment. At his court, he enjoyed card games, gambling and the company of jesters, keeping five near him. He collected books and established a library, employing a librarian to oversee his collection. The king was also fond of music, funding a court orchestra and chapel choir for his personal pleasure and official state events.

During the reign of Henry VII, the English legal and trade systems were reformed, with experienced and trustworthy advisors named to his councils, while new committees were formed to administer the judicial and treasury functions. Receipts for the royal treasury were increased by changing the methods for the collection of rents and taxes to limit corruption and waste. The Tudor kingdom's agrarian and wool industries were reformed and made more efficient. Henry's royal treasury was enriched by trading in alum, which was essential in the process of making wool and cloth. The European economies were only supplied with alum from the papacy's mines, but Henry opened up trade with the Ottoman Empire using leased Italian ships to transfer the commodity to customers in the Low Countries and England.

As his financial reforms generated increases in the kingdom's revenue, Henry began a grand building programme. During the reign of Edward IV, construction had begun of St George's Chapel at Windsor Castle, and under Henry's instructions the splendid structure was completed. When his favourite great house at Sheen was destroyed by fire in 1497, he erected a new palace on the site in the Gothic style, renaming it Richmond. Within two years, the new palace was ready for occupancy by the royal family. The private lodging was richly decorated with fourteen turrets and an unusually large number of windows. Richmond Palace was set apart from other royal houses by its large tower. The palace quickly became Henry VII's favourite residence. He also spent large amounts of money to rebuild Baynard Castle and the palace at Greenwich. With financial assistance from the Church, the king conceived and built the chapel at the eastern end of Westminster Abbey. Under his patronage, Henry founded three houses for the Franciscan Order and for the monks and nuns at Richmond, Greenwich and Newark. Furthermore, the Savoy Hospital in London was financed with money provided by the king, offering care to 100 destitute patients.

Beginning in 1502, the health of King Henry VII began to fail, becoming increasingly worse in the following years. The monarch complained about his eyesight and recurring bouts of consumption. He became gravely ill at his manor house in Wanstead in 1506, and the following year the illness returned. He suffered from pulmonary tuberculosis, which affected his breathing, leaving him weak and tired. In the spring of 1509, he was too frail to observe Holy Week and remained at his palace in Richmond. As he laid in his bed at Richmond, the king called Prince Henry to his bedside, advising him to marry Catherine of Aragon. Soon after, King Henry died on 21 April 1509 at the age of 52, ending a reign of twenty-four years.

The first Tudor king left a will with a complete description of his desired funeral. He called upon the faithful to pray for him in his time of need and ordered 10,000 Masses said for his soul in the London area churches a month after his death. Henry bequeathed 2,000 pounds for the sick and needy, and asked that silver statues of himself in prayer be placed at the shrines of St Edward the Confessor and St Thomas Becket and in Norfolk at the Chapel of Our Lady of Walsingham. The body of Henry VII was conveyed in state to London and placed in St Paul's Cathedral for the entombment service. On 10 May, the Bishop of Rochester conducted the funeral service and the king was buried in his chapel at Westminster Abbey alongside his beloved Queen Elizabeth. The sarcophagus was designed and built by the Italian Pietro Torrigiano of Florence, with portrait effigies of the king and queen lying side by side, decorated with putti, cherubs and classical images.

Selected Sources

Ackroyd, Peter, *Foundation – The History of England from its Earliest Beginnings to the Tudors* (Thomas Dunne Books, 2011).
Blum, Jerome, *The Emergence of the European World* (Little Brown, 1966).
Bevan, Bryan, *Henry VII – The First Tudor King* (The Rubicon Press, 2000).
Chrimes, S.B., *Henry VII* (University of California Press, 1972).
King, Edmund, *Medieval England* (Phaidon Press, 1988).
Lockyer, Roger, *Henry VII* (Longman Group Limited, 1968).
MacDougall, Norman, *James IV* (Tuckwell Press Ltd, 1997).
Pickering, Andrew, *Lancastrians to Tudors* (Cambridge University Press, 2000).
Read, Conyers, *The Tudors* (W.W. Norton, 1964).
Roberts, Clayton and Roberts, David, *A History of England – Volume* (Prentice Hall, 1991).
Seward, Desmond, *The Wars of the Roses* (Carroll and Graf Publishers, 2007).
Williams, Neville, *The Life and Times of Henry VII* (Weidenfeld and Nicolson, 1994).
Williams, Neville, 'Henry VII', in Fraser, Antonia, *The Lives of the Kings and Queens of England* (Alfred A. Knopf, 1975).

Henry VIII

In the aftermath of several failed military campaigns to recapture the lost English lands in France, King Henry VIII signed a non-aggression treaty with the French crown in 1518 binding the two kingdoms to continual peace. The agreement was soon expanded to include additional European powers to end the perpetual wars that had devastated the continent. To celebrate the détente, Henry VIII agreed to meet with the French king, Francis I, in the Pale of Calais at Balinghem. The two former enemies met on 7 June 1520, greeting each other in friendship. Amid the magnificent temporary palaces, chapels, banqueting halls and tents at Balinghem, more than 12,000 English and French courtiers gathered in peace. The assembly of English and French magnates and prelates served as an opportunity for both monarchs to display the grandeur and wealth of their courts. Henry's temporary palace covered over 2 acres and was richly decorated, containing a great hall, chapel and golden fountain. Over two weeks, the English and French kings took part in daily jousting events, archery competitions and numerous military games, while dining together in great feasts and attending musical performances. The assembly ended on 24 June with a Mass in an open-air church. The cloth of the many tents and clothes of the courtiers used so much golden thread that the event became known as the Field of the Cloth of Gold. Despite the promises of peace amid the magnificent grandeur of one of the great spectacles of Medieval Europe, relations between the two nations quickly worsened after Henry signed a separate treaty with the Holy Roman Empire, and England was soon at war again with France.

Prince Henry Tudor was born at Greenwich Palace on 28 June 1491, the third child of King Henry VII and Queen Elizabeth of York. The prince spent his first years at Eltham Palace under the care of guardians appointed by his mother. As the second of his father's four sons, Prince Henry was not expected to rule England and was destined for a career in the Church. He began his clerical education at an early age with the objective of occupying the Archbishopric of Canterbury in the future. Under the guidance of his grandmother, Lady Margaret of Beaufort, who directed his studies in a more secular direction, tutors were appointed for Henry's education and he was taught reading and writing, along with the languages of Latin, French and Spanish, while also receiving lessons in music, religion and mathematics. Henry developed a strong fondness for music, learning to play the lute, organ and harp, as well as composing instrumental and voice songs. When Henry was later named Duke of York, he organized his own ensemble of musicians, who became an indispensable part of his entourage. As the second son, he received no training for the future assumption of the Tudor throne, living a very restrictive life away from any association with the ruling of the kingdom, and was barred from attending council meetings and audiences with foreign dignitaries.

On 5 April 1493, the young prince received his first royal office when he was named Constable of Dover Castle. Other honours followed, and on 30 October 1494, at the age of 3, he travelled from Eltham to Westminster to receive the spurs of a Knight of the Bath. On the following day, Henry was given the title Duke of York before the assembled king and nobles in the chambers of parliament. The title was presented to Henry as a rebuke to the pretender Perkin Warbeck's false claim to the English crown.

Prince Henry was second to his older brother, Arthur, in the line of succession to the English throne, and in November 1501, when aged 10, took part in the wedding of the Tudor heir to Princess Catherine of Aragon. Henry VII had earlier sent envoys to Spain to forge a political alliance with Queen Isabella and King Ferdinand for the marriage of their daughter, Catherine of Aragon, to Prince Arthur to solidify the union between the two royal houses. At the beginning of the marriage ceremony, Henry led his sister-in-law to St Paul's Cathedral and down the aisle to his waiting brother. He witnessed the marital rites performed by the Archbishop of Canterbury, and following the service escorted Catherine out of the church to the cheers of the waiting spectators. In the wake of the marriage ritual, Prince Henry enthusiastically participated in the celebrations, greatly enjoying the dancing and musical performances.

The marriage between Arthur and Princess Catherine lasted only four months, as the prince died of consumption in April 1502. Henry was now recognized as heir-apparent to the English crown. He immediately succeeded to his brother's right to the Duchy of Cornwall, and on 18 February 1503 was created Prince of Wales and Earl of Chester, while his title of Duke of York as the second son was rescinded.

While Henry was still Duke of York, Henry VII had begun preliminary negotiations with Archduke Philip IV of Burgundy for the marriage of his second son to the archduke's daughter, Eleanor. The death of Arthur created the opportunity for a better matrimonial and political alliance, and talks with the Spanish ambassador were soon underway for the marriage of Princess Catherine to Henry. Discussions quickly stalled over the payment of the remaining dowry for Arthur, which Ferdinand refused to pay. When Henry VII proposed the marriage to Catherine, the Spanish queen demanded the return of her daughter. The marital impasse was finally resolved after the terms were revised and the marriage contract was signed. On 25 June 1503, Henry, Prince of Wales, was officially betrothed to Catherine in the Bishop of Salisbury's London house.

Despite eventually agreeing to the marriage between Catherine and Henry, the Spanish regime continued to delay the wedding and Henry VII began seeking other advantageous marital unions in the European courts for both his son and daughter. In 1506, Archduke Philip of Burgundy died, his unexpected death presenting the English king with the opportunity to expand his influence into the Kingdom of Castile and central Europe through the marriage of his daughter, Mary, to Prince Charles of Habsburg. The king sent his envoys to the Burgundian court, and in

December 1508 signed a treaty uniting the two realms. As Henry VII continued his quest for the marriage of his son to a European continental power, King Ferdinand became less interested in the wedding of his daughter to Henry, threatening to cancel the treaty. While her marriage back into the Tudor family remained in doubt, Catherine stayed in England, isolated with her small court at the palace of the Bishop of Durham. Prince Henry then began receiving ambassadors from the Holy Roman Empire for his marriage to a daughter of the Duke of Bavaria, as the Tudors steadily pressed the European courts for a bride for the Prince of Wales.

In April 1509, Henry VII grew increasingly ill, suffering from respiratory difficulties. With the king nearing death, Prince Henry remained at his bedside at Richmond Palace. In a weak and laboured voice, the monarch spoke to his son, exhorting him to marry Catherine of Aragon, defend the Church and fight against infidels. When the first Tudor monarch died on 21 April, his son was recognized as his successor to the English throne as King Henry VIII. The following day, the new monarch travelled from the palace to the Tower of London to begin his reign. From the Tower, he issued his first official act confirming the pardons recently granted by his father, but exempted several lords who had gained the wrath of the populace for their strict and merciless collections of royal taxes. The sentence of execution for the men gained Henry VIII the favour of his subjects. He stayed in London, and on 10 May attended the funeral service of his father, which was conducted by the Bishop of Rochester at St Paul's Cathedral.

Shortly after assuming the reins of power, Henry VIII proclaimed that he would honour the last wishes of his father and marry Catherine of Aragon. Following the announcement, there was widespread speculation in the European courts that the king had created the story of his father's advice to placate the Habsburgs, whose daughter had earlier been the subject of matrimonial negotiations. Talks for the marriage to Princess Catherine were resumed with the Spanish ambassador, and after the Tudor king agreed to forego the unpaid dowry, the marital treaty was signed. The wedding ceremony between Henry and the Spanish princess was held in the Franciscan Church at Greenwich on 11 June, attended by the grand nobles and churchmen of the realm.

In late June, Henry VIII departed from Greenwich to the Tower of London to begin preparations for his coronation ceremony. He planned a grand and elaborate celebration and put hundreds of carpenters, tailors, embroiderers and goldsmiths to work preparing for the pageant. On 23 June, the king and his queen proceeded through London to Westminster Palace for the crowning ritual. The roadways were richly decorated with tapestries and banners of golden cloth, and loud cheering crowds lined their route. The following day, the king and his entourage made their way to Westminster Abbey on streets covered with fine carpets and under canopies. Before the great lords, ladies and prelates of the kingdom, William Warham, Archbishop of Canterbury, placed the crown on the king's head, asking the assembled audience: 'Would you have Henry as king?' They responded with loud cries of 'Yea, yea!' Following tradition, the invited guests retired to Westminster Palace for a magnificent banquet. The coronation celebrations concluded for the day with a martial tournament that lasted until dark. The festivities were continued over the following days with jousts, pageants, tilts and hawking, while the nights were occupied with more banqueting, musical performances and dancing.

During the rule of Henry VII, the policies of the royal regime had been directed at securing internal peace in England and maintaining cordial relations with the courts of Europe. The strategies of the first Tudor monarch had brought a reconciliation with France and favourable relations with Spain and the Holy Roman Empire. After assuming the crown, Henry was occupied with jousts, hunting and touring his kingdom, receiving the adulation of his subjects. He was content to leave the affairs of state to his governing council, which was occupied by his father's advisors. During his youth, Henry had been exposed to tales of heroic knights whose exploits on the battlefields of France brought them fame and glory. He was now determined to replicate their feats by waging war in Europe. He had little interest in domestic affairs as he became drawn toward renewing the conflict against the French king, Louis XII. When he learned that a letter had been sent to the Valois monarch by his council expressing the desire for goodwill and peace between the two kingdoms, Henry exploded with anger, yelling at his counsellors: 'Who wrote this letter? I ask peace of the King of France?' Acting without the advice of the counsellors, he ordered the Archbishop of York, Christopher Bainbridge, to meet with Pope Julius II in Italy and arrange an alliance against France. Meanwhile, the royal commission acted independently, forming a union of friendship with the Valois regime.

On 1 January 1511, while Henry VIII was actively engaged in forming an alliance against France, Queen Catherine delivered a male child, to the great joy of her husband. The birth of his son was followed by rounds of grand pageants and martial tournaments. The king had his clothes decorated with 'H's and 'K's in gold thread in celebration of his successor's birth. The baby was named Henry and appointed Prince of Wales. However, the monarch's delight turned to grief two months later when his infant son suddenly died.

While Henry mourned the death of his heir, negotiations were continued under the directive of his regime to isolate France for an attack by the Tudor monarchy. Before invading England's historic enemy, Henry needed a co-conspirator to share the burden of the expense and risk of a counter-attack by a formidable foe, but the three potential continental allies – Spain, the Holy Roman Empire and the papacy – were now members of the League of Cambria, with France, against the Republic of Venice. Venice had been a friend and commercial trading partner of the English, and coming to its defence suited the king's purpose of breaking up the League to gain an ally against the French. He wrote to his father-in-law in Madrid, encouraging him to abandon the League and unite with him against France. Letters were also sent from the English crown to the Holy Roman Emperor, offering to serve as an intermediary to resolve the war against Venice, and to Pope Julius II, petitioning the reversal of the embargo placed on the Venetian Republic. When his correspondences failed to end the war, Henry VIII dispatched the Archbishop of York to Rome to secure the support of the pope. While his envoys manoeuvred in Europe to isolate Louis XII, the Tudor king began preparations at home for the coming conflict, ordering war supplies, preparing his fleet and organizing his army.

Under increasing pressure from the English regime, by the middle of 1510 the League of Cambria was dissolving, the pope forming a new Holy League to drive the French out of northern Italy. Louis XII responded by threatening to summon a Schismatic Council to meet in French-occupied Pisa to depose Julius II. The former members of the League of Cambria now rushed to unite in the Holy League against the French, which Henry was only too pleased to join.

As the allies were preparing for the conflict against France, Henry, to win the favour of Emperor Maximilian, sent a force of 300 archers to the Low Countries to reinforce the Holy Roman Empire's war against the rebellious Charles of Egmond, Duke of Guelders, who was an ally of the French. In May 1511, Henry also agreed to support Ferdinand of Spain's incursion into North Africa against the Moors with an armed contingent of 1,000 men. The expedition to Spain turned into a fiasco when the Spanish king abandoned the expeditionary force and the English were compelled to return home. However, the military aid sent to the Habsburgs succeeded in helping to defeat the Duke of Guelders's uprising in support of the French. Although Henry's first two attempts to influence European politics thus had mixed success, he had gained the friendship of the the the Holy Roman emperor, the papacy and the Spanish against the French, and in October 1511 the Holy League was formally established in Rome.

In the wake of the creation of the Holy League, Henry VIII sent an emissary to Paris to demand the abandonment of the Schismatic Council, which was quickly refused by Louis XII. With the French refusal and Pope Julius II's appeal for armed intervention against the Valois regime, Henry secured the support of his reluctant English council and a united realm was now willing to wage war in Europe. In November 1511, the English and Spanish signed an agreement for a joint assault against Aquitaine, in south-west France on the border with Spain. During the winter months, the English made ready for the expedition to Aquitaine. Henry had previously established a unit of spearmen known as the King's Spears to serve as his mounted bodyguard. The 200 horsemen, nobles especially chosen for their martial and riding skills, were included in the invasion army. As preparations proceeded, the fleet was made ready, provisions collected and troops assembled, while armouries were built at Southwark and Greenwick to supply arms and equipment. To supplement the equipment of its men-at-arms, the Tudor regime purchased hundreds of suits of armour from the European mainland. The king was determined to become a major military power in Europe, and now, following an absence of over twenty years, the English were again making war against France.

War was formally declared against King Louis XII in April 1512, and the English troopships put to sea on 3 June, carrying over 10,000 soldiers under the command of the Second Marquess of Dorset, Thomas Grey. A week later, the army disembarked at Fuentarrabia in north-west Spain, making ready to march against the enemy. Shortly after their arrival, the Spanish king failed to provide the promised horses and supplies, attempting to persuade Grey to participate in his attack against the independent realm of Navarre instead of France. When the English commander refused and pressed for the campaign against the French, Ferdinand abandoned his allies and advanced against Navarre, leaving the English at Fuentarrabia. The Tudor troops remained idle in their camps for four months before returning to England, suffering from disease and food shortages. After seizing Navarre, Ferdinand made peace with Louis XII – Henry VIII's political and martial manoeuvrings had failed to result in a war against France.

Despite the disaster at Fuentarrabia, King Henry remained determined to strike a blow against the French and a new plan of attack on France was soon drawn. While the Tudors were occupied in north-west Spain, Louis XII's army had been forced out of northern Italy by Pope Julius II and Emperor Maximilian, with the English presence at the French border acting as a positive diversion. Henry's scheming to gain allies against the French now turned in his favour, with the papacy remaining unwavering in its desire to punish France, while Maximilian's victories in northern Italy acted to unite the allies against Louis XII.

Through his envoys, Henry secured an agreement with King Ferdinand for a new attack against the French, with an English army, personally led by the Tudor monarch, marching into Picardy, while the Spanish crossed over the border to attack Aquitaine. During early 1513, the campaign was enlarged when Maximilian pledged to support the Anglo-Spanish war by invading France from the Low Countries, while the pope agreed to enter the fray from Provence.

Henry VIII spent the next several months preparing his army and navy for the campaign in Picardy. Provisions and war supplies were purchased and the fleet was assembled, containing leased vessels and newly constructed ships. Before the fleet sailed for France, Pope Julius II unseated Louis XII from his title as French king and conferred it upon Henry. The pope further promised to anoint the Tudor monarch with the French crown in Paris if he could conquer France.

In late June 1513, Henry's soldiers, led by the advance guard and rearguard, boarded their ships to cross the Channel and begin the invasion of France, soon being followed by the main army under the command of the king. Henry landed at Calais in the early evening of 30 June with a bodyguard of 300 soldiers and a retinue of 115 priests and singers from the royal chapel. Shortly after reaching the city, he rode to St Nicholas Church to pledge himself to God. The English stayed at Calais for three weeks, the king receiving ambassadors, attending pageants and finalizing the details of the campaign. He was escorted by fourteen boys dressed in coats of gold wherever he rode or walked, intent on displaying his wealth and glory. At his personal encampment, he had eleven tents erected and a grand pavilion built out of gold thread. On 21 July, 30,000 troops dressed in white and green set out in the pouring rain, eager to attack the French. After advancing only 3 miles, a bivouac was established for the night, Henry riding around the camps encouraging his soldiers by his presence. On the morning of 22 July, the English proceeded through south-east Picardy toward the town of Therouanne, which was key to the capture of the region. Following eleven days of marching, Henry reached his first objective after fending off several French probing sorties. The English established their campsites, while besieging the town and bombarding its defences with their twelve great cannons, known as the Twelve Apostles. During the siege, Henry VIII rose before dawn and rode his great warhorse into his men's encampments, visiting the artillerymen and personally adjusting the sights on their cannons, while practicing archery with his bowmen and encouraging his men. He displayed no fear, moving about in the open dressed in a golden tunic and wearing a cap decorated with a large jewel, despite the danger of being killed by an exploding enemy cannonball. A few days later, Emperor Maximilian joined the English with his smaller than expected forces, but was welcomed by the king as an ally and friend.

With the arrival of reinforcements, the siege against the well-fortified town was tightened. However, the French continued to repel the English assaults and resist the bombardments of their cannons. The enemy's field army was nearby, laying siege to the Holy Roman Emperor's town of Hesdin, and on 16 August the French commander sent 2,000 mounted men-at-arms to harass and draw the English away from Therouanne. Learning of the approaching enemy cavalry from his scouting patrols, Henry VIII led a force of 1,100 knights to challenge them. Near the town of Guinegate, the forces clashed under the hot August sun, the Tudor horsemen charging into the ranks of the French with slashing swords and thrusting lances, driving them back in bloody and fierce fighting. Following a brief battle, the troops of Louis XII galloped away in disarray with Henry, surrounded by his bodyguards, in close pursuit. At what became known as the Battle of the Spurs, King Henry won a total victory, fulfilling his quest for chivalric success on the battlefield.

The garrison at Therouanne held out for a few more days before surrendering on 23 August. The next day, Henry VIII and Emperor Maximilian rode into the town and went to the church for a Te Deum, sung by the king's choir, to thank God for victory. Therouanne was razed to the ground as punishment for its prolonged resistance to the allies. Henry and the Habsburg emperor left the town in ruins, making their way to the friendly city of Lille, where they spent three days celebrating the first victory of the war. The Tudor king attended musical performances, played the lute and pipes before the ladies of the court and danced the hours away. While in Lille, he met with the emperor and envoys from Madrid, seeking to renew their offensive the following year. They agreed to continue the war in 1514, with the Spanish moving against southern France while Henry and the emperor resumed their campaigns in Picardy.

Following the short respite in Lille, the king and his Habsburg ally rejoined the army and laid siege to Tournai. The town was encircled and bombarded by the army's large guns. After being under fire for eight days, the garrison and townspeople agreed to submit, fearing the destruction of their homes, as had happened in Therouanne. Tournai, the seat of a bishop, was fortified with double walls and seven great towers. Henry decided to spare the town from being sacked and garrisoned it with his troops, to be utilized as a second Calais and future departing point for the reconquest of the French lands lost by his predecessors. He spent three weeks in Tournai enjoying martial tournaments, jousts, grand banquets and balls before travelling to Calais and then home across the Channel.

Before Henry had departed for the French campaign, he appointed Queen Catherine as governor of his kingdom and captain-general of its armed forces, supported by advisors, to rule the realm in his name. As the king remained occupied across the Channel, the Scottish king, James IV, declared war on England, seeking to exploit Henry's involvement in the war against Louis XII. In the late summer, the Scots crossed the border to plunder the northern English counties. The royal council responded by sending the Earl of Surrey, Lord Thomas Howard, with a small army to defend the borderlands. At the Battle of Flodden, the two armies collided on 9 September in a barbaric and bloody fight, which lasted three hours and ended in a great English victory, with most of the Scottish aristocracy, including James IV, lying dead on the battlefield. If Henry had not lingered in France so long basking in the glory of his conquest, he likely could have used Thomas Howard's triumph as a spark for the conquest of Scotland.

King Henry owed much of the credit for his victories in France to Thomas Wolsey, who organized the logistics of arming, supplying and transporting the English forces during the summer campaign. The two men became close and trusted friends. Wolsey was born a commoner, the son of a cloth merchant. Unlike his father, he disdained a career in the cloth trade and chose a calling to the priesthood after studying theology at Oxford. He held several ecclesiastic posts, including chaplain to Henry VII, before entering the service of Henry VIII as advisor to his ruling council. Wolsey used his exceptional organizational skills and energy to rise to high office in the king's government and was appointed to the governing council, where he interacted frequently with Henry, displaying his many talents. Henry was reluctant to engage in detailed administrative work, so Wolsey increasingly assumed the tedious duties of drafting proclamations, negotiating with foreign emissaries and keeping the army and navy ready for war. The king preferred to spend his days hunting, jousting and playing tennis, while at night attending court with its world of dancing, gambling and feasting. Despite their wide differences, the sovereign found the services of the ambitious Wolsey highly useful. In 1514, Wolsey was named Archbishop of York, becoming Lord Chancellor and a cardinal the following year.

Henry took little interest in domestic affairs, whereas Cardinal Wolsey eagerly carried out such work. Following his return from the war in France, the king was anxious for a second more ambitious campaign, and preparations were soon underway. Although he had secured the pledges of Maximilian and the Spanish for a combined offensive, his allies had secretly negotiated a treaty with Louis XII to end their involvement in the war. Despite the defections of his allies, Henry continued his arrangements for the spring offensive. However, the English plans for a new invasion were shattered when Pope Julius II died and the newly elected Leo X had no interest in supporting Henry in his French conflict. Papal envoys were soon sent to London to encourage the king to sign a peace accord with Louis XII. Now facing France alone, Henry agreed to discuss a settlement with his enemy, and under Cardinal Wolsey's directions they came to terms. Under the provisions of the treaty, the English were ceded the captured town of Tournai, the French pledged to pay a large sum in gold and friendship was to be secured by the marriage of the king's sister, Mary, to King Louis.

In 1515, however, Louis XII died and was succeeded by the young and ambitious Francis I, who became a serious challenger to the plans of King Henry. Francis I, the only son of Count Charles of Angouleme, was born on 12 September 1497. The Angouleme family was not in the direct line of succession to the French throne, but when Louis XII died without an heir, Francis was recognized as king. Francis I's rule was dominated by his alliances of friendship with and wars against both Henry VIII and Emperor Charles V – who succeeded Maximilian upon his death in 1519 – for dominance over Europe.

Following the death of King James IV at Flodden, Henry's elder sister, Margaret, ruled Scotland in the name of her son and heir, James V. Seeking to recreate the Auld Alliance between the Scottish and French, Francis I sent John Stewart, Duke of Albany, who was a prince of the royal blood, to Scotland to seize the throne. The rule of Queen Margaret had been unpopular among the Scots, and with the support of the Scottish nobility, Stewart besieged the queen at Stirling Castle, taking control of the young James V and forcing Margaret to flee to England. With possession of the king, the Duke of Albany usurped the crown and governed as regent, pledging his loyalty to the French. Henry VIII now had an enemy on his northern border who was a close ally of Francis I and an increasing danger to his regime.

The potential hostility of the Scottish regent now prohibited Henry from leaving with his army for France, freeing Francis I to renew his predecessor's campaign of conquest in northern Italy. In August 1515, the French crossed the Alps into Lombardy with an army of more than 40,000 soldiers, defeating a force of Swiss mercenaries at the Battle of Marignano to impose their supremacy over the Duchy of Milan. To counter the French victory, Henry VIII agreed to subsidize the Swiss and Emperor Maximilian in their fight against Francis, but their campaign failed to drive him from Italy. While the allies struggled against the French in northern Italy, Ferdinand of Spain joined Henry's coalition. Yet Henry's attempts to create a grand alliance against the French were soon shattered when Ferdinand died and the Habsburg noble, Archduke Charles, succeeded to the throne, throwing his support behind the French. Charles' grandfather, Emperor Maximilian, soon joined the pro-French faction in opposition to the increasingly isolated English.

The coalition between the Valois and Habsburg regimes began to collapse the following year, however, as Maximilian and Charles resumed their anti-French policies in the quest for European dominance. Francis I responded by sending envoys to the English court to discuss a peace treaty. While the negotiations continued, Cardinal Wolsey dispatched envoys to the courts of Europe pursuing an agreement for perpetual peace. To enforce the non-aggression pact, each signatory pledged to participate in a military campaign against any nation that violated the accord. On 3 October 1518, in St Paul's Cathedral, the major powers of Europe gathered to celebrate the signing of the Universal and Eternal Alliance, with Wolsey singing a High Mass of thanksgiving to God.

The following year, Emperor Maximilian died, after which Charles of Habsburg and Francis I began contending for succession to the throne of the Holy Roman Empire, which was determined by a general election of the member states. Charles of Habsburg was born on 24 February 1500 in the Flemish city of Ghent, the son of Philip, Duke of Burgundy, and Joanna of Spain. During his lifetime, he was acknowledged as Duke of Burgundy, King of Spain and Emperor of the Holy Roman Empire through diplomatic marriages, political alliances and wars of conquest. When he was chosen emperor, becoming Charles V, the French king found himself boxed in between Habsburg Spain and the imperial princedoms, which included current-day Germany, Switzerland, Poland, Austria and the Low Countries. As part of the Universal and Eternal Alliance, Henry VIII and Francis I agreed to meet and secure their permanent peace. With Charles V now in a position to challenge the French from multiple directions, Francis was eager to meet with Henry and secure an alliance.

Cardinal Wolsey was appointed by Henry to make preparations for his meeting with England's historic enemy. To heighten the prestige of Henry's reign, Wolsey arranged for Emperor Charles to stop in England during his voyage to the Low Countries to discuss European affairs. On 26 May, the imperial fleet anchored at Dover and Charles V was escorted by Wolsey to meet the English king at the nearby castle. The two rulers embraced each other in friendship and discussed the recent political moves of the French. The following day, they rode to Canterbury for a service of thanksgiving. The next few days were filled with talks of war and peace. Charles then renewed his voyage to the Netherlands, leaving the English to finalize their arrangements for the conference between Henry VIII and Francis I to reaffirm their peace. This great spectacle, held in north-east France, became known as the Field of the Cloth of Gold.

In the summer of 1520, Henry boarded his flagship the *Great Harry* at Dover and crossed the Channel with a retinue of more than 4,000 men and women to finalize the peace with the French king, landing at Calais. Over 2,000 masons, glass workers and carpenters had earlier been sent to build a magnificent encampment of temporary grand palaces, banqueting halls, tents and pavilions, while lists and viewing galleries were set up for the chivalrous martial contests. Wolsey was in charge of the preparations, and every detail was carefully planned and implemented. The French had also been busy erecting gaily coloured pavilions and refurbishing the castle at Ardres for Francis I's living quarters. On 7 June, Henry set out to the sounds of cannon fire for his historic first meeting with the French monarch. When he reached the edge of the tournament field, he stopped, while Francis I waited on the other side. At the sounds of trumpets, both monarchs charged forward on their horses to the previously agreed site and embraced each other several times. During the next seventeen days, the two rulers dined together in their splendid palaces and participated in numerous games. The event was filled with military tournaments and archery competitions, while the nights were occupied with parties, banquets, masquerades, dancing and music. They jousted each day, but during inclement weather Henry and Francis danced and held bouts of wrestling. King Henry entered the lists on 15 June dressed in full armour, challenging all English and French men-at-arms to battle. Two days later, he appeared on the tournament field in a suit of golden armour, charging against his opponents on a warhorse adorned in gold and pearls, vanquishing all challengers. On 23 June, the two kings and their queens, along with their courtiers, attended a church service in a chapel decorated with ornate wall hangings and statues of saints, where Cardinal Wolsey sang the High Mass. At the conclusion of the religious service, the gathered crowd marvelled at a dragon kite flying through the bright sky. Created by English artisans, the dragon displayed Francis I's salamander emblem with Henry's Tudor dragon in tribute to their new friendship. The final banquets were held on 24 June, followed by an exchange of gifts. The seventeen-day gathering of former enemies was described by contemporaries as the eighth wonder of the world.

Soon after the celebration of friendship and the reaffirmation of peace between the two kingdoms, Henry met again with Charles V at Calais. During their discussions, the emperor attempted to pull the English king away from his alliance with the French. Henry refused to join an anti-Valois coalition, but the Habsburgs kept the pressure on him. By the beginning of 1521, the Tudor monarch – at the encouragement of Wolsey – favoured a partnership with Charles if a dispute with Francis erupted. The catalyst for war against France occurred in Spain when rebellion broke out against the regime of the Habsburgs. With Charles V occupied with the suppression of the Spanish rebels, Francis I seized the opportunity to attack the Habsburg Empire, marching his troops into Navarre. The war quickly spread to northern Italy and the Low Countries. The English were beseeched by both kings to form a coalition, but Henry sent Wolsey to the English Pale at Calais to moderate between the two warring realms. In August, Wolsey travelled to Calais to meet with the envoys from both states, but no peace settlement was possible as the two adversaries refused to compromise. The talks continued with no resolution to the conflict. With the French unwilling to make concessions, a treaty of support was signed by Wolsey in the name of his king on 25 August, with the English agreeing to enter the war against Francis I.

During the winter of 1522, Henry was occupied preparing for the clash against the French. As the king mustered his arms and men, Francis I responded by encouraging the regent of Scotland to plunder along the northern English border to distract the Tudors. As the adversaries moved steadily toward hostilities, in March 1522 Henry announced that England would protect the Low Countries controlled by the Habsburgs against the French, which Francis asserted was a declaration of war. As Charles was returning to Spain from Flanders in May 1522, he put in on the English coast to finalize the treaty with King Henry. Under the terms of the Treaty of Windsor, signed on 12 June, the two sovereigns agreed to a joint invasion of France.

In July, Henry VIII sent the Earl of Surrey, Thomas Howard, into France to raid the area where the grand union between the French and English had been celebrated two years earlier. The earl moved swiftly, razing numerous towns and burning farmlands. The opening campaign against Francis I accomplished little, but Henry had bigger plans for 1523. The Constable of France, Duke Charles III of Bourbon, began secret talks with the allies for the overthrow of Francis I, while the French populace grew increasingly restless over the heavy tax demands to finance the wars of the Valois regime. Henry VIII was convinced that the French were now overextended and vulnerable to attack. The English and their Habsburg allies planned a double offensive for 1523, with Henry's army invading northern France and Charles V attacking from Spain. The campaign was delayed for over three months before the English parliament finally granted the necessary subsidies, and it was not until late August that Charles Brandon, Duke of Suffolk, led an army of more than 25,000 troops across the Channel to Calais. The king and Brandon at first planned to move against the fortress at Boulogne, but were persuaded by Cardinal Wolsey and the Habsburg allies to advance the army toward Paris. The English expeditionary force remained at Calais until late September, waiting for Charles V's soldiers to mount their assault from Spain before proceeding towards Paris. When the Habsburgs launched their incursion, the English forces moved forward, capturing several towns and laying waste to the countryside, and in early November reached the River Oise, 40 miles from Paris. However, the planned uprising by the Constable of France failed to develop, while Charles V's offensive accomplished little. With the onset of winter, Suffolk was compelled to fall back to Calais. An invasion which had begun with great expectations thus ended in disappointment, with no gains of territory for King Henry and Francis I still on the French throne.

Henry VIII's participation in the war against France had exhausted the royal treasury and produced no conquests. Emperor Charles' failures to provide assistance in the coalition's attack prompted Henry to abstain from any foreign interventions in the following year and to make peace overtures to the French. He began secret negotiations at Calais with representatives from the Valois government, Cardinal Wolsey leading his delegation. Nevertheless, when Charles V's ally, the Duke of Bourbon, Charles III, invaded southern France, Henry ordered his troops to assemble in support of the attack. Duke Charles moved against the fortifications protecting Marseille, but his siege was unsuccessful and the English quickly abandoned their offensive.

Henry had inherited a large treasury from his father, but his expensive wars had steadily depleted his wealth. During the early years of Henry's reign, he largely financed his wars from his personal purse, but by the early 1520s it was necessary to call on parliament for subsidies. When the legislative assembly met in 1523 at the king's summons, his demands for increased taxes were stubbornly rejected for over three months. The Commons finally voted for half of the demanded amount to be given. In the following year, the cardinal ignored the rights of parliament to allocate taxes, sending his agents throughout the realm to collect the funds from property holders. Resistance to his collection of the money was widespread, compelling Henry to intervene and sanction Wolsey. The actions of the overbearing Wolsey generated a party in opposition led by Thomas Howard, who moved to depose the cardinal.

In October 1524, King Francis I advanced into northern Italy with an army, renewing his quest for possession of Lombardy. During his campaign, he was defeated and captured at the Battle of Pavia. With their king now a prisoner and the kingdom virtually defenceless, Louise of Savoy took control of the French regency government for her son. Anxious to secure peace with the English, Louise began secret negotiations with Henry's envoys, who were led by Thomas Wolsey. The Habsburgs had steadily expanded their presence in Europe, becoming a threat to England, and in August 1525 a treaty of friendship was signed by the Tudor and Valois regimes. Under the agreement, Henry pledged to abandon his rights to French territory in return for the payment of a large sum in gold. The pact pulled the English monarchy out of the Habsburg orbit and closer to its former enemy. The rise of the Holy Roman Empire compelled Henry to implement new policies to limit Habsburg expansion. With his reign now aligned against Charles V, Henry aggressively supported the anti-imperial League of Cognac, which was sponsored by the papacy. To solidify English friendship with the Valois government, the two realms ratified the Treaty of Amiens in late August, binding them to never sign a separate peace with the Habsburgs.

Henry VIII had remained a faithful husband to Queen Catherine until 1514, when he began an amorous affair with Elizabeth Blount, who became his mistress for five years. Their relationship resulted in the birth of a son named Henry Fitzroy in 1519. Despite several pregnancies, Catherine had failed to give Henry a healthy heir. In February 1516, the queen finally delivered a strong and healthy baby, a girl who was named Mary. Upon viewing his daughter, Henry told his gathered courtiers: 'If it was a daughter this time, by the grace of God the sons will follow.' Several further pregnancies ensued, but all the infants failed to survive and after ten years of marriage Henry still had no heir to his throne.

By 1525, King Henry had lost all hope of Catherine giving him a healthy successor. He then began promoting his illegitimate son, Henry Fitzroy, as his heir. He named his son Duke of Richmond and Lord High Admiral to expand his status among the lords and ladies of his court in order to gain their acceptance. Despite the efforts of the king to secure his son's succession to the throne, Henry Fitzroy was subjected to challenges by legally recognized Tudor heirs. Henry's attempts to legitimize his son having been largely unsuccessful, he now moved to divorce Catherine. Before his wedding with Catherine, he had received a papal dispensation to marry the wife of his dead brother. Henry was now convinced that the queen's failure to deliver a son was the result of her previous marital union with Prince Arthur, which was seen as a breach of God's teachings. When he first approached Wolsey about a divorce, the cardinal attempted to direct him on a different course. Despite the Archbishop of York's strong opposition, the king instructed him in 1527 to arrange the annulment of his marriage to the queen, believing his matrimonial union with her was a sin.

Henry VIII's quest for divorce was strengthened by his relationship with Anne Boleyn. After ending his affair with Elizabeth Blount, the king was attracted to Mary Boleyn, who became his new mistress. While Henry was involved with Mary, he was introduced to her younger sister, Anne, and fell passionately in love with her, but she hesitated to return his adoration. He wrote romantic letters to Anne telling her of his deep and boundless affection. But Anne, not wanting to be his mistress and then be cast aside like her sister, refused to respond to his love until he divorced Queen Catherine.

Rebuffed by Anne, the king ordered Cardinal Wolsey to arrange the annulment. The cardinal was the pope's legatine representative in England, and acting in this capacity he planned to approve the annulment and later secure Pope Clement VII's approval. The cardinal's plan soon fell apart due to the sack of Rome by forces of the Holy Roman Empire, when the pope became the prisoner of Charles V and was held under guard in the Castle Sant' Angelo. With his scheme shattered, Wolsey attempted to gain the pope's approval for the transfer of his papal powers to him. As Wolsey manoeuvred to secure the annulment, the king told Catherine of his intensions and she promptly sent a message to her nephew, Charles V, with an account of the divorce plans. The emperor wrote to the pope asking him to intervene to protect Catherine. With the proposed divorce at a standstill and Wolsey losing favour with his king, the cardinal travelled to France to organize an attack with King Francis' regime against the Habsburgs, while pressing his attempts to gain the pope's powers. While Wolsey remained in France, Henry VIII began to act on his own accord, sending several envoys to Rome to petition Clement VII for the annulment. The king's agents failed to gain the pope's approval, but Wolsey's friends in Rome convinced the papacy to allow the petition to be settled in London through a special papal representative, Cardinal Lorenzo Campeggio. The papal legate arrived in London in early October 1528 and held the first of many meetings with King Henry and Wolsey. While Henry pursued his divorce, the Habsburg emperor used his influence with the captive pope to prevent his aunt's divorce, and Clement VII sent secret directives to his cardinal in London instructing him to make no decision. When Catherine intervened, showing Lorenzo Campeggio the pontiff's earlier approval of her marriage to Henry, the cardinal utilized the official document to invalidate his commission, returning the petition to Rome for settlement. In late July 1529, the papal legate announced his ruling to refer the appeal to the Holy See to an enraged Henry VIII, who took out his anger against Cardinal Wolsey.

While King Henry manoeuvred to secure the papal approval of his divorce from Queen Catherine, Emperor Charles V and the French were again fighting in Lombardy. As the ally of Francis I, Henry was hard pressed by the French to support their war effort. The involvement of the English with their historic enemy was highly unpopular among the nobility and Church in England, while the populace feared a disruption of trade and an economic slowdown. As riots in protest at the intervention erupted and parliament spoke out against it, Henry VIII refused to honour his pact with the French kingdom and sent emissaries to arrange a peace agreement with the Holy Roman Emperor. In June 1529, an agreement was signed with Charles V, and the next year the warring Habsburgs and French approved the Peace of the Two Ladies, binding them to end their conflict. Under the terms of their treaty, Francis pledged to withdraw from Lombardy, leaving Charles the unchallenged ruler of Italy. With the emperor now in a stronger position and a threat to the Holy See, the pope refused to render a decision on Henry's petition for a marriage annulment and demanded to hear from Catherine before making a decision. Shortly after the delay of the appeal, papal messengers were sent to London with orders summoning Henry to Rome to settle the request.

Through his astute political manoeuvrings, Cardinal Thomas Wolsey had risen to heights of grandeur, but his failure to secure the king's divorce signalled his downfall. In mid-September 1529, Henry ordered the cardinal to surrender the Lord Chancellor's seal and the following month he was arrested on charges of bringing papal law into England. When Wolsey confessed to the charges, his lands, titles and offices were seized, but he was allowed to remain Archbishop of York. During the following year, Wolsey wrote to Francis I and Charles V petitioning them to intercede with Henry in his favour. A message was also sent to Pope Clement VII urging him to excommunicate King Henry and organize a rebellion directed at the recovery of his powers. When Henry VIII learned of the accusations, Cardinal Wolsey was arrested on 4 November 1530 on charges of treason. On 29 November, Wolset died at Leicester while travelling south to face trial.

While Henry VIII's pursuit of divorce from Catherine had been thwarted by the emperor and Wolsey's failed interventions with Rome, the king remained resolved to marry Anne Boleyn. To build a case for the dissolution of the marriage, he sent royal agents to Oxford and Cambridge universities to gather evidence in support of the divorce, while other representatives travelled to universities on the European mainland seeking opinions on the legitimacy of the monarch's proposed marital union. Looking to justify Henry's divorce, they searched libraries and archives, while interviewing ecclesiastic officials, scholars and renowned doctors. As the agents spread across Europe, they convinced universities and seminaries to pass resolutions favouring Henry's annulment. Royal representatives were next dispatched into Italy, paying academicians to write opinions favourable to the matrimonial union with Anne. As Henry pressed his quest for divorce, Pope Clement VII issued a papal bull prohibiting individuals from speaking or writing in support of Henry's right to annulment. By the end of 1530, the Tudor king was compelled to end his pursuit of information to promote his marriage after the results provided documents that mainly confirmed the pope's authority.

During Henry VIII's search for beneficial legal opinions and precedents to use against the papacy, his agents rediscovered the law charging clerics who paid allegiance to the Holy See to the detriment of the English crown. Under the edict, the king was given the right to charge and convict the offending churchmen. In January 1531, Henry prosecuted the English clergy collectively for using their Church powers in favour of the pope to the harm of their monarch. When charged with the crime, the Church leaders pleaded guilty and were fined 100,000 pounds. Following his initial success over the Church, Henry demanded his acknowledgement as protector and supreme head of the English Church. By 1532, the Tudor regime had been battling for more than six years to arrange the king's marriage to Anne, and despite the great expense and many threats, he was still without a new queen and heir.

While King Henry's pursuit of papal recognition for his divorce from Queen Catherine continued, Anne Boleyn became pregnant in early 1533, and on 25 January she and Henry were secretly married. The king now needed to move quickly to annul the marriage to Catherine so that the birth of the child would be legitimate. The Archbishop of Canterbury had died in August 1532, and to fill the vacant post the king appointed Thomas Cranmer, who had enthusiastically supported his divorce from the queen. As Archbishop of Canterbury, Cranmer was now the head of the Church of England and an advocate for Henry VIII's annulment from the queen. When his name was presented to the pope for approval, a bull was issued supporting the appointment. Acting as the leader of the English Church, Archbishop Cranmer called upon Henry to explain why he was living in sin with his dead brother's wife in violation of ecclesiastic law.

By April 1533, Anne's pregnancy and her secret marriage to the king had become public knowledge. To further secure Anne's position as queen, the dukes of Suffolk and Norfolk were dispatched to Catherine's residence to inform her of the marriage and that she must abandon the title of queen. As the widow of the deceased Prince Arthur, Catherine was now known as the Princess Dowager, while Anne was recognized as the English queen. As Henry pursued his matrimonial nullification from the English Church, in early 1533 he empowered the Archbishop of Canterbury to resolve all nuptial issues without the approval of the Holy See by arranging for parliament to enact the Act of Appeals. Under this act, all marital unions made under similar circumstances to the marriage between Henry and Catherine could be voided by the archbishop. On 10 May, the ecclesiastic court was convened at Dunstable by Cranmer to resolve the petition for divorce from Catherine. She would not acknowledge the court, refusing to attend and reiterating that she was answerable only to Rome. After four days of hearings, Archbishop Cranmer ruled Henry VIII and Catherine of Aragon had never been married and that the nuptial union between the king and Anne Boleyn was therefore valid.

Shortly after Cranmer's ruling, on 31 May 1533, Anne was anointed Queen of England. On a day with bright blue cloudless skies, she sailed down the Thames in Catherine's boat, escorted by hundreds of barges gaily decorated with flags, bells and banners, making her way to the coronation ceremony at Westminster Abbey. There, the Archbishop of Canterbury anointed her with holy oil and placed the crown of England on her head. While London had been lavishly adorned for the coronation with pageants, singing choirs and richly decorated banners, few Londoners cheered as the queen passed by and there were frequent 'boos'. A rumour had earlier spread through the city that Anne was a witch and had used her powers and potions to bewitch the king. At the traditional wedding banquet, many nobles were absent, finding excuses not to attend. Despite Henry's attempts to make the ceremony of his new queen's anointment a joyous event, the new marriage was unpopular with the people of England.

When parliament was summoned by the king in 1529, it became known as the Reformation Parliament for its far-reaching enactment of new laws. Under the leadership of Henry's first minister, Thomas Cromwell, a wave of new legislative measures was passed to increase the powers of the crown. The Act of Appeals served as the foundation of Henry's quest for authority over the Lords, Commons and Church. The statute ceded to the monarchy the right to decide both secular and religious matters independently of the legislative body or Church, and eliminated the ability of the English to appeal directly to the pope to overturn Henry's rulings. The act stated: 'This realm of England is an empire and the pontiff has no authority to interfere in its affairs.' The immediate effect of the act gave Henry the right to cancel Catherine's appeal to Rome to reinstate her marriage. Under Cromwell's directive, additional laws were passed, the Act of Dispensation giving the Tudor regime the ability to establish decrees which were contrary to established Canon Law and the practices of the Church. The Act in Absolute Restraint of Annates dictated that the payments made by new bishops to their bishoprics upon their appointment would no longer go to Rome, but to the king's coffers. Henry's authority was also increased by the ratification of the Act for the Submission of the Clergy, which prevented the clerics from making appeals directly to the Holy See and transferred the petition to the Church of England. The king further broadened his rule through the passage of the Treason Act, which made it treasonable to declare the monarch a heretic, while the Act of First Fruits and Tenths demanded a tenth of the bishoprics' net income for the royal treasury. Within a period of a few years, Cromwell gave back to Henry many of the royal rights lost by previous monarchies, while further separating the English Church from Rome.

The king's policies of the past few years had been focused on the legalization of his marriage to Anne Boleyn and the birth of a son to inherit his monarchy. Yet to Henry's great disappointment, on 7 September 1533, at Greenwich Palace, Anne gave birth to a daughter, who was named Elizabeth. Several days later, when the baby was christened at the nearby Church of the Franciscans, he did not attend the ceremony. In his relentless pursuit of a successor, the birth of Elizabeth did not correspond with his goals of providing a male heir for the continuance of the Tudor dynasty.

As the Tudor monarchy steadily broke away from the Holy See, Pope Clement VII threatened to excommunicate the king. Henry VIII's new policy initiatives were highly unpopular with the English populace. Catherine of Aragon retained her support with the people, while Queen Anne continued to be disliked. Dissent spread across the kingdom, and in Canterbury a nun named Elizabeth Barton spoke out openly against the king's attempted divorce. The nun had gained widespread fame in Kent when she was inexplicably cured of a disease in public. As the divorce proceedings continued, she used her renown to threaten the monarch if he did not abandon his pursuit of his marriage to Anne. The nun became the centre of rebellion in Canterbury and gathered around her numerous pious leaders, who incited the public against the Tudor monarchy. As the spirit of revolt multiplied, in July 1534 Barton, along with the leading opponents of the divorce, were arrested, interrogated and sent to the Tower of London. In November of that year, a large gathering of nobles, judges and counsellors were summoned to determine the fate of the prisoners. After three days of hearings, the nun and her adherents were taken to St Paul's Cross, placed on a scaffold and publicly humiliated and ridiculed as frauds. Elizabeth Barton and five others were returned to their cells and in April 1534, after the strength of the uprisings had abated, they were hanged.

The Barton uprising had sparked widespread opposition to Henry's marriage to Anne, and the king now manoeuvred to eliminate the centre of resistance. Bishop John Fisher had served on the royal council for several years but continued to support Queen Catherine, while Sir Thomas More was a celebrated lawyer and official in the royal administration but refused to recognize Henry as the head of the English Church. On orders from King Henry, the two protesters were arrested and confined to the Tower. In the following year, the pontiff promoted Fisher to cardinal, ignoring the English regime's conflict with the Holy See. The directive of the papacy was considered papal interference in the governing of the English Church, and More and Fisher were executed on charges of treason. The beheading of the two such renowned political leaders dampened enthusiasm for resistance to the monarchy, sending a clear message that dissent would not be tolerated.

In September 1534, Pope Clement VII died ,but before his death he issued his long-awaited judgment on Catherine's divorce petition, finding in her favour and against King Henry. However, the ruling was seen as meaningless by the English monarch, who was firmly on the path to a break with the See of Rome. After crushing the opposition to his rule, he moved against the wealth and properties of the Church, appointing his first minister, Thomas Cromwell, to seize the possessions of the Church of England.

In February 1536, Henry VIII recalled parliament into session to discuss the state of the Church's monasteries. The religious houses were at the centre of opposition to the king's struggle for papal recognition of his marriage to Anne. To destroy the power of the monasteries, the king's Lord Chancellor, Cromwell, sent his agents to the abbeys, nunneries and churches to compile an inventory of their wealth. After Cromwell received the results of the visitations to the numerous religious houses, the sovereign met with the House of Lords to promote their closure. When the size of the Church's income was read to the lords, there were shouts of 'Down with them'. With the support of the upper house, Henry summoned the Commons to the royal gallery, telling them: 'I hear that my bill will not pass, but I will have it pass or I will have some of your heads.' Under the strong hand of the monarch, the Act for the Dissolution of Monasteries was passed, ordering all houses with an annual income of less than 200 pounds to be repressed. A total of 419 monasteries were compelled to close, but when Cromwell and his representatives accepted bribes from the abbots, the number was reduced to 243. The Tudor regime had not moved against the large religious houses, and the displaced monks were transferred to these. The closing of the smaller institutions caused little protest, as the monarchy advanced slowly to enforce its rule over the prelates while formulating a new faith under royal supremacy. During the assembly of parliament, the Commons and Lords also passed the Court of Augmentation, dictating that all revenues from the dissolution of the monasteries be directed to the English throne.

After Anne's delivery of Elizabeth, two stillborn births and a miscarriage followed, convincing Henry that the queen was incapable of giving him a male heir. He was increasingly drawn away from Anne and became involved with several mistresses before finding another love. His new interest was one of the queen's ladies-in-waiting, Jane Seymour, the daughter of a minor nobleman, Sir John Seymour. Similar to Anne's earlier plight, Jane was reluctant to accept the king's advances, returning his gifts and unopened letters, but the more she rejected his attention, the greater Henry's desires for her grew. As the king continued to pursue the queen's lady-in-waiting, in 1534 Anne discovered his interest in Jane and flew into a wild rage. Henry replied to her outburst by telling the queen she must accept his romances. When Anne suffered another miscarriage in 1536, Henry became determined to marry again, turning to Jane Seymour as his future wife.

To clear the path for his marriage to Jane Seymour, the king ordered his first minister and the Duke of Norfolk, Thomas Howard, to lead a commission to search for evidence of treason against the queen. In less than a week, they drew up a list of five adulterous liaisons for the indictment of Anne. They charged the queen with adultery involving several members of the court – including her brother, George

Boleyn, Lord of Rochford – which were purported to be acts of treason against the kingdom. At the May Day jousting tournament at Greenwich, Queen Anne supposedly dropped a handkerchief of one of her suitors, causing Henry to sulk away in a rage. The king ordered the arrest of Queen Anne and several of her alleged lovers. On 15 May, the queen was tried on charges of treason and found guilty. She was beheaded four days later in the courtyard of the London Tower by a swordsman from Calais, at her own request to avoid the pain of the axe. While the trial was unfolding, Archbishop Cranmer officiated over a court in Lambeth that reached the conclusion that Henry's marriage to Anne was voided by his earlier adulterous affair with her sister, Mary. When Henry heard of Anne's execution, he boarded a barge and sailed to visit Jane Seymour. Their betrothal was announced the next day, and on 30 May the king and Jane were quietly married at York Place.

Henry VIII was now in his mid-40s and still without a male successor to his throne. While the king waited for his new queen to provide his much-needed son, he had parliament enact the Second Act of Succession in June 1536, which bastardized his second daughter, Elizabeth, and named any offspring from the marriage to Jane as his chosen heir. He was further given the right to name his successor, if Jane and he remained childless. Before the act was passed, Henry and his oldest daughter, Mary, were reconciled after years of separation, her mother Catherine of Aragon having recently died. She had previously been barred from her father's presence and isolated from the royal court. Mary was placed under close observation to prevent her escape to the European mainland and potential union with Emperor Charles V against her father. In the wake of Henry's marriage to Jane, Mary made arrangements with Thomas Cromwell to act as her intermediary and orchestrate a meeting with the king. She was forced to make a full capitulation to her father and admission of her illegitimacy. The submission was accepted and Mary was once again welcomed to court. The reconciliation was accepted by Henry to ensure that after his death a Tudor would succeed to his crown in the person of Mary, if Jane and he had no male heir.

As Henry VIII struggled to secure the succession to his throne, the dissolution of the English monasteries and the regime's demands for increased taxes gave cause to widespread revolt across the kingdom. On 1 October 1536, a riot erupted in Lincolnshire over demands for the removal of supposedly heretic bishops appointed by the crown and an end to the closing of the religious houses. Under orders from King Henry, the Duke of Suffolk, Charles Brandon, marched into Lincolnshire with the royal army and quickly restored order. However, a new uprising known as the Pilgrimages of Grace then broke out in Yorkshire, led by Robert Aske, who demanded the legitimization of Princess Mary and restoration of the pope's lost powers. The royal army was forced to remain in Lincolnshire to enforce the peace, leaving Henry without a force to counter the rebels in Yorkshire. He was compelled to send Thomas Howard, Duke of Norfolk, to quell the rebellion. Arranging a meeting with Aske, the duke promised a new parliament to resolve the rebels' grievances and a pardon for all who abandoned the revolt. Norfolk's terms were agreed to, thus ending the uprising peacefully.

Robert Aske and his supporters honoured the agreement with Howard, returning to their towns in peace, but one of them, Francis Bigod, proclaimed the submission was a betrayal. He raised a contingent of volunteers and attempted to take Hull by force, while the town of Carlisle was also besieged. In early 1537, King Henry responded to the threat by sending newly mustered troops led by the earls of Rutland and Shrewsbury to suppress Bigod's disobedience. The royal soldiers quickly overran the conspirators, putting down their rebellion. More than 150 rebels were publicly hanged to deter future revolts. The Pilgrimages of Grace gave Henry's regime the excuse it needed to dissolve the remaining large monasteries. By 1540, the final religious house at Waltham in north-east Lincolnshire was closed. To suppress the spirit of revolt in the northern English counties, the Council of the North was created to enforce Henry's rule over the recalcitrant local clerics and nobles. As a result of disbanding the monasteries, the crown's annual income was increased by 50 per cent and its authority stronger than ever.

During the spring of 1537, Queen Jane became pregnant, to the great joy of the king. Henry provided for the queen's every need, sending her to spend the summer at Windsor Castle to avoid the dangers of the plague outbreak in London. On 12 October, at Hampton Court, Jane delivered the king's long-awaited healthy son after a difficult birth. The king's son was born on the eve of the feast of St Edward, and the baby was christened Edward in honour of the English saint. At the time of his heir's birth, Henry was at Esher, but rushed to Jane's side after hearing the good news. He ordered great celebrations throughout the kingdom, but his joy was short-lived when Queen Jane died twelve days later from complications following the birth of Edward. Jane, who had never been crowned queen, was buried amid great royal pomp and glory at St George's Chapel in Windsor, with Henry attending the ceremony and displaying sincere sorrow and grief at her death. Indeed, in his will, he directed that he should be buried next to Queen Jane.

Following the subjugation of the revolts and with his coffers filled from the sale of the seized church properties, Henry began construction of a new royal residence to showcase his wealth and opulence. He had earlier confiscated Cardinal Wolsey's palace at Whitehall in central London and the grand country manor house at Hampton Court, but now wanted a palace of greater magnificent splendour than any in Europe. In 1538, construction began on the great building, located on 2,000 acres of land several miles from Hampton Court. Hundreds of woodcarvers, glazers, carpenters and clockmakers were imported from the mainland Europe, while gardeners from France were hired to construct the elaborate parks and fountains. While the building continued on the new palace, called Nonsuch, Henry's other royal dwellings at Eltham, Greenwich and Windsor were embellished, creating an unrivalled collection of royal residences among the European courts. Nonsuch was built with turrets, battlements and cupolas, with flags flying from every tower, while the top section was laid in timber and decorated with stucco works. The magnificent gardens were laid out with walking paths around numerous fountains, waterfalls and statues, making a glorious display of courtly beauty. Nonsuch Palace had a colourful history until it was demolished by a mistress of King Charles II in the late seventeenth century.

In 1539, Pope Paul III issued a papal bull against Henry VIII for his disobedience to the See of Rome, calling upon all Christians to attack and destroy the Tudor kingdom. In the wake of the pope's proclamation, Francis I of France and Emperor

Charles V met near Nice, agreeing to end their hostilities and unite against King Henry. Meanwhile, to the north, the Scottish king, James V, promised to attack northern England in support of the rumoured Franco-imperial invasion of England. As fears of war escalated, a fleet of sixty-five enemy warships was sighted off the English coast, spreading fear throughout the land. To defend his realm, Henry assembled his army from the shires and reviewed his fleet of 150 vessels, including the formidable *Mary Rose*, which was anchored at Deptford ready to defend the Thames. The *Mary Rose* served the king's navy for thirty-three years before it was sunk in July 1545 leading the attack against the galleys of the French invasion fleet. The vessel was manned with a crew of 200 sailors and 185 soldiers. To strengthen the defences of his kingdom against invasion, Henry VIII reinforced his shoreline fortifications and built new warships armed with the latest cannons.

As the threat of invasion continued, Henry toured the south coast, ordering new fortifications, while the defences along the Scottish border were also reinforced. The Privy Council now met daily, preparing the kingdom for war. By the beginning of May, thousands of men mustered with their weapons and armour, ready to repel the enemy should they invade. As a morale booster, Cromwell staged a mock sea battle on the Thames, with one boat flying the papal flag and the other the colours of the king. To the delight of the many spectators, the royal ship was victorious. As the king's army and navy waited for the French attack, England was spared the horrors of war when Francis I cancelled the planned invasion. The French and Habsburgs had expected the English to rise up in rebellion against the king for his recent anti-papal policies and destruction of the monasteries, but they remained faithful to his regime and the danger of invasion dissipated.

While Henry had avoided immediate war with the Habsburgs and Francis I, his realm was still under threat from them. To better defend the kingdom, the king needed allies on the European mainland. At Cromwell's direction, envoys were dispatched across Europe in search of new allies. To strengthen the negotiations, they were to propose the marriage of Henry VIII to a daughter of a European ruler. Overtures were made to the French for a marriage to Maria, daughter of the powerful Duke of Guise, but the talks quickly ended when she was betrothed to James V of Scotland. After several other proposals ended in failure, Henry's ambassadors approached Duke William of Cleves for a marital union with his sister, Anne. The duchy was strategically located on the lower Rhine and could become a constant threat to the territories of Emperor Charles V. The duke was a member of the Schmalkaldic League, formed by German princes against the Habsburg emperor. Duke William had three sisters, and King Henry sent Hans Holbein to paint their portraits. When he returned to the Tudor court, the king chose to marry the second sister, Anne, after carefully examining the portraits. Near the end of 1539, Anne arrived in England and Henry rushed to greet her at Rochester, but after seeing her told Thomas Cromwell: 'I like her not.' Nevertheless, England remained isolated and in danger from the Habsburg-Valois alliance, compelling Henry to agree to the political marriage to keep a beneficial ally. The wedding ceremony was performed at Greenwich on 6 January 1540, but Henry refused to remain with his new bride, soon ordering Thomas Cromwell to find grounds to end the marriage. Searching the legal documents, Cromwell's men discovered Anne was still bound by a previous contract to marry the son of the Duke of Lorraine. With this evidence, divorce proceedings were begun and quickly completed. Under the divorce settlement, Anne confirmed the marriage had not been consummated and pledged to cause no trouble, while Henry agreed to provide her a handsome palace and pay a large endowment if she remained in England. Anne stayed in the kingdom in properties provided by the king, living happily and quietly until her death in 1557. Cromwell had proposed and encouraged the political union with Cleves, and its failure incurred the wrath of Henry. He was arrested on 10 June 1540 on charges of treason and heresy, and soon after executed.

While the divorce proceedings were being pursued, the Duke of Norfolk, Thomas Howard, introduced his beautiful 19-year-old niece, Catherine, to the king. Before reaching the age of 10, Catherine's mother died, and soon she was abandoned by her father. He placed her under the care of her step-grandmother, but left alone, she became involved in numerous sexual affairs, including with her music teacher and her cousin, Francis Dereham. When she served as a maid-of-honour to Anne of Cleves, Catherine was widely known at court for her numerous sexual encounters. To enhance his presence at the Tudor court, the Duke of Norfolk aggressively promoted his niece to the king and advised her how to behave with him. Henry was totally infatuated by his new love's beauty and gaiety, spending more and more time with her and lavishing her with expensive gifts of clothing and jewels. She received chains of gold and pearls, jewelled crosses, diamond necklaces and dresses decorated with rich furs. Nineteen days after his marital-union to Anne of Cleves was dissolved, on 28 July 1540, Henry VIII was married to Catherine Howard, who became his fifth wife.

As King Henry grew older, he gained weight and suffered greatly from leg ulcers. The bouts of infection caused him to become depressed and remorseful. The ulcers frequently became inflamed and the pus was drained by a painful operation, which left him in a horrible mood with a raging temper. He would refuse to see his counsellors and barred his new queen from his presence.

In the summer of 1541, the leg ulcers disappeared and Henry and Catherine led a grand procession through the northern counties, which had a reputation for riot and rebellion. Henry set out to impress the often recalcitrant northerners with an escort of 5,000 horsemen and 1,500 infantry in a display of his military power. During the tour, Henry, dressed in rich clothing of gold and jewels, accepted the submissions of the local lords. Queen Catherine had been married to the king for nearly a year and now, dissatisfied by her aging husband, renewed her sexual affairs with members of the court. As the journey moved further north, she began a romantic liaison with Thomas Culpeper, a lord of the crown's Privy Chamber. With the assistance of the ladies-in-waiting, she met secretly with Culpeper and other courtiers. As the queen continued her amorous affairs, her former lover Francis Dereham went to Catherine threatening to disclose their earlier relationship. To silence Dereham, the queen appointed him private secretary and usher for her chambers, while renewing her sexual relationship with him.

As the romantic encounters of the queen continued unabated, an informant finally approached Archbishop Cranmer, telling him of the queen's many indiscretions. The archbishop questioned members of Catherine's household, who confirmed the stories. When Cranmer notified the king, he refused to believe her acts of infidelity. He ordered the archbishop to investigate the allegations, and when he and his counsellors questioned the courters, it became apparent that Catherine was guilty. Dereham was interviewed and confessed to his sexual relationships with Catherine. The queen was called to meet with the archbishop and acknowledged the encounters prior to her marriage, agreeing to sign a confession. The investigation was renewed, and when several ladies-in-waiting were interrogated, they implicated Thomas Culpeper in the adulterous affairs with Catherine. The council questioned Culpeper, who admitted being alone with the queen but not to engaging in intercourse. After collecting the evidence, Cranmer met with Henry and presented the testimonies. The king flew into a rage, threatening to kill the queen. On 1 December, Dereham and Culpeper were found guilty of treason and executed, with their severed heads impaled on London Bridge. In early 1542, Queen Catherine was taken from Syon House to the Tower of London Tower, where on Tower Green she was beheaded for her traitorous acts. On the day of the execution, Henry held a grand banquet, sitting with twenty-six ladies at his table in an attempt to forget the revulsions of Catherine Howard's scandal.

In the spring of 1542, France and Holy Roman Emperor Charles V were again at war. Henry renewed his quest for England's lost territory in north-west France, negotiating a treaty of alliance with the Habsburg regime. Before taking his army into France, the king sent a force north to eliminate any danger from France's historic ally, Scotland. Thomas Howard, Duke of Norfolk, led the 20,000 royal troops in an attack across the frontier, ravaging the southern Scottish Lowlands for six days, burning and looting towns and farms. In retaliation, James V of Scotland sent an army of over 15,000 men led by Lord Robert Maxwell to invade northern England. The local English soldiers were commanded by Sir Thomas Wharton, and his host of 3,000 men moved from Carlisle to meet the invaders. On 24 November 1542, the two forces clashed at Solway Moss. When the Scots recognized the small English army atop a hill, they hesitated, fearing a trap, which allowed Sir Thomas to send his lancers charging into their ranks, compelling them to withdraw in disarray. During the wild retreat, hundreds of Scots were drowned in the River Esk and many great Scottish warlords were taken prisoner. The Scottish border was now open to English invasion, but Henry's objective remained the seizure of his lands in France so a peace treaty was signed with the Scottish king.

In early 1543, parliament was summoned to grant a subsidy for the royal expenses of the recent Scottish campaign and the planned expeditionary force against France. While preparations for the French invasion proceeded, in July 1543, Henry VIII was married at Hampton Court to Lady Catherine Parr, the daughter of a Northamptonshire lord. Catherine, who was well educated and served Princess Mary as a lady-in-waiting, was 31 years old and had been married twice before. After the execution of his fifth wife, King Henry had become increasingly lonely and suffered from the pains of the frequent leg ulcers, which made it difficult to walk. He was encouraged by his advisors to take another wife to end his sorrow and loneliness. Under pressure to remarry, the king was drawn to Catherine Parr, who became his sixth wife. She developed a close relationship with Henry, providing him with companionship and affection. Catherine succeeded in uniting the sovereign's three children into one household, and under her influence they received a highly enlightened education. The queen brought into the court notable humanists as tutors for the royal children. Catherine was an intelligent and decisive wife, who took away some of the bleakness of the king's later years as he became largely immobile and had to be carried about in a litter.

According to the agreement signed by Henry VIII and Charles V, each realm was to field an army of over 40,000 soldiers against the French. Before the English launched their invasion of France, Scotland broke its recently signed treaty of peace with the Tudor throne and rejoined its ancient ally. The English were again compelled to bring the Scots to heel before attacking King Francis I. In early May the Earl of Hertford, Edward Seymour, was ordered by Henry to sail north and ravage Edinburgh. He was to destroy the castle and also attack Leith and St Andrews, reeking havoc on the Scots. On 6 May, Hertford landed his troops at the port of Leith, vanquishing the local defenders. The English expeditionary force then marched against Edinburgh, overrunning the garrison troops and burning much of the city. After sacking Edinburgh, Seymour advanced his forces into the surrounding countryside, continuing his campaign of destruction before returning to Leith and sailing back to England, where he was given a hero's welcome by Henry.

While the Earl of Hertford was in Scotland, the plans for the French invasion were finalized by the Tudor and Habsburg regimes. King Henry agreed to march against Paris from the west, while Charles V was to attack the city from the east. Soldiers and ships were assembled in the English ports, and in the summer of 1544 the invasion force crossed the Channel to Calais, led by the dukes of Suffolk and Norfolk. Soon after landing, the Tudor army was divided, with Thomas Howard, Duke of Norfolk, marching to capture Montreuil, while Charles Brandon, Duke of Suffolk, was sent to besiege the coastal town of Boulogne. On 14 July, King Henry arrived in Calais, and five days later Suffolk reached Boulogne, laying siege to the well-fortified town with its hilltop citadel. While Brandon attacked the defenders with his artillery and sorties, Henry set out from Calais to join Suffolk's forces. Reaching the siege, the king took charge of the army, supervising the forays against the defensive walls and placement of the artillery. The lower end of Boulogne was lightly fortified and was quickly seized, while the assaults against the upper defensive works continued with the English cannons bombarding the walls. After more than a month of assaults, the garrison commander surrendered in early September, the town falling under English control. Although Boulogne was occupied by Tudor troops, the castle still held out, repelling numerous English attacks, but after tunnels were dug under the walls, the French defenders submitted on 18 September. Henry entered Boulogne in triumph, remaining there nearly two weeks supervising the reconstruction of the fortifications. At the end of September, he departed, sailing back across the Channel and leaving an English garrison to defend Boulogne.

England and the Habsburg regime were linked by a treaty containing a provision binding Henry VIII and Charles V to launch a two-pronged attack against Paris. In spite of the agreement, the English had delayed their advance to secure their lines of communications in the rear by taking Boulogne and Montreuil. The emperor's army had struggled against the French, and Charles V was seeking terms from Francis I to end the fighting. Charles accepted the French king's unfavourable conditions, abandoning the English, whom he claimed had violated the stipulations of their treaty by delaying their march against Paris. With the Habsburgs out of the conflict, the French crown sent an army to break Norfolk's siege at Montreuil. With the Valois forces approaching, Henry dispatched orders to Thomas Howard ordering him to withdraw from the siege and take his troops to reinforce Boulogne.

Following the desertion of his Habsburg ally, Henry agreed to negotiate with envoys from Francis I, sending two commissioners to Calais to meet with the French. On 18 October the discussions began, with the English demanding French recognition of their Boulogne conquest and Francis I's pledge to abandon his alliance with the Scots. The French representatives refused to accept the terms, and in early November they left the conference with the war between the two kingdoms unresolved.

In the wake of the failed peace negotiations, King Henry prepared for an invasion by Francis I. To defend his homeland, three armies were mustered, with the Duke of Suffolk in command of the soldiers in Kent and Thomas Howard sent to defend Essex, while the Earl of Arundel led the troops in the western theatre. The English border with Scotland was protected by the Earl of Hereford, while the fleet put to sea with eighty warships to guard the coastline.

While the armies waited for the French invasion, the Valois fleet of over 200 warships set sail for England in mid-June 1545. On 18 June, they entered the Solent between Hampshire and the Isle of Wight, making for Portsmouth. Henry VIII, in southern England inspecting the coastal fortifications, was aboard the *Great Harry* when the enemy was first sighted. Under the command of Admiral Claude d'Annebault, the French naval forces were sent against the English in Portsmouth harbour, but were repelled. On 19 July, the two fleets clashed off Spithead. During the battle, the *Mary Rose* was sunk, but despite the loss, the Tudors outmanoeuvred d'Annebault's galleys, driving them off. Following the inconclusive sea battle, the French landed troops on the Isle of Wight to pillage the island, attacking the villages of St Helens and Bonchurch and Sandown Castle. When the French soldiers disembarked at St Helens, they soon clashed with local militiamen, overwhelming them and burning their homes. At the village of Bonchurch, 500 French raiders stormed ashore, encountering the waiting English volunteers. During the ensuing fighting, the Tudor militia pushed the invaders back to the sea and saved their village from destruction. A third French assault was launched against the newly constructed Sandown Castle on the east coast of the Isle of Wight, where the local English troops charged into d'Annebault's men on the beach, forcing them to fall back to their boats. After the indecisive land and sea battles, and with unfavourable winds driving the French vessels to the east, Admiral d'Annebault ordered a retreat. The cost of the war had depleted the treasuries of both kingdoms, and with the conflict at a stalemate, talks were resumed, resulting in the Treaty of Ardes that bound the English and French to honour the peace. The agreement, signed in the summer of 1546, allowed Henry to retain possession of Boulogne for eight years before abandoning it for the payment of a large French indemnity.

By 1546, King Henry VIII's health had deteriorated significantly and he was beset with frequent fevers and bleeding leg ulcers. He was almost totally immobile and had to be carried in a chair or by litter. He was unable to attend council meetings and looked to Queen Catherine for his care and support. In December, he was confined to his bed at Whitehall Palace with a high fever, which his physicians feared was fatal. Henry had earlier prepared his will, entrusting his heir, Edward, and the English kingdom to the decisions of a Regency Council, which was headed by the Earl of Hereford, Edward Seymour. With his death fast approaching, he asked for Archbishop Cranmer, who arrived near midnight on 28 January 1547. The king, now unable to speak, slowly stretched out his hand to the archbishop. When Cranmer asked him for a sign of his faith in Christ, the dying monarch pressed his hand. Shortly after, King Henry died following a reign of 37 years, leaving England to his 9-year-old son, Edward. On 31 January, parliament was assembled and the chancellor rose to announce the death of the sovereign-lord. Henry's will was read, revealing the names of the nobles who would rule in the name of King Edward VI. The body was carried in a long procession to Windsor Castle, where the funeral Mass was celebrated, and following a trumpet fanfare, Henry VIII was buried in St George's Chapel next to Queen Jane Seymour, his one true love.

Selected Sources

Ackroyd, Peter, *The History of England from Henry VIII to Elizabeth I* (Thomas Dunne Books, 2012).

Cannon, John and Hargreaves, Anne, *The Kings and Queens of England* (Oxford University Press, 2001).

Erickson, Carolly, *Great Harry* (Summit Books, 1980).

Harvey, John, *The Plantagenets* (Franklin Watts, 1948).

Lacey, Robert, *The Life and Times of Henry VIII* (Welcome Rain, 1972).

Pollard, A.F., *Henry VIII* (Harper and Row Publishers, 1966).

Read, Conyers, *The Tudors* (W.W. Norton, 1964).

Roberts, Clayton and Roberts, David, *A History of England – Volume 1* (Prentice Hall, 1991).

Scarisbrick, J.J., *Henry VIII* (University of California Press, 1970).

Simpson, Helen, *Henry VIII* (Peter Davies Limited, 1934).

Skidmore, Chris, *Edward VI* (Weidenfeld and Nicolson, 2007).

Williams, Neville, 'Henry VIII', in Fraser, Antonia, *The Lives of the Kings and Queens of England* (Alfred A. Knopf, 1975).

Postscript

In the wake of the death of Henry VIII, the English throne passed without opposition to his only surviving son, Edward VI. At the time of his accession to the kingship, he was just 9 years old, necessitating the establishment of a regency council to rule in his name. While the council governed the kingdom, the dominant Protestant members enacted new laws to suppress the Catholic faith in England. In the royal household, Edward VI attended Protestant religious services, becoming a fervent anti-Catholic. In early 1553, he developed a severe lung infection and became increasingly ill, despite the treatment of his doctors. Under the provisions of the Parliamentary Act of Succession and the last will of Henry VIII, the Tudor crown passed to Lady Mary Tudor, if Edward VI died childless. As a zealous Protestant, the king strongly opposed the acquisition of the throne by his Catholic half-sister. As his health continued to deteriorate, Edward signed documents excluding Mary from the monarchy, naming his Protestant cousin, Lady Jane Grey, as his heir. Following the death of Henry VIII's son, Jane Grey was proclaimed queen by the ruling council, but few nobles or commoners accepted her and instead threw their support behind Mary Tudor.

During the reign of Edward VI, the governing regents enacted numerous laws designed to suppress Catholic beliefs, compelling Mary to worship her faith in her private chapel with a handful of supporters. Despite threats from Edward VI's followers, Mary remained true to her religious beliefs. After the death of her half-brother, she travelled to Norfolk to muster soldiers to enforce her rights to the crown. Soon after her arrival in Norfolk, many warlords abandoned Queen Jane and rallied to Mary's cause. With her small band of soldiers, Mary moved into Suffolk, where she was joined by thousands of volunteers ready to protect her claim to the monarchy. As Lady Mary proceeded toward London, her army grew to over 20,000, while support for Jane Grey collapsed. On 3 August 1553, Mary Tudor rode into London in triumph, and she was anointed Queen of England at Westminster Abbey on 1 October, while Jane, who had reigned for only nine days, was executed in the Tower of London in February 1554.

Queen Mary I devoted her reign to the repeal of the anti-Catholic laws enacted by her father and Edward VI. She pressed parliament to restore the authority of the Holy See of Rome over England. The legislative assembly passed new laws in support of her religious beliefs, but the queen demanded the total abolishment of the Protestant Church in England. In an attempt to secure the succession of future Catholic monarchs with her birth of an heir, Mary negotiated her marriage to the King of Spain, Philip II of Habsburg, who was an ardent defender of the

Holy See. Under the influence of Philip II, the queen allowed representatives from the papacy to attend her court and new laws were passed restoring the Catholic faith in England. As the queen aggressively suppressed the Protestants, there were several armed uprisings against her rule, but Mary easily overpowered them. In 1557, Mary declared war against France in support of Philip II's military offensive against the Valois regime.

In France, the combined Anglo-Habsburg army destroyed the French forces at Saint Quentin, but in January 1558 the English-held Pale of Calais was lost to the enemy. The loss of Calais, which had been occupied by the English for over 200 years, resulted in widespread condemnation of the queen. While Mary struggled to rule her realm, she became ill in the summer of 1558 and by October was nearing death. Under pressure from her council, the queen acknowledged her Protestant half-sister, Elizabeth, as her successor. Queen Mary I died on 17 November 1558 after a reign of five years.

On 15 January 1559, amid great celebration, Elizabeth I was crowned Queen of England at Westminster Abbey. After taking the throne, she moved quickly to restore the Church of England and abolish the Catholic doctrine. Elizabeth was the only surviving child of Henry VIII, and to secure the future of the Tudor line she was encouraged by her council to marry. Despite the urging of her advisors, Elizabeth refused to consider any of the marriage proposals from the European courts. While the queen remained unmarried and childless, the heir to the English throne was the Catholic Queen of Scotland, Mary, who was a cousin to Elizabeth. In 1558, Mary was deposed in Scotland and fled to England seeking protection. Mary's presence in England was a threat to the Queen Elizabeth, who ordered the imprisonment of her cousin. Mary now served as a rallying cause for the English Catholics, the northern pro-Catholic nobles rising up in rebellion against the crown in November 1569. The rebel army marched south, but found little support for their uprising and when confronted by armed forces loyal to the queen retreated to Scotland.

Following the failed northern rebellion, the English Catholics continued to plot against Queen Elizabeth. When Spain's King Philip II began supporting conspiracies to place Mary on the English throne, relations between the two kingdoms grew increasingly strained. Philip II was involved in the Ridolfi Plot in 1571 to invade England from the Spanish-controlled Netherlands and march against London with English rebels to enthrone Mary. However, the insurrection was discovered by the queen's spies and quickly suppressed. Under orders from Elizabeth, the English launched plundering raids against Philip II's settlements in the New World, attacking his ports and treasure ships in retaliation for his interference in England.

In 1583, Elizabeth's followers thwarted a Spanish plan to land an army in England and with support from English Catholics secure the monarchy for Mary of Scotland. Mary was duly arrested on charges of treason, and was tried and declared guilty of involvement in the plot to assassinate Elizabeth. In February 1587, Mary, Queen of Scots, was executed after Elizabeth signed her death warrant. In retaliation, Philip II began preparations to invade England and seize the crown by force of arms, assembling the Great Armada of 200 ships which set sail for

England. After the fleet entered the English Channel, Elizabeth's sea captains attacked the Spanish vessels, outmanoeuvring them and sinking many of them. During the night of 27/28 July 1588, the English sent burning ships crashing into the anchored Spanish fleet near Calais, destroying numerous vessels. The remnants of Philip II's Armada then fled north, making for Scotland before limping back to Spain. The great naval victory over the Spanish Armada was celebrated throughout England with religious services of thanksgiving to God.

As Queen Elizabeth continued to reign over England in the years following the destruction of the Spanish Armada, she was compelled to fend off Spain's quest for power in Europe and maintain English sovereignty over the rebellious Irish by force of arms. During 1603, the health of the nearly 70-year-old Elizabeth began to deteriorate, but despite the pleas of her parliament and counsellors, she refused to name a successor. On 22 March, Elizabeth I died after a reign of 45 years. Following her death, her Privy Council sent envoys to Edinburgh to announce the accession to the English throne of the son of Mary, Queen of Scots, King James VI of Scotland, of the House of Stuart, who became James I of England.

The death of Queen Elizabeth I ended the rule of the House of Tudor, and for the next 111 years the Stuarts held the reins of power over England. After the death of Queen Anne in 1714, her second cousin from the House of Hanover, George I, ruled over England. The six Hanoverian monarchs reigned until the death of Queen Victoria in 1901, when her son, Edward VII, became king under the House of Saxe-Coburg-Gotha. In 1917, during the First World War, the name of the ruling dynasty was changed to Windsor due to anti-German war sentiment. The Windsors have ruled over the United Kingdom through George V, Edward VIII, George VI, Queen Elizabeth II and the recently enthroned Charles III.

Bibliography

Ackroyd, Peter, *Foundation – The History of England From Its Earliest Beginnings to the Tudors* (New York: Thomas Dunne Books, 2011).

Ackroyd, Peter, *Tudor – The History of England From Henry VIII to Elizabeth I* (New York: Thomas Dunne Books, 2012).

Allmand, Christopher, *Henry V* (Berkeley and Los Angeles: The University of California Press, 1992).

Ashley, Mike, *British Kings and Queens* (New York: Carroll and Graf Publishers, 2004).

Ault, Warren O., *Europe in the Middle Ages* (Boston: D.C. Heath and Company, 1937).

Barber, Richard, *Henry Plantagenet – 1133–1189* (New York: Barnes and Noble Books, 1964).

Barber, Richard, *The Devil's Crown – A History of Henry II and His Sons* (London: British Broadcasting Company, 1978).

Barlow, Frank, *William Rufus* (New Haven and London: Yale University Press, 2000).

Barratt, Nick, *The Restless Kings* (London: Faber & Faber, 2018).

Bevan, Bryan, *Henry IV* (New York: St Martin's Press, 1994).

Bevan, Bryan, *Henry VII* (London: The Rubicon Press, 2000).

Bingham, Caroline, *The Crowned Lions – The Early Plantagenet Kings* (Totowa, New Jersey: Rowman and Littlefield, 1978).

Brooke, Christopher, *From Alfred to Henry III* (New York and London: W.W. Norton, 1961).

Brooke, Christopher, *The Saxon and Norman Kings* (Great Britain: Fontana and Collins, 1967).

Cannon, John and Hargreaves, Anne, *The Kings and Queens of Britain* (Oxford and New York, Oxford University Press, 2001).

Carpenter, David, *The Struggle for Mastery – Britain 1066–1284* (Oxford and New York: Oxford University Press, 2003).

Chambers, James, *The Norman Kings* (London: Weidenfeld and Nicolson, 1981).

Cheetham, Anthony, *The Life and Times of Richard III* (London: Weidenfeld and Nicolson, 1972).

Chrimes, S.B., *Henry VII* (Berkeley and Los Angeles: University of California Press, 1972).

Church, Stephen, *Henry III – A Simple and God-Fearing King* (United Kingdom: Allen Lane, 2017).

Clive, Mary, *This Sun of York* (New York: Alfred A. Knopf, 1974).

Costain, Thomas B., *The Last Plantagenet* (New York: Doubleday and Company, Inc., 1962).

Davis, John Paul, *The Gothic King – A Biography of Henry III* (London and Chicago: Peter Owen Publishers, 2013).

Dockray, Keith, *Edward IV* (Phoenix Mill, Gloucestershire: Sutton Publishing Limited, 1999).

Earle, Peter, *The Life and Times of Henry V* (London: Weidenfeld and Nicolson, 1972).

Erickson, Carolly, *Great Harry – The Extravagant Life of Henry VIII* (New York: Summit Books, 1980).

Fraser, Antonia, *The Lives of the Kings and Queens of England* (New York: Alfred A. Knopf, 1975).

Griffiths, R.A., *The Reign of King Henry VI* (Phoenix Mill, Gloucestershire: Sutton Publishing, 1998).

Hallam, Elizabeth, *Four Gothic Kings* (New York: Weidenfeld and Nicolson, 1987).

Hollister, C. Warren, *Henry I* (New Haven and London: Yale University Press, 2001).

Huntingdon, Henry of, *The History of the English People – 1000–1154* (Oxford: Oxford University Press, 2009).

Hutchison, Harold F., *King Henry V* (New York: Dorset Press, 1967).

Hutchison, Harold F., *The Hollow Crown – A Life of Richard II* (New York: The John Day Company, 1961).

King, Edmund, *Henry I – The Father of His People* (United Kingdom: Allen Lane, 2018).

King, Edmund, *Medieval England* (Oxford: Phaidon Press, 1988).

Kirby, J.L., *Henry IV of England* (London: Archon Books, 1971).

Lacey, Robert, *The Life and Times of Henry VIII* (New York: Welcome Rain, 1972).

Lewis, Matthew, *Henry III – The Son of Magna Carta* (Gloucestershire, United Kingdom: Amberley Publishing, 2016).

Lockyer, Roger, *Henry VII* (London: Longman Group Limited, 1968).

Macdougall, Norman, *James IV* (East Linton, Scotland: Tuckwell Press Ltd, 1997).

Mortimer, Ian, *The Fears of Henry IV – The Life of England's Self-Made King* (London: Jonathan Cape, 2007).

Penn, Thomas, *Winter King – Henry VII and the Dawn of Tudor England* (New York and London: Simon and Schuster, 2011).

Pickering, Andrew, *Lancastrians to Tudors* (Cambridge and New York: Cambridge University Press, 2000).

Pollard, A.F., *Henry VIII* (New York: Harper and Row Publishers, 1966).

Read, Conyers, *The Tudors* (New York: W.W. Norton and Company, Inc., 1964).

Roberts, Andrew, *Great Commanders of the Medieval World* (London: Quercus, 2011).

Roberts, Clayton and Roberts, David, *A History of England – Volume 1* (Englewood Cliffs, New Jersey: Prentice Hall, 1991).

Robinson, John Martin, *The Duke of Norfolk* (Chichester, West Sussex: Phillimore and Company, 1995).

Ross, James, *Henry VI – A Good, Simple and Innocent Man* (United Kingdom: Allen Lane, 2016).

Scarisbrick, J.J., *Henry VIII* (Berkeley and Los Angeles: University of California Press, 1970).

Schlight, John, *Henry II Plantagenet* (New York: Twayne Publishers, Inc., 1973).

Seward, Desmond, *Henry V – The Scourge of God* (New York: Viking Penguin, Inc., 1988).

Seward, Desmond, *The Hundred Years War* (New York: Atheneum, 1978).

Seward, Desmond, *The Wars of the Roses* (New York: Carroll and Graf Publishers, 2007).

Simpson, Helen, *Henry VIII* (United Kingdom: Peter Davies Limited, 1934).

Smith, Goldwin, *A History of England* (New York: Charles Scribner's Sons, 1957).

Warren, W.L., *Henry II* (Berkeley and Los Angeles: University of California Press, 1973).

Watts, John, *Henry VI and the Politics of Kingship* (Cambridge and New York: Cambridge University Press, 1996).

Weir, Alison, *The Wars of the Roses* New York: Ballantine Books, 1995).

Williams, Neville, *The Life and Times of Henry VII* (London: Weidenfeld and Nicolson, 1994).

Wolffe, Bertram, *Henry VI* (New Haven and London: Yale University Press, 1983).

Index